GREAT
JEWISH
MEN

GREAT JEWISH MEN

Elinor Slater & Robert Slater

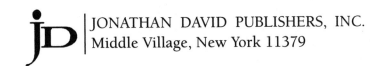

JONATHAN DAVID PUBLISHERS, INC.
Middle Village, New York 11379

GREAT JEWISH MEN

Jonathan David Publishers, Inc.
68-22 Eliot Avenue
Middle Village, NY 11379

www.jdbooks.com

2 4 6 8 10 9 7 5 3 1

Library of Congress Cataloging-in-Publication Data

Slater, Robert, and Slater, Elinor,
    Great Jewish men / Elinor Slater and Robert Slater.
        p. cm.
    Includes index.
    ISBN 0-8246-0381-8
    1. Jewish men—Biography.   I. Slater, Robert, 1943–   II. Title.
DS115.3.S63   1996
920.71'089924—dc20
                                                                95–10343
                                                                CIP

Book design and composition by John Reinhardt Book Design

Printed in the United States of America

FOR OUR GRANDCHILDREN
— *Edo Shalom, Maya Dorian, and Shai Natan Binyamini* —
WITH ALL OUR LOVE AND HOPE

ACKNOWLEDGEMENTS

WHEN WE WROTE *Great Jewish Women* (Jonathan David Publishers, 1994), we found that almost everyone to whom we mentioned that we were writing a book expressed curiosity about who we planned to include in it. We have found the same to be true with this new book about great Jewish men.

The questions put to us by friends and relatives were of great importance, for they challenged us to widen our horizons, to think more deeply about whether or not we were being too hasty in omitting someone from our list. Of course, as our research continued, we went far beyond the suggestions of friends and relatives in determining our subjects. We pored through many *Who's Whos* and countless other reference books and biographies before we drew our final conclusions.

We are deeply grateful to the hundreds of people who engaged us in serious, warmly felt, discerning discussions. Trying to thank them all individually is not possible, but we hope that everyone who helped us understands how appreciative we are for his or her contribution. In keeping the list limited to the one hundred most outstanding Jewish men in history, we know that not everyone will be satisfied. But there was no way of accomplishing such an impossible task, nor was that our intention. We simply aspired to create an interesting and informative companion volume to *Great Jewish Women*, one that recognized many of the great Jewish men in history. We hope we have succeeded in achieving that aim.

One of the most pleasing aspects of our project was personally contacting a number of the men who appear in this book and asking them to answer questions for our profiles. We wish to thank those whom we interviewed or with whom we corresponded: Saul Bellow, Isaiah Berlin, Stephen G. Breyer, Alan M. Dershowitz, Milton Friedman, Larry King, Henry Kissinger, Teddy Kollek, Ralph Lauren, Yehudi Menuhin, Amos Oz, A.M. Rosenthal, Philip Roth, Jonas Salk, Natan Sharansky, Elie Wiesel, and Herman Wouk.

A number of others helped provide background information or smoothed the way for us to interview our subjects. We thank them: Lyn Tesoro (Calvin Klein), Carol Watts (A.M. Rosenthal), Robert M. Zarem (Dustin Hoffman), Diana K. David (Henry Kissinger), Jennifer Brodlieb and Nancy Aronson (Ralph Lauren), Tonia Philips (Saul Bellow), Steve Haworth and Maggie Simpson (Larry King), Nomi Yeshua (Teddy Kollek), Kris Kelley and Tibby Rothman (Steven Spielberg), Thomas Eli Nisell (Adin Steinsaltz), Kathleen Murray and Jonathan D. Salk (Jonas Salk), Gail Muello (Alan Dershowitz), and Ruth Ann C. Evans (Stephen Breyer).

We also wish to thank Jean Max, Joel Breslau, Leonard Fein, Herb Bloom, Lee Levine, Judith Resnik, Dennis Curtis, Jack and Bea Slater, Judd and Roslyn Winick, Michael and Bobbi Winick, Mel Laytner, Lois and Barry Perlman, Ruth and Rashi Fein, George Ginsberg, Ruth Weisberg, Mel and Shoshana Glatzer, Chaim Pearl, and Joseph Applebaum.

We also wish to thank Kevin Proffitt of the American Jewish Archives on the Cincinnati campus of Hebrew Union College—Jewish Institute of Religion for helping us to obtain photographs.

We are also indebted to Shirley J. Longshore for her excellent editing of the manuscript and to Fiorella deLima of Jonathan David Publishers, Inc., for her invaluable aid in preparing the manuscript for publication.

Above all, we thank our children, Miriam and Shimi Binyamini, and Rachel and Adam, for serving as sounding boards, for thinking of people we might have overlooked, for being enthusiastic listeners and creative participants in our project, and for being part of a family of not one, but two authors.

CONTENTS

Thumbnail Sketches

CONTENTS

FOREWORD

JUST AS WITH *Great Jewish Women*, in preparing this volume we were faced with establishing criteria for our choices of which prominent Jewish men to include. We could have selected only those who had spent their lives immersed in Judaism, such as biblical heroes, sages, rabbis, and Jewish scholars. That, however, would have meant excluding too many formidable Jewish men for whom Judaism was not the major factor in their lives, and whose magnificent achievements went beyond the Jewish world. For example, we included Moses, Theodor Herzl, and Rashi as a matter of course because of their contributions to Jewish history, but we also included Henry Kissinger, André Citroën, and Norman Mailer, though none of the latter three derive their fame from their Jewish backgrounds.

What we have tried to do in *Great Jewish Men* is recognize a relatively small number of Jewish men who, because of their noteworthy deeds, have made significant contributions in their different fields. Our Major Biographies list comprises the one hundred Jewish men in history who, to our minds, have had the largest impact in their respective fields. For each of these one hundred men, we have written a profile that both describes his achievements and notes his relationship to Judaism.

Because we realize how relatively few people we are singling out in these one hundred biographies, we have added fifty Thumbnail Sketches in which we make brief mention of other Jewish men whose achievements we also find to be significant and impressive.

The professions of the men profiled are varied, including literature, sports, the performing arts, science, medicine, politics, law, and business. Our list includes those who forged the Jewish nation (the biblical figures Abraham and Moses); served as the great interpreters of the Bible and Jewish law (Rashi and Maimonides); and stood at the forefront of the Zionist movement (Theodor Herzl and Chaim Weizmann). It also includes those who are among the most important literary figures of all time (Franz Kafka and Saul Bellow) and those who wrote some of the most memorable music of our age (Irving Berlin and Jerome Kern). It is a list that honors some of the greatest minds in history (Albert Einstein and Sigmund Freud) and that takes note of those who founded and shaped the modern state of Israel (David Ben-Gurion, Moshe Dayan, and Menachem Begin).

Making our selections was easier in some cases than in others, for some occupations were crowded with great Jewish men, while others were not. Choosing among the world's great violinists, for example, or from the array of men who founded the Hollywood film industry was challenging—there were so many outstanding Jewish violinists and so many Jewish Hollywood moguls. Selecting our choices from among Jewish actors or photographers, on the other hand, was simpler, as there were fewer truly great male figures in either of these fields.

Beyond determining which men were "great" by virtue of their achievements, we had to establish criteria to decide how "Jewish" they needed to be. We felt that it was not necessary, nor desirable, to insist that to qualify for inclusion in *Great Jewish Men* an individual had to be a ritually observant Jew, nor did his work have to be involved in some way with Jewish life.

We did feel strongly that in determining whether or not a man was Jewish, we should use the Orthodox Jewish definition of a Jew. According to that definition, a Jew is someone born of a Jewish mother or who has undergone a proper conversion. We have done extensive research on this question and as a result, we believe we have chosen only those Jews who meet these criteria.

Because their mothers were not Jewish, we omitted some important men who readers might miss in a book like this and who are listed in a number of *Who's Whos* of Jewry. Among them are the controversial journalist Joseph Pulitzer and the actor Paul Newman.

We also excluded some prominent men who were born Jewish, yet left the faith. Among these are British statesman Benjamin Disraeli, German social and political thinker Karl Marx, composers Gustav Mahler and Felix Mendelssohn, Russian author Boris Pasternak, French novelist Marcel Proust, physicist Neils Bohr, and the poet Heinrich Heine. We also declined to include some who never formally abandoned their Judaism but denied any affiliation with their religion, such as American city planner Robert Moses and German physicist Max Born.

One issue we faced was what to do about Jesus and Saint Paul, both of whom were Jewish and had a tremendous impact on history. We resolved the issue this way: We rejected including either man for the simple reason that his historical importance is based entirely on the fact that he was a founder of Christianity.

We also asked ourselves whether or not we should include biblical figures. At the time that we wrote *Great Jewish Women*, we were conscious of the fact that some readers might question the historical existence of biblical personalities, while others would be horrified at the idea of even questioning their existence. We decided to include biblical women in that work because we felt that they were a part of Jewish tradition and Jews throughout the generations have counted them as part of their history. For the same reasons, biblical men were included in this volume.

The most difficult issue for us to resolve was how to define the term "great." For us, establishing standards about a person's Jewishness was reasonably straightforward. It was far more challenging to devise standards that would help in comparing the accomplishments of so many illustrious Jewish men. To get around the ambiguity surrounding the word "great," we decided to make judgments about how great a person was only within his field. This helped us avoid having to compare a Jewish scholar's greatness with that of a Hollywood mogul—Maimonides with Sam Goldwyn, for example. We certainly invite readers to decide whether or not we made the right choices in all cases. We do, however, hope that they accept our caveats and not raise such questions as: "Do you genuinely believe that Marc Chagall and Albert Einstein are equally great?"

Another problem that we encountered in selecting "great" subjects was whether or not to consider those who, while they have had an undeniably significant impact upon society, are not necessarily regarded in a positive way. For example, what about Michael Milken, the junk-bond king who was convicted in the inside trading scandals of the mid-1980s, or Meyer Lansky, whose links to organized crime have been well documented? We chose to omit both Milken and Lansky as well as others in this category because we did not want to include on our list of great Jewish men anyone whose impact on society was linked to criminal activity. Here and there, some on our list have had brushes with the law, but those incidents were marginal in terms of their total careers and were not associated with the reasons for calling them "great."

A word about how we conducted our research. We could have relied on the ample material on public record for the raw material from which to draw in writing these profiles. But we wanted to go beyond such material, to meet the person profiled ourselves, where possible, in order to hear the facts firsthand, to gather interesting additional information, and so that we could provide our own personal impressions. We therefore sought to interview our subjects, or at the very least, to engage in written correspondence with them. We are pleased that we were able to establish personal contact with many of our subjects.

Our research odyssey took us to the desert town of Arad in Israel to meet with Israeli novelist Amos Oz on September 13, 1994. He talked to us first about Israeli politics, which he seemed to find easier to discuss than his literary success. We gently shifted the subject to his writing, asking him what a typical day was like for him. When he described his mornings—usually devoted to his craft—we realized that, given the time of day we were there, he had made an exception to see us, and we were grateful for that privilege.

Five days later, we met the former Russian dissident Natan Sharansky in his office at the Zionist Forum in Jerusalem. Talking to Sharansky was an emotion-filled experience for us. We remembered that period in the 1970s and 1980s when he was in jail in the former Soviet Union and his wife, Avital, traveled around the world seeking his release. He is an easygoing, cheerful, yet soulful individual who seems to get immense joy out of life. He laughed off a slight injury to his hand suffered the day before our interview, when he fell off a ladder building his *sukkah*. We were taken with the irony of it and commented about his surviving imprisonment by the KGB only to be injured while fulfilling a religious duty in the Promised Land.

On October 19, 1994, we paid a visit to new United States Supreme Court Justice Stephen G. Breyer. He had been a member of the highest court for only a few weeks and told us how impressed he was with the quality of the people around him. Though we knew his work was pressing, he took ample time to talk with us about the pleasure he felt at being on the Supreme Court; he was especially pleased that no one had made an issue of his being the second Jew to be named to the current body. (Ruth Bader Ginsburg was the first.)

Later in the month, Larry King scheduled us for lunch at one of his favorite Washington, D.C., restaurants, Sam and Harry's. We arrived first and were seated.

"Will Mr. King know where we're seated?" we asked the maitre d', who calmly replied. "He'll know. It's his table."

King, one of the most famous talk-show hosts in the world, was charming, chatting easily with us about his childhood and his favorite interview subjects. Intrigued by our book (and pleased to be included on the list), he spent the final twenty minutes of our interview giving us advice as to whom to include and probing hard to find out why we had selected certain people and omitted others. He was especially intrigued to know why we were leaving Jesus off the list.

"Tell me your reasons for that one again," he said. At the close of our interview, we realized that King had interviewed us as much as we had interviewed him!

Two days later, on October 26, we walked along the venerable corridors of the *New York Times* main office in New York City and located the office of its former executive editor, A. M. Rosenthal. We had a long, engrossing chat with Abe Rosenthal, now a *Times* columnist. He was effusive, friendly, and barely winced when we asked a few tough questions, such as why so many people thought he had been an autocratic editor. Toward the end of our interview, Rosenthal revealed that in a few days he was scheduled for open-heart surgery, and he admitted that he was squeamish about the prospect. Some days later, we happily read on the Op-Ed page of the *Times* that Rosenthal was recovering nicely from the surgery.

We were in Boston later in the week for our October 28 interview with famed attorney Alan M. Dershowitz. Our interview was scheduled for 10:30 A.M. at Dershowitz's office at Harvard Law School. A relative with whom we were staying invited us to join her at a Ted Kennedy rally at Brandeis University at 9 A.M. Dershowitz turned out to be the master of ceremonies at the rally. We quickly introduced ourselves to him at a pre-rally reception as "your 10:30 appointment." After the rally, instead of going to his office, Dershowitz drove us to his home in Cambridge, where we conducted our interview and, incidentally, also admired his eclectic art collection. Dershowitz agreed to write the introduction to *Great Jewish Men*, and we are most grateful to him.

The following week we were in La Jolla, California, visiting the Salk Institute for Biological Studies for our meeting with renowned scientist Jonas Salk. Before our interview, one of his aides escorted us around the Institute, showing us with obvious awe and appreciation this remarkable architectural wonder, designed by another of our great Jewish men, Louis Kahn. Salk had celebrated his eightieth birthday a few days earlier. We were moved by how lovingly and proudly the famous man spoke of his accomplishments, and he expressed confidence that one day his current work in search of a cure for AIDS would produce results. Sadly, Salk died before this project was completed.

In late January 1995, we visited former Israeli Prime Minister Yitzhak Shamir in his Tel Aviv office. Nearing eighty years old, still a member of Knesset, Shamir talked at length about his childhood years in Poland, explaining that growing up in Poland had merely been an "episode" to him. His constant goal in life was to reach *Eretz Yisrael*, the Land of Israel, which he accomplished in 1934 when he was nineteen years old.

There were times in the course of our research that we had to be content with a telephone chat rather than a live interview. This was the case with both Herman Wouk and Ralph Lauren. Wouk contended that he had not agreed to be interviewed in person for twenty-five years and he refused to succumb to our charms. He did, however, answer some of our questions in writing.

Lauren took time away from designing his latest fashion collection to speak with us, vividly explaining how he had changed his original name of Lipshitz to Lauren, not to avoid his Jewishness but to put an end to his schoolmates' teasing for having a four-letter expletive in his name.

We thoroughly enjoyed writing *Great Jewish Men* and hope that it provides a glimpse into the lives of some of the most outstanding Jewish men in history.

Elinor Slater
Robert Slater
Jerusalem, Israel

INTRODUCTION

by Alan M. Dershowitz

THE EXTRAORDINARY DIVERSITY among the Jewish men selected for inclusion in this volume attests to the eclectic nature of Judaism, Jewishness, and the Jewish people. If "Jewish" were defined as only theological or religious, there would be no place for atheists, agnostics, or secularists such as Herzl, Ben-Gurion, Anielewicz, Spinoza, Freud, Spielberg, and Brandeis. Yet who could deny that these are not only great men—they are also great Jews. Their Jewishness helped form their consciences and to inform their life's work. Though these men share little *religiously* with other greats, such as the biblical patriarchs, Maimonides, Schneerson, Wise, Buber, Caro, Kaplan, Rashi, Nachmanides, Baal Shem Tov, and Soloveitchik, they *do* share a common history, civilization, and tradition. Others on the list—Wiesel, Singer, Bialik, Roth, Agnon, Chagall, Oz, Shalom Aleichem, and Wouk—have expressed the range of the Jewish experience, each from a different perspective, yet each uniquely Jewish.

Some on the list just happen to have been Jews who achieved greatness without explicit references to their Jewish backgrounds. Even *they* were almost certainly influenced by their heritage. For example, there is a definite Jewish influence in the music of Gershwin and Bernstein, as there is in the art of Chagall and Shahn, the literature of Bellow, the comedy of Allen, Marx, and Benny. For others, their status as Jewish outsiders influenced their work. Included in this category are surely Kafka, Modigliani, Soutine, Houdini, Mailer, and Pissarro. A few were Jews who simply made us proud because they were world-class athletes—like Koufax, Greenberg, and Spitz—and because they did not forget their roots.

Then there is the Jewish tradition of justice. "*Tzedek, tzedek tirdoff*" (seek justice), says Deuteronomy. The Jewish quest for justice surely has influenced the lives of those lawyers, judges, and political reformers who are included in this book. Jewish scientists, too, were often affected by the Jewish tradition of helping others or by the sense of inquisitiveness that seems characteristic of many Jewish intellectuals.

The important point is that the Jewish experience from Abraham to the end of the twentieth century has transcended religion and theology, and has been as varied and eclectic as that of any of the great civilizations. That is because, as Mordecai Kaplan aptly put it, Judaism is a civilization that transcends its religious origins. A compilation of great Catholics, Protestants, Muslims, or Buddhists would probably not include as many secular figures as this book does. This list celebrates the diversity that is Judaism.

As we enter the next century, the Jewish people will once again be struggling for survival and perpetuation, as it always has done. In past centuries, the challenge has come primarily from external forces determined to destroy Jews. They have always failed. The challenge of the next century will be directed more at the internal dynamics of the Jewish people: assimilation, intermarriage, low birth rates, secularism, fundamentalism. The diversity of Jews, as reflected in this book, may well prove to be a central ingredient in the ability of the entire people to survive its own success.

This same diversity may also pose the greatest challenge to Judaism. The nonreligious aspects of Jewish civilization are the most difficult to transmit from generation to generation, and they are also least resistant to assimilation and intermarriage. But Judaism has confronted challenge since its earliest days in the desert. That is what makes it powerful and persevering. As long as so many great men and women come from these roots—like the millions who have lived and died over the past several millennia—the challenge will be met and Jewish men and women will continue to make their mark on history.

ABRAHAM

First Patriarch of the Jewish People

> Born in Ur of the Chaldeans and died in Canaan around the nineteenth century B.C.E. Biblical patriarch. Abraham is generally regarded as the first monotheist. Abraham left his native land at the command of the god he considered the One God, who offered him protection if he promised to obey His commandments. It is by keeping this covenant with God, symbolized by male circumcision, that Abraham's descendants, the Jewish people, retain their special historical and spiritual role.

ABRAHAM'S ORIGINAL NAME was Abram, meaning "the father is exalted," but God changed his name to Abraham, which means "father of a multitude of nations."

The key details of Abraham's life are recorded in Genesis 11:26–25:10. He appears to have been wealthy and the head of a large establishment, a seminomadic tent dweller. He possessed flocks of cattle and sheep, silver, gold, and slaves, as well as commanding a private army. Clearly a man of stature, Abraham is depicted as someone who made military alliances, had contacts with kings, and negotiated the purchase of land with city officials. Of the little that we know of him, we can surmise that he was peace-loving, magnanimous, hospitable to strangers, and, above all, obedient to God and His laws.

Abraham's father, Terah, was born in Ur of the Chaldeans, in southern Mesopotamia. The Bible does not mention Abraham's mother. Abraham was the tenth generation descended from Noah, through the line of Shem. He had two brothers named Nahor and Haran. His wife was Sarai, later called Sarah, a paternal half-sister.

Around the nineteenth century B.C.E., Terah took his son Abraham, Abraham's wife Sarah, and his grandson Lot (Abraham's nephew), away from Ur, a cosmopolitan city in Babylonia. By crossing the Euphrates River, Terah and his family became the first people identified in the Bible as *Ivrim*, meaning "those who cross," which has been anglicized to "Hebrews."

Terah and his family arrived at Haran, in northwestern Mesopotamia, six hundred miles northwest of Ur, in the southern part of present-day Turkey, where Terah then died. After his father's death, Abraham was instructed by God to travel to an undisclosed place. God's covenant to the family patriarch was this: If Abraham would follow God's commandments, God would make Abraham's descendants "the chosen people," putting them under God's direct, special protection.

These events are recorded in Genesis 12:1–3. At the time, Abraham, who was already sixty-five years old, and his wife, Sarah, were childless. Abraham, Sarah, and Lot proceeded to Canaan, the land God had promised Abraham his offspring would inherit. When he arrived at

Abraham's sacrifice (Rembrandt etching).

Shechem (called Nablus today), Abraham again received a promise from God that this land would belong to his "nation." So Abraham constructed an altar to God there. He wandered further into the region between Beth-El and Ai, building another altar in that area. He then traveled south to the Negev.

Abraham and his family lived the lives of nomads. As the patriarch, he made pacts with local kings and, in his preachings, championed a monotheistic creed.

When famine struck the land of Canaan, Abraham took his family to Egypt. When he entered Egypt, he feared that Pharaoh would want the exceptionally beautiful Sarah to join his harem. Pharaoh chose only unmarried young women; if he discovered that Abraham was married to Sarah, Pharaoh would surely kill Abraham so that he might have Sarah. To save himself, Abraham advised Sarah to say that she was his sister.

Pharaoh did take Sarah into his harem, but as soon as he discovered that she was Abraham's wife, he released her. He was terribly distressed over the incident, and he said to Abraham: "Take her and be gone." He then castigated Abraham for misleading him and almost causing him to be guilty of sexual misconduct.

When the famine was over, Abraham returned to Canaan and settled in the Negev, while Lot moved to the Dead Sea region. Again, God promised Abraham nationhood; this time He also pledged possession of the land of Canaan to Abraham.

In his role as military leader, Abraham led a force of 318 soldiers against a coalition of eastern kings who had captured Lot when they plundered Sodom and Gomorrah. After rescuing his nephew, Abraham returned the booty, refusing an offer from the king of Sodom to share in the looted items.

Through a number of revelations, God had promised Abraham that He would grant him many descendants, who would grow into a great and blessed nation. In return, Abraham had promised to serve only the One God. This covenant was affirmed in a ceremony of circumcision, which Abraham performed on himself and all the male members of his household. The act of circumcision became a symbol of the immutability of God's covenant with Abraham and his descendants.

Ten years had passed since the first Divine promise of many offspring, yet Sarah remained childless. So she gave her maidservant, Hagar, to Abraham for the purpose of procreation of a child. Abraham was eighty-six years old when Hagar bore him a son, who was called Ishmael. The Bible says nothing about the thirteen years that followed. Then, one day, three tired travelers visited Abraham. At first he did not recognize them as angels that God had sent. The angels announced that Abraham, who was one hundred, and Sarah, who was then ninety years old, would have a son together. Sarah laughed at this idea. They also informed Abraham that God had decided to destroy Sodom and Gomorrah because of the wickedness of its inhabitants. Abraham asked God to spare the two cities. If as few as ten righteous men could be found in the cities, God said He would relent. But Abraham was unable to find those ten men, so the two cities were destroyed by fire and brimstone.

Sarah did bear Abraham a son that year, who was named Isaac, from the Hebrew verb "to laugh." But Isaac's birth led Sarah to fear that her son's inheritance would be threatened by Hagar's son Ishmael. She demanded that Hagar and Ishmael be expelled from their home. Abraham objected, but only God's intervention convinced him to agree. Hagar and Ishmael were banished.

The final test of Abraham's faith and covenant with God was God's demand that the patriarch make a sacrifice of his son Isaac in the land of Moriah. Without hesitation, because of his complete faith in God, Abraham agreed. He took the youngster to the mountaintop and prepared him for sacrifice. At the last moment, when the boy was bound and Abraham had raised his hand, the knife poised to kill his son as God had commanded, an angel prevented the sacrifice from occurring and Abraham was ordered to sacrifice a ram instead. Abraham had passed the ultimate test of faith.

When Sarah died at the age of 127, Abraham buried her in the Cave of Machpelah in Hebron, which he had purchased as a family burial plot. While Abraham was in his final years, Isaac married Rebekah, who had been brought to him for that purpose by Abraham's servant from the Chaldean city of Nahor because Abraham did not want his son to marry a Canaanite wife.

In his last years, Abraham married a woman named Keturah and they had six children. Abraham died at the age of 175. The Bible (Genesis 25:1–11) recounts that his two sons, Isaac and Ishmael, buried him in the Cave of Machpelah.

SHMUEL YOSEF AGNON

First Hebrew-Language Writer to Win the Nobel Prize for Literature

Born in 1888, in Buczacz, Galicia; died in 1970. Hebrew fiction writer. Shmuel Agnon is widely viewed as one of the masters of modern Hebrew prose fiction, winning the Nobel Prize for Literature in 1966. Agnon wrote his first story when he was eight years old, moved to Palestine in 1908, spent a few years in Germany, then returned to Palestine permanently in 1924. He wrote four novels and over two hundred short stories. Agnon's style has been described as "surrealistic, introspective, and dreamlike." His literary heroes are often torn by the conflict between the old world and the new, and are deeply affected by the spiritual desolation of the old-world Jewish life.

SHMUEL YOSEF CZACZKES, later renamed Agnon, was born in 1888 into a traditional Jewish home. His father, a fur merchant, liked to read his son *aggadot* (rabbinical legends). His mother told him German stories. Hasidic tradition and European culture were highly valued in the Czaczkes home in Buczacz in Eastern Galicia, then a part of the Austro-Hungarian Empire.

Private tutors instructed Agnon in the Talmud and the German language, he was also able to pore through Hebrew and Yiddish writings and satisfy his interest in reading as much as possible. He had an unquenchable thirst for knowledge and was especially attracted to Hasidic literature.

Agnon was only eight years old when he began to write, and he published his first poem at the age of fifteen. Over the next four years, Agnon managed to publish seventy literary pieces in Hebrew and Yiddish. After leaving his native Buczacz, however, he never wrote in Yiddish again. But Buczacz became the prototype for the small Jewish town or *shtetl* in Agnon's writings. The *shtetl* intrigued Agnon. He described it in one of his early works as "the city of the dead," to indicate his view of it as slowly and painfully disintegrating.

Leaving his parents behind, Agnon settled in Palestine in 1908, residing first in Jaffa and later in Jerusalem. That same year marked the publication of "*Agunot*" ("Chained Women"), the author's first story published in his new homeland. It was with the publication of "*Agunot*" that he began using the pseudonym Agnon. The story dwelt on separations, including that between the land of Israel and the Diaspora. Personally, and as a writer, Agnon was intrigued by such issues.

As a young adult on his own, Agnon supported himself by giving private lessons in Hebrew, working as a clerk, and writing. In 1913 he moved to Germany, where six years later he married Esther Marx and began a family. They had a daughter, Emuna, and a son, Shalom. Agnon associated with Jewish scholars and Zionist officials, read German and French literature, and widened his knowledge of Judaism. He began collecting rare Hebrew books. Earning income by tutoring at first, Agnon later received financial support from his publisher, Salman Schocken. Living comfortably during this time in Germany, Agnon was quite prolific. Once his works were translated into German, he acquired a growing reputation among German Jews.

A fire in 1924 brought this productive period in Agnon's life to an abrupt halt. It destroyed his home and most of his books and manuscripts. Returning to Jerusalem that year, Agnon settled in the Holy City and lived there with his family for the rest of his life.

Agnon saw himself in the tradition of the holy scribes, believing, albeit tentatively, that

Shmuel Yosef Agnon

State of Israel Government Press Office

modern Hebrew literature was a kind of substitute for these sacred texts. He had, however, abandoned the religious aspects of Judaism; his writings presented a view of Jewish life seen through his own secular prism.

In 1929 a second fire, this time occurring in his home in Jerusalem, ruined many of his remaining books and rare manuscripts. In his novel *A Guest for the Night* (1968), Agnon dwelt on the symbolic nature of the two fires, comparing them to the twin destructions of the Temple. The narrator in that novel visits his hometown in Galicia following a long absence and finds it deserted. Agnon based the story on his return to his native Buczacz in 1930. For Agnon, the city reflected, with its empty synagogues and dismal inhabitants, the spiritual loneliness of the Jewish people.

Agnon's early works were often set in Poland. In these works, he characterized the lives of the pious in a positive vein. This, however, eventually gave way to a new, more literary Agnon in the early 1930s as he focused his stories more on the real world and its conflicts: his hometown versus the state of Israel, Jewish tradition in contrast with Western culture and modern Hebrew literature. His later protagonists admire the new world but remember the old fondly, and they are therefore torn between the two. Because Agnon's themes involve the decline of the old order—including the loss of innocence, exile, and ambivalence—his stories frequently end in tragedy. For that reason, he was often compared to Franz Kafka, another writer of the era. Agnon himself denied that any similarity existed, however.

Agnon was known as a modern Hasidic storyteller. Contributing to that reputation were stories such as "*Vehaya He'akov Lemishor*" ("And the Crooked Shall be Made Straight"), published in 1911, and "*Aggadat Hasofer*" ("The Tale of the Scribe"), published in 1921 in Hebrew and translated into German. A majority of Agnon's stories of that time, especially his 1931 comic novel *Hakhnasat Kallah* (*The Bridal Canopy*), take place in the pious Jewish communities of Eastern Galicia. Besides *The Bridal Canopy* and *A Guest for the Night*, Agnon wrote two other long novels: *Temol Shilshom* (*The Day Before Yesterday*) (1945) and *Shirah* (published between 1948 and 1953). He published over two hundred short stories.

Temol Shilshom is one of Agnon's best-known novels. In it, he related the tale of Yitzhak Kummer, unable to root himself in either the neophyte society of pioneers in Jaffa or in the traditional and pious Jewish community in Jerusalem. This novel has been regarded as a critique of the ideals of both religious Judaism and secular Zionism.

Shirah recounts the story of Manfred Hebst, a lecturer in Byzantine history at Jerusalem's Hebrew University. The novel unfolds against the backdrop of Jerusalem in the 1930s and 1940s. Nearing middle age and the father of two grown daughters, Manfred is in conflict over his affection for and loyalty to his devoted wife, who has just given him a third daughter, and his romantic passion for a nurse named Shirah.

Agnon won the Israel Prize, the nation's highest award, in 1954 and 1958. In 1966, he won the Nobel Prize for Literature.

Edmund Wilson, dean of American literary critics, wrote in *Commentary* magazine: " . . . What makes Agnon so remarkable and an appropriate recipient of the Nobel Prize is that he is able to embody in his Talmudic world so much of our common humanity, and even of our common morality, so much of ironic humor, and ironic but touching pathos, that he can be read, I should think, with appreciation by anyone who knows nothing at all of it."

Agnon died in Israel in 1970 at the age of eighty-two.

WOODY ALLEN

Filmmaker and Comic Genius

Born December 1, 1935, in Brooklyn, New York. American film director, screenwriter, playwright, and actor. Originally a stand-up comedian, Woody Allen began making movies in the early 1970s, creating his own genre of seriocomic films. He is a prolific filmmaker whose best-known films are *Annie Hall, Interiors, Manhattan, Everything You Always Wanted to Know About Sex** (But Were Afraid to Ask), Hannah and Her Sisters, Crimes and Misdemeanors,* and *Husbands and Wives.*

WOODY ALLEN was born Allen Stewart Konigsberg. He and his sister, Letty, were raised in the Flatbush section of Brooklyn. His father, Martin, who according to Allen worked at "a million little short-lived jobs," and his mother, Nettie, who kept the account books for a flower shop, were Orthodox Jews. In his early stand-up routines, Allen included his parents in his jokes. "Their values," he quipped, "are God and carpeting."

Allen hated school except for English composition; his composition was usually the one read aloud to the class. A loner, he avoided family and his peers, and he often remained in his room for hours. Woody attended Midwood High School in Brooklyn, graduating with a just-passing average.

At age fifteen, signing his name Woody Allen, he wrote jokes and sent them to *New York Post* columnist Earl Wilson. After Wilson published one of Allen's jokes and gave him credit for it, he was hired by a press agent to write one-liners for the agent's clients, for which he earned twenty-five dollars a week.

Although Allen attended New York University and the City College of New York, he did not earn a degree from either school. Poor attendance and low marks at both brought him back-to-back expulsions.

In 1961 Allen was hired at $1,700 a week as a writer for *The Garry Moore Show* on television, but resigned to do stand-up comedy at Greenwich Village night clubs, modeling himself after comedians Bob Hope and Mort

Woody Allen

Brian Hamill

Sahl. A year later, he appeared on *The Tonight Show* and other television programs, giving his career a great boost.

In 1964, a turning point in his career occurred when the actress Shirley MacLaine and the movie producer Charles K. Feldman caught his act at New York's Blue Angel night club. Feldman gave Allen his first movie job, assigning him to write the screenplay for *What's New, Pussycat?* (1965), in which Allen also played a supporting role.

Allen's comedy *Don't Drink the Water*, about a Newark caterer on vacation with his wife and daughter in an Iron Curtain country, was the surprise hit of the 1966–67 Broadway season. A second comedy, *Play It Again, Sam*, was about a neurotic film critic whose wife leaves him; he subsequently seeks a new love with the help of Humphrey Bogart's ghost. The hit play ran on Broadway from February 1969 to March 1970. Allen played the lead part through most of the Broadway run and starred in a film adaptation of the play in 1972.

In 1969 Allen starred in the movie *Take the Money and Run*, a comedy about a young man who aspires to become public enemy number one, but fails to make even the Ten Most Wanted list. *Bananas*, in which Allen played a nerd named Fielding Mellish who finds himself the leader of a Latin American revolution, followed in 1971.

In 1972 Allen starred in the movie *Everything You Always Wanted to Know About Sex** (But Were Afraid to Ask)*. He played, among other roles, a sperm pale with trepidation as it waits to be ejaculated. "The remarkable thing," wrote critic William Wolf in *Cue* magazine in August 1972, "is that Allen isn't obscene, just cleverly risqué, as he masterfully satirizes movies, TV, and literature while having fun with sex."

Allen began his longtime collaboration with screenplay-writing partner Marshall Brickman on the 1973 movie *Sleeper*, in which Woody played Miles Monroe, a Greenwich Village health-food restaurant owner who checks into a hospital for a minor ulcer operation and wakes up in a defrosting lab two hundred years later. In 1976, in a change of pace, Allen starred in *The Front* as a small-time bookmaker who starts a lucrative second career lending his name to the scripts of blacklisted playwrights.

Allen acknowledged in interviews in the 1970s that in his early films he just wanted to make them funny, simply to survive and to get film credits under his belt. "Everything was coordinated with the joke—everything," he said. In his later films, he wanted to develop his ideas so that he would be seen as a more serious filmmaker. By 1975, when he made *Love and Death*, "I was very concerned with the filmmaking aspect, and with wanting to do darker things, not deal with a lot of conventional stuff." The movie was a mock epic on the scale of *War and Peace*, Allen playing a self-professed "military coward" during the Napoleonic wars. Although the critics thought the movie extremely funny, Allen was upset that the serious intent underlying his humor did not come through in the film.

To change this impression, Allen downplayed the humor in his next movie, *Annie Hall* (1977), which he originally wanted to call *Anhedonia*, a psychiatric term meaning the inability to experience pleasure—the opposite of hedonism. United Artists, producers of the film, however, talked him out of using that title. *Annie Hall* was an introspective, semi confessional story of failed relationships and was hailed as Woody Allen's best work, receiving Academy Awards for best picture, best director (Allen), best screenplay (Allen and Marshall Brickman), and best actress (Diane Keaton).

The next Allen movie was *Interiors* (1978). "If *Annie Hall* was this era's 'nervous romance,'

Woody Allen and Mia Farrow in a scene from Allen's film Hannah and Her Sisters.

Interiors is its genteel nightmare," wrote critic Janet Maslin. In a departure from his previous films, Allen wrote and directed, but did not appear in, the movie. His next film, *Manhattan* (1979), was shot in black and white, and was a paean to Allen's beloved New York. More Allen films followed: *Stardust Memories* (1980) showed Allen agonizing over his role as a comic moviemaker; *Zelig* (1983) was about a fictionalized celebrity from the 1920s.

The *Purple Rose of Cairo* (1984) explored the role of film in our fantasies by depicting on screen the wish-fulfillment of a young woman who wanted the make-believe of cinema to become a reality. *Radio Days* (1987) was set in the era of Allen's childhood and chronicles his affection for that medium. *Crimes and Misdemeanors* (1989) was a poignant and thought-provoking murder mystery.

Now considered a comic genius of mythic proportions himself, Allen has said that the comedians who influenced him the most were George S. Kaufman, Groucho Marx, Robert Benchley, and S.J. Perelman.

Allen has been accused of promoting anti-Semitism by portraying Jews in a negative light in his films. In his 1986 movie *Hannah and Her Sisters*, for instance, Allen's character is a television writer-producer stricken with metaphysical paralysis. The character denies his Jewish heritage and tries Catholicism and other religious avenues for healing before ultimately finding comfort in his film work and a new romance.

Asked if he thought of himself as a "Jewish" filmmaker, Allen answered, "Not really. I draw my ideas from everything I've done and everything that interests me . . . . You can have six hundred jokes in your film and if two gags are Jewish, the picture will be perceived as 'Jewish' comedy. This is a false perception, I think."

Allen, known for his recognizable, routine attire of a plaid shirt, corduroy trousers, and an Ivy League-style tweed jacket, was first married to Harlene Rosen, a teacher, from 1954 to 1959; then to Louise Lasser, an actress, from 1966 to 1971. He has had close, longstanding relationships with the actresses Diane Keaton and Mia Farrow.

In the early 1990s, Allen became known for the controversy surrounding the case involving his unconventional family. His liaison with Mia Farrow, who appeared in thirteen of his films, collapsed in the summer of 1992. On August 13 of that year, Allen filed suit in State Supreme Court in Manhattan for custody of his and Farrow's four-year-old son, Satchel, and for two children they adopted together, Moses, fourteen, and Dylan, seven. Tension mounted when Allen declared that he was in love with one of Farrow's other adopted daughters, Soon-Yi Farrow Previn.

Farrow claimed in another suit that Allen had molested Dylan. Stating that the evidence might not be strong enough to win a conviction, the state of Connecticut decided not to prosecute Allen on these charges, but custody of the three children was awarded to Farrow with limited visitation rights granted to Allen. He continued to date Soon-Yi, thirty-five years his junior.

In September 1992, Allen's movie *Husbands and Wives* was screened and was well received. It dealt with the problems of being married, especially infidelity. In the summer of 1994, Allen made his first movie for TV, *Don't Drink the Water*, an adaptation of his hit 1966 Broadway play. In October 1994, Allen's film *Bullets Over Broadway* opened to good reviews. It received several Academy Award nominations.

In his 1995 film, *Mighty Aphrodite*, Allen played a sportswriter who, after he and his wife adopt a baby, feels obligated to locate the child's birth mother, who turns out to be an aspiring pornography actress and prostitute. Allen won an Oscar nomination for a screenplay written for his 1997 film *Deconstructing Harry*. The protagonist, Harry Block, is a successful Manhattan novelist whose stories have focused on his own foibles as well as on unending sexual exploits and the betrayal of friends and lovers.

In December 1997, Allen married Soon-Yi Farrow Previn, in Venice, Italy. Following the wedding, Allen continued a frenetic pace of moviemaking, directing and/or starring in such movies as *Wild Man Blues* (1998); *Small Time Crooks* (2000); *Curse of the Jade Scorpion* (2001); and *Hollywood Ending* (2002).

Curse of the Jade Scorpion, set in the 1940s, has Allen playing an ace insurance investigator and Helen Hunt playing an efficiency expert with Allen's firm. They do not get along, and while hypnotized, the two discover romance. Critics assailed Allen, then sixty-five years old, for casting himself in the role of the romantic leading man.

In November 2004 Allen's play *A Second Hand Memory*, set in Brooklyn in the 1950s, was presented by Off-Broadway's Atlantic Theater Company.

MORDECAI ANIELEWICZ

Jewish Hero of the Holocaust

> Born in 1919 in Warsaw, Poland; died May 8, 1943. Commander of the Warsaw ghetto uprising. Mordecai Anielewicz was one of the outstanding heroes of the Holocaust. By virtue of the stand he took against the Nazis, Anielewicz became a powerful symbol of Jewish resistance to all forms of tyranny as well as a significant representative of the terrible sacrifices Jews have had to make in the twentieth century.

MORDECAI ANIELEWICZ was born in the slums of Warsaw in 1919. As a youngster, he joined the Ha-shomer Ha-tsair Socialist Zionist movement, eventually becoming one of its leaders. Little else is known of his childhood.

On September 7, 1939, a few days after the Germans invaded Poland, he fled Warsaw, as did many of the leaders of the Zionist youth movements. Reaching the Soviet-occupied section of Poland, Anielewicz then tried to get to Romania, from where he hoped to journey to Palestine. He was, however, arrested by the Soviet authorities, who put him in jail. Meanwhile, hundreds of thousands of Polish Jews were virtually imprisoned, forced to live in ghettos, including the one in Warsaw.

Upon his release from the Soviet jail, Mordecai made his way back to Warsaw, stopping along the way at a number of Jewish communities to find out how other Jews were faring against the Nazi threat. When he finally reached Warsaw, he stayed there only briefly, going on to Vilna, where many Zionist youths lived. Some of them wanted to travel to German-occupied Poland in order to lead the resistance movement, even if it had to be done secretly. Anielewicz volunteered to return once again to Poland.

In the summer of 1942, Anielewicz convinced the Jewish political leaders of the Warsaw ghetto that military resistance, however crazy it sounded, offered the only possible chance of survival. He also told them that speed was of the essence. The forced resettlement of the Jewish populations had reached a new level. Reports began arriving at the ghetto indicating that Jews in the German-held parts of the Soviet Union were being murdered.

That news spurred Anielewicz to create an armed Jewish underground. The first of these organizations, known as the Antifascist Bloc, fell apart even before it was fully organized.

Anielewicz learned that only sixty thousand Jews remained in Warsaw and that the Jewish Fighting Organization (JFO), a newly-created armed underground organization, was in a weakened condition. Anielewicz became the JFO commander, vowing to strengthen this brave group of Jewish fighters. He conducted seminars, built up an underground press, and searched for weapons to use in their efforts. To raise money, Jewish allies employed strong-arm tactics to squeeze out whatever funds were left among the few well-off Jews in the ghetto. With this money, a few revolvers and grenades were purchased from Italian army deserters and from members of the Polish Communist party. The weapons were then smuggled into the ghetto.

By early 1943, Anielewicz had taken over complete command of the resistance movement within the Warsaw ghetto.

On January 18, 1943, while the deportation drive was on, the first armed clashes between Germans and Jews occurred. In one brief battle, during which many Jewish fighters were killed, some of his own "soldiers" saved Anielewicz's life. For a while, the Jewish fighters lived under a pleasant illusion: The German deportation of Jews had ceased briefly, and the Jews attributed the halt to the success of Anielewicz's army. With that kind of reputation inside the ghetto, the twenty-four-year-old Anielewicz and his "soldiers" became leaders of the ghetto.

In Warsaw, pretending to build air-raid shelters, Anielewicz and his Jewish fighters instead constructed dugouts that were connected to the sewer system. They built bunkers as well, frenetically preparing for full-scale armed resistance.

On Passover eve, April 19, 1943, the German forces, including Latvian collaborators, invaded the ghetto, which they had decided to destroy. To ward off the Germans, the armed Jewish underground, under Anielewicz's command, used every available weapon to fight their attackers. Anielewicz recruited 750 fighters and managed to obtain nine rifles, fifty-nine pistols, and a few grenades.

The fighting began in the streets, then shifted to the bunkers the resistance fighters had built.

On April 23rd, Anielewicz wrote what turned out to be his final letter: "What happened is beyond our wildest dreams. Twice the Germans fled from our ghetto. One of our companies held out for forty minutes and the other, for over six hours . . . . I have no words to describe to you the conditions in which the Jews are living. Only a few chosen ones will hold out; all the rest will perish sooner or later. The die is cast. In the bunkers in which our comrades are hiding, no candle can be lit for lack of air . . . . The main thing is: My life's dream has come true; I have lived to see Jewish resistance in the ghetto in all its greatness and glory."

It was small consolation for the valiant Jewish hero, but through his example a courageous Jewish resistance, however weak and ineffective in the long run, made the battle far more difficult for the Germans than they had hoped or imagined was possible. The Jews managed to kill sixteen Germans and wound eighty-five others.

In the early days of May, the Nazis mounted a heavy offensive. On May 8, 120 Jewish resistance fighters were holed up at 18 Mila Street, the last large group of Jewish fighters in the ghetto. Though the building entrance was bombed, the Jews were unharmed, able to find shelter in a bunker.

When the Nazis discovered that there were Jews who were not hurt, they started drilling into the bunker overhead so they could shoot at the Jews from a closer range. Anielewicz ordered guards to go to the five entrances of the bunker. The drilling went on for another two hours before it stopped. The Jews waited. Someone called out in Yiddish to the Jewish fighters that they should come out and surrender. The Germans fired shots and threw hand grenades into a tunnel leading to the bunker. A Nazi soldier entered the tunnel. He was shot and killed by the Jewish defenders. The Nazis retreated.

Drilling resumed. Surprised to be still alive, Mordecai Anielewicz made a solemn promise:

He would die in this bunker, fighting the Nazis. The Nazis made another demand for surrender. It was rejected. Then the Nazi soldiers fired gas through a hole they had drilled into the bunkers, forcing a few Jewish fighters to crawl toward the exits. At that point, some of the resistance fighters tried to surrender. But Anielewicz would not, staying behind to talk to the remaining Jews in the bunker about their options, none of them good.

One of the trapped Jews, Aryeh Wilner, argued for suicide. If the Jews chose that method of dying, it had the advantage of preventing the Nazis from taking them alive. Another Jewish fighter, Michael Rozenfeld, suggested that they should die killing Nazis. Escaping and fighting to the finish were no longer realistic options, however. They could either die by suicide or die by gas. Anielewicz was against suicide. He wanted to believe that somehow the Jews could survive the gas. He ordered his "soldiers" to wet pieces of cloth in a puddle under the tap and to cover their faces. But this ploy did not work.

Mordecai Anielewicz

Givat Haviva Archives

Ultimately, Mordecai Anielewicz died along with one hundred of his fighters. The few remaining Jewish fighters who were still alive held out for another eight days. Altogether, several thousand Jews died in the ghetto resistance. Some European countries, with far better equipped armies, had been able to mount even less resistance than the brave Warsaw ghetto fighters led by Mordecai Anielewicz.

Yad Mordecai, a kibbutz near the Gaza Strip, along the Mediterranean coast, was named after this hero.

BA'AL SHEM TOV

The Charismatic Founder of the Hasidic Movement

Born in 1700 in Okop, Podolia, then southeastern Poland, now the western Ukraine; died in 1760. Hasidic religious leader. Israel ben Eliezer, known as the Ba'al Shem Tov, founded the Hasidic movement that arose among the pietistic communities of Jews in Poland, Russia, and Austria-Hungary in the eighteenth and nineteenth centuries. The movement was led by Hasidic masters called *tzaddikim* (righteous or proven men); the Ba'al Shem Tov was the first *tzaddik*.

ISRAEL BEN ELIEZER was born in Okop, in then southeastern Poland, to poor and elderly parents and was orphaned while still a child. As an adult, he became known as the Besht, an acronym for Ba'al Shem Tov, or Master of the Good Name, and was the founder of Hasidism, a mystical approach to Jewish life and thinking, still found today.

Ba'al Shem Tov

The earliest information about the Ba'al Shem Tov appeared in an 1815 biography. Most of what has been written about his youth appears to be legendary and is difficult to verify. At age twelve, Israel ben Eliezer worked as a teacher and caretaker at a *heder*, a religious elementary school. He preferred the wooded outdoors to school and resisted attempts by his elders to give him a Talmudic education. Married at eighteen years old to a rabbi's daughter named Hannah, ben Eliezer worked in a variety of capacities over the next eighteen years, among them kosher slaughterer (*shochet*) and school assistant. It was during this phase of his life that, according to disciples, he acquired a reputation as a miracle worker. On one occasion, it was reported, he encountered a group of thieves who tried to connive him with a promise of taking him to the Holy Land through an underground tunnel. Just then a wall of fire arose, separating ben Eliezer from the robbers.

While still in his twenties, accompanied only by his wife, Israel ben Eliezer retreated to the Carpathian Mountains; he lived there for seven years in seclusion, working at times as a lime digger. He claimed to be able to communicate with the biblical prophet Ahijah the Shilonite.

Ben Eliezer's reputation grew, and eventually he was considered a great spiritual figure and given the name of Ba'al Shem Tov. He was known as a healer, using folk remedies and spiritual power to work his wonders. In 1736, at the age of thirty-six, the Ba'al Shem Tov settled in Medzibozh, Podolia, where followers, sometimes as many as ten thousand at a time, flocked to see and hear him.

Prior to the Ba'al Shem Tov, Jewish mysticism had been elitist and erudite. It had stressed piety and urged asceticism. Mystics taught esoteric kabbalistic practices. The Ba'al Shem Tov, on the other hand, decided to take his message to a far larger audience, hoping to show God's accessibility to all Jews. Israel ben Eliezer spoke to the simple man and made Judaism comprehensible through stories and parables that were understood by even the least sophisticated Jew. Uneducated Jews responded to his message, especially when he told them that the way to God did not require great learning.

Although other scholars had far more impressive academic credentials, the Ba'al Shem Tov, because of his charisma and insight, became master and teacher to many Jews. He knew less of the Talmud than did others, but his forte was his wide knowledge of the Bible, rabbinic legend, and folklore (*aggada*). He addressed his followers by telling them stories and parables, and it was only through the skills and interest of his chief disciples, Jacob Joseph of Polonnoye and Dov Baer of Mezhirech, that the Ba'al Shem Tov's teachings were preserved in writing. The Besht, as he came to be called, wrote nothing more than letters.

The Besht told his stories in the marketplace during the hour of morning prayer, as he smoked a pipe, dressed like a peasant. He chatted with other Jews while evening prayers were being recited. The common people who gathered around him were cheered by the message that it was possible to observe the commandments by means other than ritual.

Greatly influenced by the mystical teachings of the sixteenth-century kabbalist Isaac Luria and his school of thought, the Ba'al Shem Tov argued that the most important goal of religious life was spiritual communion with God. That communion, or constant attention of the mind to God Almighty, could be achieved not only through prayer but in each and every part of daily life, including when one was eating, drinking, and engaging in conversation. The Besht placed emotion over rationality, faith above study, and, most importantly, joy over asceticism. To the more conservative rabbinical leaders, all of this sounded heretical, and they attacked the Besht's preachings as "licentious." But their criticism had no effect on the commonfolk who were attracted to his philosophy. To the Ba'al Shem Tov's critics, known as the *mitnaggdim* (the opponents), his teachings posed a threat to their own belief system—that all that mattered spiritually was the study of Torah.

Among the Besht's most well-known sayings are:

- In the struggle with evil, only faith matters.
- The important thing is not how many separate commandments we obey, but the spirit in which we obey them.

- There is no room for God in a person who is full of himself.
- If a vision of a beautiful woman, or of any lovely thing, comes suddenly to mind, let a man say to himself: The source of such beauty must be the Divine force that permeates the universe. So why be attracted by a part? Better be drawn after the all. Perception of beauty is an experience of the eternal.
- Pray for the suppression of evil but never for one's own material well-being, for a separating veil arises if one admits the material into the spiritual.
- If you wish to live long, don't become famous.
- As a man prays for himself, so must he pray for his enemy.
- If I love God, what need have I of the world to come?

It had been part of messianic belief that an era of ecstasy would occur at some point in the distant future. Opposing this view, the Besht argued that one could experience cycles of ecstasy within one's own life. His idea was that one's attitude toward faith need not depend upon a messianic redeemer. In a famous letter to his brother-in-law, the Besht contended that the Messiah had spoken to him in a dream, saying that he would enter the world "only when all Israel is capable of uniting the lower and upper worlds through prayer and meditation."

Legend has it that once, in a dream, the Besht met Shabbatai Zevi, the deranged Turkish Jewish mystic who, in 1666, insisted that he was the Messiah. The false messiah Zevi asked the Besht to heal him. At first the Besht tried to do just that, but he quickly sensed that Zevi was trying to tempt him into becoming the false messiah's disciple. They wrestled, and Shabbatai was thrust into the underworld. The Besht said later, "He had a spark of holiness in him, but his pride destroyed him."

It was the Besht's hope to reinvigorate Judaism and so he trained a group of disciples who went on to create a mass mystical movement called Hasidism. Within a generation, it spread to a great many of Eastern Europe's Jews.

By the time of his death in 1760, a whole set of legends surrounded the Besht: he understood the language of birds and trees; his body was completely spiritual; he walked over the Dnestr River on a piece of clothing; he could bring the dead to life; he knew every secret; every Sabbath he extracted new meaning from the Torah; he was in constant touch with the true Messiah, who announced to the Besht that redemption depended upon everyone's accepting the Ba'al Shem Tov's teachings.

The Ba'al Shem Tov was sixty years old when he died, having influenced Jewish thought and everyday life more than many scholars who lived before—and after—him.

BERNARD BARUCH

Financial Wizard

Born August 19, 1870, in Camden, South Carolina; died June 20, 1965. American stock analyst and statesman. America's most respected civilian figure during World War I, Bernard Baruch was a financier who made a fortune in investments, then devoted his life to public service, serving as an advisor to several United States presidents, especially Woodrow Wilson and Franklin Roosevelt. His efforts during both world wars helped America mobilize its industrial resources.

BERNARD MANNES BARUCH'S FATHER, Simon, was a German-Jewish physician who immigrated to the United States and became a well-known Confederate Army surgeon. His mother, Belle (Wolfe) Baruch, was American-born and came from a family of South Carolina plantation owners. Bernard was the second of four sons.

When the family moved to New York in 1881, Baruch attended public school, and in 1884 he enrolled at the College of the City of New York. Tall, muscular, and agile, he was a fine athlete, excelling in lacrosse, boxing, and baseball. He graduated from college in 1889.

Baruch's first job was with a firm that dealt in druggists' glassware. Errands for the company took him to Wall Street, where the young man became dazzled by the prospect of making money.

In 1890, working as a driller in the Colorado gold fields, Baruch was tricked into buying some valueless mining stock, thereby learning the important lesson of never investing in anything that he had not fully researched.

Baruch next worked for the brokerage firm of A. A. Housman, earning five dollars a week as an office boy. In the evenings, he took courses in bookkeeping and contract law, studied financial and commercial manuals, and acquired a reputation as a budding authority on securities. He soon saved enough to buy his first bond.

In 1896, when Baruch was twenty-six years old, Housman offered him an eighth interest in the firm and, thanks to the wise trades he executed, Baruch received $6,000 in profits at the end of that year. The next year, on a $200 speculation in the sugar market, Baruch earned a $40,000 profit. That year, Baruch bought a seat on the New York Stock Exchange and became a partner in the Housman brokerage firm.

The same year, Baruch married Annie Griffen. She was the granddaughter of an Episcopal minister and the daughter of a glass manufacturer. They had two daughters and a son. Annie died in 1938.

By the age of thirty, having learned his trade well, Bernard Baruch was a millionaire. When Baruch told his father of this financial feat, he was disappointed to discover that his father did not share his excitement. "No, my son, I am not impressed. What I want to know is: How will you spend the money you have earned?"

In May 1903, just thirty-three years old, Baruch left the Housman firm to set up his own office in the field of industrial development. Over the next fourteen years, Baruch invested money of his own and that of others in promising new enterprises. Among these were Texas Gulf Sulfur, which gave the United States control of the world sulfur market, and Utah Copper, which doubled the world's output of copper. Baruch also invested in one firm that exploited the discovery that rubber could be made from the guayule plant, and in another that made use of the fact that gold could be profitably extracted from a low-grade ore.

During his twenty-two years on Wall Street, Baruch acquired a reputation for prescience in his investment decisions. "I make no apologies," he once said. "I am a speculator." He was unsurpassed in his uncanny ability to observe which stocks were a good gamble. He was a genius in his profession.

Baruch was a commanding physical presence as well. He was nearly six feet, four inches tall and weighed 202 pounds. He liked to eat well, but rarely drank alcohol. He smoked cigarettes until he was 64 years old, then quit. He lived well into his nineties.

In 1912, Bernard Baruch turned to politics and supported an up-and-coming politician in the Democratic party named Woodrow Wilson. Baruch was a major contributor to Wilson's first presidential campaign. Wilson was elected to the United States presidency in 1913.

From early in 1915, Baruch championed the cause of America's speedy preparation for war. With the threat of war becoming stronger by 1916, President Wilson appointed Baruch a member of the Advisory Commission to the Council of National Defense, the financier's first post in the American government. Wilson liked to refer to Baruch as "Dr. Facts" because Baruch knew so much. In order to devote his attention to Wilson's administration, Baruch liquidated his holdings, resigned from his positions in various industrial firms, and sold his stock exchange seat so that he could be in Washington full time.

In March 1918, Wilson appointed Baruch chairman of the War Industries Board (WIB), which took charge of mobilizing the United States' industrial resources for the war effort. In this position, Baruch became the country's "industrial czar," with nearly unlimited power in overseeing American industries' capacity to meet wartime needs. He recruited experienced businessmen to advise him on a voluntary basis.

After the 1918 armistice, Baruch became an economic advisor to President Wilson at the Paris Peace Conference. In that capacity, he helped shape the economic clauses of the peace treaty. He described his peacemaking role in a 1920 treatise called *The Making of the Reparations and Economic Section of the Peace Treaty*.

After the war, Baruch became a commentator on current events while continuing as an unofficial economic advisor to American presidents. He was viewed as an elder statesman, a title he richly deserved. But he liked to show his humble side. He would often say that his office was in fact a New York City park bench where he frequently met with other well-known business figures.

Just before the 1929 Wall Street crash, Baruch was asked by some investors for a tip in connection with the continually advancing stock market. "Put your money into four-percent bonds," he advised them. Having apparently taken his own advice, Baruch survived the crash better than most.

In the 1930s, Baruch helped finance the campaigns of various Democratic party candidates. A friend and advisor to President Franklin D. Roosevelt and his wife, Eleanor, Baruch believed that Roosevelt should not dismiss Adolf Hitler's rise to power in Germany and that the president should prepare the nation for the possibility of war. To that end, in 1934 Baruch urged the stockpiling of two important war items: rubber and tin.

Baruch continued to be very involved in national politics and served in an advisory capacity in many areas. In January 1941, as America debated whether to get involved in the war then raging in Europe, Baruch urged the centralization of defense powers in the president's hands. The following year, Baruch chaired the Rubber Survey Committee. A year later, he became advisor to the war mobilization director, James Byrnes. In 1944, Baruch was named a member of a committee that studied postwar adjustment problems in advance of the anticipated end of the war.

Baruch wrote the first official American policy proposal on the control of atomic energy, submitting it to the United Nations on June 14, 1946. The proposal was never adopted, however. That same year, he was appointed a member of the American delegation to the United Nations Atomic Energy Commission.

Baruch did not care deeply about being Jewish. His wife was Episcopalian and their children were raised in her faith. He made it clear that he considered himself an American first, a Jew second. Yet, during World War II, he took a strong interest in the plight of European Jews and provided financial relief to Jewish refugees, suggesting that they be settled in Uganda. Baruch was at first against the establishment of the state of Israel. But at the United Nations debate in 1947 on that subject, he rallied to the Zionist cause. In later years, however, he changed his attitude again and was not an overt supporter of the Jewish state.

At the age of eighty-seven, in 1957, Baruch published the first part of his memoirs, *My Own Story*, following it three years later with the second installment, *The Public Years*. He died at the age of ninety-five in 1965.

MENACHEM BEGIN

Negotiator of Israel's First Peace Treaty

Born August 16, 1913, in Brisk (Brest-Litovsk), Poland; died March 9, 1992. Israeli political leader. An underground activist who helped expel the British from Palestine in the 1940s, Begin was called a terrorist by his Arab enemies and a warmonger by his Israeli political adversaries. He headed the political opposition from 1949 until 1977 when, on his ninth try for the premiership, he succeeded. Begin led Israel for the next six years, signing the 1979 Israel-Egypt peace treaty and overseeing the 1982 war against Lebanon.

I F THE SYMBOL OF THE HOLOCAUST was the defenseless, helpless Jew, the heroic symbol of the modern state of Israel became the fighting Jew, symbolized by Menachem Begin.

Menachem Begin was born on August 16, 1913. His father, Dov Ze'ev Begin, was a timber merchant and a leader of the Jewish community in his native Brisk. Dov met and married his wife, Hassia, in 1906. Menachem was the youngest of three children.

Begin's early childhood years in Poland were filled with violence and war. When his father was forced to flee from their home after the Russian authorities suspected him of cooperating with the German enemy, Menachem remained behind in Brisk with his mother, brother, and sister. World War I meant a life on the run for young Menachem. One afternoon, while visiting relatives in Drohicyzn, the Cossacks arrived and the five-year-old Menachem sought shelter in a stack of straw. The episode, with its lasting message of powerlessness, was chiseled into his memory forever.

Menachem displayed a quick mind and a passion for *Eretz Yisrael*, the Land of Israel. "From my early youth I had been taught by my father . . . that we Jews were to return to *Eretz Yisrael*." His father's love for his heritage had an influence on him as well. When he was fourteen, Begin refused to take a Latin exam scheduled for a Saturday, the Jewish

Begin at his office at the Prime Minister's Office in Jerusalem.

Sabbath, at the Polish government school he attended. It was his first recorded act of prideful defiance in defense of his Jewishness. His non-Jewish classmates were not sympathetic and his teacher gave him a failing grade.

In 1923, at age ten, Begin made his first mark as a budding orator. Standing on a table at a Lag B'Omer festival, he spoke in a mixture of Hebrew and Yiddish, explaining the significance of the Jewish holiday.

Begin, in 1929, joined the militant Zionist youth movement called Betar, founded by Ze'ev Jabotinsky in 1923. Betar represented Jabotinsky's revisionist views of Zionism, favoring the establishment of a Jewish state on both sides of the Jordan River. As he grew up, Begin's health was fragile and some suspected that he might be tubercular. As an adolescent, he preferred chess over sports, and books over almost anything else. Begin decided to attend law school at Warsaw University in 1931, but his heart remained with the Betar movement and so, while studying, he took a paying job in Betar's central office in Warsaw. By September 1935, he had become head of Betar's Propaganda Department and, further developing his fiery oratorical style, he spoke fervently about his cause. He graduated from the university in 1935 with a master's degree in jurisprudence.

From 1936 to 1938, Begin served as general secretary of the Czechoslovakian Betar branch. In April 1939, he was appointed commander of the Polish Betar. The following month he married Aliza Arnold. (They had one son, Benjamin, and two daughters, Hassia and Leah.) Soon after, he was arrested and incarcerated for several months for organizing mass demonstrations protesting British restrictions on Jewish immigration to Palestine, outside the British Embassy in Warsaw. Once released, he fled Warsaw just before invading German forces arrived in Poland. Begin traveled, mostly on foot, to Vilna in Lithuania.

Begin wanted to continue on to Palestine, but in September 1940 he was arrested by Communist authorities who viewed him as suspicious because of his Betar activities. He was sentenced to eight years of slave labor in the Arctic wasteland.

In 1941, following Germany's attack on the Soviet Union, Begin and thousands of other Polish prisoners were released from their Arctic prison to supply manpower for a new Polish army being organized on Soviet soil. A few months later, Begin's unit was sent to Amman, Transjordan.

While in the army in May 1942, Begin entered Palestine and became head of the Jerusalem Betar group. A year later, he was demobilized from the Polish army in exile and became commander of the Irgun Zvai Leumi, the National Military Organization, a paramilitary group also linked with Jabotinsky's Revisionist faction. It had organized a sabotage campaign against the British mandatory administration in Palestine.

By 1946, the British had placed a thirty-thousand-dollar price on Begin's head, forcing him to assume other identities. He became Israel Halperin, a Tel Aviv law student, at one point, and at another, Israel Sassover, a bearded Talmudic scholar. Through it all, he continued to secretly command the two thousand Irgun activists.

Near the outbreak of the 1948 War of Independence, the Irgun joined forces with the mainstream Jewish defense organization Haganah to fight the Arab armies. The conflict between Begin and Israeli Prime Minister David Ben-Gurion over control of Jewish military manpower reached a peak in June 1948, when the Irgun tried to land the ship *Altalena* on Israeli shores. Loaded with arms and munitions, part of which was meant for the Irgun, the ship, with Begin aboard, was fired upon and blown up on the orders of Ben-Gurion, who feared the Irgun planned

State of Israel Government Press Office

Begin visits the Western Wall in Jerusalem.

a coup against the new Israeli government. Begin at first refused to leave the ship, even after it was in flames, but was eventually dragged off by his aides.

In July, Begin and his former Irgun allies formed a new political party, the Herut (freedom) movement. Their first test came in January 1952, when Begin and his group staged a rally in Jerusalem's Zion Square to protest Israel's plan to open negotiations with the West German government for wartime reparations. The rally turned into a riot and Begin was suspended from his parliamentary seat for fifteen months.

Herut lost election after election, yet Begin continued at the helm. Finally, on May 17, 1977, only seven weeks after suffering a serious heart attack, Begin led the Likud bloc (an amalgam of Herut and other right-wing groups) to victory over the Labor party, which had Shimon Peres at its helm. Assailed by Labor party critics as a warmonger, Begin surprised his foes when he warmly accepted Egyptian President Anwar Sadat's plan to visit Jerusalem in November 1977. The two leaders began serious peace talks during that visit.

Another sixteen months passed before Israel and Egypt signed a peace treaty, the first between the Jewish state and an Arab country. For their peacemaking efforts, Begin and Sadat shared the Nobel Peace Prize in 1978.

By the spring of 1981, when Begin faced reelection, the polls strongly favored Peres's Labor party because there was a sense that the prime minister had neglected the Israeli economy, which was suffering from the effects of labor strife and an annual inflation rate of 130 percent. Begin was spared defeat, however, after he sent Israeli jet planes to destroy the Iraqi nuclear reactor on June 7, 1981, just three weeks before the election. Begin's aggressive action against the potential Iraqi nuclear threat earned him a solid following.

Begin's first term as prime minister had been marked by peaceful gestures, but his second term deteriorated into military conflicts marring his overall tenure. On June 6, 1982, Begin sent the Israeli army into Lebanon to deal with Palestinian fighters who had been launching deadly raids against Israel's northern communities. Begin hoped to contain the war in an area of twenty-five square kilometers in southern Lebanon, but his defense minister, Ariel Sharon, spurred the Israel Defense Forces to move farther north. The army reached Beirut a mere five days after the war began. The war cost the lives of over six hundred Israelis; three thousand were wounded.

By August 1983, Menachem Begin was a broken man, in part because his wife, Aliza, had died the previous November, and in part because he realized that Israel's most controversial war had dragged on at far too high a cost in human life. He resigned as prime minister and went into a self-enforced seclusion, seeing only close friends and family members in his Jerusalem apartment.

Begin died on March 9, 1992, at the age of seventy-eight. In June 2004, the Menachem Begin Heritage Center, based on the concept of American presidential libraries, opened in Jerusalem.

SAUL BELLOW

Winner of the Nobel Prize for Literature

Born June 10, 1915, in Lachine, Quebec, Canada. American writer. Although Canadian by birth, he is considered one of the United States's finest living writers. Bellow has written outstanding books for over forty years, including *The Adventures of Augie March* (1953), *Herzog* (1964), *Humboldt's Gift* (1975), and *The Dean's December* (1982). He won the Nobel Prize for Literature in 1976.

SAUL BELLOW was born in 1915 in Lachine, Quebec, a Montreal suburb, the youngest of Abraham and Liza Bellow's four children—three boys and a girl. His parents had immigrated to Canada from St. Petersburg, Russia, two years before Saul's birth. "My parents were both Jewish," Bellow wrote, "as were all my ancestors so far as anyone can be certain."

His parents were observant Jews. Yiddish was Saul's first language, but he also learned French, English, and Hebrew. His "traditional Jewish education" began at age four with the study of Hebrew. Hebrew-language lessons came to a halt in his junior year of high school, however, "when I became something of a radical," he says.

Abraham Bellow had been an onion importer in Russia. Once he had moved to Canada, he became involved in a number of business ventures, among them onions, bootlegging, and coal, with varying degrees of success.

During Saul's childhood years, the Bellow family lived in a tough immigrant neighborhood. "I saw mayhem all around me from an early age," Bellow recalled. "At the age of eight, I understood what sickness and death were."

His mother, who died when he was fifteen years old, expressed the wish that he would become a violinist or a rabbi. But Bellow wanted to become a writer. He was attracted to books, not to the Jewish scholarly works he found at home, but rather to the works of Mark Twain, Edgar Allan Poe, Theodore Dreiser, and Sherwood Anderson. As a teenager, he read his compositions to his school friends, soliciting their responses. At age seventeen, he and a friend ran away to New York, hoping, in vain it turned out, to find publishers for their writings.

Bellow entered the University of Chicago after graduating from Tuley High School in 1933. Two years later, he transferred to Northwestern University, from which he later graduated with honors in anthropology and sociology. After his graduation, he considered studying English literature at the University of Wisconsin, but instead chose to use a scholarship he had won to study anthropology. He quickly found that subject to be less to his liking. "Every time I worked on my thesis, it turned out to be a story."

In December 1937 Bellow quit school, determined to pursue a writing career. He was employed briefly by the Work Projects Administration Federal Writers' Project, preparing short biographies of Midwestern novelists.

Bellow became a naturalized American citizen in 1941. From 1938 to 1942, Bellow taught at Pestalozzi-Froebel Teachers College in Chicago. In 1943, he became a member of the editorial department of the *Encyclopedia Britannica*, where he worked on Mortimer J. Adler's Great Books project. Later, he joined the merchant marines, finding time during his stint there to complete his first novel, *Dangling Man* (1944). Capturing the tensions of wartime well, the novel, well received by critics, told the story of a dissatisfied young man from Chicago who was waiting to be drafted.

Bellow knew that he had something to say and he sensed that others were interested in it. "I think I felt it from the very outset. I published my first book forty years ago," he said in the 1980s, "and to my immense sur-

Saul Bellow

The Jewish Week

prise—although I don't think it was a very good book—people got in touch with me—hundreds of people—to say, 'This is just what we've been thinking and feeling!'"

Bellow's next novel, *The Victim* (1947), focused on the character Asa Leventhal, a Jewish woman who was mentally unstable.

From 1946 to 1949, Bellow taught English at the University of Minnesota, after which he traveled to Paris and Rome on a Guggenheim Fellowship. In Paris, he began writing *The Adventures of Augie March* (1953). The hero of the book, whom Bellow treats with poignant humor, learns how to survive in his Jewish Chicago neighborhood despite the hostile environment. *Adventures* won the 1954 National Book Award and established Bellow's reputation as a major emerging writer.

Bellow returned to a more serious mood in the novella *Seize the Day* (1956), which is set on the Upper West Side of New York. The main character is Tommy Wilhelm, an ex-salesman who is something of a failure. Bellow's next work, a novel called *Henderson the Rain King* (1959), relates the tale of an American millionaire who, on the surface, appears to have all that life can give, but suffers inside from a spiritual loneliness.

From 1950 to 1952 Bellow was a visiting lecturer at New York University and from 1954 to 1959 an associate professor of English at the University of Minnesota. In 1962, he left New York because he disliked what he perceived as the "increased politicization of writers." He returned to Chicago that year and, as a professor at the University of Chicago, he served on the Committee on Social Thought.

Bellow's bestselling novel, *Herzog* (1964), considered his masterpiece, won him another National Book Award. The hero, Moses Herzog, is a Jewish everyman who describes himself as "a learned specialist in intellectual history . . . handicapped by emotional confusion." Herzog seeks self-understanding through his writing of impassioned letters to family, friends, and famous people.

Bellow published his seventh novel, *Mr. Sammler's Planet*, in 1970. This novel tells about an elderly Holocaust survivor living on New York's Upper West Side who speculates on the decline and fall of Western culture. Bellow's most pessimistic work, the book is deeply critical of America in the 1960s and is, as one critic noted, "an onslaught on the way the vast majority of Americans live." The novel won Bellow his third National Book Award.

Bellow spent eight years writing his Pulitzer Prize-winning novel *Humboldt's Gift* (1975). Its major themes are the role of the artist in modern society and the conflict between materialism and art. When it appeared, Bellow called it a "comic book about death."

In October 1976, Bellow became the seventh American writer to win the Nobel Prize for Literature. The Swedish Academy cited his "exuberant ideas, flashing irony, hilarious comedy, and burning compassion," applauding Bellow's typical hero "who keeps trying to find a foothold during his wanderings in our tottering world, one who can never relinquish his faith that the value of life depends on its dignity, not its success." In accepting the award, Bellow referred to Joseph Conrad's conviction that the province of art is "what is fundamental, enduring, essential."

To Jerusalem and Back: A Personal Account (1976) was Saul Bellow's first nonfiction book and was based on a visit he had made to Israel the previous year. Of the intensity of life in Israel, he wrote: "These people are actively, individually involved in universal history. I don't see how they can bear it."

Bellow's next novel, *The Dean's December* (1982), deals with political and social issues. Another novel, *More Die of Heartbreak*, appeared in 1987. In 1994, in another departure from his fictional mode, Bellow published a collection of his essays and criticism entitled *It All Adds Up*.

Bellow has been married four times: to Anita Goshkin in 1937, to Alexandra Tschacbasov in 1956, to Susan Glassman in 1961, and to Alexandra Ionesco Tuleca in 1974. All of these unions ended in divorce. He had a son with each of his first three wives.

In 1996 he ate a poisonous fish while on a Caribbean vacation and was ill for a year. His twenty-second book, a 104-page novella called *The Actual*, published in 1997, is a romantic comedy set in contemporary Chicago.

Bellow proudly identifies himself as a Jew. "Here and there some loony or other will now and then identify me as an assimilationist," he wrote. "I am no such thing."

On October 17, 2000, James Atlas's 688-page *Bellow: A Biography*, which had been ten years in preparation, was released to critical acclaim. In December 2001, an anthology of Bellow's short writings was issued under the title *Collected Stories*.

DAVID BEN-GURION

Founding Father of the State of Israel

Born October 16, 1886, in Plonsk, Pale of Settlement, then Russian Poland; died December 1, 1973. First prime minister of the state of Israel.
An active Zionist since childhood, Ben-Gurion became one of the political leaders of the Jewish community in Palestine, building its social and
political institutions, preparing it for statehood. As the country's first prime
minister, he governed almost uninterruptedly for the country's initial fifteen years and was the dominant political figure of that era.

ORN DAVID GRUEN IN PLONSK, in the Pale of Settlement, which was part of what was
then Russian Poland, to a "freethinking," middle-class, Zionist family, David Ben-
Gurion was given a traditional religious education in a Hebrew-language *heder* (a Jewish school for young children) but learned secular subjects from private tutors. His father, an

David Ben-Gurion

unlicensed attorney whose house was the
center of Zionist activity in the town, infused
him with a strong belief in Zionism. David's
mother, Sheindel, died when he was only
eleven years old.

As a youngster, Ben-Gurion organized the
Zionist Ezra Society in order to promote the
study of Hebrew and Zionist ideology. Later,
in 1905, when he was nineteen, he joined
the Poalei Zion (Workers of Zion) movement, traveled on its behalf to Warsaw and
other, smaller towns, and was arrested twice
during the Revolution of 1905. However,
thanks to his father's intervention, Ben-
Gurion was released both times. As a result
of his participation in Jewish self-defense
work at the time, Ben-Gurion came to appreciate how important it was for Jews to be
able to stand up for themselves.

In 1906 Ben-Gurion traveled to Palestine,
and there he worked for several years along
the Mediterranean seacoast in the orange

groves of Petah Tikvah and in the wine cellars of Rishon le-Zion. He was chosen to join the forty-member central committee of Poalei Zion. In October of that year he helped formulate the party's first platform, stressing the obligation of everyone to settle in *Eretz Yisrael* and to use the Hebrew language, rather than Yiddish, in everyday parlance.

From 1907 to 1910, as a farmer in the Lower Galilee, Ben-Gurion became convinced that, in his words, "the settlement of the land is the only true Zionism, all else being self-deception, empty verbiage, and merely a pastime." In 1910, while writing for the new Poalei Zion organ *Ahdut* (*Unity*), he took the pen name Ben-Gurion.

Hoping to represent the Palestinian Jewish community in the Turkish parliament, Ben-Gurion enrolled at Istanbul University to study law. His studies came to a halt, however, after only two semesters because he developed malaria. He thought of returning to Palestine but was stranded in Turkey when World War I broke out. Finally arriving back in Palestine, Ben-Gurion sided with the Allies against the Turkish government. As a result, in 1915 he was expelled from Turkey because of his subversive Zionist work.

Ben-Gurion headed for the United States in May 1915. There he worked both as a writer and a political organizer for the Zionist He-Halutz movement, which advocated establishing a Jewish legion within the British army in order to liberate Palestine from the Turks. In 1917, Ben-Gurion married Paula Munweiss, a Brooklyn nurse who was also an active member of Poalei Zion. They had three children during their marriage.

Helping in 1918 to organize the newly-formed Jewish Legion, which was made up of American and British volunteers, Ben-Gurion once again traveled to Palestine, where he served in the Legion during General Allenby's operations against the Turks. After the war, Ben-Gurion helped build up the Labor party and found the Histadrut, or General Federation of Labor. In 1921 he became a political leader of the tiny *Yishuv*, the Jewish community in Palestine, and served until 1935. During the 1920s and 1930s, Ben-Gurion presided over the growth of the Histadrut's network of social institutions.

Consolidating his own personal power and that of his party, Ben-Gurion was instrumental in bringing about the merger of the major Zionist labor parties to form a new party called Mapai in 1930. Mapai dominated Jewish politics in Palestine and later in the state of Israel until 1977. Leaders of the Zionist Organization set up the Jewish Agency to represent Zionist interests in Palestine, and in 1933 Ben-Gurion was elected to the Jewish Agency Executive and then chairman of its board. Ben-Gurion was now the prime minister of the *Yishuv* in all but name.

Ben-Gurion's two main objectives in the late 1930s were to create a Jewish state and to promote Jewish immigration to Palestine. In 1937 he supported the partition plan of the British Royal Commission, contending that no matter how small Jewish sovereignty might be, it could be enough to rescue the growing number of Jewish refugees from Hitler's Nazi Germany.

After the British government issued the infamous White Paper limiting Jewish immigration to Palestine in May 1939, Ben-Gurion was put in the awkward position of having to choose whether to support the British in their struggle against Nazi Germany or to "punish" England for its decree by withholding support.

Ben-Gurion decided on a middle course. As World War II broke out, he diplomatically announced, "We shall fight the White Paper as though there was no war, and we shall fight the Nazis as though there was no White Paper."

With Zionist leader Chaim Weizmann's power declining in the 1940s, Ben-Gurion had no other challenger to lead the Zionist movement. Although others, both British leaders and Zionists, advised the *Yishuv* to take a "go-slow" approach on the question of Jewish statehood, Ben-Gurion believed firmly that statehood was essential. A 1945 visit he paid to Holocaust survivors in Germany further strengthened his resolve. The following year, the Jewish Agency chose Ben-Gurion to be, in effect, the defense minister of the *Yishuv*. His mission: to strengthen the Haganah, the fledgling Jewish defense organization in Palestine.

As the acknowledged leader of the Zionist movement, Ben-Gurion proclaimed the independence of the state of Israel on May 14, 1948. He was chosen both the new state's prime minister and defense minister. His political and military leadership during Israel's War of Independence of 1948 and 1949, shown especially in his ability to concentrate the thin Israeli forces in the right strategic locations, brought about Israel's triumph against overwhelming odds.

For the next fifteen years, David Ben-Gurion governed the state of Israel almost uninterruptedly. He went into early retirement in late 1953, and made his home at the Negev kibbutz Sde Boker, but returned to office in early 1955, promoting a policy of swift retaliation to Arab attacks. This initiative was best reflected in Israel's lightning victory during the October 1956 Sinai Campaign against Egypt.

Ben-Gurion's most important overall contribution was in fostering the concept of *mamlakhtiyut* (statism), which meant insisting that the state take over those institutions that had functioned semi-autonomously under the *Yishuv*. For example, he dismantled all of pre-state Israel's private armies, including the cantankerous Irgun. He then amalgamated their manpower and equipment into the new Israel Defense Forces.

Ben-Gurion was a realist as a diplomat. Recognizing that Israel was too tiny and too poor to go without friends among the major powers, Ben-Gurion first cultivated France, and later the United States, as important allies. Despite harsh criticism that it was too early to deal with post-Hitler Germany, Ben-Gurion made arrangements with West Germany to pay reparations to Jewish refugees who had suffered at Hitler's hands.

Marring his final days as a political leader

David Ben-Gurion

were his arguments with Mapai party colleagues. Rather than let the 1950s political scandal known as the Lavon Affair fade, as many thought it should, Ben-Gurion kept it alive. He looked for vindication for his view of events, believing that Defense Minister Pinhas Lavon was responsible for a 1954 security mishap in which Israeli agents who engaged in sabotage in Egypt were later discovered, tried, and some executed.

Splitting with many of his Mapai colleagues in 1965, Ben-Gurion, along with Shimon Peres and Moshe Dayan, formed a new party called Rafi, which won ten seats in Knesset elections.

David Ben-Gurion was described by Golda Meir as "the greatest Jew in our generation." After a bout of bronchitis and a stroke, he died in December 1973 at the age of eighty-seven, just two months after the outbreak of the Yom Kippur War. He was buried at Sde Boker.

JACK BENNY

"The World's Finest Comedian"

Born February 14, 1894, in Waukegan, Illinois; died December 27, 1974. American comedian, radio and television star. Though at first he seemed destined for a career as a concert violinist, Jack Benny embarked on an entertainment career after his comic talents were discovered while serving in the United States Navy. After brief stints in vaudeville and Hollywood, he turned his talents to radio, then television. During his forty-year career, he became one of the entertainment world's most popular figures. He was master of the slow take and the piqued stare, and he perfected the indignant, precisely timed and inflected "Well" that became his trademark.

JACK BENNY was born Benjamin Kubelsky in Waukegan, Illinois, in 1894. His father, Meyer, and his mother, Emma, were Orthodox Jewish immigrants from Europe. Meyer ran a saloon and, later, a dry goods store. Young Jack helped out in the store.

Benny was timid, but he learned how to take care of himself because his parents were so busy with their businesses. Studying the violin as a child, he showed sufficient talent for others to suggest that he become a concert artist.

At the age of fifteen, he took a job as a violinist in the orchestra of the Barrison Theater in Waukegan and was paid eight dollars a week, but playing during matinees led to his expulsion from school. At that point Benny left home and set up a touring vaudeville act with Cora Salisbury, the Barrison Theater's orchestra leader. The act was known as "Salisbury and Benny—From Grand Opera to Ragtime." Jack was the violinist; Salisbury was the pianist.

In 1913, now nineteen years old, Benny established another vaudeville act, with pia-

Jack Benny

nist Lyman Woods, known as "Benny and Woods." They performed popular tunes and made as much as $200 a week.

World War I interrupted, however. Benny joined the United States Navy. While stationed at the Great Lakes Naval Training Station, Benny's comic talents were discovered. In 1918 he was cast in a sailor revue called *Maritime Frolics*. He played the juvenile lead with great success because of his humorous way of delivering lines. His expertise as a violinist didn't count for as much as his comedic ability. Benny himself, however, would always remain attached to the violin even as he gained popularity as a comedian. "When I feel troubled and depressed, I play the violin and the bad mood goes away," he told *The Saturday Evening Post* in 1963.

Although Benny's original stage name was Ben K. Benny, he was often confused with another entertainer named Ben Bernie who, it so happened, also used a violin in his act. And so, as his career progressed, Benjamin Kubelsky became Jack Benny.

Throughout the 1920s, Benny's comedic talents won him great praise. He played New York's Palace Theater and toured with such stars as the Marx Brothers, Nora Bayes, and Frank Fay. On January 25, 1927, Benny married Sadye Marks, a salesgirl in the hosiery department of the May Company department store in Los Angeles. She adopted the stage name of Mary Livingstone and became part of Jack Benny's vaudeville act, a foil for her husband's humor, until her retirement from show business in 1957. They had an adopted daughter, Joan.

Benny made his film debut in 1929, but really won his stardom in the 1930s on radio, and later on television. His best-known films included *Charley's Aunt*, *George Washington*, and *To Be or Not to Be*. In the latter film, Benny played the head of a Polish theater troupe who becomes a spy during World War II.

Benny's radio debut occurred on March 29, 1932, when he was invited as a guest on newspaper columnist Ed Sullivan's program. Benny opened his monologue this way: "Ladies and gentlemen, this is Jack Benny talking. There will be a slight pause while you say, 'Who cares?'" But, in fact, they turned out to care a lot. Within a few weeks, Benny had his own program which, for the next twenty-three years, was heard at 7 P.M. on Sunday nights. From 1934 to 1936, the program was the most popular radio program on the air; from 1937 until 1955, when it finally went off the air, it was rarely out of the top ten programs.

Benny's television program debuted in 1950 and was called *The Jack Benny Show*. It began as an occasional special, becoming biweekly, then weekly, and remained on television until 1965. Benny won Emmys for the program in 1957 and 1958.

Jack Benny created a style of humor that left American radio and television audiences rolling in laughter. He did not tell jokes nor was he a slapstick comedian. He was funny because of his mannerisms, his deadpan looks, his slow burn. Benny got laughs not for what he said, but for what he seemed to be thinking and his droll manner. All it took was a facial expression and a brief remark such as "Well!" or "Hmmm," or "Now cut that out!" followed by a perfectly timed pause.

In 1948, when Benny played the London Palladium, someone in the audience tapped a critic on the shoulder during one of the entertainer's prolonged pauses and asked when Jack would actually do something. "I explained," the critic later said, "that Jack Benny never did anything, which was his particular genius."

Through his comedy routines, Benny acquired the reputation of being show business's most famous miser. He once put on a jeweler's glass to appraise the diamond ring of the girl he was embracing. He liked to tell the story of the holdup man who demanded, "Your money or your life." After a long pause the holdup man asked, "Well?" To which Benny indignantly replied, "I'm thinking it over."

Vanity was also a large part of Benny's comedy routine. So concerned was Benny with maintaining his youth that he insisted, when asked, that he was thirty-nine years old—year after year. This became so much a part of the American psyche that when Americans want to conceal their age, they also become "thirty-nine."

Jack Benny continued to rely on his love of the violin, but only for comedic effect in his routines. He played what became his signature tune, "Love in Bloom," ineptly on purpose, winning more laughs.

Benny became the first comedian to let some of his straight men share in the laughs, whether it was his valet, Eddie (Rochester) Anderson, singer Dennis Day, or announcer Don Wilson. Once, Wilson pitched an idea for a script in which Benny would play a triple role: "a man, a boy, and a dog." "How can I play a dog?" Benny asked. "You have to take your glasses off," singer Dennis Day offered helpfully as part of the skit.

"The show itself is the important thing," Benny once said. "As long as people think the show is funny, it doesn't matter to me who gets the punch lines." But he wasn't interested in pointed sarcasm. When he stated his philosophy about comedy, it was: "There are enough basic concepts in life to poke fun at. Funny things happen to us all the time . . . . If a gag is hurtful, I don't need it."

Ed Wynn, another great comic, described Jack Benny as "the world's finest comedian—comedian meaning a man who says things funny, as opposed to a comic, who says funny things."

Benny was a proud Jew. Once, preparing for his Sunday program, set to begin at 4 P.M. in Los Angeles on the eve of Yom Kippur, Benny realized that on the East Coast, sundown would already have occurred. This meant that the high holy day would be ushered in before his program ended. He told an assistant: "I wouldn't want people to think I'm desecrating this holiday by working on it." The assistant, trying to joke, said all the Jews on the East Coast would be in synagogue and wouldn't know of his indiscretion. But Benny stood firm. "I wasn't thinking of the Jews. I wouldn't like the Gentiles to think I didn't respect my religion," he said.

When Benny died in 1974 at the age of eighty, people the world over mourned a comedian who had brought great pleasure to audiences for many decades.

ELIEZER BEN-YEHUDA

The Father of Modern Hebrew

> Born in 1858, in Luzhky, Lithuania; died December 16, 1922. Hebrew writer and lexicographer. Eliezer Ben-Yehuda was seized early in his life with the idea that the Hebrew language should be revived as the main language for Jews. Eventually he made his way to Paris and then to Palestine. Once in Palestine, he virtually single-handedly made Hebrew the everyday language for all Jews there.

THE FATHER OF MODERN HEBREW was born Eliezer Yizhak Perelman but used the pseudonym Ben-Yehuda in his literary efforts, officially adopting the name when he traveled to Palestine in 1881. His father was a Habad Hasid (a follower of the Lubavitcher Rebbe). He died when Ben-Yehuda was five years old.

When he was thirteen, Ben-Yehuda was sent to an uncle so that he could attend a yeshiva in nearby Polotsk. The yeshiva's director introduced Ben-Yehuda to secular literature, including a Hebrew translation of Daniel Defoe's *Robinson Crusoe*. Ben-Yehuda's commitment to making Hebrew a modern language used for secular as well as religious purposes began at this time.

Ben-Yehuda's uncle was concerned that his nephew was straying from traditional Jewish learning, so the boy was sent to study in a yeshiva in the Vilna district. There he met another Habad Hasid named Samuel Naphtali Herz Jonas, a writer for Hebrew periodicals. Jonas convinced Ben-Yehuda that he should continue formal study so that he could graduate from high school. Jonas's eldest daughter, Deborah, taught Ben-Yehuda Russian, French, and German. A year later, Ben-Yehuda entered the Dvinsk Gymnasium, graduating from the school in 1877 at the age of nineteen. He then traveled to Paris to study medicine.

Ben-Yehuda had become a sympathizer with the Russian revolutionary movement, further detaching himself from traditional Jewish activities. When Russia and Turkey went to war in 1877, the struggle of the Balkan nations for their independence persuaded Ben-Yehuda that Jews, too, should strive for a national revival. He hoped to settle eventually in Palestine.

In 1879, Ben-Yehuda wrote an article called "*She'elah Lohata*" ("A Burning Question") for the Hebrew-language magazine *Ha-Shahar*, using the name E. Ben-Yehuda in print for the first time. In the article, he advocated Jewish immigration to Palestine, arguing that only in a country with a Jewish majority could a living Hebrew literature and a distinct Jewish nationality develop and survive. He argued that Jews should speak Hebrew as their everyday language.

While studying medicine in Paris, Ben-Yehuda contracted tuberculosis and believed that he had little time left to live. He was hospitalized at the Rothschild Hospital, where he met a Jerusalem scholar, A.M. Luncz, who told Ben-Yehuda that the Jews in Jerusalem used the Sephardic pronunciation in speaking Hebrew. Ben-Yehuda became convinced that this pronunciation was closer to the biblical one.

Ben-Yehuda regularly sent timely articles promoting Jewish settlement in Palestine to a Jerusalem-based Hebrew-language journal called *Havatzelet*, but he became increasingly concerned that he would be branded a hypocrite for urging this immigration while he remained in Paris. He never wavered in his resolve on the issue. "In those days," he wrote, "it was as if the heavens had suddenly opened, and a clear, incandescent light flashed before my eyes, and a mighty inner voice sounded in my ears: the renascence of Israel on its ancestral soil."

Eliezer Ben-Yehuda

State of Israel Government Press Office

In time Ben-Yehuda did follow his own lead. In 1881, halting his medical studies midstream, he decided to immigrate to Palestine at once. While en route, in Vienna, he reunited with Deborah Jonas, and they were married in Cairo before reaching Jaffa together that year.

In a daunting way to begin a marriage, Ben-Yehuda announced to his new wife that from now on they would only speak Hebrew to each other. Deborah agreed. Her husband decided that they would use the Sephardic pronunciation.

Only a few people spoke casual Hebrew in Jerusalem. Because they thought it a holy language, Orthodox Jews would not consider uttering Hebrew outside of the synagogue. The few secular Jews in Palestine, whose descendants were European, also had no interest in speaking Hebrew. Yet, as the new associate editor of *Havatzelet*, Ben-Yehuda set for himself the task of making Hebrew the language of his Jewish people.

When Ben-Yehuda learned that Deborah was pregnant, he asked her to pledge that their child would be the first in centuries to hear only the Hebrew language at home. Again, she went along with her husband's wishes. Their first son, Ben-Zion (later called Ithamar Ben-Avi) thus became the first modern Hebrew-speaking youngster. This was not, however, without its strains. For all of the Ben-Yehudas' five children, using Hebrew as their everyday language meant that they lacked friends with whom they could communicate and play.

Ben-Yehuda went about ingratiating himself to the Orthodox Jews of Jerusalem, believing that they would be the easiest segment of the Jewish community to convert to speaking modern Hebrew. He grew a beard and earlocks and convinced his wife to wear a *sheytl* (wig). But these efforts were all to no avail. The Orthodox Jews reviled Ben-Yehuda, accusing him of debasing the holy tongue through everyday use. They threw stones at him and denounced him to the Turkish authorities. He was even jailed briefly by the Turkish authorities for sedition.

Ben-Yehuda persisted in his mission, however, founding the Hebrew Language Council in 1890, the forerunner of the Academy of the Hebrew Language, and establishing the first Hebrew-language newspaper for children. He also encouraged Jews to take a Hebrew-language surname, as he had done in exchanging Perelman for Ben-Yehuda, a practice followed by most Israelis in later years.

Tragedy struck the Ben-Yehuda household in 1891. First Deborah died at age thirty-seven from tuberculosis contracted from her husband. Then, within the next three months, three of their children also perished. The cause of their deaths is unclear. Ben-Yehuda then married his wife's sister, Hemda, who aided her new husband in his literary work and, after his death, devoted herself to the continued publication of his Hebrew-language dictionary.

By 1897, Ben-Yehuda's dream was coming true. The Hebrew language was increasingly being adopted as the everyday tongue of Jews in Palestine. The real breakthrough came not in Jerusalem, where the Orthodox Jews continued to dismiss Ben-Yehuda, but in the isolated farming communities in the outlying parts of Palestine. By persuading the schools in these villages and settlements to use Hebrew exclusively in their teaching, Ben-Yehuda ensured that Jewish youngsters, after they grew up and married, would use the language in their homes.

Books and plays began to appear in Hebrew. Ben-Yehuda started working on his *Dictionary of Ancient and Modern Hebrew*, a task he remained at for the rest of his life. His goal was to make Hebrew literature simple and concrete, to do away with the florid rhetoric that had characterized Hebrew in the past.

Ben-Yehuda initially sought old, established words for inclusion, but when none existed to describe some modern aspects of life, he coined new words. He introduced these words into his daily language and into his writings, and he also encouraged his family to use them. The dictionary he compiled, however, which is the greatest testament to his mission, was compiled by others. Most of it was published after his death, the last of the seventeen volumes appearing in 1959.

Most of the words Ben-Yehuda invented became common parlance in the Jewish community in Palestine. By 1914, when Ben-Yehuda had completed half of his dictionary, World War I began, and he halted his work and moved to a safer haven in the United States. Returning to Palestine after the fighting was over, he was greeted by the British governor of Jerusalem with the Hebrew phrase, *Shalom aleichem* or "Peace be unto you." Ben-Yehuda was thrilled that a British official had welcomed him back to Palestine using Hebrew.

At the time of Ben-Yehuda's death in 1922 at the age of sixty-four, due to complications from his tuberculosis, Hebrew had become the main language of the *Yishuv*. The British, now in charge after conquering Palestine from the Turks in World War I, recognized Hebrew as one of the country's official languages.

HENRI BERGSON

Outstanding French Philosopher

Born October 18, 1859, in Paris, France; died January 4, 1941. French philosopher. The winner of the 1928 Nobel Prize for Literature, Henri Bergson is also known as a brilliant philosopher who argued that a life force, which he called the *élan vital*, controlled the world, rather than lifeless mechanical laws. Bergson spent a good deal of his life elaborating on this theory. He argued that evolution embodied the endurance of the *élan vital*, or vital impulse. He also maintained that there are two opposing tendencies in the world, one the *élan vital*, the other, the resistance of the material world to that force.

HENRI BERGSON, born October 18, 1859, was the son of a Polish Jew, Michael Bergson, the scion of a Hasidic family. Michael was a pianist and composer who had been a pupil of the musical composer Frederic Chopin. He emigrated to France as an adult and married Kate, an English Jew. Henri himself remained in and around Paris throughout his life.

Bergson studied at the École Normale Supérieure. After his graduation in 1881, he taught high school philosophy in several provincial towns, including Anger and Clermont-Ferrand. It was at the latter school that he gave lectures on laughter that became famous. It was there as well that he conceived the idea of the vital, continuous, and regenerative impulse of the universe. Beginning in 1884, while still in his twenties, Bergson elaborated on this theory, which he named the *élan vital*, in different forms.

In 1889, after returning to Paris, Bergson published his doctoral dissertation, "Time and Free Will: An Essay on the Immediate Data of Consciousness." He also lectured at the École Normale Supérieure. From that time on he devoted his life to philosophical reflection and writing.

Henri Bergson.

54

In 1900, Bergson was appointed professor at the Collège de France. Students, as well as the elite of Paris society, flocked to his lectures. For all his popularity, Bergson was unable to secure a post at the prestigious Sorbonne. Ironically, however, his lectures and books helped him win fame in France and throughout the world.

Bergson made an impression on other famous writers. His antirationalist thinking and his doctrine of creative evolution influenced the writings of British playwright George Bernard Shaw, who became enthusiastic about Bergson's belief in the unlimited potential for the progress of humanity.

Bergson was politically active at times, heading a French delegation to the United States. At one point, he was president of the League of Nations' Committee for Intellectual Cooperation.

According to Bertrand Russell in A *History of Western Philosophy* (1945), Henri Bergson was the chief representative of what Russell called "practical philosophers," those who considered action as the supreme good, happiness as an effect of action, and knowledge as the instrument of successful activity.

In developing his philosophy, Bergson reacted to the materialists who argued that, to understand life, one must understand the way one's physical surroundings worked. Bergson rejected this view, insisting that time, not physical space, was far more important as a building block of the universe.

Bergson thought the world was divided into two disparate portions: life and matter. In his mind, the entire universe was the result of the clash and conflict of life, which climbed upward, and matter, which fell downward. Life, he felt, was one great force, a vast vital impulse that ultimately met the resistance of matter.

Bergson's fundamental philosophical thought focused on a "life-drive," the *élan vital*, the great power that permeates all that is alive, creating life's constant movement and its energy. He posited this view in contrast to the mechanistic world view that had previously dominated nineteenth-century thinking. Bergson's views were considered by some to be antirationalistic and mystical.

Bergson's best-known work is *Creative Evolution*, published in French in 1907 and in English four years later. Evolution was not primarily explicable, Bergson argued in this book, by adaptation to environment; instead, it was a truly creative process, like the work of an artist.

Bergson's greatest work was called *Matter and Memory* (1911). He wrote the book after making a long, intensive study of memory. Until then, the prevailing view had been that there is a psychophysical connection between mind and body. But Bergson rejected that notion and argued that memory was independent of the body and only utilized the body for its own ends. Bergson gained great acclaim for this work and soon a school of thinking called Bergsonism arose.

Bergson's thinking was rooted in evolutionary theory, and he maintained that evolution embodied the endurance of the *élan vital*. There were two opposing tendencies in the world, he believed: one the *élan vital*; the other the resistance of the material world to that force. Bergson liked to say: "Action is what matters. We are present where we act." He also observed: "What is found in the effect was already in the cause." And: "There is no state of mind, however simple, which does not change every minute."

Bergson was thought of at times as more of a poet than a philosopher, and his literary style was greatly admired. In 1914 he was elected a member of the Academie Française, and in 1928 he was awarded the Nobel Prize in Literature.

Bergson had little affection for Judaism. In the latter part of his life, he actually found Catholicism appealing, believing it to be the fulfillment of Judaism. But in the final analysis, he was never able to take the critical step of renouncing his Jewish faith, being influenced greatly by the widespread prevalence of anti-Semitism as World War II loomed on the horizon.

When the Nazis occupied France during World War II, Bergson refused an offer from the Vichy Government that would have exempted him from the anti-Jewish laws and would have treated him as a kind of honorary Aryan. Though in ill health by then, Bergson insisted on standing in line, along with every other Jew, to be registered as being Jewish. It is said that this act alone worsened his health and hastened his death in 1941 at the age of eighty-two.

IRVING BERLIN

America's Most Beloved Songwriter

Born May 11, 1888, in Temun, Siberia, eastern Russia; died September 21, 1989. American songwriter. Irving Berlin wrote uncomplicated songs. He once said there were only six tunes in the world and from those six tunes he wrote nearly a thousand songs, including such classics as "God Bless America," "White Christmas," and the song that in 1911 made him a household name, "Alexander's Ragtime Band." *Life* magazine chose him as one of its one hundred most important Americans of the twentieth century in a special 1970 edition. Another famous American songwriter, Jerome Kern, once said of him, "Irving Berlin has no place in American music. He *is* American music."

IRVING BERLIN was born Israel Baline, one of eight children of Moses and Leah (Lipkin) Baline. His father was a cantor and a *shochet*, one who certifies that meat and poultry are slaughtered according to Jewish dietary laws.

Berlin's parents fled the Russian pogroms in 1893 and took young Irving, then age six, to New York City, where they lived in a tenement at 300 Cherry Street on the Lower East Side. Two older children remained in Russia.

When Irving was eight years old, he dropped out of second grade in order to support his family, at first selling newspapers, then, from 1905 to 1907, singing while waiting on tables at the Pelham Cafe. "Once you start singing," he said, "you start thinking of writing your own songs. It's as simple as that."

Berlin, who became his nation's greatest popular song composer, had no musical training. He taught himself to play the piano, black keys only, at the cafe. The myth grew that Berlin played with only one finger, but it was not true. He played with all ten fingers, but only on the black keys.

Because he could not read or write music, Berlin used an invention called the transposing piano, which had a lever that moved the keyboard, changing the key signature. When he played the piano, he changed whatever music he wanted to play into the only key he had mastered, F sharp.

Berlin wrote his first song in 1907 and called it "Marie from Sunny Italy." The name of the composer that appeared on the cover was I. Berlin. It was incorrect, but it stuck. He earned all of thirty-seven cents for this, his first published lyrics. The second song he wrote, "Dorando" (1908), earned him $25 as well as employment with a music company. Later he became a partner in the firm.

Berlin's first great composing success was "Alexander's Ragtime Band," published in 1911. Ragtime had a strongly syncopated melody and a regularly accented accompaniment. Until that time, ragtime, which originated in the African-American community, was popular to listen to, but it became a dance craze as a result of Berlin's hit tune. He became a household name because of this song, which has been credited with ushering in the jazz age. It sold over one million copies of sheet music in a short time.

Berlin's first complete Broadway score was *Watch Your Step*, which starred Irene and Vernon Castle and opened on December 8, 1914. It popularized the song "Play a Simple Melody."

In February 1913, Berlin married Dorothy Goetz, but a short while later, on July 17 of that year, she died of typhoid contracted during their honeymoon in Cuba. After this tragedy, Berlin began adding serious ballads to his repertoire of novelty songs. He wrote his first real love song, "When I Lost You," in Dorothy's memory.

Irving Berlin

John Miehle

Berlin was drafted into the United States Army as an infantry private in 1917 and served at Camp Upton, Long Island, an embarkation point for troops who were leaving for Europe. His classic army hit, "Oh, How I Hate to Get Up in the Morning," written in 1918, was inspired by Berlin's desire to sleep until noon. After being discharged in 1919, he formed his own music publishing firm, the Irving Berlin Music Company.

During his lifetime, Berlin composed nearly a thousand songs, including the scores for nineteen stage musicals and eighteen films. His song "A Pretty Girl is Like a Melody" was written for the *Ziegfeld Follies of 1919* and became the unofficial theme song of all the Ziegfeld shows. By the early 1920s, Berlin was no longer writing just individual hits but complete stage scores. With partner Sam H. Harris, Berlin financed the building of the Music Box Theater on West 45th Street, near Broadway, in 1921. It was the first theater designed to showcase the revues of one composer. Berlin wrote "Say It With Music" as the theme song for the theater.

In 1926, Berlin married Ellin Mackay, the daughter of a leading Catholic layman and president of the Postal Telegraph Company. Because her father objected to Berlin, the couple married in secret. But when the marriage of the Lower East Sider to the socialite Mackay was revealed, the fact became one of the biggest news events of the 1920s because it was both an interfaith wedding and the union of two prominent people. The Berlins had three daughters during their marriage.

In 1927, the classic song "Blue Skies" was included in the historic film *The Jazz Singer*, which was part talkie. As silent movies grew less prevalent, Berlin also wrote songs for the films *Top Hat* (1935); *Follow the Fleet* (1936); *On the Avenue* (1937); *Holiday Inn* (1942); and *Easter Parade* (1948).

On Armistice Day 1939, singer Kate Smith introduced "God Bless America," written by Berlin earlier for his World War I Army show. In 1954, President Dwight D. Eisenhower presented him with a special gold medal for composing the song that had become an unofficial American anthem. Berlin signed over the royalties from the song to the Boy Scouts and the Girl Scouts, organizations he and his wife supported for many years. "A patriotic song is an emotion," he said in a 1962 interview with *Look* magazine, "and you must not embarrass an audience with it, or they'll hate your guts. It has to be right, and the time for it has to be right."

Holiday Inn was one of two movies Berlin wrote for Bing Crosby and Fred Astaire. It contained the classic "White Christmas." He also wrote the music for the Broadway shows *Annie Get Your Gun* (1946) and *Call Me Madam* (1950). It was from the former that the entertainment classic "There's No Business Like Show Business" emerged. All his life, Berlin had trouble sleeping and he also worked at a feverish pace. When it was decided that *Annie Get Your Gun* needed another song, he rushed home and six minutes later, phoned the show's director. "Listen to this," he said, playing the first verse of "Anything You Can Do." He had written the song in the taxi going home.

Berlin tried to retire in 1954. Golfing, fishing, and painting became avocations, but he could not stay away from songwriting. He wrote the score for *Mr. President* in 1962, becoming one of the oldest composers to write a score for a musical comedy. Critics called the score "corny," but Berlin barked back in an interview in *Variety*, "If some of Berlin's songs are corny, then it's because they're simple, and all I know is that some of the corniest and simplest songs have lasted, be they 'White Christmas,' 'Easter Parade,' or 'My Old Kentucky Home.'"

Berlin knew what made his music so timeless and popular. "A good song," he said once, "embodies the feeling of the mob, and a songwriter is not much more than a mirror which reflects those feelings. I write a song to please the public—and if the public doesn't like it in New Haven, I change it!"

Irving Berlin made millions of dollars from his music and, in his lifetime, was a generous donor. After he wrote "This Is the Army," he turned over all ten million dollars in royalties to the American government.

Berlin died in 1989 at the age of 101. His obituary in the *New York Times* stated accurately that "Irving Berlin set the tone and the tempo for the tunes America played and sang and danced to for much of the twentieth century."

ISAIAH BERLIN

Intellectual Giant

Born June 6, 1909, in Riga, Latvia; died November 5, 1997. Philosopher and political scientist. Isaiah Berlin is considered one of the intellectual giants of the twentieth century. In 1932, at the age of twenty-three, Berlin became the first Jew to be elected a fellow of All Souls College at Oxford, England. His best-known work is *The Fox and the Hedgehog* (1953), an essay on Tolstoy's philosophy of history. Over the years, Berlin inspired thousands of Oxford students. He became known throughout Britain because of a series of talks he gave that were broadcast on the BBC in 1952 and 1955.

ISAIAH BERLIN was born in Riga, Latvia, in 1909, the son of a timber merchant, patriarch of a middle-class family. He had what he described as "an ordinary middle-class Jewish education," attending synagogue seven or eight times a year and having a bar mitzvah. One incident during the Russian Revolution of 1917 left an indelible mark upon the eight-year-old Isaiah: He watched helplessly as a man was overpowered by the police and forcibly dragged away. "I've never forgotten the sight of him struggling," he said later. "It left me with a horror of violence." It also left him a lifelong anticommunist.

Taught to read the Bible in Hebrew by a Zionist student in St. Petersburg, where his family was then living, Isaiah had a "tremendous appreciation" for Hebrew but a distaste for Yiddish because it was the language of the Diaspora and, according to him, "of slavery and poverty, both spiritual and material." Berlin became a Zionist during his formative years, believing that the Jews had to have a land of their own and, in his words, "*that* was plainly Palestine." Later in his life, Berlin credited the Hebrew language with bringing about the success of the formation of the state of Israel and the Zionist movement. He had a long-standing personal friendship with several Zionist leaders, especially Chaim Weizmann.

Berlin spent a good part of his early life in Russia, but in February of 1921 he and his parents immigrated to England. Many years later, Berlin said: "I'm an Anglophile. I love England. England's my home. I have been very well treated in this country. But I remain a Russian Jew."

Isaiah was educated at St. Paul's School, where he discovered the writers James Joyce, T. S. Eliot, and Aldous Huxley. He won a scholarship to Corpus Christi College at Oxford and majored in philosophy there. He became one of the English poet W. H. Auden's successors as editor of the journal *Oxford Outlook*, received top grades, and, in 1932, at the age of twenty-three became the first Jew to be elected a fellow of All Souls, one of the colleges at Oxford. Berlin left All Souls in 1938 and became a fellow of New College at Oxford, where from 1938 to 1950 he lectured and engaged in research in philosophy. He remained at Oxford because

". . . I wanted to learn, I wanted to talk to people in my subject. There were a lot of people in Oxford with whom I felt I could develop intellectually." In 1939, Berlin wrote the first of his important literary works, *Karl Marx*, considered one of the finest discussions of Marx's thinking.

By the 1940s, Berlin ceased studying and teaching philosophy because he had lost interest in the subject. He felt that "later thought did not make obsolete earlier thought; I wished to know more at the end of my life than I had at the beginning." As a result, he became a historian of ideas.

In 1941, Berlin joined the staff of the British Ministry of Information, having moved to New York from England. A year later he settled in Washington, D.C., where he served at the British Embassy, writing highly informative weekly summaries of American opinion for numerous British officials. Some called those summaries "Churchill's favorite reading," though Berlin himself did not subscribe to this view.

In 1952, Berlin captured the imagination of his listeners when he delivered six broadcasts on the BBC's *Third Program* on political philosophers who had helped formulate contemporary political opinion—Helvetius, Rousseau, Fichte, Hegel, St. Simon, and De Maistre. Berlin was also the commentator for another BBC series, in 1955, on the "marvelous decade" (1838 to 1848) in Russian literary history.

One of Berlin's best-known works is *The Fox and the Hedgehog* (1953), an essay on Tolstoy's philosophy of history. Based on the idea that the fox knows many things, and the hedgehog knows but one big thing, Berlin divided humanity into two groups: those who "relate everything to a single central vision . . . a single, universal, organizing principle," and those who "pursue many ends . . . seizing upon the essence of a vast variety of experiences and objects for what they are in themselves." Dante belonged to the first category, he said; Shakespeare to the second. Tolstoy, Berlin felt, was by nature a fox, although his writings indicated that he philosophically believed in being a hedgehog.

Berlin spent much of his research time trying to identify the intellectual roots of such modern developments as nationalism, romanticism, populism, liberalism, and historicism. Two eighteenth-century thinkers, Giambattista Vico, an Italian philosopher, and Johann Gottfried von Herder, a German philosopher, had impressed Berlin with their creative thinking, and he discussed their ideas in his 1976 work *Vico and Herder*.

Not a believer in any laws of history, Berlin postulated that there were, however, "large, impersonal factors which determined human history—climate, geography, the development of agriculture, technology, etc." He did not think, however, that those factors totally determined human behavior; he thought there was room for freedom of action, not caused by these variables. He laid out such thoughts in "Historical Inevitability," published in *August Comte Memorial Lectures* (1953–62, 1964), and *Four Essays on Liberty* (1969), which points out the key errors and distortions that are found in historical determinism. Berlin's thinking is thoroughly documented in the four volumes of his *Collected Papers* (1975–80).

The concept of liberty interested Berlin greatly. In his *Two Concepts of Liberty* (1958), he made a distinction between those who try to find liberty within a framework of mutual restraints while recognizing the diversity of human need and behavior, and those who, while advocating one all-embracing and dogmatic notion of liberty, seek to "force men to be free" only to wind up enslaving them.

In 1957 Berlin became professor of social and political theory at Oxford. In 1968 he was appointed the first president of the newly-founded Wolfson College in Oxford, a new graduate college of the University, which opened that year. He retired in 1975.

Stephen Spender, the English poet and critic, once said to Berlin: "What would you most like to see in your lifetime?" Berlin replied: "The collapse of the totalitarian system in Russia and Eastern Europe." When that actually happened, Berlin suggested that totalitarianism had given way partly for economic reasons and partly "because they were in prison." Commenting further on that event, he noted that "the collapse of an empire, without losing a major war, or invasion by some hostile people, is a unique event in human history."

Berlin received many commendations during his lifetime. In 1946, he was named a CBE, Commander of the British Empire; in 1957, knighthood was bestowed upon him and he was also given a Fellowship in the British Academy; in 1971, he was appointed to the Order of Merit.

In 1956, Berlin married Aline de Gunzbourg, the French-born daughter of a Russian-Jewish banker; he has three stepsons from this marriage.

It is said of Sir Isaiah Berlin that he is the embodiment of the Oxford spirit: dispassionate, eclectic, undogmatic, elegant in expression, and displaying a great sense of humor. A marvelous conversationalist and a lecturer of great renown, Berlin, one critic noted, "shows that it is possible to preserve within a scrupulous academic framework the wide and high courtesy of private conversation."

Berlin died on November 5, 1997, at the age of eighty-eight, in Oxford, England, after a long illness.

LEONARD BERNSTEIN

The Greatest Maestro of His Era

Born August 25, 1918, in Lawrence, Massachusetts; died October 14, 1990. American musician. Leonard Bernstein is regarded as one of the most versatile musicians of the twentieth century. *West Side Story*, which he composed in 1957, ranks as one of the greatest musical theater pieces written by an American. Bernstein's uninhibited and spirited conducting style made watching his symphony orchestra concerts as much fun as listening to the music itself. His television concert series brought classical music into America's living rooms and made him a household name. Several of his compositions were inspired by Jewish themes; he was troubled that his popular compositions were more successful than his serious ones.

LEONARD BERNSTEIN was born in 1918 in Lawrence, Massachusetts, to a family that had emigrated from the Ukraine. His father ran a beauty supply business and inculcated a strong sense of Judaism into his family's life.

Bernstein's father wanted his son to enter the family business. In fact, he opposed his son's musical career for many years, to the point where Bernstein had to pay for his own piano lessons. Later in life his father admitted, "You don't expect your child to be a Moses, a Maimonides, or a Leonard Bernstein."

The future composer attended the prestigious Boston Latin School, then Harvard University, and later, persisting in his career ambitions, the Curtis Institute in Philadelphia. There he was a pupil of conductor Fritz Reiner. Accomplished conductors Artur Rodzinski and Serge Koussevitzky were impressed by Bernstein's talent and encouraged him in his chosen career.

In 1943, Rodzinski named Bernstein his

Leonard Bernstein

assistant at the New York Philharmonic. Said Rodzinski, "I finally asked God whom I should take and God said, 'Take Bernstein.'" Shortly thereafter, Bernstein had to substitute as conductor, with a few hours' notice, for the ailing Bruno Walter at a performance of the New York Symphony Orchestra which was to be broadcast on the radio. His debut was so magnificent that it was reported on the front page of the *New York Times*. At the age of twenty-five, Bernstein became an overnight sensation. (At this point in his career, some wanted him to change his name so that it would sound less Jewish, but he refused: "I'll perform as Bernstein or not at all.")

In 1953, Bernstein was the first American to conduct at Italy's La Scala, and he became a popular guest conductor with the Vienna and Israel Philharmonic Orchestras. He first conducted in Israel as early as 1947, returning the following year to conduct concerts near the front lines during the War of Independence. Many years later, in 1988, he conducted Mahler's *Resurrection Symphony* in a large open-air concert in Jerusalem to mark Israel's fortieth anniversary.

In 1958 Bernstein became conductor of the New York Philharmonic, the first American-born conductor to head a major orchestra, as well as the youngest in the Philharmonic's history. During his tenure, which lasted until 1969, the New York Philharmonic enjoyed a golden age; millions of recordings of its concerts were sold, making it extremely popular to general audiences. Bernstein became a spokesman for classical music, enlightening television's mass audiences with his *Omnibus* and *Young People's Concert* programs in the 1950s and 1960s.

After the 1967 Six-Day War in Israel, Bernstein conducted the Israel Philharmonic in a concert on Mount Scopus, which was reunited with Israel's capital of Jerusalem. The concert was a dramatic symbol of worldwide Jewish solidarity, as manifested by Bernstein's presence and the great popularity he was enjoying.

Bernstein was known for his emotional and energetic style of conducting. The editors of *Time* magazine wrote, "Through exaggerated gestures that would have done Barrymore proud, he cajoled his orchestra. He pleaded. He commanded. He looked heavenward for inspiration. At times he would even levitate, jumping into the air as if to transcend the forces that kept him earthbound." When Igor Stravinsky watched Bernstein conduct a performance of Stravinsky's *Symphony of Psalms*, his response was, "Wow!"

In 1969 Bernstein retired from conducting orchestras to devote himself to composing, but he remained a sought-after guest conductor for many years.

Leonard Bernstein wrote both popular and serious music. Among his earliest compositions was *Jeremiah*, written in 1944. It features a vocal solo based on the Hebrew text of Lamentations and is a serious piece. On the other hand, he also wrote the ballet *Fancy Free*, which was choreographed by Jerome Robbins and later became the Betty Comden and Adolph Green musical *On the Town*.

Bernstein used many ideas and forms for his musical pieces. He wrote *Symphony No. 2*, subtitled *The Age of Anxiety*, based on a poem by W. H. Auden, utilizing jazz rhythms. Later came a one-act opera, *Trouble in Tahiti*, and *Candide*, an operetta that was performed on Broadway. Bernstein's masterpiece was the 1957 musical drama *West Side Story*, for which Stephen Sondheim wrote the lyrics. The story is an adaptation of Shakespeare's *Romeo and Juliet*, updated to take place in a modern-day New York City setting. The rivalry between two youth gangs representing different cultures forms the backdrop for the action. It is considered by many the greatest musical written by an American.

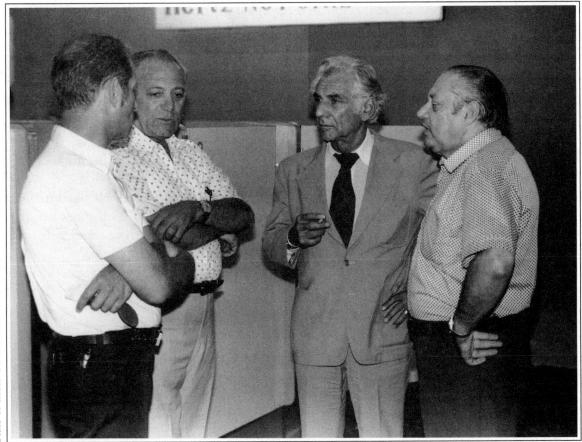

State of Israel Government Press Office

Members of Israel Philharmonic Orchestra greet Leonard Bernstein (second from right) upon his arrival in Israel August 11, 1979.

It seemed to embarrass Bernstein that his best-received works were those written for the popular stage. His more serious compositions did not enjoy the success of his other music. Among them are the *Kaddish* symphony, which he conducted for the first time in Tel Aviv in 1963; *Mass*, which inaugurated the new Kennedy Center in 1971; and most troubling to Bernstein of all, the opera *A Quiet Place* (1983), which was meant as a sequel to *Trouble in Tahiti* but did not do well.

Bernstein was never able to repeat the success of *West Side Story*. A less serious later musical did not begin to rival it. In 1976 a Bernstein musical about the presidency, *1600 Pennsylvania Avenue*, closed after just seven performances. Critics universally panned it.

Leonard Bernstein married the Chilean actress Felicia Montealegre Cohn in 1951. They had three children: Nina, Alexander, and Jamie. When Felicia died in 1978, Bernstein was so despondent that he stayed in bed for six months. Nine years later Joan Peyser's controversial biography revealed that the maestro was bisexual. However, his involvement with men was always an open secret in the music community.

Bernstein's Jewishness, when expressed in his music, was intense. Many of his musical works were replete with Jewish feeling and reference. His first symphony, *Jeremiah*, contained aspects of synagogue chant: the cadence for the Ashkenazi intonation of the festival *Amidah*, for example. In his operetta *Candide*, there is a parody of *shofar* calls. His third symphony, *Kaddish*, in 1963, is considered a deeply Jewish work. To the regret of Jewish music circles, Bernstein wrote only one piece of music directly for use in the synagogue, *Hashkeveinu* (1945).

Bernstein had never thought he would live to an old age. However, he did live into his seventies. A few years before his death from emphysema and a pleural tumor, he said, "I smoke. I drink. I stay up all night. I'm overcommitted on all fronts. I was told that if I didn't stop smoking, I'd be dead at thirty-five. Well, I beat the rap."

One of Bernstein's final performances was in the summer of 1990, when he conducted Beethoven's *Ninth Symphony* with the Berlin Philharmonic on the site of the destroyed Berlin Wall. He substituted the word *freiheit* (freedom) for *freude* (joy) in the choral finale.

Leonard Bernstein once said that making music made him feel immortal. He liked to boast that he had outlived the doctor who first diagnosed his emphysema when Bernstein was still in his twenties. On October 8, 1990, he announced that owing to poor health he was finally *really* retiring from the concert stage. Six days later he died at the age of seventy-two.

At the time of his death, the *London Times* wrote, "Bernstein was the most spectacularly versatile of all American musicians of the twentieth century. Exuberantly gifted, he possessed an uncanny touch of success with all kinds of music and all manner of musicians."

CHAIM NACHMAN BIALIK

Israel's National Poet

Born January 11, 1873, in Radi, Russia; died June 30, 1934. The father of modern Hebrew poetry. Chaim Bialik is generally considered the greatest Hebrew writer of the modern era as well as the poet-prophet of Jewish nationalism. In virtually every one of his poems, Bialik referred to the aspiration of the Jewish people for a national revival. When he emigrated from Russia to Palestine in 1924, he immediately became one of the Jewish community's most important cultural icons.

THROUGH CHAIM NACHMAN BIALIK'S WORK, one can tell that the poet thought of his childhood as a lost paradise of fields and woods. That happy youth came to an abrupt end with his father's death when Chaim was only seven years old. Sent to live in Zhitomir, Russia, Bialik was raised by a stern, scholarly Hasidic grandfather. The youngster found his grandfather's style of life suffocating.

State of Israel Government Press Office

Chaim Nachman Bialik

Bialik was also pained by this forced separation from his widowed mother. The themes of widowhood, orphanhood, and poverty permeate his later writings. Drawing from his own personal experience, Bialik wrote about the struggles of humanity, the suffering that artists go through, the oppression that people are forced to endure.

When Bialik was sixteen years old, he went to the yeshiva at Volozhin, the prestigious Lithuanian Talmudic academy. There the future poet spent several months immersed in Talmudic studies in the hope that he could discover a way to build an intellectual bridge between the Jewish Enlightenment and Orthodoxy. As a young person, Bialik was attracted to the secular world and its ideas, and he began questioning the convictions and dogmas of Judaism. He utilized this experience as the basis for his poem *Hamatmid* (*The Diligent Student*, 1894–95).

67

Bialik was a good student, although he found the life that Orthodox Jews lived in the ye-shiva too constraining. In 1890 he had the opportunity to travel to Odessa, in southern Russia, which was a wonderful literary center. There Bialik started to win some acclaim as a Hebrew poet. He came under the intellectual spell of the spokesman of Jewish national revival, Ahad Ha'am. Around this time, Y. H. Ravnitzki, editor of *Hapardes*, accepted Bialik's *El Hatzipor* (*To the Bird*), a philosophically Zionist poem which was well received. In this poem, Bialik asks the bird on his windowsill for news from the land of his ancestors. It was the publication of *El Hatzipor* that brought Bialik his first public recognition.

Bialik contributed frequently to *Hapardes*. His poetry also appeared in *Hashiloah*, another prestigious journal founded by Ahad Ha'am. Consistent with Ha'am's Zionist cultural outlook, Bialik's poems were about love and nature and relied heavily on Jewish themes.

While in Odessa, Bialik found it hard to make ends meet, so he returned to Zhitomir, where he married Manya Auerbach in 1893 and began working in his father-in-law's lumber busi-ness. He continued to write prolifically. Eventually he tired of the lumber business, finding it too difficult and not as professionally fulfilling as his poetry.

Bialik returned to Odessa in 1900 and lived there for the next twenty years, except for one year in Warsaw (1904). From 1896 to 1900, he taught Hebrew in several Jewish community schools. At the same time, he wrote essays, poems, stories, and both published and edited Hebrew-language literary journals. The bulk of his poetry was written during these two dec-ades. Critics noted that Bialik was maturing as a poet, especially as his ideas became less parochial.

In 1902 Bialik wrote an allegorical poem in epic form called *Metei Midbar* (*The Dead of the Desert*). The poem was based on a Talmudic legend that the Exodus generation had not really died but lay dormant in the desert, awaiting rebirth at the time of the coming of the Messiah. To Bialik, the Exodus generation symbolized both a passive Jewish people waiting for redemp-tion and humanity's struggle against mortality. He was critical of Jewish apathy and a number of his poems assailed his fellow Diaspora Jews for not being more aggressive in trying to over-come the difficulties in their lives.

In 1903, when the Kishinev pogrom left forty-five Russian Jews dead and hundreds injured, the Odessa Relief Committee, undoubtedly aware of his lofty reputation, asked Bialik to probe the tragedy. After he met pogrom victims, he composed two poems, *Be'ir Haharegah* (*In the City of Slaughter*) and *Al Hashehitah* (*On the Slaughter*). The first poem, written in biblical cadences, had an immense effect on Russian Jewry; Bialik himself translated the poem into Yiddish. It attacked the Kishinev survivors as parasitic and cowardly and was a critical factor in the creation of the Jewish self-defense movement. Bialik wrote a number of other such "poems of wrath" between 1903 and 1906.

Collaborating with Y. H. Ravnitzki and S. Ben Zion, Bialik helped found a publishing house called Moriah, whose specialty was in the printing of textbooks. Bialik and Ravnitzki also edited a classic omnibus of rabbinic legends called *Sefer Ha-aggadah* (*The Book of Legends*). In 1904 Bialik was the editor of *Hashiloah*, moving to Warsaw to work at the magazine's editorial offices. There he wrote a series of "folk poems" as well as the experimental prose-poem *Megilat Ha'esh* (*Scroll of Fire*, 1905).

With the advent of modern Zionism, Bialik became one of the movement's spiritual leaders and was known as the poet-prophet of Jewish nationalism. A modest man by nature, however, he was embarrassed by the appellation. His poetry inspired Zionists both inside and outside Palestine. In 1916 Bialik visited Palestine and the Jewish community there acclaimed him as its national poet. Wherever Hebrew was taught, Bialik's poetry was studied. Bialik wrote poems according to the Ashkenazic style, which meant that rhythms and rhymes were composed differently from the Sephardic pronunciation used in Israel today.

In the years leading up to World War I, Bialik ceased writing poetry, a period his critics have called his "silence." During this "silent" period, he wrote essays on Hebrew literature and on the Hebrew language. Those essays became important to the development of modern Hebrew literature.

After 1916 Bialik wrote fewer poems than he had in earlier periods. He published *Safiah* (*Aftergrowth*), hoping to base a future novel on this poem, but he did not accomplish that in his lifetime. In the poetry that he wrote during this period, he appeared to question whether Ahad Ha'am's dream of creating a synthesis between Judaism and Western culture would ever occur.

In 1921 the Soviet government gave its approval to Bialik and several other Hebrew language writers to immigrate to Palestine. After leaving Russia, Bialik first lived in Berlin for three years; there, he established a new publishing house called Dvir.

In 1924 Bialik settled in Tel Aviv and established the Hebrew Writers' Association, along with its periodical, *Moznayim*. He became preoccupied with public activities; as a result, his literary output declined once again. He did, however, have several major literary achievements. He collected and edited the works of the major Hebrew-language poets of Spain and a book of the legends of the rabbinic tradition known as *Aggada*. His 1930 prose-poem *Aggadat Shlosha Ve'arba'ah* (*The Legend of Three and Four*) ranks as one of his most important works.

Bialik died in 1934 of a heart attack suffered in Vienna. He was sixty-one years old and at the height of his fame. His death was considered a national tragedy for the Jews in Palestine. His home in Tel Aviv is now the Bialik Museum.

LOUIS BRANDEIS

The First Jewish United States Supreme Court Justice

Born November 13, 1856, in Louisville, Kentucky; died October 5, 1941. American jurist. Brandeis was the first Jew appointed to the United States Supreme Court, on which he served for twenty-three years. He supported the social legislation that was known as the New Deal. In addition, he emerged as a leader of American Zionism, encouraging many American Jews to embrace the establishment of a Jewish homeland in Palestine without any sense of diminishing loyalty to the United States.

L OUIS BRANDEIS was the youngest of the four children born to Adolph and Frederika (Dembitz) Brandeis, immigrants from Prague to the United States. His mother was a descendant of followers of the pseudo-messiah Jacob Frank. Brandeis's parents prized intellectual achievement but had little interest in Judaism.

Louis Brandeis

Brandeis was especially fond of one of his uncles, Lewis Dembitz, a scholarly attorney, author, and Zionist known as "the Jewish scholar of the South." Brandeis even changed his middle name from David to Dembitz in honor of his favorite uncle.

Brandeis grew up in Louisville and graduated from high school at age fifteen. About that time, in 1872, the family grain business was dissolved because of financial setbacks and the Brandeis family made an extended visit to Europe. Between 1873 and 1875, young Brandeis attended the Annen Realschule in Dresden. He disliked German academic discipline, noting, "In Kentucky you could whistle."

Encouraged by his Uncle Lewis to return to the United States, Brandeis entered Harvard Law School. To pay the tuition, he borrowed money from his older brother and also tutored other students. He graduated first in his class before his twenty-first birthday.

Brandeis practiced law in Boston, defending the rights of consumers and labor unions, interests that until then had not enjoyed much advocacy. He was called the "people's attorney" because he always appeared to be defending those with little representation, often the poor. He was described as ascetic, compassionate, and commanding. It was said that Brandeis reminded people of Abraham Lincoln. By the mid-1890s, he was considered one of America's best lawyers.

In 1908, Brandeis submitted a brief to the United States Supreme Court in which he defended an Oregon statute that regulated working hours for women. That document, containing over one hundred pages of supporting facts, became known as the "Brandeis Brief." It helped pave the way for the introduction of sociological data in the defense of public policy before the judiciary system.

Brandeis acquired a reputation as one of the leading progressive reformers in the country. In 1912, when Woodrow Wilson was elected president, he turned to Brandeis, seeking the jurist's counsel in translating ideas of political and social reform into practice. It was Brandeis' notion of a highly competitive economy that served as the basis for Wilson's New Freedom, which aimed at establishing more economic opportunities in the United States by freeing the American economy from restrictive tariffs.

During the early part of his life, Brandeis had no special feeling for Judaism, but later his religion's emphasis on justice and ethical values warmed him up. In 1911, Brandeis gained an understanding of the Jewish working class for the first time when he arbitrated the garment workers' strike in New York City. These workers' intelligence and their ability to see issues from the point of view of the other side impressed Brandeis.

Heightening his Jewish consciousness that same year was his fateful meeting with Jacob De Haas, editor of the *Jewish Advocate*, a Boston newspaper. De Haas, secretary to Theodor Herzl in London, managed to get Brandeis excited about Jewish history and especially the burgeoning Zionist movement. Brandeis devoured every word of the reading material De Haas gave him. He then asserted, "My sympathy with the Zionist movement rests primarily upon the noble idealism which underlines it and the conviction that a great people, stirred by enthusiasm for such an ideal, must bear an important part in the betterment of the world."

Just before World War I, Brandeis became chairman of the Provisional Committee for General Zionist Affairs in the United States, a post that essentially made him the leader of American Zionism.

Using the same organizational skills he had honed as a political reformer, Brandeis turned American Zionism into a major political force in the life of American Jewry. He favored, as every Zionist did, the reestablishment of a Jewish homeland in Palestine with American democratic ideals. This Brandeisian Synthesis, as it came to be called, enabled American Jews to sympathize with Zionism without undue concern about having to choose between dual loyalties. Brandeis also advocated what was eventually called cultural pluralism. "Every American Jew who aids in advancing the Jewish settlement in Palestine, though he feels that neither he nor his descendants will ever live there, will be a better man and a better American for doing so," he said.

In 1916 President Wilson nominated Brandeis to the Supreme Court, setting off a controversial four-month Senate debate over confirmation. A Jewish reformer was difficult for some of the conservatives in the Senate to accept, but they were unable to block his nomination.

Harris & Ewing/Collection of the Supreme Court of the United States

Louis Brandeis

Brandeis became the first Jew to serve on the high court.

Brandeis' closeness to President Wilson has been credited with securing American support for the Balfour Declaration, the statement of British policy issued in 1917 that supported a Jewish national home in Palestine.

Following World War I, Brandeis became the honorary president of the World Zionist Organization. A rift occurred at that point between Brandeis and his American associates and Chaim Weizmann and the East European Zionists. Assailing the way Zionist funds were being handled, Brandeis was determined to place the Zionist movement on a sounder, more efficient economic underpinning, but he was rebuffed in this effort by Weizmann. So contentious was the controversy that Brandeis and his American allies withdrew from the Zionist Organization, although they continued to support its ideals.

During his tenure on the Supreme Court, Brandeis was one of the few justices to support President Roosevelt's New Deal. At a time when a majority of the Court was striking down new social legislation, Brandeis voted to accept minimum-wage laws, price-control laws, and legislation that protected trade unions against injunctions in labor disputes. Franklin Roosevelt labeled Brandeis "Isaiah" because, in FDR's mind, Brandeis was a great teacher and seemed so much like a prophet.

Brandeis was known as one of the most gifted legal craftsmen in the Court's history during the twenty-three years he served as a justice. He supported "judicial restraint," the view that courts should not engage in second-guessing the legislative branch on the wisdom of public policy. He also believed that the courts had a special role to play in the area of civil liberties. He once said, "Order cannot be secured merely through fear of punishment; it is hazardous to discourage thought, hope, and imagination; fear breeds repression; repression breeds hate; hate menaces stable government." He also was a strong believer in dispersing power among the states rather than allowing too much power to be concentrated at the federal level.

Some believe that, had he not been Jewish, Brandeis might well have become Chief Justice of the Supreme Court.

Louis Brandeis died just before his eighty-fifth birthday; he did not live to see the founding of the state of Israel in 1948. But a kibbutz there, *Ein Hashofet* (Spring of the Judge) was named for him. And in Waltham, Massachusetts, near Boston, where he began his career, a highly regarded major American university established by Jewish sponsors bears his name.

STEPHEN G. BREYER

United States Supreme Court Justice

Born August 15, 1938, in San Francisco, California. United States Supreme Court justice. A Harvard Law School graduate, Stephen Breyer was a law professor at his alma mater, and chief counsel to the Senate Judiciary Committee in the 1970s before being appointed to the United States Court of Appeals (First Circuit), Boston, in 1981, and chief judge of that court in 1990. He was appointed to the United States Supreme Court in June 1994 to fill the vacancy created when Justice Harry Blackmun announced his retirement from the bench.

STEPHEN BREYER'S PATERNAL GREAT-GRANDFATHER emigrated from Romania to the United States, settling in Cleveland, where Breyer's grandfather was born in 1870. His grandfather's wife came from Berlin at the turn of the century. His maternal grandparents relocated to San Francisco from Konigsburg in East Prussia. They were members of Temple Emanuel, a reform congregation in San Francisco. Both sets of grandparents eventually settled in San Francisco.

Breyer's father, Irving Breyer, was an attorney. As a youngster, Stephen attended Sunday school and went to synagogue on the holidays. He had his bar mitzvah in San Francisco and for a few weeks attended a Jewish youth camp south of the city. The rabbis at his temple and the camp had a "significant positive influence upon me," he has said. Fortunately, Breyer experienced "very little" anti-Semitism during his childhood.

As a young man, Breyer worked at various blue-collar jobs. One summer he dug ditches for a utility company in San Francisco; he was also a janitor for the city school system. He cites these jobs as proof of his ability to be in touch with the common man. "My ideas about people do not come from libraries," Breyer said at his Senate confirmation hearings in July 1994.

Because of his mother Anne's encouragement, he chose as an undergraduate to attend Stanford University rather than Harvard. His parents expected him eventually to practice law in California. They were concerned that if he went to Harvard, he would choose to remain in the East and become an academic instead of a practicing lawyer. Breyer graduated from Stanford in 1959 and spent the next two years as a Marshall Scholar at Oxford University. Eventually he did go to Harvard Law School, from which he graduated in 1964.

In 1964 and 1965, late in his twenties, Breyer clerked for then-Supreme Court Justice Arthur Goldberg. Between 1965 and 1967, he served as a special assistant to the Assistant Attorney General in the Department of Justice. Breyer was an assistant professor of law at Harvard Law School from 1967 to 1970, becoming a full professor there for the next ten years. He was also

Stephen G. Breyer

professor of government at Harvard's Kennedy School of Government from 1978 to 1981.

In 1973, Breyer served as assistant prosecutor on the Watergate Special Prosecution Force; in 1974 and 1975, he was special counsel to the Senate Judiciary Committee. One achievement of which he is most proud is his part in drafting the plan that helped lead Congress to deregulate the airline industry in 1978. His efforts won him supporters among Republicans. Breyer served as chief counsel to the Senate Judiciary Committee from 1979 to 1981.

President Jimmy Carter appointed Breyer to the United States Federal Court. Shortly thereafter he lost the 1980 election. Breyer had not yet been confirmed at that point, but despite the fact that the Democrats had also lost control of the Senate with Carter's defeat, Breyer won Congressional confirmation.

Breyer was appointed a Federal Court of Appeals judge for the First Circuit in 1980 and chief judge of the First Circuit in 1990.

Breyer has a moderate-liberal judicial record, though his rulings on both criminal and civil rights cases do not easily fall into a single category, neither liberal nor conservative. He takes a scholarly, balanced approach on the majority of legal issues.

Breyer was a member of the United States Sentencing Commission between 1985 and 1989, and helped write federal guidelines for criminal sentencing. Those guidelines required judges in all parts of the country to give roughly equivalent sentences for comparable crimes.

In 1993 Breyer wrote a book called *Breaking the Vicious Circle: Toward Effective Risk Regulation*, which focused on how government regulated health and safety risks. He describes the present system as wasting resources and believes that, with better priorities, the system could utilize the same expenditures more effectively and save far more lives. The regulators, he charges, are too sensitive to fluctuating public opinion. To take one example: While exaggerated public fears about the potential damage of breathing asbestos led to a major financial commitment to remove the material from buildings, with no significant life-saving result, the government neglected paying for mammograms, which could save many lives at a lower cost but is overlooked by the public.

In the spring of 1993, Breyer was among those considered to fill the seat being vacated by Supreme Court Justice Byron White. White House officials listed as one Breyer attribute the fact that his appointment would allow President Bill Clinton to honor his pledge to appoint the first

Jew to the bench since Abe Fortas resigned in 1969. However, two days before his interview with Clinton, Breyer was hit by a car while bicycling through Harvard Square. He suffered two broken ribs and a punctured lung. Probably due to his weakened physical condition, his initial interview went poorly and Clinton decided that Breyer was "too stiff and a little too eager."

Breyer also had a "nanny problem," so named because of other Clinton appointees who were not confirmed due to similar situations. It was reported that Breyer had not paid Social Security taxes for his domestic cleaning woman, an employee since 1980. Breyer eventually paid the taxes; in fact, the Internal Revenue Service determined that he did not owe as much as was first thought. White's vacated seat was subsequently filled by Ruth Bader Ginsburg (also a Jew).

Breyer received a second chance at the Supreme Court when Justice Harry Blackmun announced his retirement in 1994. This time President Clinton chose Breyer to replace Blackmun. At his Rose Garden nomination ceremony, Breyer described a judge's task as making sure that the mass of statutes and constitutional provisions "fit together." What the law "is supposed to do, seen as a whole, is allow people . . . to live together in a society where they have so many different views . . . so that they can work productively together." Breyer, this time, sailed through the Senate confirmation process.

During his hearing, Breyer stated that he thought America's most important Supreme Court rulings were *Brown* v. *Board of Education* and *Cooper* v. *Aaron*, both of which ordered desegregation of public schools. Asked his view on religious freedom, Breyer said, "I think of Jefferson. I think of a wall." This was in reference to Thomas Jefferson's view that the Constitution required a wall of separation between church and state.

Breyer was pleased that his Jewish background had not been an issue in his being appointed to the Supreme Court. "Here I am, absolutely Jewish," he said. "I am appointed to the Supreme Court, and there's already another Jewish member, and there's no issue for or against. My parents and grandparents would never have believed it. It's the kind of ideal that many people have aspired to in terms of the place of a Jew in public life. It's neither a qualification nor a disqualification."

When asked how his Judaism had affected his public career, Breyer responded, "It's a little corny but I think of what Hillel said: 'If I am not for myself, who am I for?' I've always thought of the practical nature of Jewish religious beliefs and the way they're involved in making this world a better place, requiring people to have a sense of justice and to think about other people."

By 2000 and 2001, in several major court decisions, Breyer teamed up with conservative colleague Sandra Day O'Connor. Those rulings struck a more moderate tone than the stance the court's majority had taken in the landmark 2001 *Bush* v. *Gore* case. Breyer has been more moderate than the court's other liberals: John Paul Stevens, David Souter, and Ruth Bader Ginsburg.

Breyer has emerged as an effective behind-the-scenes conciliator among Supreme Court justices, and he has written the majority opinion in several important cases. In June 2000, in *Stenberg* v. *Carhart*, with the help of O'Connor's key fifth vote, Breyer explained why the court had decided to strike down a Nebraska ban on a controversial abortion procedure. His opinion acknowledged that the abortion issue sharply divided the nation. Then, in April 2001, in *Hunt* v. *Cromartie*, again with O'Connor as the fifth vote, Breyer penned the majority opinion upholding a heavily black North Carolina congressional district that white voters claimed was unconstitutional.

MARTIN BUBER

Modern Jewish Theologian

Born February 8, 1878, in Vienna; died June 13, 1965. Jewish philosopher. Martin Buber was one of the leading spiritual figures of his generation and had a deep impact on Christian as well as Jewish thinking. In his books, especially *I and Thou* (1937), Buber developed a personalist philosophy of God, man, and society, a philosophy of dialogue that was a major influence on contemporary thought. He became a great enthusiast of Hasidism, and it was through Buber's writings on Hasidism that its message was brought to the attention of the Western world.

MARTIN MORDECAI BUBER was born in 1878 in Vienna. When he was three years old, his mother disappeared without a trace, and Buber was brought up by his grandfather, Solomon Buber, a noted Midrash scholar in Lemberg.

Beginning in 1896, when Martin was eighteen years old, he traveled to Leipzig, Zurich, and Berlin, where he heard the lectures of philosophers Wilhelm Dilthey and George Simmel. He also studied philosophy at the University in Vienna. Having abandoned his ties to Judaism as a child, Martin renewed them around this time, embracing Zionism as well. What particularly interested Buber about Zionism was the opportunity it presented to revive the Hebrew language and to nourish Jewish and Yiddish culture.

In 1898, when he was twenty years old, Buber joined the Zionist movement, and a year later was a delegate to the Third Zionist Congress. While attending the Congress, he spoke on behalf of its Propaganda Committee, arguing that Zionists would be better off if they concentrated their energies on education rather than propaganda.

In 1900 Buber married Paula Winkler, a non-Jew from Munich. The next year, at the initiation of Theodor Herzl, the founder of

Martin Buber

modern Zionism, Buber was appointed editor of the official Zionist journal, *Die Welt*. In the pages of this newspaper, Buber argued that it would be possible to achieve full Jewish creativity and spirituality only after the majority of the Jewish people returned to their homeland in Palestine.

At the Fifth Zionist Congress in 1901, Buber became a member of a new group called the Democratic Faction, which championed the cause of cultural activity as the best way to promote Zionist aims, as opposed to Herzl's strategy of pursuing political activity. Resigning as editor of *Die Welt* because of his dispute with Herzl, Buber and his friends founded the *Juedischer Verlag* in Berlin, which became a publisher of books of high literary quality. In 1904 Buber became a great enthusiast of Hasidism as he came to acquire an understanding and appreciation of the religious side of Judaism. Abandoning all Zionist activities, Buber devoted himself during the next five years to the study of Hasidism. In that same year, Buber wrote his doctoral dissertation, entitled *Towards a History of the Problem of Individuation—Nicholas of Cusa and Jacob Boehme.*

Buber developed an existential Jewish philosophy that came to be known as Neo-Hasidism. He rejected those parts of Hasidism that he felt were made up of superstition and bigotry, focusing instead on those stories and myths that he thought taught a genuine religiosity. Buber was taken with such Hasidic traits as cleaving to God (*devekut*), humility, enthusiasm, and joy. It was through Buber's writings on Hasidism that its message was brought to the attention of the Western world.

Through his study of Hasidism, Buber gained new insights into and a greater appreciation of Judaism. He wrote lovingly of the great things that Judaism still had to offer to its people: "For Judaism has not only a past, despite all it has already created, it has, above all, not a past but a future. Judaism has, in truth, not yet done its work, and the great forces active in this most tragic and incomprehensible of people have not yet written their very own word into the history of the world."

Buber settled in Berlin in 1916, where he founded a monthly periodical called *Der Jude*; it developed into one of the most important publications on Jewish thought in Central Europe. In 1923 Buber published his most famous literary work, *Ich und Du* (*I and Thou*, 1937), which elaborated on his philosophy of dialogue.

Buber argued that the world could be divided into two fundamental forms of relationship. The I-Thou, the relationship between one person and another, implies mutuality, openness, directness, and presentness, and involves meeting in person and engaging in direct encounters. The I-Thou relationship cannot last, and invariably deteriorates into the I-It relationship.

Buber described the relationship between man and God as an I-Thou relationship, arguing that God, the Eternal Thou, can not be known through cognitive propositions or through metaphysical reasoning, but only through the I-Thou relationship. The one Thou that can not be changed is God, whose presence is inherent in every dialogue. Only in the I-Thou relationship can one conduct a "dialogue" with a partner as an equal.

In 1925, working closely with the German-Jewish philosopher Franz Rosenzweig, Buber produced the first volume of a German translation of the Bible, attempting to preserve the original character of the Hebrew Bible. After Rosenzweig's death in 1929, Buber continued the translation effort, completing the project in 1961.

Buber taught Jewish religion and ethics at the University of Frankfurt in 1925, and five years later was appointed professor of religion there. He held that post until 1933, but was forced to leave the university when the Nazis came to power. Shortly thereafter, he founded and led the Central Office for Jewish Adult Education, established in the wake of the ban on their attending German educational institutions.

In 1938 Buber settled in Palestine and was appointed professor of social philosophy at Jerusalem's Hebrew University. He taught there until his retirement in 1951. His first book written in Hebrew, *Torat ha-Nevi'im* (*The Prophetic Faith*) was published in 1942. In this history of biblical faith, Buber argues that the covenant between God and Israel indicates that the existence of the Divine Will is real.

Buber applied his concept of dialogue to the Jewish-Christian relationship. A pioneer of innovative post-World War II thinking, Buber considered it possible to acknowledge someone else's view of spirituality, encouraging Jews and Christians to recognize one another's religions. He called Jesus "my brother."

In relation to his peers, Buber had iconoclastic political thoughts. He looked toward a cooperative effort between Jews and Arabs in developing a joint Arab-Israeli state. To this end, he founded, along with Judah Magnes, Ernst Simon, Leon Roth, and others, the *Ichud*, or unity movement, which advocated the establishment of this joint state. Buber also helped to found the College for Adult Education Teachers, the goal of which was to train teachers from among Israel's growing new immigrant population.

Martin Buber was not a popular figure among some groups in Israel. He antagonized Orthodox Jews because of his idiosyncratic views of Jewish tradition and his feeling that the Arab-Israeli conflict could be resolved by establishing one Arab-Jewish state. Nonetheless, in 1960, when he was eighty-two years old, Buber was named the first president of the Israel Academy of Sciences and Humanities. He served in that position for two years. After suffering a fall, he died at the age of eighty-seven in Jerusalem on June 13, 1965.

BENJAMIN CARDOZO

Great American Justice

Born May 24, 1870, in New York City; died July 9, 1938. American lawyer and justice of the United States Supreme Court. Cardozo has been ranked as one of the ten most outstanding figures in American judicial history. When he served on the New York Court of Appeals, from 1913 to 1932, it enjoyed the reputation of being the most important state court. Cardozo was appointed to the United States Supreme Court in 1932 and served until his death at the age of 68 in 1938. He was known as a compassionate liberal who cared deeply about social welfare issues. In response to Adolf Hitler's increasingly horrific oppression of European Jews in the 1930s, Cardozo became a strong supporter of the Zionist movement.

BENJAMIN NATHAN CARDOZO, born in New York City, in 1870, came from a family descended from prominent Sephardic Jews who had settled in the United States prior to the American Revolution. Several Cardozo family members became infamous by signing the repeal of the Stamp Act. Over the years Cardozos had been rabbis and presidents of Jewish congregations. Although Benjamin Cardozo's parents were Orthodox Jews, he did not grow up to share their interest in religious observance.

Benjamin was the youngest child of Albert Cardozo, who had been one of the judges appointed to the New York State Supreme Court by William M. Tweed, the corrupt boss of the New York Democratic party machine. In 1872, when the young Cardozo was two years old, his father had to resign his seat in disgrace because of the scandal surrounding Tweed's administration. Albert Cardozo was threatened with impeachment for allegedly misusing his office during that time. Throughout his childhood, young Cardozo was deeply affected by the disgrace that occurred to his father.

As a youngster, Benjamin was taught at home by private tutors. He had one brother and two sisters, but he was especially devoted to his older sister, Nel. Following the death of their parents, Nel assumed the task of raising Benjamin. He continued to live with his sister until her death.

At the extraordinarily young age of fifteen, Cardozo entered Columbia University. He was elected vice-president of his class and often engaged in public debates. He earned his bachelor's degree in 1889 and his master's degree a year later. Cardozo then enrolled in Columbia Law School and was admitted to the New York State bar upon his graduation in 1891.

Joined by his brother, Albert, Cardozo started a private law practice. Although his father's

Benjamin Cardozo

reputation was tarnished, it did not impede Benjamin Cardozo's own growing reputation as a legal expert, based in large measure on his ability to describe complex issues in understandable language. Some lawyers referred to him as a "walking encyclopedia" of law.

Most of Cardozo's legal practice consisted of arguing cases before the New York Court of Appeals. Considered a brilliant scholar, he was also thought to be charming and sensitive. A "lawyer's lawyer," in the words of fellow attorneys, he devoted much of his time to small claims, seemingly uninterested in higher-priced work. He charged on a sliding scale, helping those clients who could not afford his regular fees to utilize his services.

At the age of thirty-three Cardozo published *The Jurisdiction of the Court of Appeals of the State of New York* (1903), a book that was considered authoritative.

In 1913 Cardozo was elected as a reform candidate to a lower court justiceship. After only six weeks he was appointed to fill a sudden vacancy on the New York Court of Appeals. Soon thereafter he was elected to the post permanently and served as an associate judge on that court for another fourteen years. Cardozo was made chief justice in 1927, a position he held for five years.

While on the Court of Appeals, Cardozo's decisions were often used as precedents in other courts in the United States. One example was *MacPherson* v. *Buick Motor Co.*, a 1916 case that involved implied warranty. Cardozo ruled that a person who purchased faulty merchandise had a right to expect compensation from the manufacturer, even though the retailer was the actual owner of the product immediately before the purchase.

In 1920 Cardozo was asked to give the prestigious Storrs lectures at Yale Law School. His most famous literary work, *The Nature of the Judicial Process* (1921), was an outgrowth of this lecture series. In 1924 Cardozo wrote *The Growth of Law*, a book that was based upon his lectures on constructive legal philosophy, legal outcomes, and the functions and ends of law. His *Paradoxes of Legal Science* (1928) was a collection of lectures he originally delivered at Columbia University.

Cardozo was a staunch defender of President Franklin Roosevelt's New Deal legislation. A fervent liberal, he attributed his beliefs to the lessons he had learned in reading about twenty centuries of Jewish oppression.

Benjamin Cardozo was an active member of New York's Sephardic congregation and was deeply interested in Jewish education, giving his time to the Jewish Educational Association. At first he avoided Zionist activities, but as Jews in Europe began to suffer greater humilations

Courtesy of the Library of Congress

Benjamin Cardozo (upper right corner).

and atrocities in the 1930s, he increasingly sympathized with the notion of a safe haven for Jews in Palestine.

In 1932, after the resignation of Justice Oliver Wendell Holmes, many people called upon President Herbert Hoover to appoint Cardozo to the Supreme Court. Justice Harlan Stone waged an aggressive battle to secure Cardozo's appointment, fearing that Hoover would otherwise select a conservative.

President Hoover nominated Cardozo, then sixty-two years old, to fill Holmes's vacancy. As had been the case when Cardozo was a candidate for high judicial office in earlier days, the newspapers, showing respect for Cardozo's achievements, avoided any mention of his father's controversial departure from the New York court.

Cardozo did run into critics, however. They labeled him a bleeding-heart liberal who put individual rights above the concerns of big business. Other opponents of his nomination felt that one Jew on the Supreme Court was enough (Justice Louis D. Brandeis was serving at this time). Justice Stone continued to express his strong support for Cardozo, threatening to resign at one point if Cardozo wasn't confirmed and thus openly battling Cardozo's opponents.

As a Supreme Court justice, Cardozo's decisions frequently required that he take into account the social and economic needs of the public, which he did very well. Benjamin Cardozo served on the United States Supreme Court for only six years. He died from the combination of heart disease and a stroke in 1938. The lifelong bachelor was sixty-eight years old.

Franklin Roosevelt wrote of Cardozo, "I know of no jurist more learned in law, more liberal in its interpretation, more insistent on simple justice, keeping step with the progress of civilization and bettering the lot of the average citizen who makes up mankind."

Cardozo has been ranked as one of the ten most outstanding judges in American judicial history.

JOSEPH CARO

The Codifier of Jewish Law

Born in 1488, in Toledo, Spain; died in 1575. Codifier of rabbinic law. Joseph Caro is best known as the author of the *Shulchan Aruch* (*Prepared Table*), a shortened version of his earlier work *Beit Yoseph* (*House of Joseph*). Commonly referred to as the *Code of Jewish Law*, the *Shulchan Aruch* quickly became the definitive compilation of Jewish law. Caro's reputation was greater than that of any rabbi since Maimonides and his work has had a major influence on the development of Jewish law since the sixteenth century.

JOSEPH BEN EPHRAIM CARO came from a family of distinguished Spanish scholars. Soon after the Spanish Expulsion in 1492, four-year-old Joseph and his family wandered about for several years until they finally took refuge in Constantinople, Turkey, in 1498, where a vibrant Jewish community had been developing. After living there for twenty years, Caro moved to Adrianople, a Turkish city that had become a center of Jewish learning.

In 1525 he moved to Palestine and settled in Safed, where he founded a yeshiva. It was here that he began working on a four-volume work called *Beit Yoseph* (*House of Joseph*), his great codification of Jewish law that was published in 1555. Caro's aim was to bring order out of the chaos that had existed as a result of the variety of often conflicting codes that had been written over the years. Caro believed that those codes had failed to dig deeply into the sources and had not accounted for the various points of view that comprised Jewish law.

Joseph Caro

In his presentation, Caro relied primarily on the codes of Isaac Alfasi, Moses Maimonides, and Asher ben Yehiel. Whenever the three disagreed, Caro accepted the majority view. *Beit Yoseph* was widely studied, but was not as popular as his later work, the *Shulchan Aruch* (*Prepared Table*), a shortened version of *Beit Yoseph*.

The *Shulchan Aruch*, recognized as the basic guide to Jewish religious practice, is accepted as the most authoritative book on Jewish law ever written. With its publication rabbinic law became accessible for the first time, not only to scholars but laymen as well.

In its original format, the *Shulchan Aruch* was embraced only by Sephardic Jews because it presented only customs and practices relating to the Sephardic community. After a hue and cry by the Ashkenazic community made itself heard, a supplement to it, written by Polish-born Moses Isserles in a tract known as the *Mappah*, meaning "Tablecloth," was appended to Caro's text. Since the new text reflected views of the German, French, and other non-Sephardic communities, the *Shulchan Aruch* became fully acceptable to all Jews as the standard code of Jewish law.

Louis I. Rabinowitz, Deputy Editor-in-Chief of the *Encyclopedia Judaica*, wrote that "for encyclopedic knowledge and complete mastery of the subject, for thoroughness of research, and for keen critical insight, this work is unmatched in the whole of rabbinic literature . . . . It is an indispensable guide for anyone desirous of following the development of any individual law of the Talmud from its source to the stage of its development in the sixteenth century."

Caro kept the code deliberately brief so that its study would take no more than thirty days. A pocket edition appeared in 1574 "so that it could be carried in one's bosom" and "referred to at any time and any place, while resting or traveling."

Ironically, from the standpoint of Talmudic scholarship, the *Shulchan Aruch* ranks as the least important of Caro's works. Caro dismissed the work as just a digest for his young students. He quoted the *Beit Yoseph* rather than the *Shulchan Aruch* in his response to questions addressed to him on matters relating to Jewish law.

While living in Adrianople in his formative years, Caro came under the influence of the charismatic kabbalist Shlomo Molcho, who infused in him mystical thoughts and led him to believe in dreams and visions which Caro believed were revealed to him from a Higher Being. This mystical bent accompanied Caro when he settled in Safed, a hotbed of mysticism. When Molcho died as a martyr on the stake in 1532, Caro began to wish that he too would meet such a noble end.

Caro's love of learning, however, could not be surpressed, although it was influenced by his mystic tendencies. Much of this is revealed in a kind of diary called *Maggid Mesharim* ("Teacher of Righteousness") which is ascribed to him. In it are recorded his "discussions" with his heavenly mentor and the intellectual and spiritual guidance which was provided him.

Joseph Caro married at least three times. He had six children: five sons and a daughter. Sketches of Caro that have survived show a man with a thin face, a long flowing white beard, and a turban-like covering on his head. He died at the age of eighty-seven in Safed, where he was buried.

MARC CHAGALL

Quintessential Twentieth Century Jewish Artist

Born July 7, 1887, in Vitebsk, Russia; died March 28, 1985. Russian painter. Considered one of the greatest Jewish painters, Marc Chagall painted memorable scenes from his childhood days in Russia. He was best known for his paintings "I Am the Village" and "The Rabbi of Vitebsk." He was also recognized for his etchings, mosaics, tapestries, and stained glass. The Bible was one of the most important inspirations for Chagall's paintings. In the 1930s, his work included many Christian motifs as he sought to emphasize a universal message.

MARC CHAGALL was born into a large, poor, and pious Hasidic family. His father was a herring packer, his grandfather a cantor and kosher butcher. One of his uncles was an amateur violinist. In his youth, Chagall was influenced by a rabbi from Mohiliff who taught him about Judaism. Becoming a more observant Jew, he gave up swimming on Saturdays to study the Bible.

Chagall's interest in becoming a painter was a cause of dismay to his mother, but in 1906, with the support of an uncle, it was arranged for Chagall, then nineteen, to study with a Vitebsk artist named Yehuda Pen. The following year Chagall moved to St. Petersburg, where he attended a private institution of learning known as the School of the Imperial Society for the Protection of the Arts. However, because he was Jewish, he was forced to live outside the city. He later studied at the Swanseva School in order to work with the famous Jewish artist Leon Bakst, the designer for the Diaghilev Ballet.

In 1910, Chagall obtained a subsidy from a liberal Jewish attorney and politician named Maxim Vinaver that permitted him to move to Paris, then the artistic capital of the world. He painted scenes inspired by his native town and of the village of Lyozno, where he often visited his grandfather. Depicted in these scenes were family, friends, homes, aspects of the life of the Jewish community, landscapes, and skyscapes.

Chagall's paintings had a dreamlike, fairy-tale quality. Although he continued to paint scenes from his childhood, as his work matured, he left behind the dark tones and naturalism of his earlier works and began to rely more on the bright colors reminiscent of Fauvism and the faceted planes taken from Cubism. Now living in Paris, Chagall attended the art schools of La Palette and La Grande Chaumière. He eventually moved to La Roche.

While his paintings, with their lively colors, showed the influence of both Cubism and Fauvism, it is still very difficult to put Marc Chagall in one category or another. In the period

Marc Chagall (second from left) with Dr. Miriam Freund, former President of Hadassah, (right) Rose Halprin, chairperson of the Jewish Agency, and Charles Marq, a French art expert, before the dedication ceremony of the stained windows at the Hadassah Synagogue in Ein Kerem, Jerusalem, February 6, 1962.

before 1914, Chagall's paintings were filled with light and images of the world in which he lived. He painted the Eiffel Tower, trains, and scenes of village life.

In 1914, the Der Sturm gallery in Berlin held a one-man exhibition of two hundred pieces of Chagall's work. The artist traveled to Berlin to be on hand for the exhibition, then journeyed on to his native Vitebsk. There in 1915 he married Bella Rosenfeld, who had been his childhood sweetheart. He painted a number of pictures featuring his new wife and the familiar surroundings of his hometown; he was enthralled with what he called the town's "special sky." Chagall's imagination was rich, as is evidenced by his fantasy-based paintings that included flying cows, dancing fiddlers, airborne violins, and soaring brides—all in that sky he loved. Frequently, he painted two lovers, who most supposed were himself and his bride, hovering over the roofs of houses.

When World War I began, Chagall was drafted into Russian military service and stationed in St. Petersburg. At that point, he became effectively stranded in his native land. In 1918, swept up in the Soviet revolution, Chagall was appointed Commissar for Arts in Vitebsk. Soon after this appointment, he became disillusioned with the new regime and moved to Moscow. There he produced murals and stage designs for the Kamerny State Jewish Theater and the Habimah Theater.

Chagall's stained glass windows at the Hadassah Synagogue in Ein Kerem, Jerusalem.

Leaving the Soviet Union finally in 1922, Chagall was considered a nonperson by the Soviets because he was Jewish and a painter whose work did not celebrate the heroics of the Soviet people. He spent a year in Berlin. There, the Jewish artist Herman Struck taught him printmaking. Chagall then returned to Paris. He made the first of many journeys to Palestine in 1931 for the opening of the Tel Aviv Museum, doing 105 biblical etchings; these have been described as some of the finest masterpieces of the art of etching.

From 1941 to 1948, Chagall lived in the United States, although France always remained his true "home." On the other hand, he never forgot Vitebsk. In 1962, Chagall offered to turn over some of his paintings to the town, but Soviet officials still considered him a traitor to the motherland and the offer was spurned. A Marc Chagall Museum was built in Vitebsk in 1992, but it was a private effort and houses only replicas of the artist's works.

Chagall's first wife, Bella, died in 1944; eight years later he married Valentine Brodsky, a hat designer. Chagall's only child was his and Bella's daughter, Ida. Bella and Ida appeared in many of the artist's early and most famous paintings.

Chagall had a complex relationship with Judaism. On the one hand, he credited his Russian Jewish cultural background as being crucial to his artistic imagination. However ambivalent he was about his religion, he could not avoid drawing upon his Jewish past for artistic material. He once said in the 1920s that "[all] the little fences, the little cows and sheep, all the Jews, looked to me as original, as ingenuous, and as eternal as the buildings in Giotto's frescoes." On the other hand, he was not a practicing Jew as an adult and he increasingly tried to suggest that his paintings had more universal messages as he attempted to reach out to non-Jewish audiences with Christian themes.

During the 1930s, Chagall often used these motifs in his paintings, often depicting the Crucifixion and suggesting that it was meant to be a metaphor for modern suffering, which, in his mind, was the suffering of the Jewish people. Chagall produced many stained glass images for Christian churches. He was given only one commission to decorate a synagogue: He created the Chagall Windows for the Hadassah Hospital in Jerusalem. Those windows, each one dedicated to one of the twelve Tribes of Israel, are one of the major tourist attractions in Jerusalem.

Chagall did other important and significant work in stained glass, including the Peace Window for the United Nations Secretariat in New York, and windows for the Vatican and for the cathedral of Metz in France. He painted the ceiling of the Paris Opera and two large murals for New York's Lincoln Center.

The poet of the Cubist era, Blaise Cendrars, wrote of Chagall: "He grabs a church and paints with the church. He grabs a cow and paints with the cow . . . . He paints with an oxtail . . . with all the dirty passion of a little Jewish town . . . with all the exacerbated sexuality of provincial Russia."

Chagall, more than most of his contemporaries, served as a valuable inspiration to many novice painters because of his unique artistic abilities. The sheer number of Chagall's paintings is said to have rivaled Picasso's.

Art critic Robert Hughes called Marc Chagall "the quintessential Jewish artist of the twentieth century." This great and prolific artist died at the age of ninety-eight on March 28, 1985. In the early 1990s Chagall's daughter, Ida, arrived in Israel with six suitcases of works by her father. She turned them over to Jerusalem's mayor, Teddy Kollek, as a gift to the Israel Museum.

ANDRÉ CITROËN

Major French Industrialist

Born February 5, 1879, in Paris, France; died July 3, 1935. French industrialist. Credited with helping France prevail during World War I by assuring the steady flow of ammunition to the French army, André Citroën was also largely responsible for creating the automobile industry in France. Because of this, he was dubbed the French Henry Ford. His company failed during the Depression, however, and Citroën was forced to sell most of his interest in it to his largest creditor, Pierre Michelin, head of the Michelin Tire Company. The *New York Times*, in its obituary of Citroën, said, "The rise and fall of the house of Citroën is one of the most dramatic stories of modern industry."

OF DUTCH ANCESTRY, the Citroën family lived in Paris, where André, who was considered a brilliant student, studied engineering at the École Polytechnique.

After completing his studies, André Citroën struggled to earn a living. In 1908, at age twenty-nine, he bought the failing Mors automobile company. At the time, Mors was producing 125 cars a year. By 1914, Citroën had increased annual production to twelve hundred vehicles.

When World War I began, Citroën was a lieutenant in the artillery; he served some time with the engineers corps and proposed to the Ministry of War that it increase munitions production to meet wartime needs. As a result, the French government gave him responsibility for overseeing arms production. Citroën sent engineers to the United States to purchase machinery and he established a large factory on the Quai de Javel, which produced twenty-eight million shells for the French Army.

Citroën did more than produce munitions during the war. He created facilities for soldiers to buy food and other items; he invented a food card in order to eliminate confusion in the commissary department; he regulated coal distribution; and, later, reorganized the Army's postal service. Citroën was credited by the *New York Times* with contributing more than any other person to the French victory by assuring a constant output of ammunition for the army.

Citroën's Quai de Javel factory showed him how important mass production was for industry. Within seven months after war hostilities ended, Citroën had converted his munitions factory into an assembly line that produced automobiles. He wanted to mass-produce a small, affordable car. It was a ten-horsepower vehicle, calculated to be widely available and to popularize the automobile in France. The factory averaged thirty cars a day in 1919, a figure that increased to three hundred in 1924 and to nearly 120,000 in 1929.

Two models were produced: a small four-cylinder car and a six-cylinder car, both economical to operate. By 1928, Citroën had ten large factories employing thirty thousand workers. He took charge of the financing, designing, and manufacturing and assembling systems.

Citroën visited the United States three times—in 1912, 1923, and 1931. He met Henry Ford while in Detroit, and the two motor magnates became good friends. Like Ford, Citroën believed that the best way to make a large profit was to operate mass production efficiently and with a small margin of profit on each automobile. The buyer got ample value for his or her money and a large volume of business would more than compensate for the small profit on each sale. Contrary to the attitude of most French automobile manufacturers, Citroën believed in giving better value by reducing the price of the car. He did not believe in expensive improvements, nor did he seek to cater to a desire for comfort or luxury. Citroën wanted to make his auto available to the greatest number of people.

André Citroën

Citroën advertised on a large scale. Thousands of tourists gazed at the huge Citroën sign on the Eiffel Tower; it had two hundred thousand electric lamps flashing in different colors, spelling out the letters of Citroën's name. It would go dark and then burst forth with a giant barometer to show the temperature; go dark again, and then display the time on an electric clock.

As a way of further popularizing his cars, Citroën sought to develop trade routes through the Sahara Desert by sponsoring the Citroën Central African automobile crossing in 1922. This first car trek across the Sahara desert had the effect of linking Algeria with western Africa; it also established outposts all along the route, which linked the African colonies. The cars were equipped with specially designed wheels that could negotiate the nearly impassable country from Algeria to Nigeria, British East Africa, the Belgian Congo, and the Union of South Africa, leading all the way to Cape Town.

In 1932, Citroën and the National Geographic Society backed the Georges-Marie Haardt Expedition, during which an eight-thousand-vehicle caravan from Beirut to Beijing was sucessfully completed.

Citroën contributed to civic improvements in France; he helped to organize the traffic system and planned the floodlighting of Paris. He was also responsible for vastly improving bus service throughout the country.

However, Citroën lost control of his company when the worldwide Depression of the early 1930s arrived. The growth of competition from other automobile producers hurt sales at a time when purchasing power was declining. Citroën failed to make adjustments for this new economic situation, and by 1932 he was able to produce only 58,000 cars a year. On December 21, 1934, the firm went into liquidation. Over twenty thousand workers had to be dismissed as the company continued to lose money. The fall of the Citroën car firm, considered one of the worst commercial disasters in French history, left Citroën himself shattered and disillusioned. The *New York Times*, in its obituary of Citroën, referred to this debacle, saying, "The rise and fall of the house of Citroën is one of the most dramatic stories of modern industry."

C. R. Hargrove, writing in the *Wall Street Journal* on January 9, 1935, talked about why Citroën had risen so fast in the beginning. It was "because he is a man of wide vision, great enterprise, high ambition," characteristics suited for "years of peace and plenty. But the Depression required that Citroën restrict his energies, ambitions, vision. He could not do that. And he fought against it in a manner that astonished all who have been negotiating with him these past nine months."

Citroën was forced to turn over most of his stock in the company to his largest creditor, Pierre Michelin, the head of the Michelin Tire Company. Although the Citroën company experienced a slight recovery the following year, André Citroën did not. His financial setback was a personal disaster for him.

He and his wife had three children: two sons and a daughter.

Gambling was one of Citroën's passions. Much of his time was spent with his wife at the casinos in Deauville, Biarritz, and Monte Carlo. Once, at Deauville, he lost forty thousand dollars. He kept on smiling while his wife, angry at the loss, wept openly.

Illness plagued Citroën for the last few years of his life and he was confined to a hospital bed in his final months. He died at the age of fifty-seven in 1935.

The impact Citroën made on French life and industry was immense. In addition to aiding his country's triumph in World War I, he was largely responsible for creating the automobile industry in France. In 1934, a year before his death, one third of the 1.8 million cars in France were Citroëns.

ELI COHN

Israel's Most Daring Spy

Born December 16, 1924, in Alexandria, Egypt; died May 18, 1965. Israeli spy. Upon being asked to join the Mossad, Israel's intelligence service, Eli Cohn at first refused. Later he agreed, and was sent to Syria in the mid-1960s as a spy. Spending three years under cover, Cohn penetrated the senior ranks of Syria's political and military establishments. The information that he sent back to Israel during this time proved invaluable and helped the Jewish state defeat the Syrians in the 1967 Six-Day War. His spy activities were finally discovered, and Cohn was hanged by the Syrians in 1965.

ELI COHN was born in Alexandria, Egypt, in 1924. His father was a shopkeeper who had lived in northern Syria. Cohn was an excellent student, both in high school and at the Midrasha, the Institute of Higher Hebraic Studies.

Identifying himself as a patriotic Egyptian as well as a Jew, during his free time Eli worked on behalf of the Nationalist Movement for a Free Egypt. On occasion he took part in anti-British street demonstrations. He had two hobbies that later proved useful: photography and collecting photos of weapons.

At Farouk University, Eli began to study applied electricity, but when the state of Israel was founded in 1948 and a wave of anti-Semitism struck the school, he and other Jewish students were forced to give up their studies. Devoting himself to underground Zionist efforts, Cohn was recruited by a ring of young Egyptian Jews and played a role in what became known in Israel as the Lavon Affair. Sent to Tel Aviv for three months of intelligence training, Cohn was part of a group that was ordered to sabotage public buildings in Alexandria. The aim was to damage American and British property as a way of creating discord.

Cohn was arrested and served four months in jail. He was arrested once again following the 1956 Suez operation, and detained by the Egyptian government aboard the ship *Marianis Rosso*. Upon his release, Cohn was expelled from Egypt.

When he arrived in Israel in 1957, Cohn began working as a translator at the Ministry of Defense. At that point, the Mossad, Israel's equivalent of the CIA, tried to recruit him. The first time he turned them down. The second time he agreed.

Eli Cohn was sent to Syria in order to infiltrate the higher ranks and send valuable intelligence information back to Israel. He used the name Kamel Amin Tabet. To establish his cover, Cohn was first sent to Buenos Aires, where he posed as a successful businessman who wanted to return to his native Syria. He was accepted into the expatriate Syrian society while in

State of Israel Government Press Office

Eli Cohn

Argentina. Among the valuable contacts he made there was Amin al-Hafez, the military attaché who would later become chief of staff and president of Syria. After several months in Argentina, Cohn had gathered letters of recommendation to present to senior leaders in Syria.

Cohn spent the next three years in Syria. So accepted was he as a Syrian businessman that two weeks before he was captured, he was put forward by members of the National Revolutionary Council to become the next minister of information in the wake of a recent cabinet shuffle. Several key officers proposed that he be appointed deputy minister of defense.

To those who met Cohn in Syria, he seemed a committed Marxist, a member of the Arab socialist Baath Party, and an up-and-comer. He rose through party ranks; what he learned about the political scene in Syria he was able to relay back to Israel through text, photos, or microfilm, all invaluable to the Israeli military in the months and years before the 1967 Six-Day War.

When Cohn claimed to his Arab friends that he was doubtful that Syria's army was battle-ready, he was asked by Syrian defense officials to inspect the lines along the border with Israel periodically. From those visits, Cohn passed along to the Mossad sketches of bunkers and precise coordinates of artillery placements, hiding the secret information in the backgammon boards that he exported to Europe as part of his business.

He also acquired crucial information about the new MiG 21 fighter jets that had been supplied by the Soviets to Syria. The Israelis had asked Cohn to check Syrian plans for diverting the waters of the Jordan, plans that could have threatened Israeli irrigation and its water supply. Feigning interest in purchasing land in the area, Cohn managed to obtain a map that delineated the planned diversion project. The Israeli Air Force blew it up based on this information.

Cohn knew that living in Damascus would be difficult for his wife, Nadia, and their three children; they therefore remained in Israel. He promised his wife that he would conclude his work by May of 1965. She, however, was skeptical.

One day, in January 1965, while he was sending a message to Israel, Cohn was picked up by new tracking equipment that detected his secret transmitter. When his apartment was searched, the Syrians found a photography lab, microfilm, two transmitters, and a tape recorder that had been built into the wall of a guest room. When questioned by the Syrian authorities, Cohn insisted that he was an Arab immigrant from Argentina.

The Syrians forced him to send a message to Israel stating that the Syrian Army had gone on alert. Cohn broadcast the message at a different speed, and that was how Tel Aviv learned that Eli Cohn had been caught.

At first the Syrians believed him to be an Arab who was working for Israel, not a Jew. But when he was interrogated in depth about Muslim customs, it was clear to them that he was not an Arab. The Syrian interrogators tortured him until he finally admitted, "I am an Israeli operative employed by the Mossad. My name is Eliah ben Shaul Cohn, and I live with my wife and three children in Bat Yam, near Tel Aviv. All I will add is that I have operated in the best interests of my country."

A Syrian military court condemned him to death.

Appeals for clemency came from the Pope, French President Charles de Gaulle, and other high-placed officials worldwide, but nothing changed his sentence. He was publicly hanged on May 18, 1965, in Damascus.

As his last wishes, he asked to write a letter to his wife and his family, and he requested a rabbi. The Syrians agreed to these requests.

The Israelis have frequently sought to have Eli Cohn's body returned to Israel, but the Syrians have always refused. At one point, Israeli agents penetrated Syria and were able to retrieve his remains, but the mission had to be aborted when border guards pursued them. They were forced to leave Cohn's body behind.

In a preface to *Our Man in Damascus: Eli Cohn*, Cohn's wife, Nadia, noted: "I said goodbye to him in the last days of November 1964, with a clear feeling that this would be our last meeting. When they informed me two months later that he had been caught, my heart ached, but I was not surprised. 'Your husband was a hero,' they said in May. 'His exploits will go down in history.' When the Six-Day War ended, I knew that indeed that's what he was, and now I see that history will also remember him."

AARON COPLAND

Dean of American Composers

> Born November 14, 1900, in Brooklyn, New York; died December 2, 1990. American composer. As the creator of a genuinely American musical form, Aaron Copland had a major influence on two generations of composers. His goal was to establish a "naturally American strain of so-called serious music." Copland was trained in Europe, yet he was one of the first American composers to incorporate American folk tunes into his music. His output was prodigious, and he composed music in just about every form, from ballets and operas to instrumental solos. His orchestral piece *Music for the Theater* (1927) was the first to win him fame, but he is perhaps best known for his ballet pieces *Billy the Kid* (1938), *Rodeo* (1942), and *Appalachian Spring* (1944).

AARON COPLAND was born in Brooklyn, New York, in 1900, the youngest of five children. Copland's parents, Harris Copland and Sarah Mittenthal Copland, were of Russian-Jewish descent. Harris Copland owned a department store in Brooklyn. Aaron's family, apart from his elder sister, an amateur pianist, displayed little appreciation for music. But when he was eleven years old, his sister taught him to play the piano. Two years later, Aaron convinced his parents to allow him to take lessons with Leopold Wolfsohn, a neighborhood teacher.

The Copland family belonged to a synagogue in Brooklyn where the rabbi, Israel Goldfarb, had composed a world-famous melody for "Shalom Aleichem," and some have suggested that young Copland was influenced by Rabbi Goldfarb's achievement. While Copland celebrated his bar mitzvah at the synagogue in Jewish tradition, he later acknowledged that religious observance was "more of a convention than a deep commitment."

By age fifteen, Copland had committed himself to pursuing a career as a musical composer. In the fall of 1917, when he was seventeen and in his senior year at Boys' High School, Copland studied harmony, counterpoint, and composition with music teacher Rubin Goldmark. In time, however, he grew disenchanted with Goldmark's German bias and switched to other teachers, first Victor Wittgenstein, then Clarence Adler. Copland developed a personal style in composing that inculcated many of the new musical forms played by the European modernists.

Despite his seeming lack of interest in Judaism, at age nineteen Copland wrote *Lament* (for cello and piano), which incorporated a traditional Rosh Hashanah melody for the Hebrew prayer *Adon Olam*.

In June 1921, Copland traveled to France, the first student to enroll in the newly established Conservatoire Americain at Fontainebleau. Studying composition there under Paul Vidal, Copland visited Nadia Boulanger's harmony class and was so thoroughly taken with her teaching methods that by the end of the summer session he had decided to live permanently in Paris. He studied composition with Boulanger for the next three years, the first of many American composers to study with her.

In June 1924 Boulanger asked Copland to send her a composition for her forthcoming American tour. Thus it was that on November 16, 1924, the *Organ Symphony* became the first of his works to be performed in the United States. Copland, however, thought *Organ Symphony* was "too European in inspiration." He introduced a jazz idiom into his next compositions, *Music for Theater* (1925) and *Piano Concerto* (1927). Music critic Oscar Thompson regarded the former as "the

Aaron Copland

most impressive symphonic work in the jazz idiom that any composer, American or European, has placed to his credit." At its Boston premiere, however, some in the audience expressed dislike for the piece.

By this time, Copland had opened and closed, for lack of students, a piano studio. However, another music critic, Paul Rosenfeld, liked Copland's *Organ Symphony* enough to connect Copland with a patron who began sending the composer a monthly stipend.

In 1925 Copland became the first composer to be awarded a Guggenheim Fellowship; it was renewed the following year. In 1927 he began ten years of teaching modern music at the New School for Social Research in New York. Around this time, Copland concluded that he had done all that was possible as a music composer within the limited scope of the jazz idiom.

His *Symphonic Ode*, written between 1927 and 1929, exemplified a new phase in Copland's evolution as a musical composer as he tried to make his music more accessible to larger audiences. Soon thereafter, he produced such major works as *Piano Variations* (1930), *Short Symphony* (1932–33), and *Statements* (1933–35). These were said by music critics to be more spare in sonority and lean in texture. According to Paul Moor, writing in *Theatre Arts*, "Dissonance abounded along with nervous, irregular rhythms and angular, jagged, nonmelodic thematic material."

In 1929 Copland wrote his most important work on a Jewish theme: a work for three instruments (violin, cello, and piano) called *Vitebsk: Study on a Jewish Theme*, which had a clear-cut Hasidic sound.

In the late 1930s, Copland felt that his music was reaching only an elite audience, and not getting to the wider public. He began writing a number of unquestionably American musical pieces that ultimately attained great popularity. These included the ballet scores *Billy the Kid* (1938) and *Rodeo* (1942), and such concert pieces as *El Salon Mexico* (1937) and *Lincoln Portrait* (1942) as well as his most popular composition, *Appalachian Spring* (1944), first written as a ballet score commissioned by Martha Graham. Copland was awarded a Pulitzer Prize for this musical piece. He also composed music for the films *Of Mice and Men, Our Town,* and *The Heiress,* for which he won an Academy Award in 1948.

Copland became a key music administrator during the 1930s. He was president of the American Composers Alliance, director of the League of Composers, and a member of the faculty of the Berkshire Musical Center at Tanglewood, Massachusetts. He was also involved in early television musical programming.

Music critics sometimes found Copland's Jewish heritage implicit in his composing. It was said by some, for example, that in the first of *Four Motets* (1921), which were psalm paraphrases, Copland subconsciously paraphrased the tones emanating from Yiddish folk songs. In 1937, he arranged *Banu,* a Palestinian hora with words by Natan Alterman. His 1947 cantata, *In the Beginning,* which took as its subject the Genesis story, had no obvious Jewish musical theme, but still evoked Hebrew prayer for many listeners.

Copland was asked once how a Jewish boy from Brooklyn could write *Rodeo,* and he replied, "I preferred to imagine being on a horse without actually getting on one."

Music critic Rosenfeld said of Copland that he "was like a colt—all legs, head, and body, cantering past on long, uncertain stilts—the colt of American brass and momentum, all that's swift and daring, aggressive and unconstrained in our life."

Leonard Bernstein paid Copland this compliment: "He was the leader to whom all young composers brought their compositions."

In 1964 Copland was awarded the Medal of Freedom by the American government. He stopped composing after 1970, concentrating his energies on lecturing and conducting. At his death in 1990 at the age of ninety, the *New York Times* called Aaron Copland "America's best-known composer of classical music and a gentle yet impassioned champion of American music in every style."

Copland's goal had been to establish a singularly American strain in the serious music of his age. He went far beyond that, becoming one of America's greatest musical composers. He never forgot his Jewish roots. "I think of music as Jewish," he told one interviewer, "because it's dramatic, it's intense, it has a certain passionate lyricism to it."

MOSHE DAYAN

Israel's Warrior-Statesman

> Born May 4, 1915, at Kibbutz Degania, Palestine; died October 16, 1981. Israeli military and political leader. For millions of people around the world, Moshe Dayan, with his black eyepatch, was the most visible symbol of the state of Israel. As chief of staff of the Israel Defense Forces (IDF) in the 1950s, he shaped the IDF into the most potent military force in the Middle East. A military hero who led Israel to victory in both the 1956 Sinai Campaign and the 1967 Six-Day War, Dayan was later blamed for Israel's lack of preparedness at the start of the 1973 Yom Kippur War and was forced to resign as defense minister. His career ended on a high note, however, when he helped shape the 1979 Israel-Egypt Camp David peace treaty.

MOSHE DAYAN'S LIFE and achievements took on immense meaning for the Jewish people because he seemed a genuine original. He was the first child born at Degania, the first Jewish kibbutz in Palestine. His parents had emigrated there from Russia. When Dayan was six, he moved with his parents to Nahalal, the first moshav established in Palestine. A moshav, also a kind of collective community, is less centrally organized than a kibbutz.

Dayan became familiar with military life at an early age, handling his first gun when he was only ten. At the age of fourteen he joined the Haganah, the clandestine Jewish self-defense organization, and learned how to use a pistol and to practice judo.

In 1939, when Dayan was twenty-four years old, he and forty-two others were imprisoned by the British authorities for illegally possessing weapons. He was released in June 1941. When serving as a scout in southern Lebanon for British troops, Dayan was shot by a sniper and lost his left eye. From then on, he wore a distinctive black eyepatch.

During the 1948 War of Independence, Dayan commanded the 89th Battalion when it captured Lod and Ramle. In September 1948, he was appointed Jerusalem commander, and for the next two years he secretly negotiated with Jordan's King Abdullah. These talks culminated in an Israeli-Jordanian cease-fire and the draft of a nonaggression pact between the two countries.

Dayan became Israel's fourth chief of staff in November 1953. He and Prime Minister David Ben-Gurion were the architects of Israel's policy of massive retaliation against Arab terrorist incursions into Israel. Dayan's whole approach to the military was unorthodox. He shaped the Israel Defense Forces and set its battle standards by insisting that all that mattered was whether or not a soldier could and would fight, not how he looked or how he marched. Dayan valued initiative over disciplined behavior in soldiers.

In October 1956, Dayan led Israel's hundred-hour war against Egypt; the operation was known as the Sinai Campaign. During this conflict, Israel captured the Sinai Peninsula, but the land was returned to Egypt the following March in response to heavy American pressure.

Dayan retired from the IDF in 1958 and studied briefly at Jerusalem's Hebrew University. The following year he was elected to the Knesset, Israel's parliament, as a member of the ruling Mapai party, a forerunner of today's Labor party. He served as minister of agriculture until 1964. The following year, he joined Ben-Gurion's breakaway Rafi party. In 1966 Dayan traveled to Vietnam and covered the war there for the *Sunday Telegraph* of Britain and *Ma'ariv* of Israel.

As tension mounted on the eve of the 1967 Six-Day War, the public was uncomfortable with Israel's seemingly uncertain political and military leadership. This pressure from the populace led to Dayan's being appointed defense minister. Though he made few changes in the existing war plans, Dayan led Israel to a smashing victory and became the war's hero.

Moshe Dayan

State of Israel Government Press Office

In this period Israelis had a love-hate relationship with Dayan. They held him in awe for his military prowess, yet they recoiled at his contempt for the law and his flouting of convention. It was widely believed that he thought nothing of helping himself to archeological finds to enrich his private collection. When some Israelis sought to have Dayan punished for taking relics for his own personal use, he was protected by the majority of citizens, who believed that he was indispensable to Israeli security and therefore should not be punished.

Following the 1967 war, in his position as defense minister, Dayan ruled over Israel's occupation of the lands it had recently captured: the Golan Heights, the West Bank, the Gaza Strip, East Jerusalem, and the Sinai Peninsula. He appeared ready to negotiate peace arrangements with the Arabs, but said they must make the first step. When they did not, Dayan gradually built up an Israeli presence in "the territories," including civilian settlements that would make it that much more difficult for Israel to contemplate returning the occupied lands.

Despite the formidable presence of Golda Meir as prime minister during this period, Dayan was the strong man of the government. He set the tone for Israel's attitude toward the Arabs, imbuing Israelis with the false notion that the country was safe from future Arab attacks because the Jewish state had beaten the Arabs so soundly during the 1967 war.

When Egypt and Syria launched surprise attacks against Israel on October 6, 1973—Yom Kippur—Golda Meir and Moshe Dayan were blamed for their country's lack of preparedness. While Dayan had served as an inspiration to the military forces in 1956 and 1967, he seemed uncertain and insecure during the Yom Kippur War. At times he appeared ready for Israel to lay down its arms and hope for a decent cease-fire with the Arabs, one that would have yielded

Israeli territory to the Arabs. Israelis lost confidence in Dayan for not making sure that the country was prepared for war and for behaving erratically once war broke out.

After Egypt and Syria had made substantial initial gains at the outset of the 1973 war, Israel counterattacked—but not before the Jewish state had suffered many fatalities, five hundred on the first day of fighting alone. The public blamed Dayan. When a blue-ribbon commission led by Chief Justice Shimon Agranat essentially cleared Dayan and Golda Meir of any responsibility for the lack of Israeli preparedness on war's eve, the public did not accept the commission's verdict. In April 1974, public demonstrations led to the resignation of Prime Minister Meir and her Cabinet, including Dayan.

Three years later, in May 1977, the newly elected prime minister, Menachem Begin, leader of the right-wing Likud bloc, selected Dayan to be his foreign minister. Dayan happily accepted, viewing the appointment as a chance to rehabilitate his career.

In a secret visit to Morocco in the fall of 1977, Moshe Dayan met with a senior Egyptian official and began negotiating the terms for an Israel-Egypt peace treaty, paving the way for President Anwar Sadat's historic visit to Jerusalem in November 1977. During the September 1978 Camp David meetings, Dayan played a pivotal role in the negotiations that eventually led to the peace treaty, which was signed in March 1979.

Dayan retired as foreign minister in October 1979 after discovering that Prime Minister Begin was not sufficiently enthusiastic about going forward with the peace process.

For years Dayan's personal life was beset with problems. When he was twenty years old, he married Ruth Schwartz of Jerusalem. The marriage produced three children: Yael, born in 1939, Ehud, born in 1942, and Assaf, born in 1945. But the marriage was troubled, and Dayan was thought to have had affairs with several other women. In 1955 Dayan met Rachel Rabinovitch, who was also married at the time. They began an eighteen-year affair. In 1971, Moshe and Ruth Dayan were divorced; two years later Dayan married Rachel.

Not content to stay in retirement and eager to remain in politics, Dayan formed a new party, Telem, in advance of the June 1981 elections. The Telem party won only two seats in the election, a terrible disappointment. By this time, Dayan's health was also suffering badly. He had been diagnosed with cancer.

The following October (1981), Dayan died at the age of sixty-six. He left nearly all his assets to his second wife, Rachel, virtually disinheriting his three children. Moshe Dayan's sons were unforgiving of their father, but his daughter, Yael, defended and mourned him publicly.

Moshe Dayan was one of the state of Israel's legendary heroes, the builder of its army, a conqueror of Arab foes, and ultimately a peacemaker who helped forge his country's first peace treaty with an Arab neighbor.

ALAN M. DERSHOWITZ

Famous American Lawyer

Born September 1, 1938, in Brooklyn, New York. American law professor, attorney, and author. Alan Dershowitz is one of America's best-known and controversial lawyers. His reputation has been built on taking cases that permitted him to defend the constitutional right of free speech. Dershowitz became an appellate lawyer of last resort, defending such high-profile figures as porn star Harry Reams, former heavyweight boxing champion Mike Tyson, former hotel owner Leona Helmsley, and socialite Claus von Bülow. His book *Reversal of Fortune*, based on the von Bülow case, was made into a movie. In 1994 Dershowitz joined the defense team of former football star O.J. Simpson, who was subsequently acquitted of murdering his former wife, Nicole Brown Simpson, and Ronald Goldman.

ALAN DERSHOWITZ, born in 1938, grew up in an Orthodox Jewish home in Borough Park, Brooklyn. His father, Harry Dershowitz, owned a wholesale clothing store, and his mother, Claire (Ringel) Dershowitz, was a bookkeeper.

Dershowitz attended Yeshiva University High School and observed all Jewish rituals. He prayed three times a day. "My Orthodoxy, my observance, totally filled my Jewish quota," he said. "I didn't have to think of anything else."

Yet doubts surfaced. "I was never that theological," he explained. "I was always something of a skeptic and a doubter. I was a terrible yeshiva student because I was always raising questions. I had to reconcile evolution with the story of creation. So I was a bad religious student, but I was observant. My father's attitude was: It doesn't matter if you have doubts: come to synagogue."

Dershowitz excelled in his studies at Brooklyn College, where he obtained a B.A. degree *magna cum laude* in 1959 and was elected to Phi Beta Kappa. He was the first Orthodox Jewish president of the Brooklyn College student body.

Dershowitz married Sue Barlach on the day that he graduated from Brooklyn College; they had two children, Elon, a Hollywood producer, and Jamin, an attorney who is legal counsel for the National Basketball Association. Dershowitz divorced his wife in 1975. He later married neuropsychologist Carolyn Cohen. They have a daughter, Ella.

Dershowitz had always aspired to be an attorney because "I never thought I had talents in anything else. I was told by my yeshiva teachers that I wasn't too bright, but I had a good mouth so I should either be a lawyer or a Conservative rabbi. It was one of the most insulting things you could tell a young Orthodox Jewish boy. I didn't want to be a rabbi so I became a lawyer."

In the fall of 1959, Dershowitz was admitted to Yale Law School and displayed an aptitude for constitutional and criminal law. During his second year, he was elected editor-in-chief of the *Yale Law Journal*. Harvard Law School offered him a teaching position when he finished his degree. He graduated first in his class in 1962.

Postponing the Harvard offer, Dershowitz clerked with Chief Judge David L. Bazelon of the United States Court of Appeals in Washington, D.C. He was admitted to the District of Columbia bar in 1963 and served a one-year clerkship with Supreme Court Justice Arthur Goldberg. In deference to Dershowitz's strict Sabbath observance, Goldberg sometimes held emergency Saturday meetings at his law clerk's home.

Dershowitz began teaching at Harvard Law School in 1964. Soon thereafter, he stopped his strict Orthodox observance. "It didn't have meaning for me, and I had two young

Alan Dershowitz

The Jewish Week

children to whom I had to be able to explain my actions. I found it difficult to explain all the rituals to them. I found it easier to explain my other Jewish activities."

Yet abandoning the daily rituals left him with "a tremendous void in my life, a Jewish void." At that point he decided to become an activist on behalf of the state of Israel and of Soviet Jewry. Dershowitz noted that "I identified so strongly with the Soviet Jewry movement because I felt that I could have been a Soviet dissident."

In 1967, at the age of twenty-eight, he became the youngest tenured law professor in Harvard's history. As a teacher, Dershowitz specialized in criminal law, but he retained his strong interest in the relationship of mental health to legal issues.

Dershowitz's most controversial free-speech cases were in the area of pornography. In 1969, appearing before the United States Supreme Court for the first time, he defended the Swedish film *I Am Curious (Yellow)*, the first explicit sex film to be distributed in the United States. The movie had been banned in Boston and Dershowitz fought in court for its right to be shown, arguing successfully that a movie exhibited to consenting adults in a discreet setting must be constitutionally protected under the First Amendment.

Dershowitz's intense interest in Soviet Jewry led him to defend Jewish dissident Natan Sharansky, whom the Soviets had accused of being an American spy in 1977; the Soviets denied Dershowitz permission to represent Sharansky, who was convicted and sentenced to thirteen years in jail. Dershowitz likes to say that his biggest fee came not from any of his celebrity trials but from seeing Natan Sharansky set free.

Claus von Bülow was Dershowitz's first celebrity client. Dershowitz successfully appealed socialite von Bülow's 1982 conviction for attempting to murder his wife, the heiress Martha "Sunny"

Crawford von Bülow, by injecting her with insulin. Dershowitz argued that von Bülow's constitutional rights had been violated when a private investigator searched his apartment without a warrant. That evidence was withheld from the defense; he also provided sworn statements from Sunny's acquaintances that suggested that she used large amounts of dangerous drugs.

In 1986 Dershowitz wrote a book about the von Bülow case called *Reversal of Fortune*, which his son Elon then made into a Hollywood film. Ron Silver played Dershowitz, with Jeremy Irons portraying von Bülow, and Glenn Close the role of Sunny.

After critics charged that Dershowitz engaged in too much courtroom trickery and defended too many people whom he knew to be guilty, he noted that he considered it a professional obligation to represent guilty, "despicable" defendants in the most challenging, difficult, and precedent-setting cases he could handle.

In other high-profile cases, Dershowitz appealed a tax-evasion conviction against former hotel owner Leona Helmsley; he succeeded in having all the State charges dismissed, though he failed to overturn the Federal conviction. He was also unable to overturn the 1991 rape conviction of former heavyweight boxing champion Mike Tyson, although he was successful in reducing the prison sentences of Wall Street financier Michael Milken, jailed for securities law violations, and evangelist Jim Bakker, convicted of bilking his followers out of millions of dollars. In the mid-1990s, by preparing legal briefs, Dershowitz helped successfully defend O.J. Simpson against murder charges.

Dershowitz is a prolific writer. The book *Chutzpah* (1991), which described Dershowitz's personal look at American Jewish life set against his own experiences, was a surprise bestseller. He wrote the book because, until then, "I was very well known as an American lawyer who happened to be Jewish. People like Ted Koppel who had me on his [*Nightline*] show all the time didn't even know that I was a committed Jew."

Dershowitz has written both fiction and nonfiction. His first novel, *The Advocate's Devil* (1994), is a thriller that deals with ethical issues; in it, a basketball player is accused of rape. *The Abuse Excuse*, which appeared in late 1994, is a series of essays about people who admit to violent crimes but argue that they should not be held legally responsible for them because they themselves were victims of abuse.

In 1996, Dershowitz's book on the O.J. Simpson trial and the criminal justice system entitled *Reasonable Doubts* was published; soon thereafter it reached the *New York Times* list of bestselling books.

In his book *The Vanishing American Jew: In Search of Jewish Identity*, published in 1997, Dershowitz predicts that American Jewry will disappear if it does not take steps to protect itself. In 1999 he published a second novel, *Just Revenge*, about an aging Jewish professor who accidentally comes across the chief perpetrator of the atrocity that saw his family wiped out in the Holocaust. This was followed by a June 2001 nonfiction work entitled *Supreme Injustice: How the High Court Hijacked Election 2000*, which analyzes the U.S. Supreme Court's controversial ruling in *Bush* v. *Gore*. Dershowitz argued that the Supreme Court justices "hijacked Election 2000 by distorting the law, violating their own expressed principles, and using their robes to bring about a partisan result."

In August 2003, Dershowitz's *The Case for Israel*, which responds to such questions as Israel's alleged torture of Palestinians and its alleged colonialist, imperialist tendencies, was published. This was followed by the 2004 release of his *America on Trial*, a look at some of the most famous American legal cases.

ÉMILE DURKHEIM

The Founder of Modern Sociology

Born April 15, 1858, in Epinal, France; died November 15, 1917. French sociologist. Émile Durkheim is credited with founding modern sociology and establishing the field as an academic discipline and a social science with practical objectives. As the author of *The Rules of Sociological Method* (1895), *Suicide* (1897), and *The Elementary Forms of the Religious Life* (1915), Durkheim gave modern sociology its basic shape.

ÉMILE DURKHEIM came from a long line of Alsatian rabbis, and it was assumed that young Émile would follow the family tradition. He did study for the rabbinate but turned away from Judaism as a young man, remaining an agnostic and freethinker for the rest of his life.

In 1879, at the age of twenty-one, he enrolled at the École Normal Supérieure and started studying for a degree in philosophy. A serious student, he found his teachers unsatisfactory and somewhat shallow. They were not particularly interested in substantive research and scientific progress, he thought, emphasizing instead what he called "surface polish" and rhetoric.

Durkheim became a teacher of philosophy in 1882. During the next five years he taught in a number of provincial high schools outside Paris. He took a leave of absence in the 1885–86 academic year to study the state of the social sciences in France and Germany.

Durkheim wanted to be a social scientist; to him that meant that he would also have to be a moral philosopher and a scientist of moral behavior. As a result of his year of research, he produced two surveys that dealt with the state of philosophy and science of ethics in Germany. These surveys greatly enhanced his reputation as a serious scholar.

Émile Durkheim

In 1887 the University of Bordeaux offered him a post as lecturer in sociology and education. When he joined the faculty, Durkheim became the first person to hold a chair in sociology at a European university. He received his doctorate in 1893 after writing a dissertation, *The Division of Labor in Society*, within the University of Bordeaux philosophy department. Durkheim's spirited defense of his doctoral research against skeptical professors helped to launch modern sociology as a legitimate scholarly discipline.

Around this time he married Louise Dreyfus; they had two children, Marie and André. (His wife was not related to the Alfred Dreyfus of the Dreyfus Affair.)

Half a century earlier, in the middle of the nineteenth century, Auguste Comte had coined the term "sociology," combining the Latin word *societas* (society) with the Greek term *logos* (study). But it was Durkheim's dissertation in 1893 that was the first major sociological work employing a rigorously scientific methodology.

Durkheim's most important work, *The Rules of Sociological Method*, was published in 1895. The book developed the framework for sociological method and was the seminal work in establishing sociology as an independent academic discipline.

In 1898 Durkheim founded a yearbook called *L'Année sociologique*. Serving as its editor-in-chief, Durkheim published the first volume, 563 pages, that year. A compilation of the research and theory appearing in the field of sociology each year, the yearbook was published annually until the outbreak of World War I. It was an important resource for Durkheim's fellow sociologists.

Durkheim tried to show that it was possible to define rules of human behavior despite people's subjective motives. He insisted that the physical, biological, and psychological elements operating in people's social lives must be taken into account. However, society's products, including art, moral standards, and institutions, are entities that should be held apart from humankind and studied on their own.

Durkheim also developed the notion of social solidarity, a concept he used in his studies on the division of labor, morality, conscience, suicide, and religion. He argued that since the whole of society stands above individual human beings while simultaneously affecting them greatly, it remains the only thing that can inspire awe and reverence in humans. Only society as a whole can submit individuals to rules of conduct, to privations, and to the kind of sacrifices without which society would not exist.

Durkheim taught that the values that give pattern and meaning to human activity come essentially from social structure, demonstrating that the roots of morality lie in the social system and not in individual self-interest nor in Divine will. "If a morality exists," Durkheim declared, "it can only have as an objective the group formed by a plurality of associated individuals—that is to say, society."

In his *Sociology and Philosophy*, published in 1929, Durkheim asserted that "it is never possible to desire a morality other than that required by the social conditions of a given time." In effect, sociologists would be wrong to ask what goals a humane society should seek to realize or how well that society was realizing those goals. Instead, they should examine how well a society is integrated, how thoroughly it has succeeded in "socializing" its members to its value system, whatever that system happens to be.

The very notion of Divine authority, Durkheim argued, was a sublimation of society. Religion, in this sense, he said, derived not from the nature of humans but from the nature of society. Suicide, he suggested, was not a function of race, or climate, or religious doctrine, or even economic conditions. Rather, it was related to critical social facts—in short, the breakdown of social solidarity and a resulting "anomie" or lawlessness. Groups that had little social cohesion, he maintained, had higher suicide rates.

Although he was a professed atheist, Durkheim's analysts believe that his social philosophy, with its stress on collective group solidarity and the connection between morality and law, was inspired to some degree by his awareness of Jewish law and ethics. He never wrote on Jewish topics, but he always seemed to be conscious of his rabbinic heritage.

In 1902, Durkheim became professor of sociology and education at the Sorbonne, where he remained for the rest of his life. In addition to teaching, he also did research in the science of moral phenomena and religion. Throughout his academic life, he searched for a secular, scientific, rational basis for a system of ethics.

In 1913 a separate department of sociology, which he chaired, was established at the Sorbonne. When World War I began, Durkheim volunteered his services as a sociologist to France. He was named secretary of the Committee for the Publication of Studies and Documents on the War. In 1915 he published *The Elementary Forms of Religious Life*, his final major work.

Durkheim insisted that sociology was a method or system for doing research on social phenomena. He also thought that sociologists could gain insights from other areas of the social sciences and humanities such as history, geography, and psychology. He strongly favored interdisciplinary approaches to sociological research.

In 1915 Durkheim's only son, André, was killed in battle. It was believed that Durkheim's grief over his son's untimely death hastened his own in November 1917. He was just fifty-nine years old.

PAUL EHRLICH

Curer of Syphilis

> Born in Strehelen (then Germany, now Strzelin, Poland) in 1845; died in 1915. German medical researcher. Paul Ehrlich played a crucial role in developing the fields of hematology and immunology. He was also a pioneer in the field of chemotherapy. In 1908 Ehrlich was awarded the Nobel Prize in Medicine for his work in immunology. Attempting to find what he called a "magic bullet," Ehrlich searched for drugs that would kill bacteria without harming the patient. He found one—Salvarsan—a drug that cured the dreaded disease of syphilis, which had been a scourge throughout Europe for four hundred years.

BORN IN GERMANY IN 1845 to a well-to-do family, Paul Ehrlich was the only son of a distiller and innkeeper. His mother was congenial and highly intelligent. He studied at several universities in Germany. Mathematics appealed to him, as did the study of Latin, but it was only when he discovered natural sciences and chemistry as a college student that he developed an excitement for his studies. He graduated from Berlin University in 1878 and began his scientific work as an assistant there. Ehrlich then studied medicine at the University of Leipzig. Although he lacked a background in experimental chemistry and applied bacteriology, Ehrlich conducted independent research in these fields. So impressed were his colleagues that he was asked to continue his research at the Charité Hospital in Berlin.

At first Ehrlich specialized in the histological, or tissue, structure of cells, and in hematology, the study of blood. A certain amount of research had been done on the effect of dyes on cells and tissues; Ehrlich was intrigued by the possibility of improving the diagnosis of disease by using these dyes more effectively.

Paul Ehrlich

One of his first achievements was developing staining methods for bacteria as well as methods for staining dead and eventually live cell specimens. In 1882 Ehrlich devised a crucial diagnostic technique for staining the tuberculosis bacillus. Teaming up with a German physician named Robert Koch, Ehrlich also closely studied the causes of tuberculosis. He ran into personal bad luck, however, while researching the tubercle bacillus: he contracted the disease himself. He was cured two years later.

Ehrlich's later discoveries included the effective use of methylene blue dye in treating nervous disorders. He also developed diagnostic tests for typhoid and produced medication for fever. His discovery of the "diazo" reaction was a very important medical breakthrough. Through this chemical reaction that he isolated, aromatic compounds in the urine of typhoid fever sufferers were identified, which helped in diagnosing the disease.

In his paper "The Requirement of the Organism for Oxygen," Ehrlich determined that the consumption of oxygen varied according to the kind of tissue involved; these variations affected cell processes.

In 1889 Ehrlich became an associate professor at Berlin University while also working at the Robert Koch Institute for Infectious Diseases. There, he collaborated with another researcher, Emil von Behring, to develop a serum against diphtheria. Von Behring had created the antitoxin, but the serum only attained its maximum effectiveness when relying upon a technique Ehrlich invented. It included the use of blood from live horses.

After 1890, Ehrlich's research efforts focused largely on problems of immunization. By virtue of his groundbreaking research, he established the fundamental concepts of applied immunology: active and passive immunization. Once he came up with a stable antitoxic serum that could be preserved over the long term as a standard serum, he was able to develop a procedure for identifying antitoxic serums. It was one of the most important landmarks in the history of immunology.

In 1896 Ehrlich became director of a new Berlin institute for serum studies called the Royal Institute for Serum Research, which three years later became the Royal Institute for Experimental Therapy in Frankfurt. At this time his relationship with von Behring deteriorated when Ehrlich saw the limits of serum therapy. He began then to engage in research to investigate chemical substances that would selectively kill bacteria and other microorganisms without harming their host cells. This research pioneered modern chemotherapy. In 1904 Ehrlich was named honorary professor at the University of Göttingen.

In 1907 Paul Ehrlich began his research into a cure for syphilis. He had good financial backing and an excellent staff. Once the bacteria had been identified, the challenge was to find the "magic bullet" that would strike at the bacteria without harming the body.

Ehrlich discovered a dye, called trypan red, that stains trypanosomes, the organisms that were responsible for African sleeping sickness, which is transmitted by the tsetse fly. Trypan red, injected into the blood in sufficient doses, can kill trypanosomes without killing the patient. Ehrlich was not satisfied; he wanted something that would be more certain to kill microorganisms.

Ehrlich began to test arsenic compounds, one after the other, methodically numbering them as he progressed. In 1909 one of his students, Sahachiro Hata, tested compound #606 on the bacterium that caused syphilis. Although it failed to combat the trypanosomes that cause sleeping sickness, 606 did prove deadly against the microbe that breeds syphilis.

Ehrlich realized he had come across something more crucial than a cure for trypanosomiasis, a disease that could take the form of sleeping sickness and was so far confined to the tropics. Syphilis, on the other hand, had been a scourge throughout Europe for over four hundred years. He called his discovery—his "magic bullet"—Salvarsan (safe arsenic); its chemical name is arsphenamine.

Ehrlich's discovery was the most significant achievement in the medical fight against this dreaded disease. His method of discovery had even wider implications. Because of Ehrlich's scientific work, a new area of chemotherapy developed; pharmacology, the study of the action of chemicals, other than foods, upon organisms, became a field of medicine. With Ehrlich's discovery, drugs, or synthetic compounds, rather than plants (which had been used as medication until then), began to be used more frequently to combat disease.

Ehrlich cooperated with a manufacturer who provided large quantities of the "bullet" without charge to physicians around the world in order to try to eradicate the spread of syphilis. There were, however, some negative side effects to the drug and this problem led rivals to attack Paul Ehrlich's work. As a result, he had to badger hospitals into using it.

In 1908 Ehrlich was awarded the Nobel Prize for Medicine for his groundbreaking work on immunity to disease. In 1914 he became a professor at Frankfurt University. He was given many other honors, including being decorated with numerous royal orders. He was given Prussia's highest honor when he was made privy councillor; he was also awarded honorary degrees from the National University at Athens, the University of Oxford, and the University of Chicago.

Ehrlich had a reputation among colleagues for being kind, considerate, possessed of a good sense of humor and a love for animals. These personal qualities are evident in a 1940 movie based on his life story, *Dr. Ehrlich's Magic Bullet*, in which Edward G. Robinson portrays Ehrlich.

Ehrlich had little interest in religion but he was curious about Jewish affairs. He was a member of the Supporters of Zion (*Lema'an Tzion*) movement. He was also associated with, and supported, the Nordau Institute, one of the forerunners of the Hebrew University of Jerusalem.

"The whole world is in his debt," the *London Times* commented upon Ehrlich's death in 1915 at the age of seventy.

ALBERT EINSTEIN

Profoundly Influential Theoretical Physicist

Born March 14, 1879, in Ulm, Germany; died April 18, 1955. German-American physicist. The most famous physicist of the twentieth century, Albert Einstein is regarded as one of the greatest scientists of all time. Best known for formulating the theory of relativity, he won the Nobel Prize for Physics in 1921 for his research into the photoelectric effect on metal and other discoveries in theoretical physics. It is ironic that although Einstein was emphatically opposed to war and violence, he nevertheless has been credited with helping to found the nuclear age because of the relationship of his theory of relativity to nuclear physics and the development of nuclear weapons.

ALBERT EINSTEIN was born in Ulm, Germany, in 1879, but from the time he was two years old he lived in Munich, where his father and uncle had established a small electro chemical plant. His parents were not observant Jews, and therefore Albert was not raised in a religious atmosphere.

Einstein displayed special talents in mathematics and music early on, but rather than concentrate on his schoolwork, the young Einstein would stare into space and think about the physical world around him. His teachers thought he was simply daydreaming; they had no idea that he was brilliant.

Einstein locked himself in his own world, reading books on philosophy, poetry, and mathematics. Like his teachers, his father worried that he might be mentally slow. However, when given a pocket compass and a book on geometry, Einstein was inspired at that early stage in his life to be curious about science. Later he joked that "to punish me for my contempt for authority, fate made me an authority myself."

Detesting all things German and specifically the military-like discipline of German schools, Einstein renounced his German heritage. He dropped out of school at the age of fifteen and went with his parents to Italy, spending a few years there. He completed his secondary education in Aarau, Switzerland. From 1896 to 1900, he continued school at the Swiss Federal Institute of Technology (ETH), where he studied physics and mathematics. He graduated when he was twenty-one years old. Einstein wanted to teach at the Institute, but because he was Jewish and lacked Swiss citizenship, he could not do so. In 1901 he took a junior appointment at the patent office in Bern.

Albert Einstein's true passion was trying to discover the basic laws of the universe. Asking himself the most fundamental questions about life and existence, he sought to understand time and

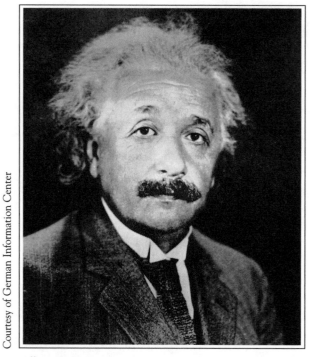

Courtesy of German Information Center

Albert Einstein

space, gravity, mass, and energy. He was convinced that the world did not operate by happenstance; it was merely the inadequacy of human intelligence that prevented people from gaining an understanding of how the universe worked. Einstein set his mind to the task of discovering the keys to these mysteries.

During the seven years between 1902 and 1909 that Einstein worked as a patent examiner, he revolutionized the world of physics through his scientific inquiries. Amazingly, Einstein never performed a single experiment, but what he discovered through his complex thought process—his theories of time and gravity—provided the foundation for much of modern science.

In 1903 Einstein married Mileva Marec, a fellow ETH physics student of Serbian descent, with whom he had a daughter and two sons.

In 1905, his "miracle year," as some called it, Einstein published papers that detailed what were to become three significant discoveries in physics. The first provided a mathematical analysis of Brownian motion, the irregular movement of tiny particles such as dust or bacteria suspended in gas or a liquid; Einstein's findings constituted one of the first indications that atoms and molecules exist. The second offered an explanation of the photoelectric effect as it applied to light, proving it to be a shower of particles.

The third was his special theory of relativity, which presented for the first time the now-famous equation $E=mc^2$. The theory was unique because it focused only on bodies at rest or moving with uniform motion. This last discovery changed the way physicists thought about the world.

Discarding classical Newtonian views of time and space, Einstein argued instead that man exists in a four-dimensional space-time continuum in which time can speed up or slow down and distances can shrink or expand—in short, that mass and energy are different aspects of the same thing and can be converted one into the other. Dealing with the motion of bodies moving freely, the theory assumes that nothing traveled faster than light and nothing could be said to be at rest unless it was motionless with respect to some other entity.

In 1909 Einstein was named to his first academic position at the University of Zurich, becoming an adjunct professor. He was later made a full professor at the German University in Prague (1911 to 1912) and a chaired professor at the Swiss Federal Institute of Technology in Zurich (1912 to 1914). In 1914 Max Planck, Einstein's colleague, obtained a professorship for him at the Prussian Academy of Science in Berlin, a research institute where Einstein could devote his entire time to scientific investigations.

In 1916 Einstein made two further major contributions to physics. In his general theory of relativity, he dealt with the phenomenon of systems accelerating instead of moving at constant velocity relative to one another, as in his original special theory of relativity. The general theory incorporated gravitation into the concept of relativity, explaining gravitation geometrically. Gravitational attraction, Einstein argued, was due to the bending of the four-dimensional space-time continuum by material bodies.

Einstein's name became a household word when the Royal Society of London announced in 1919 that its scientific expedition to Principe Island in the Gulf of Guinea had taken photos of the solar eclipse on May 29 that verified Einstein's theories in a way the public could understand. Their calculations proved that the precise angle of deviation of light passing close to the sun was exactly what the general theory of relativity predicted.

Soon after moving to Berlin and the Prussian Academy, Einstein separated from his first wife. In 1919 he married his cousin, Elsa Einstein.

Einstein won the Nobel Prize for Physics in 1921 for his research into the photoelectric effect and his other significant contributions to theoretical physics. Apparently because those giving the prize did not understand Einstein's theory of relativity sufficiently, the theory that revolutionized modern physics was not cited as a reason for his receiving the award.

Einstein opposed war and violence, and later in his life urged that the atomic bomb be outlawed, yet, ironically, he is credited with helping to usher in the nuclear age. His theories proved that a great deal of energy could be liberated by the conversion of a small amount of mass. This discovery led to the creation of nuclear weapons.

Not formally religious, Einstein did believe in a "supreme intelligence," about which he said, "God does not play dice with the world." He kept a menorah in his home. "God is subtle," he once said, "but He is not malicious."

In 1934 the Nazis stripped Einstein of his German citizenship and took away his property. Though a pacifist, Einstein believed that Nazism had to be defeated no matter what it took. Escaping Germany and the war's horrors there, Einstein accepted a post at the Institute for Theoretical Physics in Princeton, New Jersey, serving there from 1933 to 1945. He became an American citizen in 1940.

In 1939, representing a group of leading scientists, Einstein wrote to President Franklin D. Roosevelt expressing the view that it was now possible to release atomic energy. Although he dreaded such an eventuality, he thought it better that the United States build the bomb before the Germans did. That letter led to the secret American project that resulted in the development of atomic weapons.

Einstein described as one of the great moments of his life being asked by Prime Minister David Ben-Gurion to become the state of Israel's second president, upon the death of Chaim Weizmann in 1952. Einstein had visited Palestine in the 1920s and worked hard to help establish the Hebrew University in Jerusalem. Feeling unqualified for the presidency of the new state, however, Einstein declined.

In 1955 he agreed to appear on a nationwide television and radio program to celebrate the Jewish state's seventh anniversary and promote its continued growth. A few days before, however, Einstein became ill and was unable to participate. He died shortly after at the age of seventy-six.

Einstein was thought by most authorities to be a brilliant man, a true genius. People were fascinated with him. His physical appearance, with his long, unruly, wavy hair, was memorable. He received mail from children demanding that he get his hair cut. His ideas also created a stir. One 1947 postcard to him from someone in Boston demanded: "You will immediately stop calling space curved." Einstein's scientific discoveries radically changed the way people think about the world.

FELIX FRANKFURTER

Longtime United States Supreme Court Justice

Born November 15, 1882, in Vienna; died February 22, 1965. United States Supreme Court justice. After graduating first in his class from Harvard Law School, Felix Frankfurter worked in various capacities for the federal government, largely helping to resolve labor-union problems. He served on the High Court from 1939 to 1962. His major contribution to the Supreme Court was his tireless pursuit of equal protection under the law for all minorities.

FELIX FRANKFURTER was born into an Orthodox Jewish-Viennese family, the third son among six children. His forebears had been rabbis for generations, spanning three hundred years.

The anti-Semitic atmosphere in Austria prompted the Frankfurter family to immigrate to the United States in 1894, when Felix was twelve years old. They settled on the Lower East Side of New York City, where his father became a tradesman, selling linens.

Frankfurter graduated from the City College of New York in 1902, third in his class. He received his "real education," he liked to say, from devouring the books and newspapers at the public library, and at the city's numerous coffee shops. His passion for reading continued into adulthood. He was a skilled debater and public speaker.

In 1906 Frankfurter graduated with the highest honors from Harvard Law School, ranked first in his class. At Harvard he acquired a great appreciation for the values of the Anglo-American system of government and its laws.

After a few months in private practice, Frankfurter became an assistant to Henry L. Stimson, the United States Attorney for the

Felix Frankfurter

Southern District of New York. During his three-year stint with Stimson, from 1906 to 1909, Frankfurter learned that it was possible to enforce criminal law effectively without compromising individual rights—a valuable lesson that influenced his career throughout his life.

In 1911, when Stimson became secretary of war under President Taft, Frankfurter served as his personal assistant. In this capacity he had special responsibility for the legal affairs of overseas United States territories and for the conservation of water resources. During this period, Frankfurter began his long friendship with Supreme Court Justice Oliver Wendell Holmes. Both men shared a strong belief in the concept of judicial restraint.

Louis Brandeis, then a Boston attorney, was convinced that Frankfurter would become a great teacher. He contributed funds to Harvard that allowed the University to pay Frankfurter more than the average law professor earned, thus encouraging his tenure there. Frankfurter joined the law faculty in 1914 and taught at Harvard for the next twenty-five years.

During World War I, Frankfurter served as legal advisor on industrial problems to Newton Baker, the secretary of war. Frankfurter was also secretary and later legal counsel of the President's Mediation Commission. He was named chairman of the War Labor Policies Board in 1918.

Because of these positions, Frankfurter became deeply involved in the labor struggle of that era, acquiring a reputation as a liberal for ruling in favor of the unions in several significant cases. For example, in one 1917 case, striking copper miners were deported from Arizona for alleged membership in the radical Industrial Workers of the World. Frankfurter sided with the strikers in that case.

During World War I, Brandeis, who had become a justice of the Supreme Court in 1916, urged Frankfurter to take a more active interest in Zionism. Frankfurter and Brandeis worked to secure President Woodrow Wilson's backing for the 1917 Balfour Declaration, in which the British government supported a Jewish homeland in Palestine.

At the request of Justice Brandeis, Frankfurter attended the Paris Peace Conference at the end of World War I. His mission was to represent the Zionist cause to the peacemakers, including President Wilson, James Balfour, and Prince Feisal, the representative of the Arab people. Frankfurter continued to support Zionism's aims, although both he and Brandeis withdrew from the formal Zionist organization in a dispute over the issue of fiscal autonomy for the American Zionists.

In 1920 Frankfurter was one of the founders of the American Civil Liberties Union as well as the *New Republic* magazine. He served as legal advisor to the National Association for the Advancement of Colored People (NAACP) and was counsel to the National Consumers League. At this juncture he married Marian A. Denman, the daughter of a Congregational minister.

Frankfurter gained national attention in 1927 when he fought for a second trial for Nicola Sacco and Bartolemeo Vanzetti, both immigrants who had been convicted of robbery and murder, and were sentenced to death. Frankfurter asserted that their conviction was the result of prejudice because of their foreign backgrounds and the xenophobia created by the Red Scare of the 1920s. The case polarized opinion between liberal-radicals and conservatives in the United States. It was widely felt that Frankfurter was risking his position at Harvard by taking such a liberal position so publicly, but he was able to emerge unscathed.

During the late 1920s and early 1930s, Frankfurter was an advisor to two governors of New York—first Alfred E. Smith, and then Franklin D. Roosevelt. After Roosevelt became presi-

Felix Frankfurter (top row, second from right).

dent of the United States in 1932, Frankfurter continued to advise him, providing counsel on New Deal legislation.

On January 5, 1939, after the death of Justice Benjamin Cardozo, Roosevelt appointed Frankfurter to the United States Supreme Court. The appointment was controversial. There were objections to Frankfurter's nomination because of his association with the American Civil Liberties Union, his defense of Sacco and Vanzetti, and his Jewish background. Roosevelt stood firm in backing his appointee and Frankfurter was confirmed.

As a member of the High Court, Frankfurter made a number of decisions that concerned the legal protection of minority groups. He claimed that many of his judicial decisions related to minorities were influenced by his Jewish heritage. Frankfurter's Jewish background and his frustrating experience with intolerance when he championed the Zionist cause were reflected in a landmark case on group libel, *Beauharnais* v. *Illinois* (1952). This case involved the publication of a pamphlet containing derogatory information about the black race. Frankfurter wrote the opinion for the Court, declaring that protection for minority groups was essential.

He rejected the claim, however, that freedom of speech, assembly, and religious beliefs were absolutes. His position was that they must be weighed against the legitimate concerns of society. In his dissenting opinion in *West Virginia State Board of Education* v. *Barnette* (1943), Frankfurter spelled out his judicial philosophy succinctly. In that case, a compulsory flag-salute exercise in the public schools had been resisted by members of the Jehovah's Witnesses as an affront to their religious tenets. Frankfurter felt that the government had not exceeded its proper bounds in seeking to inculcate national pride and loyalty in all schoolchildren, regardless of their religious backgrounds.

"One who belongs to the most vilified and persecuted minority in history is not likely to be insensible to the freedoms guaranteed by our Constitution," Frankfurter wrote in this decision. "Were my purely personal attitude relevant, I should wholeheartedly associate myself with the general libertarian views in the Court's opinion, representing as they do the thought and action of a lifetime. But as judges, we are neither Jew nor gentile, neither Catholic nor agnostic. We owe equal attachment to the Constitution and are equally bound by our judicial obligations whether we derive our citizenship from the earliest or the latest immigrants to these shores . . . ."

Felix Frankfurter was proud to be Jewish and defended the Zionist cause. He fought anti-Semitism but did not participate in religious worship. After his college years, he described himself as a "reverent agnostic." He defended slurs against Jews no matter who made them. He also sought to make Americans conscious of the Nazi treatment of Jews. One of his college professors once made an anti-Semitic remark to Frankfurter about his name, to which the future Supreme Court justice replied, "Some day you will be proud to have known the owner of that name."

Frankfurter had a series of strokes and retired from the Supreme Court, on which he had served for twenty-three years, in 1962. A year later he was awarded the Presidential Medal of Freedom with Special Distinction. He died at the age of eighty-two in 1965.

SIGMUND FREUD

Founder of Psychoanalysis

Born in Freiberg, Moravia, (now Pribor, Czech Republic), on May 6, 1856; died on September 23, 1939. Austrian physician. Sigmund Freud explored the workings of the human mind, creating the discipline of psychoanalysis. Freud's theories about human psychology and sexuality made him one of the most influential thinkers of this century. His ideas had an immense impact not only on medicine but also on art and literature.

SIGMUND FREUD was born in Freiberg, Moravia, the eldest of seven children. His father, Jacob, was a merchant. In 1859 the family moved to Vienna, where Freud remained until 1938, nearly his entire life. The only language his mother, Amalia, could speak fluently was Yiddish. Freud was given some religious instruction as a child and was made acutely aware of anti-Semitism.

After completing high school, Sigmund studied medicine at the University of Vienna, where he encountered firsthand the anti-Semitism he had learned about in his early years. Freud always remembered bitterly his father's recounting of being physically attacked by gentile thugs on a Vienna street, insisting he leave at once, which he did. Freud was furious over his father's humiliation. He found refuge in Ernst Bruecke's physiological laboratory, where his presence was welcomed. There Freud began doing research with Bruecke after graduation from medical school. He conducted experiments with cocaine, then a new drug, hoping to show that it could be a treatment for depression and fatigue. Its side effects, especially addiction, led him to give up that research.

In 1882 Freud entered clinical practice as a resident at the Vienna General Hospital. He worked under the brain anatomist T. H. Meynert. Freud was also drawn to the work of neurologist Jean Charcot in Paris and, as a result, began studying clinical manifestations of organic diseases of the nervous system.

Freud won a traveling fellowship in 1885 and became Charcot's student at the Salpetrière mental hospital. He grew increasingly interested in studying hysterical paralysis. He observed the use of hypnosis in treating hysterical disorders, which led him to search for hidden factors in abnormal behavior.

In 1886 he married Martha Bernays, to whom he had been engaged for four years. They had six children. One of them, their daughter Anna, went on to further develop her father's theories and become famous in her own right.

In his private practice in Vienna, Freud specialized in nervous disorders. Dissatisfied with the effectiveness of hypnosis in treating neurotic and hysterical symptoms, he searched for other techniques. In time he developed the most important technique of psychoanalysis: free association, in which the patient is asked to relax and express whatever comes to mind. As the patient speaks, hints of his or her unconscious inevitably emerge.

By encouraging the patient to recall his repressed memories, Freud could analyze the "forgotten" experiences that caused the patient's neurosis. As he worked with patients, Freud became aware of the conflict each often felt between an instinct "unacceptable" to society and the person's resistance to it. Repudiating the instinct or desire, repressing it in the unconscious, the person sought substitute methods of gratification, which often caused troublesome mental or physical symptoms. The task of psychoanalytic therapy, in Freud's view, was to discover the repressed urges and permit normal judgment to accept or reject the repudiated impulse. Freud also

Sigmund Freud

The Jewish Week

believed that the repressed impulses were often sexual desires that the patient was resisting.

In an effort to understand his patients better, Freud analyzed himself. He concluded that what he called the "dream-thought" is an impulse that is really a wish. However, since the idea of it is often repellent to the person, and therefore disavowed, it results in subconscious thought, resulting in dreams that serve as a fulfillment of the repressed wish. Freud's book *The Interpretation of Dreams* expounded this theory. He was pleased that psychoanalysis could explain forms of behavior that many in his field had formerly concluded were accidental slips of the tongue or forgetfulness; these psychological phenomena could be interpreted as a conscious action growing out of an unconscious thought—hence the term "Freudian slip."

Through distortions introduced by an internal "dream censor" unhindered by the accepted rules of logic, the person in Freudian analysis finds disguised images of his or her own long-submerged infantile yearnings in dreams. The yearnings are frequently sexual and too forbidden to be permitted more direct expression. In Freud's view, if these repressed desires become too powerful to remain in the unconscious and too repellent to be openly acknowledged, a neurosis may result.

Hysteria was one way that neuroses manifested themselves. Freud worked with Viennese physician Josef Breuer on the treatment of this ailment. In 1885 they wrote *Studien ueber Hysterie* (*Studies in Hysteria*), which first described the theory that repressed emotions could lead to symptoms of hysteria or extreme emotional excitability. Freud and Breuer concluded that symptoms might disappear if a patient could be made to express the repressed emotions that made them unable to cope with normal daily life.

Freud postulated that sexual desires experienced during the first four or five years of life are the principal human drive for both normal and neurotic personalities. He felt that these sexual instincts make the child fantasize about replacing the parent of his or her gender as a partner for the other parent. The manner in which the child copes with this first love, and with the inevitable disappointment that ensues when he or she realizes the truth, will have an influence on all later personality development. Freud called this phenomenon the Oedipus Complex.

When he was nearly seventy, Freud made the determination that the human mind was composed of three elements: the ego, the id, and the superego. The ego represents reason and reality, and, consciously or unconsciously, tries to mediate between the id and the superego, or between inner needs (the id) and outer reality (the superego).

In contrast to the ego, the id contains the passions and unbridled desires with which people are born. The superego is the carrier of human conscience, which is capable of determining many human actions, even aggression (which could lead to suicide). The human ego therefore has to deal with a number of competing demands from the id, superego, and reality, all the time trying to keep anxiety to a minimum.

For much of his life, Freud believed that the libido, or sexual drive, decides human behavior. Later in life, perhaps influenced by the many deaths during World War I or his own experience with cancer, Freud suggested that everyone also has a death instinct, which is equally strong and seeks to destroy a person.

Freud's theories of how the human mind works and how it affects behavior influenced art and literature as well as medicine. Some of his books are considered among the great works of modern literature, including *The Interpretation of Dreams* (1899), *The Psychopathology of Everyday Life* (1904), *Totem and Taboo* (1913), *Civilization and Its Discontents* (1929), and *Moses and Monotheism* (1939).

Freud's relationship to his Jewish heritage was complex and ambiguous. On one hand, he was hostile to all religious beliefs and practices. He was an avowed atheist who thought religion was a kind of massive neurosis in which society reverted to an infantile wish to overcome helplessness through an omnipotent father-figure. He preferred the dominant liberal and humanitarian ideas in vogue in Austria in the 1860s and 1870s to the rituals of Judaism. Around 1870, he even changed his given name. His father had named him Sigismund, in honor of a sixteenth-century Polish monarch who was tolerant toward Jews. Freud changed it to the Germanic-sounding Sigmund.

Many of Freud's Jewish colleagues chose to be baptized to gain acceptance in German society, and although Freud briefly pondered converting, ultimately he did not. In his 1925 book *Selbstdarstellung* (*An Autobiographical Study*), he wrote: "My parents were Jews, and I remained a Jew." Always aware of the existence of anti-Semitism, Freud was worried that psychoanalysis would be regarded as "Jewish psychology," since so many of its adherents were Jewish.

Freud moved to London in 1938. He was a heavy cigar smoker and suffered the last sixteen years of his life from a malignant cancer of the jaw. After numerous operations and the insertion of a prosthesis, which impaired his ability to speak, he died at the age of eighty-three on September 23, 1939.

Freud's theories, although controversial to this day, revolutionized the ideas of the psychiatric community and had a dominant effect on the study of human behavior and motivation.

MILTON FRIEDMAN

Nobel Prize-winning Economist

Born July 31, 1912, in Brooklyn, New York. American economist. One of the most important economists in the United States, Milton Friedman won the Nobel Prize in Economic Science in 1976. Rejecting Keynesian notions that justified big government, Friedman argued that the less government intervention in people's lives, the better off they would be. His economic theories have had a strong influence on leaders in both the United States and Europe.

MILTON FRIEDMAN WAS BORN in 1912 in Brooklyn, the youngest of the four children of Sarah Ethel (Landau) and Jeno Saul Friedman. His parents emigrated as teenagers from Carpatho-Ruthenia (then Hungary, now Russia) to the United States, settling in Rahway, New Jersey, when Milton was thirteen months old.

Friedman's mother managed a small retail dry goods store and his father pursued a string of largely unsuccessful jobbing ventures. The Friedmans always seemed to be plagued by financial problems. "The thing I recall most," Friedman said, "is the family paying off somebody while postponing somebody else."

As a child, Friedman had strong ties to Judaism, studying in a *heder*, a Jewish elementary school. He was, in his own words, "rabidly religious, obeying every Orthodox religious requirement. At about the age of twelve or so, I became persuaded that I was wrong, lost my faith, and became an agnostic." Even so, Friedman had a bar mitzvah. Since then, however, he has not practiced Judaism, although he still gives credit to his parents for helping him to identify himself positively as a Jew.

Friedman's father died when he was a senior at Rahway High School, from which he graduated shortly before his sixteenth birthday. At Rutgers University, Friedman majored in mathematics and economics, hoping to become an actuary. During his time at Rutgers, he encountered the two men who would have the greatest influence on his career: doctoral student Arthur F. Burns, and Homer Jones, a University of Chicago graduate student temporarily teaching at Rutgers. From Burns, Friedman learned to appreciate economic research; from Jones, he acquired a sense of the excitement and relevance of economics.

Upon his graduation from Rutgers in 1932, Friedman was offered, at Jones's recommendation, a graduate scholarship to the University of Chicago economics department. Friedman wrote his master's thesis on factors influencing railroad stock prices. He received his master's degree in 1933, then spent the 1933–34 academic year on a fellowship at Columbia University, studying for his doctorate. He then returned to the University of Chicago to be a research assistant to Henry Schultz, a professor, for one year.

From 1935 to the fall of 1937, Friedman held various jobs as an economist in Washington, D.C. During the summer of 1935, he worked at the National Resources Committee, helping with the design of a large consumer budget study, which eventually formed a partial basis for his 1957 book, *A Theory of the Consumption Function*. Starting in the fall of 1937, Friedman worked at the National Bureau of Economic Research in New York, assisting economist Simon Kuznets with his studies of professional income.

In June 1938, Friedman married a fellow graduate student at the University of Chicago, Rose Director, and they spent their honeymoon working on their doctoral dissertations. They have two children, Janet and David.

From 1937 to 1940, Friedman was a part-time lecturer at Columbia University. In 1940–41, he was a visiting professor of economics at the University of Wisconsin. Later, from 1941 to 1943, he was principal economist in the Treasury Department's Tax Research Division. From 1943 to 1945, Friedman was again at Columbia University, serving as associate director of the Statistical Research Group, which was engaged in war research. He spent the 1945–46 academic year at the University of Minnesota.

In the fall of 1946, Friedman formally joined the faculty at the University of Chicago, where he remained for the next thirty-one years. That year, he received his doctoral degree from Columbia University; his dissertation was published as a book, coauthored with Kuznets, called *Incomes from Independent Professional Practice*.

Friedman became the leader of the Chicago school of economics, a system of thought that rejected the theories of British economist John Maynard Keynes, who believed that only through heavy government spending could a nation prosper. Accordingly, Friedman opposed such bureaucratic subsidies as social security, welfare, and Medicare. To get across the point that society, through the private sector, had to carry the responsibility for making the economy flourish, Friedman often used a phrase which he did not coin but has become associated with him: "There is no such thing as a free lunch."

In his classic book *Capitalism and Freedom* (1962), Friedman insisted that he was not championing a return to complete laissez-faire economics but rather trying to avoid encouraging a type of society that would diminish the individuality of people. He found no logical reason to assume that governments that try to order the economic lives of their citizens will automatically do a better job than those citizens will do when left largely on their own.

Government's main function, he argued, was to keep markets open and monitor the amount of money in circulation. Friedman asserted that only a change in a nation's money supply caused an economy to grow or stagnate, not government intervention. Pioneering a monetarist approach to economics, he argued that to bring about stability—the steady expansion in jobs and incomes without inflation—the Federal Reserve System should keep the money supply growing slowly and steadily. When the Federal Reserve permitted the nation's money supply to decline by a third in the 1930s, what began as a recession grew into the Great Depression. Friedman spelled out these ideas in *A Monetary History of the United States, 1867–1960* (1963), which he coauthored with economic historian Anna Schwartz.

In 1964 Friedman moved into the public arena, serving as economic advisor to Republican senator Barry Goldwater when he ran for the United States presidency. Friedman was one of

Richard Nixon's economic advisors in his successful presidential campaign four years later. In 1966 Friedman began writing a tri-weekly column on current affairs for *Newsweek* magazine. He steadfastly turned down offers of full-time political appointments in Washington, preferring to engage in his own academic research.

Friedman was awarded the 1976 Nobel Prize in Economic Science for, in the words of the prize committee, his "independence and brilliance." Friedman, though "happy and pleased," downplayed his selection, denying that it was the high point of his career. "The true judges of my work," he insisted, "are today's economists." Winning public prizes mattered to him far less than whether or not his economic ideas would still be considered important in fifty years.

After retiring from the University of Chicago in 1977, Friedman became a Senior Research Fellow at the Hoover Institution of Stanford University.

Courtesy of Milton Friedman

Milton Friedman

Milton Friedman's economic theories have had international impact as well as significance in the economic life of the United States, with a particularly strong influence on the economic policies of former American President Ronald Reagan and former British Prime Minister Margaret Thatcher. Menachem Begin, Israel's prime minister from 1977 to 1983, was also a big proponent of Friedman's ideas.

Friedman and his wife, Rose, participated in a ten-part television series that formed the basis for their bestselling book *Free to Choose* (1980), which argued that the less a government intervenes in its citizens' lives, the better off those citizens will be.

Though not an observant Jew as an adult, Friedman is proud of his heritage. While his parents were alive, he observed the Jewish holidays and participated in Passover seders at his in-laws' home in Portland, Oregon. As he explained it: "I do not go around making a great fuss about the fact that I am a Jew, but when the issue comes up, I am very frank that I am Jewish."

Many in the media call Friedman the most important conservative American economist, yet he prefers to be called a free-market or a libertarian economist. In its special Fall 1970 edition, the editors of *Life* magazine called Friedman one of the hundred most important Americans of the twentieth century.

In July 2002, the ninety-year-old Friedman was honored at a White House ceremony as the greatest economist of the twentieth century. President George W. Bush hailed him as "a hero of freedom." In turn, Friedman offered a brief analogy to convey his philosophy: "When a man spends someone else's money on someone else, he doesn't care how much he spends or what he spends it on. And that's government for you."

GEORGE GERSHWIN

American Composer

Born September 26, 1898, in Brooklyn, New York; died July 11, 1937. American composer. Though George Gershwin wrote numerous songs that have become classics of the musical comedy genre, he constantly sought to rise above being known solely as a composer of popular music. With his brother Ira as lyricist, Gershwin wrote twenty-two musical comedies and seven hundred songs, including such famous melodies as "I Got Rhythm," "The Man I Love," "They Can't Take That Away from Me," and "Our Love Is Here to Stay." With aspirations to be considered "serious," Gershwin wrote the full-length opera *Porgy and Bess* (1935), only to learn that the public and critics alike were unhappy with the play. Only after Gershwin's death in 1937 did *Porgy* acquire its reputation as a theater classic. Gershwin's most successful classical piece of music was the symphonic composition *Rhapsody in Blue* (1924).

GEORGE GERSHWIN was born Jacob Gershovitz, the son of immigrant parents from St. Petersburg, Russia. His father, Morris, Americanized the family name to Gershvin, amended by George to Gershwin after he began his professional career. Gershwin's father was involved in small businesses, including Turkish baths and restaurants, mostly unsuccessful. The family had to move twenty-five times while Gershwin was a child.

A poor student, Gershwin preferred to play and fight in the streets. His father told him he would be "nothing but a bum." Gershwin eventually developed a deep interest in music even though none of his family was musically inclined. Morris purchased a piano for the musical education of George's older brother, Ira. The instrument, however, proved a boon to the eleven-year-old George, who immediately claimed the piano as his own. Three years later, he began piano lessons with the brilliant pianist Charles Hambizer, who introduced his student to classical and modern music theory, harmony, and composition.

Gershwin found work as a staff pianist for a Tin Pan Alley publisher called Remick's, which published his first song in 1916. A year later, Max Dreyfuss, of Harms, another music publisher, employed Gershwin as a song composer.

Gershwin was not a practicing Jew, but he never denied his family origin. In 1915 he was asked by the Yiddish actor and director Boris Thomashevsky to collaborate with Sholom Secunda to write a Yiddish operetta, but Secunda rejected the idea. Then, in 1929, Gershwin signed a contract with the Metropolitan Opera to compose a work based on the play *The*

Dybbuk. He even planned to travel to Europe to study Jewish musical practice, but the project fell through.

The first musical revue Gershwin wrote was called *Half Past Eight* (1918); it preceded his first hit musical, *La La Lucille*, by a year. The next year, when Al Jolson sang "Swanee," the Gershwin number from the musical revue *Sinbad*, it caused a sensation. In 1919 Gershwin applied to songwriter Irving Berlin to become Berlin's musical secretary. "You would be better off going off on your own as a composer," Berlin advised Gershwin, who accepted the advice.

In 1924 bandleader Paul Whiteman, called the King of Jazz, organized a "serious jazz concert" and called it "Experiment in Modern Music." Whiteman commissioned Gershwin to compose a jazz symphony and what resulted was the classic *Rhapsody in Blue*, written for piano and orchestra. When it was first performed in New York in 1924, Gershwin was at the piano. *Rhapsody* made it respectable to play jazz on the American concert stage. Though he had been a rising star before then, Gershwin, thanks to *Rhapsody in Blue*, became a major celebrity.

Gershwin's Jewish heritage did find its way into his music, especially the liturgical synagogue melodies that were a part of his childhood. According to Gershwin experts, the clarinet solo that opens *Rhapsody in Blue* contains influences of Jewish cantorial style.

After writing *Rhapsody in Blue*, Gershwin was encouraged to try writing more serious music, which he aspired to do. He composed the *Concerto for Piano in F Major* (1925); the following year, *Three Preludes for Piano*; then, in 1928, *An American in Paris*; in 1931, *Second Rhapsody*; and the following year, *Cuban Overture*.

In the 1920s, Gershwin gained fame as a great composer of songs for musical comedy. He pioneered a whole new era in American popular music with his songs. They had their own special rhythms, clever lyrics (often written by brother Ira), and melodies that stuck in one's mind. Gershwin biographer Joan Peyser said of him: "He had an absolute genius for melody—writing a song came as naturally to him as breathing."

Gershwin's aim to write serious music was again manifested in a play he had in mind in the summer of 1934. He spent two months living in a shack on Folly Island, off the South Carolina coast, in order to steep himself in African-American culture. The following year, he produced a play based on DuBose Heyward's play *Catfish Row*, which recounted the life of southern African-Americans. The play was Gershwin's attempt to incorporate their music into an operatic framework. Gershwin called the play *Porgy and Bess*; it was not well received when it opened on Broadway in October 1935. It closed after only 124 performances, losing money for his backers and producers. Ironically, *Porgy* was later recognized as Gershwin's best work and referred to by some theater critics as America's greatest musical drama.

Collaborating with his brother Ira, Gershwin enjoyed theatrical successes with *Tip Toes* (1925); *Funny Face* (1927), written for Fred and Adele Astaire; and *Of Thee I Sing* (1931), a political satire and the first musical to win a Pulitzer Prize. Gershwin's most successful musical revues were *Lady Be Good* (1924), also written for the Astaires; *Oh, Kay!* (1926); *Strike Up the Band* (1927); and *Girl Crazy* (1930).

The list of the songs that George and Ira Gershwin wrote that remain part of the contemporary American musical scene is long. Here are some of them: "But Not For Me," "Embraceable You," "A Foggy Day," "Fascinating Rhythm," "I Got Rhythm," "It Ain't Necessarily So," "Somebody Loves Me," "Someone to Watch Over Me," "They Can't Take That Away from Me," "Let's Call the Whole Thing Off," "Our Love Is Here to Stay," "The Man I Love," "Love

George Gershwin

Walked In," "Lady Be Good," "Nice Work If You Can Get It," "Strike Up the Band," "Summertime," and "They All Laughed."

In the summer of 1937, when Gershwin was only thirty-eight years old and at the peak of his career, he mysteriously took ill. Despite constant pain, he continued to write songs. Some friends thought he should see a neurosurgeon for his symptoms, but Gershwin's psychoanalyst disagreed, suggesting that all of his complaints—smelling burning garbage when there was none, intense headaches, dizziness—were simply signs of neurotic depression. Gerhswin's family accepted the diagnosis. Later, while working on songs for the film *Goldwyn Follies*, Gershwin went into a coma. Two days later he was operated on and doctors discovered a brain tumor; Gershwin died during surgery. Funeral services were held for him simultaneously at synagogues in Hollywood and Manhattan.

According to biographer Peyser, George and Ira Gershwin, though they made beautiful music together, were not as close as it might have seemed. The day after George died, Ira filed papers in court in Los Angeles to gain control of his brother's assets. Four days later, in New York City, their mother also filed for the same authority, challenging Ira's claim. She won control of the funds.

George Gershwin was a pathbreaking composer, using the musical elements of different cultures—African-American, East European Jewry—as well as exploring the sounds of the classical traditionalists, and creating both the ageless catchy melodies and the longer symphonic and operatic pieces that marked him as a true musical genius.

SAMUEL GOLDWYN

Early Hollywood Mogul

Born August 27, 1882, in Warsaw, Poland; died January 3, 1974. American film executive. Samuel Goldwyn began his career as the owner of a successful glove factory, but in 1913 he entered the movie business, producing the first Hollywood-made feature-length film, *The Squaw Man*. Goldwyn formed the Goldwyn Pictures Corporation and later converted his interest in the company to start Metro-Goldwyn-Mayer. His films set a standard of high quality for Hollywood and he became a legend in the film industry.

SAMUEL GOLDWYN was born Shmuel Gelbfisz in Warsaw in 1882. His family was large and poor. In 1895, at age thirteen, he left his native Warsaw and began traveling, working and begging his way across Europe. He eventually settled with an aunt who lived in Birmingham, England, and there he pushed a coal cart, trying to save enough money for his passage by boat to America.

Goldwyn finally traveled to the United States in 1899. Reaching Ellis Island, he met a Hebrew Immigrant Aid Society (HIAS) agent who placed Goldwyn in a job in a glove factory in upstate New York. His last name was changed from Gelbfisz to Goldfish.

Five years later, the future Hollywood mogul won a job as a road salesman for the glove firm. Just prior to turning twenty, Goldwyn was earning what for him and in that era was the astronomical sum of ten thousand dollars a year. Moving to New York City in 1910, Goldwyn became acquainted with Jesse and Blanche Lasky, who were brother and sister. They were from San Francisco, the grandchildren of German-Jewish immigrants. Accompanied by their mother, the Laskys had toured the United States in a vaudeville group, settling in New York City, where they opened a successful theatrical booking office. Shmuel, or Sam, as he was called by now, fell in love with Blanche and within six weeks they were married.

Goldwyn persuaded Jesse Lasky to enter the motion-picture business with him, making his brother-in-law a lucrative offer for the use of his name, which was well-known in the theater, as the trademark of a new film company. In 1910 Goldwyn and Lasky formed their own film company, called the Jesse L. Lasky Feature Play Company. Lasky became president, Goldwyn was named vice-president and business manager, and Sam's wife, Blanche, became treasurer. Cecil B. De Mille was named artistic director-in-chief.

The Lasky Company's first venture was in 1913. Goldwyn and Lasky took twenty thousand dollars of their family's money and produced a Broadway hit play called *The Squaw Man*. De Mille arranged to take his production crew out West to make the movie. Goldwyn remained in New York to sell the distribution rights for the six-reeler. Completed in less than a month on a shoestring budget, the movie they produced is considered the first Hollywood-made feature-length film; it was an overnight success, grossing $244,000 within six months.

The Goldwyn/Lasky/De Mille trio was on its way to prosperity and stardom. Goldwyn and Lasky purchased the screen rights to every major play they could acquire, hiring every famous Broadway actor available. De Mille turned out twenty-one movies in the next six months.

By 1914 their movies were getting longer and better, and in time won the attention of Adolf Zukor, another important fledgling movie mogul. (Goldwyn, in 1915, divorced Blanche. He married Frances Howard, a Broadway actress, in 1925; they had one son, Sam Goldwyn, Jr.) In 1916, Zukor approached Goldwyn and Lasky and made them an offer they couldn't refuse, a fifty-fifty partnership with Zukor as president, Lasky as vice-president, and Goldwyn as chairman. In June 1916, the merger became official.

The new firm was called the Famous Players-Lasky Corporation, better known in time by the name of Paramount, which they eventually adopted. Zukor wanted to get rid of Goldwyn, finding him intrusive and quarrelsome. Lasky also was distressed with Goldwyn, resenting his brother-in-law's deteriorating relationship with Blanche. Goldwyn was voted out of the new firm and paid nine hundred thousand dollars for acquisition of his stock.

In 1918 Goldwyn (still using the name Goldfish) convinced the New York theatrical producers Arcel and Edgar Selwyn to join him in a new production company, which he called Goldwyn Pictures, forming the name by using the first syllable of Goldfish and the last of Selwyn. At that point he also took the name Goldwyn as his own surname.

Goldwyn moved Goldwyn Pictures to a large studio in Culver City, California. The studio made films of high quality and attracted such major film stars of the day as Mabel Norman and Mae Marsh. But, lacking its own network of exhibitors, the company eventually suffered financially. New investors were found, but they quickly voted Goldwyn out of the company in 1922, paying him a million dollars to leave.

For the remainder of his film career, Goldwyn was an independent producer. He released his films during the 1920s and 1930s through United Artists, then through RKO. He made fewer films, but they won high marks for their quality of production and were filled with big-name actors including Greta Garbo, Ronald Coleman, Gary Cooper, David Niven, and comedians Eddie Cantor and Danny Kaye.

In 1924 Goldwyn converted the interest he had maintained in Goldwyn Pictures in order to help form Metro-Goldwyn-Mayer with the mogul Marcus Loew. Loew, who had controlled Metro Pictures Corporation, merged Metro with Goldwyn Pictures and brought in film executive Louis Mayer as studio chief. Under Mayer, Metro-Goldwyn-Mayer, or MGM, as the new corporation was called, became the most prestigious Hollywood studio.

Goldwyn's films created a whole new standard of quality for the movie industry. Goldwyn believed that the customer was always right. "If the audience don't like a picture," Goldwyn said, "they have a good reason. The public is never wrong."

Goldwyn was responsible for such films as *Bulldog Drummond* (1929), *Stella Dallas* (1937), *Wuthering Heights* (1939), *The Westerner* (1940), *Little Foxes* (1941), *The Best Years of Our Lives* (1946), *Guys and Dolls* (1955), and *Porgy and Bess* (1959). He hired such well-known dramatists as Lillian Hellman and Robert Sherwood. The beautiful, long-legged girls who appeared in his famous and still popular musicals became known as the Goldwyn Girls.

Goldwyn mangled the English language and often talked in amusing contradictions that were repeated by many, becoming part of the everyday phraseology of the times. They often made sense in their own way. These Goldwynisms are now famous and many have entered the vernacular as popular phrases:

- "Gentlemen, kindly include me out."
- "Why did you call your baby 'John'? Today every Tom, Dick, and Harry is called John."
- "This atom bomb is dynamite."
- " I'll give you a definite maybe."
- "Anyone who goes to a psychiatrist should have his head examined."
- "We are dealing in facts, not realities."

However Goldwyn felt personally about being Jewish, he took steps to downplay an actor's Jewishness on the screen. In 1940, when Goldwyn hired Danny Kaye to star in the film *Up in Arms*, he was concerned that Kaye looked too Jewish in the screen test. "Well, he *is* Jewish," said Goldwyn's gentile second wife, Frances. "But let's face it, Jews are funny-looking," Goldwyn answered.

After further agonizing, Goldwyn finally resolved the issue by having Kaye's reddish-brown hair dyed blond to make him look less Jewish. A few years later, Goldwyn cast Frank Sinatra in the role that Sam Levene had played in the Broadway version of *Guys and Dolls*. "You can't have a Jew play a Jew. It wouldn't work on the screen," Goldwyn explained.

In 1969, Goldwyn suffered a serious stroke, and he spent the next five years at home bedridden. Obese and partly paralyzed, he could only stare into space, occasionally uttering a few words. He died in his sleep at the age of ninety-one in 1974. Responsible for many of the major advances in the screen industry because of his vision and keen instincts for what the public would appreciate, Samuel Goldwyn's legacy lives on in the MGM name gracing many of the finest feature films today.

BENNY GOODMAN

"The King of Swing"

Born May 30, 1909, in Chicago, Illinois; died June 13, 1986. American clarinetist and orchestra leader. Benny Goodman personified the big band era of the 1930s and 1940s in America. He formed the Benny Goodman Orchestra in 1934 and became very famous after his appearance in 1935 at the Palomar Ballroom in Hollywood. He presented his first jazz concert at New York City's Carnegie Hall in 1938. Goodman was the first major white bandleader to put black and white musicians together on stage.

THE FUTURE ORCHESTRA LEADER was born Benjamin David Goodman, the eighth of twelve children, in Chicago, Illinois. Goodman's father was an immigrant tailor from Warsaw who never earned more than twenty dollars a week.

At the age of nine, Goodman and his brothers borrowed musical instruments from the neighborhood synagogue, Kehalah Jacob. Benny got a clarinet. His brother Harry, the largest of the Goodman boys, got a tuba; Freddy, next in size, a trumpet. Later, Goodman wondered what kind of career he would have had "if I had been twenty pounds heavier and two inches taller."

Goodman first studied clarinet at the well-known Jane Addams' Hull Settlement House in Chicago. After that, he studied for two years with Franz Shoepp, a clarinetist in the Chicago Symphony, whose self-discipline and musical training had a great impact on Goodman.

By age fourteen, Benny was making forty-eight dollars a week, playing four nights in a neighborhood band. That year, he left high school to devote himself to a full-time career as a musician.

Goodman was fascinated with the jazz beats growing in popularity in Chicago in the 1920s. When he was sixteen, he joined drummer Ben Pollack's band, one of Chicago's best jazz groups. Goodman recorded his first solo with Pollack's band on December 17, 1926. He remained in the band, of which Glenn Miller was also a member, for four years.

In the fall of 1929, Goodman left Pollack's band to freelance as a musician on radio and for records. He earned $350 to $400 a week even though it was the beginning of the Depression. In 1933 Goodman met promoter John Hammond, a young jazz fan. Hammond had been commissioned to make some jazz records for release in England; he asked Goodman to lead a band for this purpose. Choosing some of his musician friends to join him for the recording sessions, Goodman cut some records that were then released under the title *Benny Goodman and His Orchestra*.

The following year, with Hammond's support, Goodman hired Fletcher Henderson as his arranger and formed his first formal band. The twelve-member ensemble opened at Billy Rose's Music Hall in New York City.

"There were practically no hot bands using white musicians at the time," Goodman recalled, "and there was a lot of talent around town, both in jobs and laid off, that hadn't gotten the breaks." Soon the band appeared on NBC's nationwide radio program *Let's Dance*. Because the Goodman band played on the midnight section of the show, it at first became better known on the West Coast than the East.

Goodman's biggest break came at the Palomar Ballroom in Los Angeles on the evening of August 31, 1935. At that point, Goodman was on the verge of giving up his fourteen-piece band to return to freelancing as a clarinetist. He had always adapted his style to what he had been told audiences wanted—pop tunes and waltzes—the "sweet music" of that era. But that night at the Palomar, believing that this might be the band's final engagement, Goodman decided that he would fail on his own terms.

Benny Goodman

International Musician

"I called out some of our big Fletcher Henderson arrangements," he remembered, "and the boys seemed to get the idea." He played some of his own favorite arrangements, including "Sugar Foot Stomp" and "Blue Skies." As he played "Sugar Foot Stomp," the jazzy sounds of Goodman's clarinet filled the ballroom and the crowd stopped dancing to listen. A roar went up from the dance floor. Benny Goodman was amazed, stunned. That roar "was one of the sweetest sounds I ever heard in my life," he said later.

It was the beginning of the swing era, swing being defined as a form of jazz. From that night forward, Goodman was its king, and two years later he found himself earning $125,000 as the country's leading jazz musician and conductor while President Roosevelt earned $50,000.

In 1938 the Benny Goodman Band (with players from the Duke Ellington and Count Basie bands, including Count Basie himself) played its historic date in Carnegie Hall, taking jazz and swing into a new social and musical milieu. Just before the performance, Goodman was asked how long an intermission he would require. "I don't know," he replied. "How much does Toscanini [the foremost classical symphony conductor of the day] get?"

Swing dominated popular music until the end of World War II. Millions loved to hear Goodman play "Sweet Georgia Brown" and "Stompin' at the Savoy." His theme song was "Let's Dance" and his closing number was "Goodbye." Other favorites that became classics are "After You've Gone," "One O'clock Jump," "Don't Be That Way," and "Sing, Sing, Sing."

In the 1930s, Goodman created the Goodman Quartet featuring Gene Krupa (drums), Teddy

Wilson (piano), and Lionel Hampton (vibraphone). Hampton and Wilson were African-Americans, creating an unusual mix in the group for the 1930s. The quartet brought a chamber music approach to jazz.

"The most important thing that Benny Goodman did," Hampton said, "was to put Teddy Wilson and me in the quartet. It was instant integration. Black people didn't mix with whites then. Benny introduced us as Mr. Lionel Hampton and Mr. Teddy Wilson. He opened the door for Jackie Robinson [the first black to play baseball in the major leagues]. He gave music character and style." Goodman's band became a training ground for many musicians, both black and white, who became notable bandleaders.

Goodman's acquaintances called him "the Professor, " largely because of his rimless glasses, which gave him a scholarly look, and his apple-cheeked face. When it came to technical brilliance mated with controlled emotion, Goodman was one of the great clarinetists of all time. He expected the same high standards from members of his band. "He'd look over his glasses and stare at you—really nail you down with his eyes," recalled Hampton. "And all the time he'd be making some of the most difficult passages on his clarinet. He wouldn't stop playing, and he wouldn't stop glaring."

Goodman appreciated how difficult it was to excel at each performance. "It's always discouraging when you're trying to play good music," he said in an interview with the *Washington Post* in February 1986, a few months before his death. "It's a life of discouragement. But that's the way it goes. In the first place, you've got to meet that instrument every day in practice if you're serious about it. It isn't like the piano or violin; you use your wind. Your body has to be in shape."

After World War II, popular musical tastes changed and big bands were no longer in vogue. Goodman was a purist when it came to his music. He was critical of "bop," a newer form of jazz, and later rock and roll.

In March 1942, Goodman married Alice Duckworth, a sister of John Hammond, who had helped Goodman start his band. They had two children, Rachel and Benjie. In his later years, Goodman spent most of his time with his wife and children in their Manhattan apartment or at their retreat in Connecticut. Alice Goodman died in 1978. Twelve years later, Benny Goodman died at the age of seventy-seven.

In 1955 Goodman's story was the subject of a film starring Steve Allen as *The King of Swing*. Generations of jazz lovers owe many hours of listening pleasure to Goodman, who helped jazz achieve a lasting following.

JUDAH HA-NASI

Compiler of the Mishnah

> Born c. 135 C.E. and died c. 220. Talmudic scholar. Judah Ha-Nasi, the leader of the Jewish community of *Eretz Yisrael*, compiled the Mishnah, the basic codification of the Oral Law. Judah Ha-Nasi's Mishnah formed the basis for the Talmud, which is an elaboration on its rulings. He received his name, which means Judah the Prince, because of his great stature and influence over other scholars of his era.

JUDAH HA-NASI, son of Simeon ben Gamaliel, succeeded his father as head of the patriarchate that was reestablished by the Romans after the failed revolt of Bar Kochba. The Romans recognized Judah as the leader of the Jews not only in *Eretz Yisrael* but also in the Diaspora. He had a commanding presence and was attended by servants as though he were a secular potentate. Legend has it that he and the Roman ruler Antonius developed a very close personal relationship.

So superb was Judah Ha-Nasi's scholarship that he was known simply as "Rabbi." Some called him Rabbenu ha-Kadosh—our holy teacher—because he was so observant and pious. Judah Ha-Nasi was so esteemed that it was said "from the time of Moses to the time of Rabbi, Torah and greatness were never so concentrated in one person."

Judah Ha-Nasi was a wealthy man who owned a great deal of land. He raised cattle and manufactured wool and linen. Using his own boats, he was involved in exporting and importing as well. Much of his wealth was used to support scholars, the best of whom were rewarded by eating at the head of his table.

Judah Ha-Nasi held the office of patriarch for fifty years. He set up an academy at Bet Shearim, not far from the Israeli port city of Haifa, to train scholars. He spent his last seventeen years at Sepphoris, where the air was clean, to help him cope with ill health.

Judah Ha-Nasi had unlimited authority in his post as the leader of the Sanhedrin, the Supreme Court. He appointed judges and teachers, and viewed as his mission the rebuilding of the Jewish community, which had been decimated spiritually and economically as a result of its defeat by the Romans and the destruction of the Temple. He was also a generous man. When famine struck, he made sure to open his private storehouses to the Jewish community.

Judah Ha-Nasi became known as Judah the Prince because of his great stature as a leader. He was called an "intellectual elitist of the most uncompromising kind" by one historian. But he was also an elitist who placed education above all else, noting to others, "It is the unlearned who bring trouble into the world."

Eighteen hundred years in advance of Eliezer Ben-Yehuda, who almost single-handedly introduced modern Hebrew into the Jewish community in Palestine in the early twentieth century, Judah Ha-Nasi insisted on speaking only Hebrew with his family and friends, although Aramaic was the spoken language of the day. It was said that even his maidservant knew Hebrew and could explain the meaning of rare words. He spoke Greek to Roman officials.

Unquestionably, Judah Ha-Nasi's most enduring legacy is his compiling of the Mishnah. Before his time, the laws governing Jewish life were transmitted orally, because it was believed that only the Torah itself was worthy of being committed to writing. Judah feared that the law derived from interpreting the Torah was growing so voluminous that it would be forgotten if not written down. Judah broke the taboo and the Mishnah, meaning to repeat or study, (as in oral instruction), came into being. Assisted by his coeditor Nathan, Judah Ha-Nasi completed the task just before his death, around 220 C.E.

Judah collected all the accepted rulings of all the scholars and presented them in six categories:

1. *Zera'im* (seeds): mostly the agricultural laws; they also dealt with prayers and blessings.
2. *Mo'ed* (appointed time): the laws of the Sabbath, feasts, and fast days.
3. *Nashim* (women): the laws governing marriage, divorce, and vows.
4. *Nezikin* (damages): civil and criminal law.
5. *Kodashim* (holy things): the laws of sacrifices and consecrated objects.
6. *Tohorot* (cleanliness): the laws of ritual purity and impurity.

The Mishnah was essential in helping define Judaism as it shifted from a Temple-centered religion to one focusing on Jewish law. Judah the Prince's work was enlarged upon by scholars over the next two hundred fifty years. All these later discussions and new rulings constitute what is called the Talmud.

Of the many teachings of Judah Ha-Nasi recorded in the Talmud, these are most noteworthy:

- A man should revere his father and mother as he reveres God, for all three are partners in him.
- What is the virtuous path which a man should follow? Whatever brings honor to his Maker and honor from his fellow man.
- Contemplate three things and you will avoid transgressions: above you (in Heaven) is an eye that sees, an ear that hears, and all your deeds are faithfully recorded.
- I have learned much from my teachers, more from my colleagues, but most from my pupils.
- Be as punctilious in observing a light as a weighty commandment, for you do not know their relative reward.
- Fulfill God's precepts joyfully, just as Israel accepted the Torah at Sinai with joy.
- Do not be deceived by the outward appearance of age or youth; a new pitcher might be full of good, old wine while an old one might be empty altogether.

During his final years, when Judah Ha-Nasi was confined to bed, he told his followers that he had given all of his strength to the perpetuation of the Torah. He is buried in Bet Shearim. His tomb has become a site for Jewish pilgrimage.

Judah was one of the most remarkable Jews of his generation. His intellectual leadership assured the supremacy of Palestine in Jewish life during his era. He labored hard and succeeded as well in guaranteeing that Jewish religious leadership would depend upon Palestine.

THEODOR HERZL

Founder of Modern Zionism

Born May 2, 1860, in Budapest, Hungary; died July 3, 1904. Viennese author and journalist. As a journalist in Paris, Theodor Herzl covered the famous Dreyfus treason trial and was struck with how widespread anti-Semitism had become. He searched for solutions to the question of whether, and where, Jews should organize themselves politically, and found one in the notion of a Jewish state. To gain support from major powers, Herzl engaged in active diplomacy, meeting with European leaders, as well as organizing several World Zionist Congresses. He died forty-three years before the United Nations approved the creation of a Jewish state in Palestine, the dream he, more than anyone else, had helped make happen.

THEODOR HERZL WAS BORN in Budapest, Hungary, on May 2, 1860. His father, an assimilated Jew, was a wealthy merchant. A fledgling writer even in high school, Herzl published his first newspaper article anonymously. During his last year in high school, Herzl's eighteen-year-old sister Pauline died. As a result, his mother suffered a psychological setback and his father decided to move the family to Vienna.

In Vienna, Herzl studied law at the university. He joined a student fraternity, but left it abruptly after the fraternity adopted a resolution barring Jews from becoming members in the future. In 1884, when he was twenty-four years old, Herzl earned his doctorate in law. Working gratis as a clerk in a judge's office, Herzl occasionally traveled to Salzburg, where he began writing plays. Over the next few years some of his plays were produced and were warmly received.

In 1886 he met his future wife, Julie Naschauer, the eighteen-year-old daughter of a wealthy industrialist. They were married in June 1889 and had three children. Hans and Pauline committed suicide; Trude, after a near lifetime in a psychiatric clinic, died in a Nazi concentration camp. The direct line ended when Trude's only son, Stephan Theodor, committed suicide in 1946.

In 1891 Herzl joined the staff of the *Neue Freie Presse*, the mouthpiece of the liberal, assimilated Viennese-Jewish bourgeoisie, and became the publication's Paris correspondent. Prior to covering the Dreyfus Affair for the paper, an experience that had a profound effect on his thinking, Herzl had odd ideas about how to solve the dilemma of Jewish integration into European society. At one stage he even suggested that all Jews should convert to Christianity! The Dreyfus trial and its overt anti-Jewish overtone, however, turned him into a fiery Zionist.

Herzl returned to Vienna after the trial, in July 1895, to become the newspaper's literary editor. That same month, writing in what he described as a "white heat," Herzl poured his ideas into a pamphlet that he called *Der Judenstaat* (*The Jewish State*). Published the following February, the pamphlet argued that Jews are a nation, not simply a community of believers. To Herzl, neither civil emancipation nor cultural assimilation were adequate solutions to the problem of Jewish identity.

In this era of nationalism, Herzl stated, the Jewish "problem," because it was essentially "political," required a political solution. He maintained that a Jewish commonwealth had to be established, one that welcomed all Jews, particularly those who were not wanted elsewhere. The commonwealth would serve the additional advantage of normalizing the lives of Jews left behind in the Diaspora.

Herzl was not clear at first as to whether the commonwealth should be located in Palestine or some other territory, perhaps in

Theodor Herzl

North or South America. In time, however, he concluded that Palestine was the logical choice because only the Land of Israel would appeal to large numbers of Jews.

Herzl used his connections to seek support for his ideas. The Zionist writer Max Nordau liked Herzl's thinking and introduced him to the British writer Israel Zangwill. Zangwill arranged for Herzl to speak to London's Maccabean Club, whose members were sympathetic to Zionist urgings. Convinced that only with the joint support of the major powers could a Jewish state be established, Herzl sought to win approval from the German kaiser, the Russian czar, and the Turkish sultan.

To his surprise and regret, Herzl soon realized that most of the Jewish lay and spiritual leadership in Europe disapproved of the establishment of a Jewish state, yet he was not put off. Paradoxically, in spite of the controversial nature of his ideas, Herzl was tremendously popular. He was able to gain entrance to the inner sanctums of the most powerful leaders of Europe. In June 1896, for example, he managed an audience with the Grand Vizier in Constantinople.

In August 1897, Herzl organized the highly successful First Zionist Congress in Basel, Switzerland. He later wrote in his diary, "At Basel I created the Jewish State. If I were to say this out loud, everybody would laugh at me. In five years, perhaps, but certainly in fifty, everybody will agree." His words proved prophetic.

A year later, following the Second Zionist Congress, Herzl paid his only trip to *Eretz Yisrael.* More meetings with political officials followed, with the kaiser in Germany and with the Grand Duke of Hesse in Holland. To obtain the results he wanted from these leaders, Herzl tried to bargain. In 1901 he offered this deal to Sultan Abdul Hamid II in Constantinople: Herzl would pay the entire Turkish debt in exchange for the sultan's support of Jewish settlement in Palestine. Unfortunately for Herzl, the sultan was not in a bargaining mood.

A year later, however, the sultan softened his stand and offered the Jews areas to settle in Mesopotamia, Syria, or Anatolia—but not in Palestine. Sorrowfully, Herzl said no. Herzl weighed in with a new offer of 1.6 million pounds to the sultan, but the Turkish leader declined.

In his pivotal novel *Altneuland* (1902), Herzl envisioned a Jewish state in Palestine and the creation of an ideal society. He urged that science and technology be used to develop the new state; he advocated tolerance, especially between Jews and Arabs, and he believed that the society should be organized on a cooperative or "mutualist" basis. The slogan of the book, "If you will it, it is no dream," became a motto for countless Israelis in their efforts to build a Jewish state.

In 1902 a bright light appeared on the horizon when the British Colonial Secretary, Joseph Chamberlain, offered El Arish in the northern Sinai Peninsula in Egypt as a venue for Jewish settlement. The offer was contingent upon the approval of the British representative in Egypt, Lord Cromer. Encouraged by Herzl, the Zionist Organization sent an expedition to El Arish in January 1903, and the plan appeared to be gaining momentum, only to be rejected eventually by Lord Cromer.

No sooner had the El Arish proposal fallen by the wayside than the British Foreign Secretary, Lord Lansdowne, offered the Jews some territory in Uganda. Inclined to accept the offer, Herzl encountered heavy opposition at the Sixth Zionist Congress in August 1903. The Uganda proposal ran aground, and consequently Herzl agreed to renew his efforts to promote a Jewish homeland in Palestine.

Although he continued his diplomatic wanderings, Herzl was exhausted by all his activities on behalf of Jewish settlement. Seeking rest at Edlach in Austria, he died there on July 3, 1904, only forty-four years old, from complications resulting from a long-standing heart condition. He was buried in Vienna, but forty-five years later, in August 1949, fifteen months after the new state of Israel came into existence, Herzl's remains were appropriately transferred to Jerusalem. Theodor Herzl was reinterred on Mount Herzl in Jerusalem.

On the long, tortuous, obstacle-strewn road to the creation of the Jewish state, Theodor Herzl gets credit as a great visionary in the effort. He was the catalyst for all that would come after his death and in the wake of his plans and dreams. He has been faulted for having little appreciation of Jewish tradition, and for not championing the Hebrew language as part of the Jewish renaissance in Palestine. But such criticisms appear petty compared to his main contribution as the founder of modern Zionism. Other Zionists had preceded him; few of his ideas were new. Yet it was his flair for public relations and his readiness to undertake, at times, a one-man diplomatic mission on behalf of Zionism that helped shift the movement into high gear and create a homeland for all Jews.

DUSTIN HOFFMAN

One of Hollywood's Best Actors

Born August 8, 1937, in Los Angeles, California. American movie actor. Considered one of the finest actors in Hollywood, Dustin Hoffman has played a variety of roles during his career. Among his best-known films are *The Graduate* (1967), *Kramer vs. Kramer* (1979), and *Rain Man* (1988), the last two winning him Academy Awards as Best Actor. He has also been nominated for Academy Awards for his performances in *The Graduate*, *Midnight Cowboy* (1969), *Lenny* (1974), and *Tootsie* (1982).

D USTIN HOFFMAN, born to Jewish parents in Los Angeles on August 8, 1937, is one of America's most versatile actors. He has played a shy, innocent college graduate, a down-and-out would-be pimp, and a suicidal comic as well as a newly divorced father and one of the journalists who uncovered the Watergate scandal.

Hoffman's father was an assistant set decorator at Columbia Pictures and later a furniture designer. Hoffman's mother, Lillian, long denied the widespread report that she named her son after the silent western film star Dustin Farnum. According to Lillian Hoffman, she "just . . . liked the name." Dustin Hoffman has one brother, Ronald.

Hoffman described himself as "a kid who was always too short, wore braces on his teeth, and had one of the worst cases of acne in California." He was so short in junior high school that he easily won the part of Tiny Tim in a student production of *A Christmas Carol.*

At Los Angeles High School, Hoffman felt alienated, although it's not clear why. "I was suddenly thrust out of the inner circle," he told an interviewer for *Newsday* in 1968. "I was an outsider, an observer. That's the way I'll prob-

The Jewish Week

Dustin Hoffman

137

ably always see life." In that same interview, Hoffman attributed his poor grades to his inability to concentrate or to develop any academic self-discipline. He was too small in stature to be good at tennis, a sport he wanted to play, so he turned to weight lifting. He also studied piano.

After his high school graduation, Hoffman considered becoming a concert pianist; he entered Santa Monica City College as a music major. An elective he took in theater arts, however, became his favorite course and influenced his life from then on. He left college a year later to enroll in acting classes at the Pasadena Playhouse. In 1958, after completing a two-year course there, Hoffman went to New York City, partly, he quipped, because "it would be easier to fail at that distance." In New York he studied acting with Lee Strasberg.

For seven years his career seemed to go nowhere. He lived in a cold-water flat on the Lower East Side and auditioned for on-and off-Broadway acting roles, while working as a psychiatric attendant, janitor, typist, and as a toy demonstrator for Macy's department store.

Hoffman's first stage appearance was in the late 1950s in a Sarah Lawrence College production of Gertrude Stein's *Yes Is for a Very Young Man*. In 1961 he debuted on Broadway in a walk-on part in *A Cook for Mr. General*, a play that lasted only twenty-eight performances. Between 1958 and 1964, Hoffman did some summer stock and minor roles on television. He toyed with the idea of becoming a full-time theater director, having worked as an assistant director on Arthur Miller's *A View From the Bridge*.

Then Hoffman won some encouraging publicity when he portrayed Immanuel, the crippled German homosexual, in a dark comedy called *Harry, Noon and Night* at a workshop theater in Lower Manhattan during the 1964–65 theater season. Shortly after that performance, Hoffman was chosen to replace Martin Sheen as the young son in the long-running Broadway hit *The Subject Was Roses*. Hoffman was forced to back out, however, because of severe burns he sustained from a kitchen fire.

In the spring of 1966, Hoffman won the Obie Award as the best off-Broadway actor of 1965–66 for his portrayal of the nasal-voiced Zoditch, a bitterly introverted Russian clerk in *The Journey of the Fifth Horse*.

Hoffman's big break came when he was tapped to play the lead in the film *The Graduate* (1967), the story of a new college graduate named Benjamin Braddock whose initiation into sex and love form the basis for a memorable comedy. Benjamin has a famous fling with Mrs. Robinson, the wife of his father's law partner, but eventually finds true love with the Robinsons' daughter, Elaine. Mike Nichols, the film's director, had seen Hoffman do some off-Broadway theater, specifically in *Eh?*, a farce for which Hoffman won the Theatre World and Drama Desk awards, and was greatly impressed with his acting ability. Nichols was looking for an actor who could project credible youthful bewilderment and picked Hoffman to do the part. Hoffman's screen test was a love scene with Katherine Ross, who played Elaine. Hoffman was so convincing at playing the part of a young man in his early twenties that few realized that the actor was in fact thirty-one years old.

The Graduate, a low-budget, low-expectation, movie became the third largest box office hit in Hollywood history. The film grossed eighty million dollars in its first year alone, although Hoffman was paid only twenty thousand to do the role. Hoffman was nominated for the Oscar as Best Actor.

He also became an overnight star. "He is the anti-star hero," Lloyd Shearer noted in *Parade* magazine in 1969, "the one actor who looks least like such Establishment heroes as Gregory

Peck, John Wayne, and William Holden." One critic called Hoffman "the most delightful film hero of our generation."

Hoffman did not want to be typecast as an innocent and shy young man like Benjamin, so he chose a role for his next film that was as far from Braddock as possible—the touching petty con man, Ratso Rizzo, in *Midnight Cowboy* (1969). Hoffman received $250,000 for that role, a big leap past his salary for *The Graduate*.

Hoffman played the title role in the film *John and Mary* in 1969. The film, which costarred Mia Farrow, is about two young people who meet, but don't exchange names, in a Manhattan singles bar, go to bed together, spend the next day together, then go to bed again, this time finally introducing themselves to each other, which was the gimmick. On the basis of his two earlier blockbuster successes, Hoffman's pay rose to $450,000 for the film.

When Dustin Hoffman made *Little Big Man* (1971), a movie portrayal of the history of the American frontier as told through the adventures of the pro-Indian white man Jack Crabb, Hoffman received $500,000. He was swiftly moving up in the Hollywood world.

The 135-pound Hoffman, known as Dusty to his friends, is five feet, six-and-a-half inches tall. Lloyd Shearer wrote in his *Parade* magazine article that "with his short stature, hook nose, beady eyes, and unkempt hair, he looks like a loser, and it is precisely because of that loser image . . . that the younger generations . . . have made him their winner."

Hoffman married a former ballerina named Anne Byrne in 1969 in a Reform Jewish ceremony. They had two daughters together, but were eventually divorced. In 1980, Hoffman married Lisa Gottsegen. They have two sons and two daughters.

Hoffman's acting roles were never limited to films. In 1984 he starred in a highly acclaimed Broadway revival of *Death of a Salesman*. He earned the Drama Desk Award as Best Actor as well as an Emmy for his portrayal of the doomed Willy Loman. In 1989 Hoffman played Shylock in *The Merchant of Venice* in London. He later reprised the role on Broadway and was nominated for a Tony Award.

Other films in which Hoffman appeared are *Straw Dogs* (1972); *Papillon* (1973); *Lenny* (1974), for which he was nominated for an Academy Award; *All the President's Men* (1976); *Marathon Man* (1976); *Kramer vs. Kramer* (1979), for which he received the Best Actor Academy Award; *Tootsie* (1982), for which he was nominated for an Academy Award and won a Golden Globe Award; and *Rain Man* (1988), for which he received the Best Actor Academy Award. He also appeared in *Dick Tracy* (1990); *Billy Bathgate* (1991); *Hook* (1991); and *Hero* (1992).

In the 1995 release *Outbreak*, Hoffman played a scientist in the midst of a modern-day plague. In 1996 and 1997 Hoffman had one of the busiest film-making periods of his career. He starred in *Sleepers*, *Mad City*, *Wag the Dog*, and *Sphere*. He was nominated for best actor for his role as a manipulative Hollywood producer in *Wag the Dog*.

In September 2002, Hoffman appeared in writer-director Brad Silberling's *Moonlight Mile*, the filmmaker's fictionalized account of the aftermath of the 1989 murder by a stalker fan of his girlfriend, actress Rebecca Schaeffer (of television's *My Sister Sam*). Since then, Hoffman has starred in *The Runaway Jury* (2003), based on the John Grisham novel, and *Meet the Fockers* (2004), a sequel to *Meet the Parents* (2000). Hoffman also starred in the 2004 movie *I Heart Huckabees*.

Hoffman is a perfectionist. Watching *Rain Man*, for which he won an Oscar in 1988, the actor noted: "I watched half a scene and I turned it off so fast—because I didn't like what I was doing and thought I could do that scene so much better."

HARRY HOUDINI

The Greatest Escape Artist of All Time

Born March 24, 1874, in Budapest, Hungary; died October 31, 1926. American magician and escapologist. The son of a rabbi, Harry Houdini became the most famous of illusionists and escape artists. He boasted that he could escape from anything, and he did. So clever was Houdini that his fans believed he had supernatural powers, but the truth was that he was a great showman, a spectacular trickster, and a fine athlete who took pride in showing that Jews could perform physical as well as intellectual feats.

HARRY HOUDINI was born Erick Weisz, later Americanized to Erich Weiss, in Budapest, Hungary, the son of Rabbi Mayer Weisz. In 1874, when Houdini was a few weeks old, his parents moved to Appleton, Wisconsin, where his father became the rabbi of a small Orthodox synagogue.

In 1882, at the age of eight, Houdini worked as a trapeze artist in a five-cent traveling circus to earn some money. He ran away from home on his twelfth birthday to look for work. His family eventually moved to the Lower East Side area of New York City, where Eri, as he was called at the time, joined them. He had become fascinated with the French magician Jean Eugène Robert-Houdin and studied Houdin's memoirs, deciding at some point to change his surname to Houdini, a variation of his idol's name. In 1894 Houdini married Beatrice Rahner. Together they developed a magic and escape act that they performed in circuses and on the vaudeville circuit.

Houdini developed a specialty of executing seemingly incredible escapes from every conceivable kind of restraint—handcuffs, prison cells, the straitjackets of insane asylums, coffins, giant milk cans that had been bolted shut. He accurately boasted that he could escape from any restraining device that had ever been made. (Among his other tricks was one in which he made a live elephant disappear before the eyes of an amazed audience, a feat he performed for the first time in 1918 in New York.) Houdini's ability to extricate himself from seemingly impossible places led his fans to believe that he possessed either supernatural powers or some amazing secret. The fact was that Harry Houdini was a marvelous showman and a fantastic trickster as well as a superb athlete.

To achieve his magic, Houdini taught himself to be an expert swimmer, to manipulate his muscles at will, and to regurgitate swallowed picks for locks when needed. He also had an encyclopedic knowledge of locks and how they worked. The expert escapologist also took great pride in showing that Jews, known far and wide for having great mental prowess, could perform physical as well as intellectual feats. To Houdini, however, Judaism seemed to have been very much a private matter. His biographers barely mention his Jewishness.

"Houdini," said Walter Gibson, who wrote about illusions and escapes and was an associate of the master, "had an unusual act . . . . Other magicians had bigger tricks, but no one had his style."

Early in his career, Houdini offered to explain his tricks to four New York daily newspapers for a mere twenty dollars, but none expressed any interest. Later, when Houdini became famous, he refused to give away the secrets that he had been willing to sell cheaply during those early years.

According to his biographer, William Gresham, Houdini's greatest illusions and escapes were achieved with a combination of masterful planning and athletic skill. One example: When he dived, manacled and chained, into an icy river, Houdini would swim free a few moments later because the chains were phony and the locks had been rigged to open at his touch. But to be on the safe side and to be prepared for the worst, he had also spent months practicing for his act by submersing himself in a bathtub of ice-cold water.

Harry Houdini

Houdini knew that most of the handcuffs manufactured at the time could be opened with the same key. He kept one hidden on his body. Handcuffs that could not be unlocked with this master key could be opened by rapping them on a hard surface. When Houdini challenged an audience to place him in handcuffs, he always happened to have a piece of metal strapped to his thigh. Once, he tricked Scotland Yard detectives into trying their handcuffs; they locked Houdini's arms around a stone pillar and left him there. By simply banging the handcuffs on the pillar, Houdini was able to escape.

The turning point in Houdini's career came in 1900, when he began a four-year tour of Europe. He packed audiences into London's Alhambra Theater nightly, delighting them with his act. His fame and popularity grew.

While in Europe, Houdini demonstrated his skills to members of both Scotland Yard and the Moscow Police Department. In 1903 his reputation was enhanced when he escaped from a horse-drawn Russian police van equipped with steel bars; it was used for transporting political prisoners to Siberia and considered escape proof. Houdini had been stripped to his underwear and examined by physicians before being locked in the van. But when his wife kissed him in a tearful farewell, she managed to pass him, mouth-to-mouth, a small, coiled-spring saw and can opener to cut through the zinc floor of the cage in which he was locked.

Harry Houdini was called "The World's Greatest Magician" and he became the highest-paid entertainer of his day. Among his famous feats were walking through a wall, escaping from a straitjacket in which he had been left hanging upside down several feet in the air, and swimming free of a weighted packing case in which he had been manacled and lowered into the sea—each trick accomplished in less than two minutes. The crowds loved it.

Houdini was committed to keeping himself at the peak of physical fitness to remain capable of performing his daring acts. He learned to fly airplanes, and in 1910 he bought one and had it disassembled and shipped to Australia, where he hoped to be remembered as a pioneer aviator. He made the first successful airplane flight in Australia on March 16, 1910.

Houdini wrote a book in 1908 called *The Unmasking of Robert-Houdin*, in which he debunked his former idol. Houdini also made a great effort to expose fake mediums and mind readers. He offered a large reward to anyone who could credibly demonstrate the actual existence of supernatural phenomena. At the same time, he believed that he himself might reappear after death. In fact, he left behind coded letters which only his spirit could answer, to be found after his death. He offered a ten-thousand-dollar reward for any "supernatural" manifestation that he could not duplicate.

On August 5, 1926, Houdini had himself put in a sealed casket, and lowered into the pool of New York City's Sheraton Hotel. He stayed there for ninety-one minutes, setting a new record. Hours after he escaped his underwater prison, he wrote a letter to a consultant for the Bureau of Mines in which he described in great detail his efforts to live on what scientists had thought was only a five-minute supply of air. Houdini stressed that he had managed the feat by remaining still and carefully controlling his breathing, not through tricks or supernatural powers. This letter was discovered in 1974, long after his death.

On October 22, 1926, Houdini was performing his show in Montreal, Canada. An admiring college student approached the entertainer and asked if he, the student, could confirm the showman's celebrated physical toughness. Houdini, leisurely looking through his mail, allowed the student to punch him in the stomach, which knocked him from his feet. The resulting injuries included a broken ankle and serious damage to the stomach. Houdini performed another three shows before permitting himself to be taken to a hospital. Peritonitis developed and Houdini died nine days later at the age of fifty-two.

At the time of Houdini's death, his widow, Beatrice, issued a statement saying that only she and her husband's technical adviser, James Collins, knew the secret of Houdini's tricks.

Houdini's story was the subject of a compelling 1953 film, *Houdini*, which starred Tony Curtis. As the film biography of a highly skilled and talented entertainer, it remains a classic depiction.

AL JOLSON

American Entertainer

> Born May 26, 1886, in Srednik, Lithuania; died October 23, 1950. American actor and singer. Al Jolson's father wanted him to be a cantor, but following the story line of his most famous movie, *The Jazz Singer* (1927), Al Jolson preferred to do his own kind of popular singing. Jolson liked to refer to himself as "The World's Greatest Entertainer." *The Jazz Singer* was the first talking movie and was one of several firsts for Al Jolson, who also appeared on the first radio program that used a monologue combined with singing format. Jolson was most famous, however, for wearing blackface for his performances, and for his melodramatic trademark gesture of falling down on his knees when he sang his signature tune, "Mammy."

AL JOLSON was born Asa Yoelson in 1886 in Lithuania. While still a small boy, just seven, Jolson immigrated to the United States with his family, which settled in Washington, D.C. His father, Moses Yoelson, was a cantor and rabbi who tried to groom both of his sons, Asa and Harry, to pursue the same career. He offered them voice lessons, which Asa refused. As he grew older he exhibited some interest in a cantorial career, but he later became more interested in acting. Harry was attracted to show business as well.

The brothers actually began their careers on the streets of Washington. As teenagers, they ran away to New York often, trying to break into show business. Jolson never took the voice lessons available to him; he believed that his innate talent would serve him well enough eventually.

In 1899 Jolson made his first appearance on the stage, in a mob scene in Israel Zangwill's *Children of the Ghetto*. After this debut, he found more work on the vaudeville circuit, performing acts with Harry as well as with other entertainers.

Jolson constantly ran away from home but always returned. He sang in cafes and saloons, and chased after circuses, hoping to find work. When he ran out of money, he was either sent back home or to other relatives. He was willing to try anything to be on his own. When he was fifteen years old, he tried to join a Spanish-American war regiment, but to no avail.

Jolson's big break came in 1909 when he sang "Mammy" for the first time, in blackface, in a San Francisco minstrel act. This act made a tremendous impact on audiences from that day on. Grown men, it was said only half jokingly, were known to rush to the post office to send a night letter to their mothers after hearing "Mammy." The crowds loved him, and Jolson loved to feel that emotional response to his performing. Jolson came up with one of his memorable lines after one performance: "All right, all right, folks. You ain't heard nothing yet."

Al Jolson

Touring the United States in 1911, Jolson won a spot on the opening night bill of the new Winter Garden Theater in New York City. He won the audience over, dominating the evening. He was at home on the stage and thrived on the adulation he received. At times he would stop the performances of others in mid-act to ask the audience whom they had come to see. To his glee and to the disenchantment of the performer on stage, the audience always went wild with enthusiasm when they saw him, shouting for him to come out early. He would then perform for hours.

He appealed to former Yiddish theater fans who searched for entertainment that, while more American than Yiddish, retained a familiar Jewish style. Jolson seemed unashamed of being Jewish and laced his act with spicy Yiddish—to entertain, not to malign, his fellow Jews.

At some point Asa Yoelson became Al Jolson. For the next fourteen years Jolson appeared on the stage in a series of productions that were known loosely as Winter Garden Shows. He starred in a number of extravaganzas, among them *La Belle Paree* (1911), *Honeymoon Express* (1913), *Robinson Crusoe, Jr.* (1916), *Sinbad* (1918), *Bombo* (1921), *Big Boy* (1925), and, later, *Wonderbar* (1935).

Gilbert Seldes, the critic, wrote of Jolson that no one else held an audience in his hand so well. "I have heard Jolson in a second-rate show before an audience, listless or hostile, sing [an] outdated and forgotten song and . . . saw also the tremendous leap in vitality and happiness which took possession of the audience as he sang it."

Jolson's unique style was a blend of frenzied rhythm and unabashed sentiment. Obsessed with his work, he not only became a recording star but also a star of the new medium of the day, radio. Yet he was happiest when he was in front of a live audience where he could hear the applause that was so addictive to him. He needed to be close to his fans, literally, and sometimes he would actually leap into the audience to accomplish that.

Jolson was married three times. His wives were Henrietta Keller, whom he wed in 1906; Ama Osborne (known on the stage as Ethel Delmar), whom he married in 1922; and Ruby Keeler, who became his wife in 1928. In 1935, Jolson and Keeler, an ex-Ziegfeld Follies girl and well-known film star in her own right, adopted a son. In 1939, however, the two divorced. The nation was fascinated with the ups and downs of Jolson's marriages. When he was courting someone, his fans were pleased for him; when one of his marriages was breaking up, those same fans took the news sadly.

In 1927 Jolson began making movies, taking his career to new heights by making what became a true Hollywood classic. Warner Brothers signed him to appear in *The Jazz Singer*, the first full-length talking film. It told the story of a young man who rejected the wish of his father, a cantor, for him to follow the same path, in order to become a popular singer. It was Al Jolson's own life story, as it turned out. The film netted three million dollars.

Jolson's next talking film was called *The Singing Fool*; in it he sang a song that also became a classic, "Sonny Boy."

Jolson returned to Broadway in 1931, this time in a more sophisticated role in a show called *Wonderbar*. That performance became his swan song; it was his final theater appearance. He then opted for the stardom of the movies and radio. Among the movies he made were *Say It with Songs* (1929), *Big Boy* (1930), *Hallelujah I'm a Bum* (1933), *Go Into Your Dance* (1935), *The Singing Kid* (1936), and *The Rose of Washington Square* (1939).

Jolson had a major influence on the film industry in general, for he was given a great deal of say over what movies, not just his own, that Warner Brothers decided to make. During the 1930s he made fewer and fewer films, however, concentrating instead on radio. His programs alternated songs with monologues, which was a new approach to broadcast entertainment.

One critic wrote that Jolson's main character trait was his inexhaustible vitality. "He is a . . . lean man with a rolling eye and an irresistibly droll smile." Jolson was an avowed sentimentalist. When he sang "Sonny Boy," he made sure to have a young boy stand near him on the stage. He liked to "confide" in his audiences, telling them about how much money he had put into the show he was performing, or what he thought of Ruby Keeler, or how much he liked his newly adopted son. He loved to gamble—on horses and on the stock market.

Two more pictures in addition to *The Jazz Singer* were made that were based on his life: *The Jolson Story* and *Jolson Sings Again*. In 1944, Jolson became a film producer; by then he was also the star of his own radio program.

Al Jolson was the first performer to travel overseas with the United Service Organization (USO). Jolson initiated the idea, calling the White House and asking to be sent overseas to entertain the troops. At that point, he felt that his popularity was sinking. The shows he did during World War II helped boost his image, however.

In 1950, during the Korean War, Jolson performed his last shows for the troops. When he returned to the United States, at the age of sixty-four, he suffered a fatal heart attack. His will stated that 90 percent of his three-million-dollar estate be divided equally among Jewish, Catholic, and Protestant groups.

Al Jolson may have wandered from the kind of career his father had hoped him to pursue, but, in becoming one of the leading entertainers of his generation, he felt that he was being true to himself and true to the Judaism that he knew and loved.

FRANZ KAFKA

Influential European Novelist

Born July 3, 1883, in Prague, Czech Republic; died June 3, 1924. Czech writer. Only after his death was Franz Kafka recognized as one of the greatest figures of modern European literature. His most famous novels are *The Trial* (1925), *The Castle* (1926), and *America* (1927). Plagued by tuberculosis, Kafka spent much of his adult life a sickly, miserable figure. When he realized that death was imminent, he left instructions with his close friend Max Brod to destroy all of his manuscripts. However, Brod disobeyed him, setting the stage for Kafka to achieve international fame.

FRANZ KAFKA was born in Prague in 1883 into a middle-class family. A lonely child, he was deeply affected by his relationship with his authoritarian father Herman. Ironically, however, Kafka's father encouraged him to write fiction, which eventually made him famous and gave him a place in history. Franz was the eldest of six children, three girls and three boys. His two brothers died in infancy. Herman worked in a dry goods business; his wife Julie came from a family of wealthy brewers. Although Kafka's parents were Jewish, they were largely assimilated into Prague's German-speaking community. Kafka himself did not feel very Jewish. (He once wrote in his diary, "What have I in common with Jews? I have hardly anything in common with myself.")

Kafka's high school studies were in the German language. He began to write creatively while in high school, but he burned all his compositions. After high school, Kafka studied law at Prague University. He continued to feel a certain loneliness in his life, but relieving his sense of isolation, if only a little, was the series of visits he made to the Reading and Lecture Hall for German Students at the university. It had in fact been turned over to the university's Zionists to use as their clubhouse. Kafka was not even certain he would be allowed to enter the clubhouse at first because he was certainly not a Zionist.

As the story is told, Kafka walked into the room. No one asked him if he was a Zionist. Until this time, he had never actually sought out friendship, but apparently he did want to be part of a group. He sat at the table with the others and listened intently to the debate that was going on; throughout the entire session, Kafka made only one small remark.

Several weeks later, while visiting again, Kafka noticed that people started paying attention to what he was saying. When he talked, conversations would suddenly stop. He thought it ironic, since his father had told him that he had no worthwhile opinions. Once he overheard one student say to another, "That Herr Kafka, he's hit the nail on the head again."

Max Brod was one of the members of this club who most admired Kafka and the two began to converse. Kafka was glad to find someone with whom he could share his thoughts. He talked so much that at times he apologized to Brod for being so dominating.

Kafka became one of the first Jews to work in public service when, in 1909, at the age of twenty-six, he was hired to work at the partially state-run accident insurance company for industrial workers. While he had the desire to write, the long hours at the job left him little extra time. Yet he was compelled to satisfy his creative urges and so he wrote under the most unfavorable circumstances, late at night or while on sick leave. Unfortunately he had contracted tuberculosis, which was diagnosed in 1917.

Kafka transferred to a different firm where he also worked hard, but the hours at the new job were shorter, permitting him more time to write. He often napped in the afternoons when he got home so that he had the stamina to write late into the night. He would often arrive at work exhausted the next morning. Eventually he had to quit the job because of his ill health.

Kafka developed close friends among members of the Jewish community in Prague. He also had several intense relationships with women. He was twice engaged to Felice Bauer, in 1914 and in 1917, but the relationship ended in part because she wanted children and he did not. Bauer is reported to have been one of the two major influences, joining his father, upon Kafka's writings.

In his books and short stories, Kafka wrote about human alienation in society and conveyed a world of frustration and utter hopelessness, a world that, even so, appeared to have its own logic. This world that Kafka depicted so well brought the word *Kafkaesque* into the English lexicon. It is used today to describe the loss of self in a world that trades individual rights for general good. In some of his shorter fiction, written during World War I, Kafka also hints at the decay of civilization; these works include *Die Verwandlung* (*The Metamorphosis*, 1915), *Der Neue Advokat* (*The New Advocate*, 1917), and *Ein Altes Blatt* (*An Old Manuscript*, 1917). In *Das Urteil* (*The Judgment*, 1913), a father sentences his son to death, and the son obediently drowns himself. In *In der Strafkolonie* (*In the Penal Settlement*, 1920), Kafka describes precisely how prisoners condemned by an arbitrary judicial system are tortured to death by a machine that inscribes the violated law on their bodies.

Because of his tuberculosis, Kafka spent lengthy periods of time in various sanatoriums and took early retirement in 1922, though he was only thirty-nine years old. He gave all his unpublished manuscripts to Max Brod, leaving word that all of these writings should be destroyed upon Kafka's death. Among the manuscripts were what would become Kafka's greatest novels. Brod knew it was high-quality, important work, and he could not bring himself to put a match to the manuscripts after Kafka's death in 1924. Because Brod disobeyed Kafka's instructions, Kafka eventually attained great fame, however much the disaffected and troubled author wished it otherwise.

In Kafka's final years, he renewed his interest in Judaism and even considered immigrating to Palestine. In the final year of his life Kafka spent some time in Berlin. He then returned to Prague and died at the age of forty-one in a sanatorium near Prague. Kafka was buried in the Prague Jewish cemetery in his family's tomb. Later, three of his sisters were killed in Nazi concentration camps.

Most of Kafka's writing was published posthumously. His best-known novels are *The Trial* (1925), *The Castle* (1926), and *America* (1927), all written in German; probably his most famous is *The Trial*. It recounts the story of a successful banker who is charged with a crime that is never identified, he falls under the power of a mysterious court, becomes helpless in the quest to fight it, and finally is executed.

Kafka's novels study institutions and their implications for society and the individual in great detail; the bureaucracy, for instance, is the subject of *The Castle*. The book includes narrative in which Kafka's characters distort logic in order to serve their own interests. Because of his early legal training, Kafka was able to show believably how authorities misuse legal machinery to incriminate the accused. From his days as a bureaucrat, he was able to write comic descriptions of officials who enjoyed harassing and obstructing those in lower positions.

Kafka's great literary originality lay in his ability to create dreamlike images with many layers of implication, sometimes even contradictory to each other. Kafka's heroes express revulsion at their lives, and that revulsion makes them enjoy a certain lack of restraint that isolates them from society. They become solitary; often they have none of the pressures of work or family.

Franz Kafka

Austrian Press and Information Service, Washington, D.C.

Intellectually curious and widely read himself, Kafka may have been influenced by the Jewish mysticism he learned about as an avid and well-informed reader. He wrote that "not one calm second is granted to the Western Jew. Everything has to be earned, not only the present and the future but also the past—something after all which perhaps every human being has inherited—this too must be earned; it is perhaps the hardest work."

Kafka's detailed diaries and letters reveal a great deal about the torments of his life. His illness, which as time went on isolated him more and more from others, gave him a great deal of time to reflect on the social and religious questions of the day. In his final year, Kafka appears to have finally found some happiness in life through his relationship with Dora Dymant, with whom he lived in Berlin during the winter of 1923 to 1924.

Kafka's books have had a major impact on both the literature and philosophy of the twentieth century. His critical, insightful, and cautionary view of a world where human beings are estranged emotionally and where the bureaucracy erodes and endangers their freedom has influenced not only readers but also leaders and educators.

LOUIS I. KAHN

Outstanding Architect

Born February 20, 1901, on Oesel Island, Estonia; died March 17, 1974. American architect. Unorthodox and innovative, Louis Kahn believed that architectural design must follow the "will" of space and construction materials. He acquired an international reputation for his dramatic geometrical buildings. Through his popular architecture courses, he also had a major influence on future architects. Kahn's finest work was the Richards Research Building at the University of Pennsylvania in Philadelphia, completed in 1961 and called "probably the single most consequential building constructed in the United States since World War II" by officials of New York's Museum of Modern Art.

LOUIS KAHN was born in 1901 in Estonia, then part of the Russian Empire. His father, Leopold Kahn, was a stained-glass worker; his mother, Bertha (Mendelsohn) Kahn, was a harpist. At the age of three, Kahn was burned on the face by a flare-up of live coals; the scar tissue on his cheeks resulted in lifelong deformity. The Kahns immigrated to Philadelphia when Kahn was five years old. When he was fifteen, he became an American citizen. His facial blemish made him shy around students, but his teachers liked him because of his aptitude in drawing. The facial scar was not noticeable and had no visible influence on him or his career in later years.

While still a child, Louis won awards for his painting and drawing; he also displayed talent as a musician. At Philadelphia's Public Industrial Art School, he studied modeling, carving, and drawing, hoping to become an artist, and graduated in 1917. In 1919 and 1920, while taking courses at the Fleisher Memorial Art School, Kahn won first prizes for the best drawings in Philadelphia high schools in competitions sponsored by the Pennsylvania Academy of Fine Arts.

After hearing a lecture on Greek and Roman architecture by William F. Gray, a college professor, at Central High School in Philadelphia (whence Kahn graduated in 1920), he decided to become an architect. He enrolled at the University of Pennsylvania's School of Fine Arts and graduated from there in 1924. One of his major influences was Paul P. Cret, a well-known American advocate of the French-inspired Beaux-Arts tradition in architecture.

During the summers of 1921 and 1922, Kahn worked as a draftsman in two Philadelphia architectural firms, Hoffman and Henon, and Hewitt and Ash. John Moliter, then the city architect, hired Kahn in July 1924, giving him responsibility for the drafting and design of buildings for Philadelphia's Sesquicentennial Exposition.

150

In March 1927, Kahn joined the staff of Philadelphia architect William H. Lee. The following year, he traveled to Europe, where he drew sketches of ancient Greek and Roman structures as well as Italian Romanesque architecture, all of which became influences in his own work.

Soon after Kahn returned to Philadelphia from his European tour, he met Esther Israeli, a research assistant in the Department of Neurosurgery at the University of Pennsylvania. They were married in 1930 and had a daughter, Sue Ann, born in 1940. Kahn worked as a designer for Paul P. Cret in 1929 and 1930, leaving there for the architectural firm of Zantzinger, Borie, and Medary, where he worked for two years. Khan worked on the drawings for the Chicago Centennial of 1933 and the Folger Shakespeare Library, in Washington, D.C.

Louis Kahn

During the years of the Depression, Kahn was frequently unemployed. Once it was over, however, his career began to grow more stable. From March 1932 until December 1933, he organized and directed the Architectural Research Group, some thirty unemployed architects and engineers who studied Philadelphia housing conditions, planned housing projects, made city planning and slum clearance studies, and probed new construction methods.

In 1937 Kahn completed his first project as an independent architect, Philadelphia's Ahavath Israel Synagogue. During 1942 and 1943, he helped create a number of federally sponsored projects, among them the Carver Court Housing Development in Coatsworth, Pennsylvania, considered one of the best housing projects of the World War II era. Kahn worked in private practice from 1947 until 1953. In 1947 he was named a visiting critic of architectural design at Yale University. Soon after that appointment, he became a professor of architecture there, a post he held until 1957.

Among the important projects he worked on in the late 1940s and early 1950s were the Morton Weiss residence in East Noriton Township, Pennsylvania, the occupational therapy building for the Philadelphia Psychiatric Hospital, and the Samuel Radbill Building for the same hospital. In the occupational therapy building, finished in 1950, Kahn used light steel openwork and joists in order to span the structure; in later buildings he decided to design only in concrete and masonry.

In 1950 and 1951, Kahn was resident architect at the American Academy in Rome and once again studied ancient architecture firsthand. He won his first important public recognition for his design of the Yale Art Gallery in 1951, also the first modern building at the university. Winning rave reviews for Kahn's design, the Art Gallery was considered by some critics to be the most outstanding academic building produced by the modern movement in architec-

architecture. For the sake of flexibility, Kahn left the interior clear and used movable panels to serve as walls for creating classrooms and exhibit space.

Kahn differed from many architects in being a kind of architect-philosopher with his own thoughts about the meaning of buildings. He believed that all things start with a "psychic existence-will" and that the architect's mission is to create a building that "wants to be."

"A rose wants to be a rose; a brick wants to be an arch," Kahn once said. "A great building, in my opinion, must begin with the unmeasurable," he also observed. A great building, according to Kahn, "must go through measurable means when it is being designed and in the end must be unmeasurable. Everything must begin with poetry and end as art."

Kahn's design of the Alfred Newton Richards Medical Research Building on the University of Pennsylvania campus, completed in 1961, was the clearest statement of Kahn's philosophy of architecture. It was honored with an unusual one-building show at the Museum of Modern Art in New York and described in the Museum's official bulletin as "probably the single most consequential building constructed in the United States since World War II." In his design for the Richards Building, Kahn's seven-story laboratory towers form a pinwheel around a service tower that contains such facilities as elevators, stairs, and air vents. Hence there is a clear division of "servant" and "served" areas.

Between 1959 and 1965, Kahn worked closely with Jonas Salk to design the breathtaking Salk Institute Laboratories along the Pacific Ocean in La Jolla, California. That commission led to Kahn's obtaining important assignments abroad, including the design of the Institute of Management (1963–74) in Ahmesdabad, India.

In the late 1950s and early 1960s, Kahn worked on a Jewish community center in Trenton, New Jersey, an AFL-CIO medical center, the United States Consulate in Portuguese Angola, and a dormitory for Bryn Mawr College. In his Trenton building, a cross-axial plan he designed showed the influence of the Beaux-Arts tradition. Here and in the Yale Art Gallery, Kahn's design work illustrated the use of the column as a means of defining space.

Kahn coauthored with architect Oscar Stonorov *Why City Planning Is Your Responsibility* (1943) and *You and Your Neighborhood: A Primer for Neighborhood Planning* (1944).

From 1957 until his death in 1974 at the age of seventy-three, Kahn was a professor of architecture at the University of Pennsylvania. He had a profound and lasting effect on the young architects he taught there as well as at Yale University and at other schools where he was invited to lecture. Ada Louise Huxtable, the architecture critic for the *New York Times*, wrote that Kahn was a "poet-philosopher-artist" and a "small, serene man of strong, unconscious magnetism" whose "pronouncements often read like a kind of Zen Architecture."

In 2003, Louis Kahn's son Nathaniel produced and starred in *My Architect*, a film depicting his five-year investigation into the question of why Louis Kahn chose to have three families, only one of which, the one with Esther Israeli, he publicly acknowledged. Nathaniel, a product of that marriage, was only eleven years old when his father died; he had seen him only once a week.

In addition to Nathaniel, Kahn had a daughter with Esther Israeli. And, Nathaniel's research revealed, Kahn had also fathered two illegitimate children by two women with whom he had maintained long-term relationships. Only at his father's funeral did Nathaniel meet relatives from the other Kahn "families" for the first time. *My Architect* is a son's attempt to explore his father's unconventional private life while examining his remarkable achievements in architecture.

MORDECAI KAPLAN

Founder of the Reconstructionist Movement of American Jewry

Born June 11, 1881, in Svencionya, Lithuania; died November 8, 1983. American religious thinker. Mordecai Kaplan was the founder of the iconoclastic Reconstructionist Movement within American Jewry. This movement rejected notions of a supernatural God and other worldly concepts of salvation, and urged that Judaism be interpreted not as a religion but as a civilization. Kaplan was widely thought to be American Jewry's most important religious thinker between the 1920s and 1940s. He inspired much of the Jewish community's life outside the synagogue, including its cultural and educational activities as well as its social welfare and antidiscrimination efforts.

MORDECAI KAPLAN was born in Lithuania in 1881, but at the age of seven was taken by his parents to New York, where his father served on the New York rabbinical court. The Kaplan home was observant, and young Kaplan attended a yeshiva. In 1900 he received his B.A. from the City College of New York and two years later was ordained a rabbi at the Jewish Theological Seminary.

In 1903, Kaplan was appointed rabbi of the prestigious, moderately Orthodox Kehillat Jeshurun Synagogue in New York City. In 1906 he met and married Lena Rubin, whose family was prominent in the New York Jewish community. They had four daughters. Six years later, at the invitation of Solomon Schechter, who established Conservative Judaism in the United States, Kaplan was appointed dean of the newly opened Teachers' Institute at the Jewish Theological Seminary. Kaplan was thrilled at being chosen for the prestigious position because he had no great interest in serving as a congregational rabbi. He directed the Institute into the 1940s and was also a professor of homiletics there. But in 1915 he returned to heading a congregation when he became rabbi of the Jewish Center, a new New York City synagogue.

Rejecting both Orthodox and Reform Judaism, and sensing that Conservative Judaism needed a new direction, Kaplan thought long and hard about his religion. He wanted to make it intellectually relevant for American Jews. In a pathbreaking article entitled "A Program for the Reconstruction of Judaism," published in the *Menorah Journal* in 1920, Kaplan outlined a new approach for Judaism.

Recoiling from the traditional adoration of a supernatural God and supernatural views of salvation, Kaplan proposed that Judaism replace these concepts of God and instead dwell on the moralistic genius of the Jews as a people. He wanted Judaism to take a pragmatic rather than a traditional approach to religion. "Any religious idea that has come down from the past will have to prove its validation by being a means of social control and betterment," Kaplan wrote.

Predictably, Kaplan found few sympathizers among members of the traditional denominations. The Orthodox community thought his views were "poisonous," labeling Kaplan a "wolf in sheep's clothing" and thus far more dangerous than any Reform or secular Jew. When Kaplan published a series of prayer books that he believed more suited to the modern Jew than existing prayer books, the Union of Orthodox Rabbis burned them during a ceremony in New York in which they excommunicated Kaplan. Conservative Jews also thought little of his "re-constructionist" ideas. The readers of the *Menorah Journal*, however, liked what he had written.

Kaplan's first and most influential book was the widely acclaimed *Judaism as a Civilization* (1934). In it he wrote that "the Jewish people are not here to maintain Torah. Torah exists for the sake of the Jewish people." Judaism, he argued, should be interpreted not as a religion but as a civilization encompassing "language, folkways, patterns of social organization, social habits and standards, and spiritual ideals, which give individuality to a people and distinguish it from other peoples."

Kaplan also wrote that the religious element within that civilization did not have to be based on otherworldly views of salvation. The Jewish religion should be reconstructed to interpret salvation as the "progressive perfection of the human personality and the establishment of a free, just, and cooperative social order." Kaplan thought that Jewish ritual, including the dietary laws, should be practiced only "whenever they do not involve an unreasonable amount of time, effort, and expense."

Kaplan refused to call the Jews "the Chosen People," and he suggested that God's miracles should not be taken literally since, in his view, they were largely folklore. He rejected any reference to the Messiah and to priestly castes, and he renounced the notion of resurrection. God, Kaplan argued, was the name given to the power in the universe that propels us toward righteousness. Faith in God means, he felt, that a person believes that, ultimately, righteousness will triumph. He thought that prayer was not an appeal to an undecided God but an act by which the worshiper sought the highest potential within himself or herself.

Kaplan, as the founder of Reconstructionism, now permanently acknowledged as a way of thought for contemporary Jews, wrote and talked about God a great deal, but he did not seem to believe in Him. "God is the warm personal element in life's inner urge to creativity and self-expression," he once said. "God is that aspect of reality which elicits from us the best that is in us and enables us to bear the worst that can befall us."

Kaplan had no desire to make Reconstructionism another sectarian stream of Jewish life like Conservatism or Reform Judaism, nor did he wish to replace existing synagogues and community institutions. He wanted his ideas to inform daily life for Jews. Toward this end, he founded a biweekly magazine called *The Reconstructionist* and set up the Jewish Reconstructionist Foundation, which had as one of its projects the revision of Passover and ritual guides. He wrote a Reconstructionist *Sabbath Prayerbook* in 1945. During the 1940s, Kaplan's Reconstructionist Foundation listed over three hundred Conservative and Reform rabbis as members, along with 250 Jewish educators, social workers, and lay people. However, Kaplan's decision not to give his new approach to Judaism an organizational component had the unfortunate effect of stifling the dissemination of his ideas.

Kaplan was also a pioneer in establishing the bat mitzvah ceremony for girls. In 1922 his daughter Judith was the first girl to have a bat mitzvah. He also fought openly for religious rights for women in synagogue life. He was, in a sense, the inspiration for much of the contemporary Jewish community's life outside the synagogue—its cultural and educational activities, and its social welfare and antidiscrimination efforts as well.

According to literary critic Hillel Halkin, Kaplan was "the right man at the right time and in the right place. He began writing and preaching as the American Jewish community was trying to become American while retaining some Jewish identity. While Jews were wrestling with the question of whether to center Jewish life around the synagogue, Kaplan argued persuasively that Judaism could and should embrace every aspect of life."

Kaplan created a common denominator between the Friday night service, the Temple Sisterhood, and a whole array of nonritualized events held under the sponsorship of synagogues. A model Jew could thus be anyone

Mordecai Kaplan

who took part in local Jewish community center activities, not necessarily one who attended synagogue faithfully. For, wrote Kaplan, "Divine is whatever possesses the quality of furthering man's perfection or salvation. 'Torah-like' is whatever possesses the quality of rendering the Jewish people aware of its function to further the process of man's perfection or salvation. 'Israel-like' is the people that identifies itself with that process."

Kaplan was one of the great ideologists of the Jewish community center movement in the United States, and he hoped that it would become the focus of Jewish life. Kaplan's biographer, Mel Scult, wrote in his 1993 book *Judaism Faces the Twentieth Century: A Biography of Mordecai M. Kaplan* that Kaplan developed "new ways of thinking about God, Israel, and the Torah that radically departed from traditional opinions and were completely within the context of twentieth-century thought. He created a new paradigm regarding the nature of Judaism for both his supporters and detractors."

Kaplan enjoyed a long life. He moved to Jerusalem in his nineties, but he returned to the United States at the age of ninety-eight. He died four years later, in 1983, at the age of 102.

JEROME KERN

Great Composer of American Musicals

Born in New York City, on January 27, 1885; died November 11, 1945.
American composer. Famous for his 1927 play *Showboat*, Jerome Kern is
considered a great and prolific composer of the American musical theater.
He took part in over a hundred stage and screen productions, and composed over a thousand songs. His 1914 classic "They Didn't Believe Me"
established the basic pattern for modern show songs. Among his famous
songs are "Smoke Gets in Your Eyes," "Old Man River," "All the Things
You Are," "The Way You Look Tonight," "Long Ago and Far Away," "Can't
Help Loving That Man," "I Won't Dance," "A Fine Romance," "Look for
the Silver Lining," and "The Last Time I Saw Paris."

JEROME KERN'S FATHER, Seligman Kakeles, was born near Prague. In the early 1840s Seligman
married Bertha Amselberg (or Anselberg). Seligman sailed alone to New York City in
1846, bringing his family there two years later and settling on Delancey Street on the
Lower East Side of Manhattan.

Jerome Kern, born in 1885, was the Kerns' sixth boy. Legend has it that his mother was
riding home from Jerome Park when she felt her child about to be born, and so named her
newborn son after the park.

Seligman Kakeles was a successful businessman. He wanted young Jerome to follow in his
footsteps, but he eventually gave up the idea when he saw that his son had no real business
talent. Once his mother realized that her son had musical abilities, she encouraged him to
push in that direction.

In 1897, when Jerome was twelve years old, the Kerns bought a home in Newark, New
Jersey. Kern entered Newark High School in the fall of 1899 at age fourteen and, although he
was not academically gifted, his skill at piano playing won him attention. He was often asked
to perform at school assemblies. He began writing songs during this time as well.

On September 5, 1902, when he was seventeen years old, Kern had his first song, "At the
Casino," published. This short piano piece was not especially memorable but it *was* his first
effort to be recognized.

In 1903 Kern graduated from the New York College of Music, the city's oldest independent
music school. There he had proved to be a good but not exceptional student. Kern then
traveled to Europe, hoping to soak up the musical atmosphere in more exotic places. As it
turned out, he fell in love with England, and visited there as often as he could during his
lifetime. Upon his return to the United States in 1905, Kern wrote what became his first hit
song, a memorable tune entitled "How'd You Like to Spoon with Me?"

In 1908 he fell in love with actress Edith Kelly, and later married her. They had a daughter, Eva.

In the years leading up to World War I, many of Kern's songs were written to be included in the New York production of London stage shows. In 1914 he wrote the classic song "They Didn't Believe Me." By the next year Kern was collaborating with Guy Bolton and P. G. Wodehouse to write what became known as the Princess Theater shows, a series of lighthearted, witty musicals that were extremely popular. These Princess Theater musicals "brought musical comedy into the twentieth century," according to Kern's biographer Gerald Bordman.

During the 1920s, Kern began working with Oscar Hammerstein II and Otto Harbach, partners with whom he wrote many successful songs. He also produced two hit shows, both of which starred Marilyn Miller, a big star of the day. One was called *Sally*, the other *Sunny*.

Jerome Kern

Kern's most ambitious work was his 1927 musical *Show Boat*. Kern thought the title of Edna Ferber's novel of the same name was "a million-dollar title." He felt that the novel's other main strength was the romantic plot it weaved against the highly colorful background of a floating theater on the Mississippi River. No one had ever tried to integrate songs into a plot in quite the way that Kern did in this play. This classic of the Broadway stage ultimately gave Kern a place of honor in the history of musical theater.

The show opened in New York in the Ziegfeld Theater on December 27, 1927, with a cast of ninety-six actors. Among its memorable tunes are "Old Man River," "Can't Help Loving That Man," "You Are Love," and "Bill." The plot recounts the bittersweet romance between a riverboat gambler, Gaylord Ravenal, and a showboat captain's daughter, Magnolia. Ravenal's gambling destroys their marriage. After Ravenal leaves, Magnolia is forced to sing in night clubs in order to support their daughter. She eventually decides to return to the family showboat. Years later, Ravenal appears on the scene again, bringing about a reunion as the final curtain descends.

Theater critic Arthur B. Waters, recalling that Kern had not had a hit score for some time, noted, "It is a pleasure to record that Jerome Kern has staged a definite and certain comeback. His score is a thing of many delights, in orchestration, in tunes, and in the manner he has caught the atmosphere of the 'mauve decade.' For once, there doesn't seem to be a single 'filler' song number in the entire list of twenty-six."

Although, over the years, critics came to find the play's treatment of blacks patronizing and racist, they generally agreed that Kern's music was wonderful. In the fall of 1994, a revival of

Jerome Kern

Show Boat on Broadway, staged by Harold Prince, received rave reviews.

Kern had other stage successes as well, including *Music in the Air* and *Roberta*. Later in his career, while working in Hollywood, Kern produced well-received scores for the films *Swing Time* and *Cover Girl*. Kern won an Academy Award for Best Song of the Year in 1936 for "The Way You Look Tonight" from the movie *Swing Time*; and again in 1941 for "The Last Time I Saw Paris" from the film *Lady Be Good*.

In the fall of 1945, Kern was in the midst of working on a musical about Annie Oakley when he was taken ill with a cerebral hemorrhage. On November 11, 1945, as Kern lay dying in a New York hospital, Oscar Hammerstein II, keeping a bedside vigil, lifted Kern's oxygen tent at one point and began singing one of Kern's favorites of his own compositions, "I've Told Every Little Star." Within seconds, Kern died. He was sixty years old.

At Kern's funeral, Oscar Hammerstein's eulogy characterized his friend and colleague this way: "His gaiety was what we will remember most—the times he made us laugh. It's a strange adjective to apply to a man, but you'll understand what I mean: Jerry was 'cute.' He was alert and alive. He 'bounced.' He stimulated everyone. He annoyed some. He never bored anyone at any time. There was a sharp edge to everything he thought or said."

Washington's *Evening Star* called Kern "one of the greatest melodists who ever lived." the *New York Times* was even more to the point. "His music will not die," it said in its headline. President Harry Truman noted, "I am among the grateful millions who have played and listened to the music of Jerome Kern . . . . His melodies . . . are the kind of simple, honest songs that belong to no time or fashion."

In his lifetime, Kern took part in over a hundred stage and screen productions and composed over a thousand songs. Many of them are classics recognized worldwide. Among them are "Smoke Gets in Your Eyes," "All the Things You Are," "Long Ago and Far Away," "I Won't Dance," "A Fine Romance," and "Look for the Silver Lining." He ranks as one of the most innovative composers of the American musical theater.

LARRY KING

America's Premier Talk Show Host

> Born November 19, 1933, in Brooklyn, New York. American broadcaster and newspaper columnist. Larry King began his broadcasting career as a Miami disc jockey in the 1950s, honing his interviewing skills by doing a radio show from Miami's Pumpernik's Restaurant in which he talked with anyone who happened to walk into the establishment while he was on the air. In 1985 he began hosting *Larry King Live* on the Cable News Network, turning the show into the most prestigious interview program on television.

L AWRENCE HARVEY ZEIGER was born in 1933 in Brooklyn, the second child of Jennie (Gitlitz) and Eddie Zeiger, both of whom were Russian-Jewish immigrants. King's home and upbringing were "very, very Jewish." His home was kosher, and he celebrated his bar mitzvah. "Jewish culture was very much a part of my being," King has stated.

The Zeiger's first child, Irwin, who was born in 1927, died of appendicitis shortly before King was born. He has one other brother, Martin. From the age of five, King wanted to be in radio. "I would look at the radio, sit and listen to it. I wrote in for everything."

King's parents ran a successful bar-and-grill restaurant in the Brownsville section of Brooklyn, but his father sold the business when World War II began and took a job at a defense plant in Kearny, New Jersey. On June 10, 1944, King's father died of a heart attack while he was working there. This forced the family to accept welfare payments.

Ten-year-old Larry, who idolized his father, was shocked by his premature death. King abandoned his studies and became a troublemaker at Brooklyn's Junior High School 128. His father's death also forced King to examine his attitude toward Judaism: "Somewhere along the line I stopped liking the God of the Old Testament. I asked great Jewish and other religious leaders why there was a Holocaust or why Hitler lived to sixty-six and a child dies at age eight. I never got good answers."

Eventually, in 1951, Larry graduated from Lafayette High School, but with a sixty-six grade average, only one point above the minimum to pass.

Although he was still interested in a career in radio, King worked as a delivery boy and mail clerk, and did other odd jobs in Brooklyn. Then, in the spring of 1957, someone told King, then twenty-three, that he might be able to break into radio in Miami. He traveled there immediately. He got his foot in the door, even though it was sweeping floors at WAHR (which became WMBM).

Larry King

When the regular disc jockey for the station's morning nine-to-noon program suddenly quit on May 1 of that year, Larry, who had let everyone know he was eager to get on the air, was asked to take his place. Fifteen minutes before the show, the manager asked King what name he planned to use. His own, King replied. "It's a little ethnic," the manager countered. A *Miami Herald* was open to a page with an advertisement for King's Wholesale Liquors on Washington Avenue. "How about Larry King?" the manager asked. "Okay," the new Larry King answered. King was paid fifty-five dollars a week to announce music, news, and sports, beginning that day.

In late 1958, King joined WKAT, a larger Miami station, and was given the morning "drive-time" slot. Later, he was hired by a Miami restaurant, Pumpernik's, to host a four-hour radio show that was broadcast live from the restaurant in an effort to boost the establishment's ailing breakfast business. King interviewed whoever happened to be eating there at the time, including then-unknown comedians Don Rickles and Lenny Bruce, as well as pop singer Bobby Darin. As the show grew in popularity, which was due to King's skill as an interviewer, other celebrities began to stop into Pumpernik's.

In 1962 Larry moved to Miami's WIOD, continuing his Pumpernik's routine for that station. The next year, he switched to evenings and began broadcasting from a houseboat as well as doing a late-night television talk show on Sundays for Miami's WLBW. He left WLBW in 1964 to do a weekend TV show on another station, WTVJ. In 1965 King began writing a column for the *Miami Beach Sun-Reporter*, then for the *Miami Herald* and the *Miami News*. By 1966 King was earning seventy thousand dollars a year from all his jobs in the communications industry.

King gambled on horses, bought expensive clothes, and rented Cadillacs, putting himself deep in debt. "At my most egotistical moments, of which there were many, I felt as if I owned Miami—and I lived as if I did, too . . . ," he said in his autobiography. "I felt that whatever Larry King wanted, Larry King should have."

King's friendship with the financier Louis Wolfson, whom he met in 1966 at the Hialeah race track, nearly ruined his career because of a miscalculation on King's part. In 1968 Wolfson handed King five thousand dollars to give to Jim Garrison, the New Orleans district attorney, to aid in the DA's probe into the assassination of President John F. Kennedy. King used the money to pay his taxes. Though King offered to pay the money back, the financier pressed grand larceny charges against King, who was arrested in December 1971. Eventually the charges were dropped because the statute of limitations had expired.

The scandal, however, was a major career setback for King. He lost his jobs as WIOD's disc jockey and color commentator for the Miami Dolphins games, his WTVJ television talk show, and his *Miami Beach Sun-Reporter* column. Thirty-eight years old and heavily in debt, King had to start over.

From 1972 to 1975, King struggled to earn a living as a freelance writer and broadcaster. He quit gambling on horse races. Still, unable to repay debts totaling $352,000, King declared bankruptcy in 1978.

Shortly before he declared bankruptcy, the Mutual Broadcasting Network offered King a national late-night talk show. On January 30, 1978, *The Larry King Show*, broadcast from Washington, D.C., debuted in twenty-eight cities over the Mutual Broadcasting System. It was the first national radio talk show and was eventually carried by 250 Mutual Broadcasting affiliates, having gained a weekly audience of three to five million people.

King says he finds it an advantage not to do his homework before airtime. "The less I know in advance, the more curious I am on the air," he said. "I don't want to know too much . . . . My wish is to do a show where I don't know the guest. I started in Pumpernik's by not knowing who the guests were. Jimmy Hoffa walked in. I couldn't plan for him. I got to like that. I trust my insatiable curiosity. I've been innately curious since my earliest memory. I was never the kind of kid who wanted an autograph. I'd run along the street asking [the Brooklyn Dodgers] questions like 'Why did you bunt?'"

King's favorite interview? The 1964 Frank Sinatra interview: "Because he was so hard to get, plus he was great." His hardest interview? Robert Mitchum: "He gave one-word answers. He had no ability to look at himself."

In 1982 the University of Georgia honored King's show with a George Foster Peabody award, the first talk show to get such an honor. King considered this prestigious recognition the highlight of his career.

In 1985 King agreed to do a similar call-in interview show—*Larry King Live*—for the Cable News Network (CNN) for $250,000 a year, doubling his pay. King's interviews with President Bill Clinton, Ross Perot, Marlon Brando, and many other celebrities made *Larry King Live* the top interview program on television.

In February 1987, King suffered a heart attack, and the following December he had open-heart surgery. His personal life has been marked with the same ups and downs as his career. His first marriage was annulled; he then wed Alene Akins, a former Playboy bunny (1961 to 1963; 1967 to 1971); Mickey Sutphin, a radio producer's assistant (1964 to 1966); Sharon Lepore, a math teacher (1976 to 1982), and Julie Alexander (1989–1992). Each marriage ended in divorce. He and Alene Akins have a daughter, Chaia, born in 1967. In early September 1997 King was married for the seventh time, to thirty-seven-year-old Shawn Southwick.

Larry King continues to be one of TV's most popular personalities, appearing in cameo roles in Hollywood movies and even hosting a January 2001 pre-inaugural event for George W. Bush. Although later that year his interview show was losing ground to Fox News Channel's *The O'Reilly Factor*, the talk star let it be known he might abandon CNN for another network. But early in 2002 he re-signed with CNN for a reported $6.5 million a year.

In November 2004, at the age of seventy-one, King continued his CNN show, broadcasting exclusive interviews with such notables as Alexis Stewart, who for the first time publicly discussed her mother Martha's jail experiences, and Hillary Clinton, who reflected on the legacy of husband Bill Clinton, whose presidential library had just opened in Little Rock, Arkansas.

HENRY KISSINGER

Nobel Peace Prize Recipient and Creator of Shuttle Diplomacy

Born May 27, 1923, in Furth, Bavaria. American diplomat and scholar. During his academic career, Henry Kissinger wrote groundbreaking studies of American foreign policy, as specifically related to national security and nuclear weapons issues. As President Richard M. Nixon's National Security Advisor and later as secretary of state, Kissinger extricated the United States from Vietnam (for which he won the Nobel Peace Prize in 1973) and was instrumental in improving America's relations with both China and the Soviet Union. He made his mark, however, by pioneering shuttle diplomacy through his mediated peace accords between the Arabs and the Israelis after the 1973 Yom Kippur War.

HEINZ ALFRED KISSINGER, the older son of Louis and Paula (Stern) Kissinger, was born in 1923 in the Bavarian city of Furth, near Nuremberg. His parents belonged to an Orthodox synagogue in Furth, and young Kissinger grew up in a strongly Jewish, middle-class atmosphere in Germany. His Jewish education, Kissinger recalls, was "considerable." In school Kissinger received good, but not outstanding, grades. In fact, he preferred soccer to studying.

In 1933, after Hitler's rise to power, the Kissinger family was subjected to increasing discrimination. Louis Kissinger lost his job as a teacher at a girls' secondary school. His son was barred from entering a gymnasium (secondary school) and forced to attend an all-Jewish school.

In 1938 the Kissingers immigrated to the United States. They settled in the Washington Heights section of New York City. Louis Kissinger found jobs as a clerk and bookkeeper; his wife worked as a cook in the homes of well-to-do families.

After graduating from George Washington High School in 1941, where he was a straight-A student, Heinz Kissinger, renamed Henry, studied accounting at City College in the evening. During the day, he worked in a shaving-brush factory.

In 1943 Kissinger became a naturalized citizen; that same year he was drafted into the United States Army. He was eventually assigned to the 84th Infantry Division and sent to the European Theater of Operations, where he saw action in the Battle of the Bulge. Kissinger served as a German interpreter for his commanding general and as an intelligence specialist.

Once Germany surrendered in 1945, Kissinger had the task of reorganizing municipal government in the town of Krefeld; he served as a district administrator with the military government of occupied Germany. He won a Bronze Star during his wartime service and was discharged from the Army in 1946.

In September of that year, when he was twenty-three, Kissinger entered Harvard College as

162

State of Israel Government Press Office

Henry Kissinger at Israel's Ben-Gurion International Airport near Tel Aviv in 1974.

a government major, receiving his B.A. degree *summa cum laude* in 1950. He was a teaching fellow at the university from 1950 to 1954, during which time he also served as a consultant to government agencies.

In 1951 Kissinger became executive director of the Foreign Student Project at Harvard, later renamed the Harvard International Seminar, which he directed until 1969. He was awarded his master's degree from that university in 1952 and received his doctorate in 1954. That same year he was appointed a lecturer on government at his alma mater. In 1957 Kissinger's doctoral dissertation was published as a book entitled *A World Restored: Castleraegh, Metternich, and the Problems of Peace*.

Kissinger was appointed director of an eighteen-month-long research program sponsored by the Council on Foreign Relations that explored alternative methods to full-scale war. The goal was to cope with the Soviet nuclear challenge. Kissinger's book *Nuclear Weapons and Foreign Policy* (1957) resulted from that project. He won the prestigious Woodrow Wilson Prize for this work, which established him as one of the leading "defense intellectuals" in America. In it, he presented the notion of "flexible response" as an alternative to the "massive retaliation" doctrine that served as America's current policy in case of nuclear warfare. By 1961 Kissinger's more rational approach had become the nation's official policy.

In 1956 Nelson Rockefeller appointed Kissinger director of the Rockefeller Brothers Fund special studies project. Five years later *The Necessity of Choice*, an outgrowth of that project, was published.

Henry A. Kissinger

Ron Hall

Kissinger became a lecturer in government at Harvard University's Center for International Affairs in 1957; he was associate director of the center from 1958 to 1960. In 1959 he was named associate professor in the government department and promoted to professor in 1962. From 1959 to 1969, Kissinger served as director of Harvard's Defense Studies Program as well. His course in foreign policy was among the most popular at Harvard. In 1965, two other books by Kissinger were published: *The Troubled Partnership: A Reappraisal of the Atlantic Alliance* and *American Foreign Policy: Three Essays.*

President Lyndon Johnson sent Kissinger to participate in secret meetings in Paris with North Vietnamese diplomats. This led in 1968 to the start of peace talks that ultimately resulted in the end of the Vietnam War.

Despite the fact that Kissinger had served as foreign policy advisor to Nelson Rockefeller in his unsuccessful attempt to capture the Republican party's presidential nomination, President-elect Richard M. Nixon asked Kissinger to become his main foreign-policy advisor in November 1968. Shortly afterward, in January 1969, Kissinger was named Assistant to the President for National Security Affairs.

During 1970 and 1971, Kissinger continued his secret meetings with North Vietnamese representatives in Paris. These negotiations culminated in the eventual withdrawal of American troops from Southeast Asia, finally ending a controversial and devastating war. For this achievement, Kissinger won the Nobel Peace Prize in 1973.

In July 1971, Kissinger made a secret trip to Beijing that led to a radical change in American foreign policy toward China, ending two decades of American hostility toward the Chinese Communist regime. The trip prepared the way for Nixon's historic visit to the Chinese mainland the following February. Kissinger was also a key figure in negotiating the SALT I Agreement with the Soviet Union in May 1972.

Nixon appointed Kissinger secretary of state in August 1973; the new secretary retained his post as head of the National Security Council. After the Yom Kippur War ended two months later, Kissinger began negotiating cease-fires between Israel and Egypt and between Israel and Syria. Jetting from one Middle East capital to another, day after day, he pioneered the strategy that became known as shuttle diplomacy, as he mediated between Israel and its Arab neighbors on an ongoing basis.

The same year, Kissinger forged the "separation of forces" agreements between Israel and Egypt, then Israel and Syria. In 1975 he helped bring about the Israel-Egypt Sinai Interim Accord, which laid the groundwork for the 1979 peace treaty between those two countries. Even after Nixon resigned as president in August 1974, Kissinger was active in United States foreign policy. President Gerald Ford retained him as his secretary of state, a position Kissinger held until November 1976 when Jimmy Carter, a Democrat, defeated the Republican Ford in the presidential election.

When Kissinger left public service in 1977, the *New York Times* editorialized, "Henry Kissinger has not been President of the United States for the past eight years; it only seemed that way."

After leaving office, Kissinger wrote a series of memoirs. His book *Diplomacy*, published in 1994, provided a historical survey of international diplomacy, including a discussion of his own groundbreaking efforts. He also founded his own consulting firm, Kissinger Associates, which offered services as an advisor to major clients, giving them the benefit of his knowledge of foreign leaders and foreign-policy issues. In recent years, Kissinger has also frequently appeared on television to provide commentary on American foreign policy.

Kissinger married Ann Fleischer on February 6, 1949. They had two children, Elizabeth and David, and were divorced in 1964. In 1974 Kissinger married Nancy Maginnes.

Combining a keen intellect with an immense appreciation of the uses of military and political power, Kissinger was the dominant diplomatic force in America from 1969 to 1976. He is still looked to today as an influential leader and advisor because of his knowledge and experience in the worlds of politics, government, and diplomacy.

In October 2000, Kissinger suffered a heart attack, from which he fully recovered. Two years later, in December 2002, President George W. Bush chose him to lead a panel investigating the September 11, 2001, terrorist attacks against the United States. Kissinger accepted the appointment, only to resign several days later out of fear that he would either have to completely sever his association with his consulting firm or would be forced to disclose the identities of the firm's clients.

In 2004, at the age of eighty-one, Henry Kissinger continued to be in demand as a foreign-policy expert. In October 2004, transcripts of 3,200 phone conversations held between Kissinger and members of the media during his tenure as secretary of state were released under the Freedom of Information Act. A certain chumminess existed between the secretary and some journalists, as revealed in an exchange with Ted Koppel when he was ABC-TV's diplomatic correspondent. "It has been an extraordinary three years for me, and I have enjoyed it immensely," Koppel told Kissinger shortly before he was to leave office. "You are an intriguing man, and if I had a teacher like you earlier, I might not have been so cynical." To which Kissinger replied: "You have been a good friend."

CALVIN KLEIN

Pioneer in Casual Chic

Born November 19, 1942, in the Bronx, New York. American fashion designer. In 1969 Calvin Klein produced a small collection of six coats and three dresses that impressed the president of Bonwit Teller. Klein's impressive career took off thereafter. Thanks to Calvin Klein, American fashion has, starting in the 1970s, come into its own, rivaling French designs for top billing at the international shows. Klein helped pioneer casual chic, the unstructured style in couture that has become very popular.

BORN IN THE BRONX IN 1942 to Leo and Flore (Stern) Klein, Calvin Klein, even as a small child, wanted to own his own business. He inherited his preoccupation with clothes from his mother, who was a seamstress for the dress designer Hattie Carnegie. While other children played sports, Klein was sewing, sketching designs for clothes, and frequently visiting Loehmann's, a high-fashion discount store in the Bronx, looking for ideas and inspiration.

Klein grew up in a neighborhood of second-generation Jews and celebrated his bar mitzvah at the Mosholu Parkway Synagogue. He attended P.S. 80 and earned high grades there, though he claims that he had no great love of learning. In 1962, at the age of twenty, Klein graduated from Manhattan's Fashion Institute of Technology. He began working in the garment district, earning seventy-five dollars a week as an apprentice designer for manufacturer Dan Millstein.

In 1968, with two thousand dollars of his own money and ten thousand from his close friend Barry Schwartz, Klein founded his own firm, initially called Calvin Klein Ltd. For its first five years, the firm was located in a small suite at the York Hotel on Seventh Avenue. Klein then bought out Millstein and moved his firm, now named Calvin Klein Inc., to the heart of New York City's fashion district.

Klein made his first splash in the fashion business with an attractive trench coat. He capitalized on the fashion industry's early-1970s slump, a result of the new informality in clothes exhibited by many young people in a move to reject the dictates of high fashion by "dressing down."

Calvin Klein's first big order came from the fashionable New York department store Bonwit Teller for fifty thousand dollars worth of the trench coats. Although the store had ordered only the coats, Klein took advantage of an opportunity and personally wheeled his samples the twenty blocks up Seventh Avenue and over to the office of Bonwit's president, Mildred Custin. "What impressed me most," she said later, "was the purity of his line and the simplicity of his designs. 'Young man,' I said, 'you better raise your prices by ten dollars or you'll never make any money.'"

In his first year, Klein shipped one million dollars' worth of orders. His sales rose dramatically in subsequent years as his clothing became more in demand. Until 1972, Klein designed mainly two-piece suits and coats that gained great popularity for their simplicity and clear lines. He then started to create the "flexible" collections of interchangeable separates that made his clothes so popular. His clothes were described by one writer as "at once sporty and elegant, trim and fluid, that offer women—and, to a lesser extent, men—a wide range of clothes for round-the-clock wear."

Klein focused his design efforts on sportswear. "I felt that the American lifestyle had changed and that there was certainly a need for clothing to express and relate to that change." He worried that young women were avoiding the purchase of new clothes, rummaging through their attics to search for more vintage, comfortable clothing. In response to this trend, Klein was impelled to create new fashions that he hoped would appeal to young people enough to encourage their purchase and that would accommodate their lifestyles. He was in the forefront of the transition to longer lengths in skirts and coats.

As Klein told a reporter in the early seventies, "I never try to overpower the woman who wears my clothes . . . . It is ridiculous to spend everything on wearing apparel. Therefore I design for the new look, but with an everlasting feeling."

Klein believes that his ideal customer is not one of the "trophy wives or the woman who likes to decorate herself for her man. I dress the woman who is very busy. She has a job and children and boardroom meetings and lunches. She goes out to the theater or to see friends. For this she needs clothes, but clothes that are soft, easy, comfortable."

At first Klein's clothes were priced for the more inexpensive market and were made available to about a thousand stores. But by 1973 he had become more exclusive, distributing to only one fourth that number of stores. As the success of his designs grew, Klein's prices climbed, in part because he stopped using less expensive man-made fabrics. "Polyester feels slimy," he said. "It represents everything I hate. It's synthetic, it's fake, it's cheap."

Klein was one of the first American designers to translate the Paris-inspired full-skirted style into proportions that were suitable for American women who were trying to keep a slim figure. He emphasized how perfectly he had designed the coordination aspect of his fall line when he had models exchange coats and jackets as they passed on the runway.

In a nationwide poll of four hundred fashion reporters, Klein was chosen a winner of the 1973 Coty American Fashion Critics Awards. The citation commended his "superlative and consistent taste, his innate but nonconformist sense of classic line, never banal but always strong and feminine, and his unique understanding of today's blend of casualness, luxury, and moderate price."

The fashion show Klein staged at New York's Lincoln Center that year included nearly identical men's and women's styles of fur-collared melton overcoats, wool turtlenecks, slacks, and pea jackets. His men's clothes, Klein said, were designed with the same philosophy as his women's apparel: "to make a person feel comfortable without taking over his personality."

In 1974 and 1975, Calvin Klein won his second and third Coty "Winnies," and on June 25, 1975, he was elected to the American Hall of Fame of Fashion.

Reviewing the spring fashion collections of November 1977, Beverly Stephen wrote in the New York *Daily News*, "Thank God there are designers like Calvin Klein . . . who understand how to interpret the current fashion trend of bigger, looser clothes in sophisticated, subdued ways. You can never go wrong wearing one of Calvin Klein's unconstricted linen blazers, linen pants, [or] shawl collar charmeuse shirts. The clothes are young and sophisticated, but not bizarre."

Months before each collection is finalized, Klein visits Europe, mainly France, to look at fabrics. Returning to the United States, he works with domestic mills, sampling about fifty yards of each fabric to see how it feels, drapes, and cuts. Then he sketches his designs, after which his cutters, patternmakers, drapers, and button and trim buyers do their jobs. About eight-hundred pieces of clothing are actually made into samples and photographed before the final selection is made.

Klein married Jayne Centre in 1964; they were divorced ten years later. Klein's name dominated the nonfashion news when their daughter Marci was kidnaped on February 3, 1978, by a former babysitter. Klein paid the ransom and she was released unharmed—all within ten hours. Klein married his second wife, Kelly Rector, in 1986. In the spring of 1994, an unauthorized biography of Klein entitled *Obsession* appeared in bookstores. Among other revelations was the claim that Klein is bisexual, creating more headlines for the designer.

When Klein's underwear designs appeared for the first time in stores in 1983, he had no idea that the collection would be so successful. Klein designed underwear first for men, then for women. "I just tried to take it beyond the classic and the predictable, to give it more meaning," said Klein. "So now people lounge in it, swim in it, go out in it." Klein's underwear ads are known for their eroticism and controversy. Klein, however, sold his underwear company to Wernicke in early 1994 for nearly seventy million dollars.

Fragrance design by Klein was another surprise success. Klein's fragrance business, owned by Unilever, did $500 million a year of business in the United States and Europe in 1994, gaining a big profit for an American clothing designer trying his hand at perfume marketing.

Klein's business ran into financial problems in 1993, which caused some difficulty in repaying several debts he owed. David Geffen, the Hollywood producer and a longtime fan of Klein's, rescued the business by buying up all its outstanding debt securities for $45 million. With his financial difficulties behind him, Klein began talking of expanding, hoping to open Calvin Klein shops in many more major cities, including Hong Kong, Geneva (Switzerland), and Singapore. The Calvin Klein organization says its worldwide sales at wholesale prices are now over one billion dollars a year, including licensed products.

In 1995 Klein undertook a series of advertising campaigns that sparked a great deal of controversy. When critics likened his jean ads, which used minors as models, to child pornography, he was forced to withdraw them. A second ad campaign featuring a young man showing off his Klein briefs was attacked as pornography by the American Family Association.

In its June 17, 1996 issue, *Time* magazine named Klein one of America's twenty-five most influential people, saying that he "remained Seventh Avenue's most devout modernist, its preeminent avatar of form-follows-function thinking."

Calvin Klein has injected a whole new practicality, sensibility, and sophistication into the fashion world. His designs continue to be more popular than ever and have definitely made their mark around the world.

On December 16, 2002, Calvin Klein surprised many by announcing that he was selling his eponymous company to Phillips-Van Heusen, America's largest shirtmaker, for $400 million in cash plus $30 million in stock and as much as $300 million in royalties linked to revenue over a fifteen-year period. The sale afforded the Calvin Klein company the financial capability to expand into Asia and Europe. Klein himself pledged to remain with the firm.

TEDDY KOLLEK

Longtime Mayor of Jerusalem

Born May 27, 1911, in Nagybaszony, Austro-Hungarian Empire. Israeli political figure. A kibbutznik at first, Teddy Kollek helped accumulate weaponry from the United States for Israel's 1948 War of Independence. Kollek served as director-general of Prime Minister David Ben-Gurion's office from 1952 until 1964 but is best known as the feisty, outspoken mayor of Jerusalem, a post he held from 1965 to 1993. After the 1967 Six-Day War, when Israel captured East Jerusalem, Kollek won the respect of the city's Arabs and presided over a much-praised Israeli-Arab coexistence in the Holy City.

TEDDY KOLLEK was born in 1911, the son of Alfred Kollek and Margaret (Fleischer) Kollek, in Nagybaszony, a small town on the Danube River near Budapest in the Austro-Hungarian Empire. He was named after the founder of modern Zionism, Theodor Herzl. His father was an employee of a Hungarian timber company owned by the Vienna Rothschilds. When Kollek was a few months old, the family moved to Vienna, where Alfred Kollek managed a branch of the Rothschild bank.

Even as a youngster, Kollek had Zionist convictions. While studying at the Vienna Gymnasium (secondary school), he worked for a Zionist youth organization called *T'helet Lavan*. In 1931, at age twenty, he was associated with the Palestine-based He-Halutz, teaching young Jews living in Europe self-defense skills. In 1935 Kollek immigrated to Palestine. His parents reached Palestine three years later.

In 1937 Kollek helped found kibbutz Ein Gev on the eastern shore of the Sea of Galilee (Lake Tiberias), and served as its treasurer. On peaceful days, he carried bags of gravel to construction sites; on less peaceful days, he helped Ein Gev defend itself against Arab attacks. In May of that year, Kollek married Tamar Schwarz, a rabbi's daughter whom he had known in Vienna; they have a son, Amos, and a daughter, Osnat.

Between 1938 and 1940, Kollek traveled in Europe representing He-Halutz. In 1939, while in Vienna, he convinced Adolf Eichmann to allow three thousand Jewish youngsters, then in concentration camps, to leave Europe for England. In 1940 David Ben-Gurion, the unofficial prime minister of the *Yishuv* in Palestine, sent Kollek to Istanbul to work with Allied intelligence in contacting the Jewish underground. After the war, Kollek helped thousands of Holocaust survivors reach Palestine and settle there.

Kollek arrived in New York in 1947 on a secret mission, sent by the Haganah, the defense arm of the *Yishuv*, to locate and secure weapons for its anticipated war against the Arabs. From his base in a New York hotel, Kollek directed a network of clandestine arms dealers

State of Israel Government Press Office

Teddy Kollek

who diverted surplus military supplies to Israel. In 1948, the year the state of Israel was established, Kollek negotiated a deal that sent a number of warplanes, including B-17s, to Israel.

In 1949 Kollek was appointed head of the United States division of the Israel Foreign Ministry, through which he developed close ties to the American intelligence community. As Israel's plenipotentiary in the United States, Kollek sought American aid for Israel and set up the first Israeli bond drive in 1951.

Prime Minister Ben-Gurion recalled Kollek to Jerusalem in 1952 to become director-general of his office, a post Kollek held for the next thirteen years. He handled a range of responsibilities including making arrangements for the trial of Adolf Eichmann and creating the Israeli government tourist office.

When Ben-Gurion stepped down as prime minister in 1963, Kollek stayed on and worked for the new prime minister, Levi Eshkol, in the same capacity. He left the government in 1964 to become chairman of the board of the Israel Museum, which opened in 1965.

That year Kollek joined Ben-Gurion when he broke with Eshkol and the Mapai party to create the dissident Rafi party. Ben-Gurion urged a reluctant Kollek to challenge the incumbent Mordechai Ish-Shalom for election as mayor of Jerusalem, which he did. Kollek was elected and took office on December 1, 1965.

During the first eighteen months that Kollek presided over West Jerusalem, then divided from Jordanian-controlled East Jerusalem by a ten-foot wall, shooting incidents occurred from time to time between the two opposing factions; this presented him with a major challenge as he sought to make the city seem more attractive to residents and visitors alike.

During the Six-Day War of June 1967, after Jordan began shelling West Jerusalem, Kollek toured the city by car to maintain calm among Israeli residents and to assure them that emergency repairs to damaged areas were being carried out. Kollek's area of responsibility suddenly broadened when Israel captured East Jerusalem, including the historic Old City, on June 7.

The East Jerusalem Arabs refused to recognize Israeli sovereignty over their neighborhoods, but Kollek nevertheless worked diligently to unite the two parts of the city by linking the newly annexed Arab area to Israel's existing water, telephone, and electricity systems. He often displayed a sensitivity to Arab concerns and needs that left him unpopular with more hard-line members of the Israeli government.

In 1968 Kollek assailed the Israeli leadership for not translating into Arabic the government proclamations that affected East Jerusalem. He also scolded Israeli government officials who demanded that residents of East Jerusalem line up for processing without separating the sexes as Muslim custom dictated. "Some people seem to think that if we make it hard for the Arabs, they'll leave," Kollek noted. "Believe me, they won't."

Kollek knew that he had his work as mayor cut out for him. "They tell us that unifying Berlin is problematic," he once said, "but Berliners are all Christian and speak the same language. So I say that we need patience, but eventually there will be harmony in Jerusalem."

Kollek considered the restoration and rejuvenation of the city of Jerusalem a personal mandate. He personally oversaw the construction of its playgrounds, libraries, clinics, youth centers, museums, and parks. Because of his efforts, the holy city hosted an international book fair, international cultural festivals, and countless other events. In contrast with the divided, dangerous, unpleasant pre-1967 Jerusalem, Kollek helped the united Jerusalem attract more than one million tourists a year.

In Naomi Shepherd's 1988 book entitled *Teddy Kollek, Mayor of Jerusalem*, the biographer described him as "a doer, a filler of vacuums, a man always in search of a hole to dig or a stockade to put up." Kollek set up the Jerusalem Foundation to attract overseas donors for social and cultural projects; these would not otherwise have been developed because of the lack of government funds to execute them.

Kollek's success as mayor depended to a large extent on keeping up good relations with the Arab residents of East Jerusalem, and his methods worked because he made sure that Israeli rule did not interfere with the Arab way of life. Arabs were allowed to retain control over their education system as well as the Temple Mount and other Islamic holy places. They were also allowed to retain Jordanian citizenship. Kollek's fairness won him respect among many East Jerusalem Arabs. All official letters coming from the mayor's office bore a stamp that read, "Let's be more tolerant."

For two decades, Kollek kept Jerusalem from exploding; for that he was frequently called "the most important mayor in the world." Even during the Palestinian uprising known as the intifada, which began in December 1987, Jerusalem was less a source of Arab unrest than the West Bank or the Gaza Strip.

In 1993, at the age of eighty-two, it seemed to Kollek that he should retire rather than seek a seventh term as mayor. Labor party Prime Minister Yitzhak Rabin, not wanting to lose Jerusalem's governance to the Likud party, begged Kollek to run one more time. The Likud candidate, Ehud Olmert, years younger than Kollek, used the mayor's age as a ploy to defeat the popular incumbent. Olmert's campaign slogan was "It's time for a change," an obvious reference to Kollek's age and length of office. Olmert thus defeated his octogenarian opponent.

In 2001 Kollek celebrated his ninetieth birthday with a big bash at the Jerusalem Biblical Zoo. The next year, President Moshe Katzav surprised him with a party at the President's Residence in Jerusalem.

That same month, Kollek told Israel's army radio station that Palestinians should be granted control over some parts of Jerusalem, including disputed holy sites in the Old City. "I think there needs to be an arrangement and we need to give something to them [the Arab residents of Jerusalem] and have part for ourselves. Listen, they [the 200,000 Arabs living in East Jerusalem] . . . feel that it is theirs. You can't achieve calm if you don't give them part of what they want and can control. There's no solution without this."

SANDY KOUFAX

One of Baseball's Best Pitchers

Born December 30, 1935, in Brooklyn, New York. American baseball player. Sandy Koufax is considered one of baseball's greatest pitchers. He was the first player in the major leagues to pitch four no-hit games. Koufax won the Cy Young Award three times in four seasons, and in 1972 he was the youngest player to be admitted to the Baseball Hall of Fame in Cooperstown, New York. He was the *Sporting News* Pitcher of the Year each year from 1963 to 1966. During his career, Koufax struck out 2,396 batters, pitched forty shutouts, and set numerous major-league records, among them the most seasons (three) with three hundred or more strikeouts.

SANDY KOUFAX was born in the Borough Park section of Brooklyn, the son of Jack and Evelyn (Lichtenstein) Braun. His name at birth was Sandford Braun. When he was three years old, his parents divorced. Koufax and his mother lived for a time with her parents. When Sandy was nine years old, his mother remarried, and Koufax always thought of his mother's second husband, Irving Koufax, an attorney, as his real father.

In the fall of 1949, Sandy Koufax enrolled in Brooklyn's Lafayette High School. He played on its basketball and baseball teams, playing first base for the latter. After his high school graduation, Koufax was awarded an athletic scholarship to the University of Cincinnati because of his basketball record. In the fall of 1953, he began school there as an architecture major.

Despite his basketball scholarship, Koufax excelled at baseball in college. In the first two games Koufax pitched for the University's baseball team, he struck out thirty-four batters. A sportswriter, Jimmy Murphy, informed the Brooklyn Dodgers of Koufax's pitching talents and the Dodgers offered the student a spot on the team. His yearly salary of six thousand dollars was supplemented by a fourteen thousand dollar bonus, giving him a very good total income for that era. Two weeks before Koufax turned nineteen, on December 14, 1954, he signed with the Dodgers.

One condition of his getting the bonus was that Koufax had to spend two years with the Dodgers, thus robbing him of valuable experience playing in the minor leagues before hitting the big-time pressures. Spring training in 1955 proved difficult for him. "I was so nervous and tense, I couldn't throw the ball for ten days." Koufax remembered. "When I finally started pitching, I felt I should throw as hard as I could. I wound up with an arm so sore that I had to rest for another week."

Sandy Koufax inducted into the Hall of Fame at Cooperstown, N.Y., August 7, 1972.

Koufax's first start for the Dodgers was on July 6, 1955. He pitched just over four innings, striking out four batters and walking eight. On August 27th, in his second start, he did better: he shut out the Cincinnati Reds on two hits, striking out fourteen batters, the most in a game by a National League pitcher that year. In his two other starts that season, he lasted one inning in one and shut out the Pittsburgh Pirates on five hits in the other.

For the next six years, Koufax had, as he said, "good periods, bad periods—mostly bad." In his first six seasons, he won thirty-six games and lost forty. He had one day of glory in 1959 when he struck out eighteen batters, tying the major-league record set two decades earlier by Cleveland Indian pitcher Bob Feller.

In 1960, with the Dodgers now in Los Angeles, Koufax was 8-13, ready to throw in the towel. Vowing to work harder during the next spring training, he asked to pitch more frequently in order to improve his control. Dodger pitcher Don Newcombe encouraged him to run more. That season, 1961, Koufax was 18-13, striking out 269 batters to break a league record held by the legendary Christy Mathewson. From 1961 to 1966, Koufax won 129 games and lost only 47.

During the 1962 season, when he was well on his way to a great season, Koufax was forced to stay out of uniform at its midpoint because of an injury. He was 14-14, with 209 strikeouts, an earned-run average of 2.06, and a no-hitter under his belt, when his index finger on his pitching hand grew numb, and he could not produce a curve ball. Physicians thought his finger might have to be amputated, which would have ended Koufax's career. But in the end his doctors were able to treat his injured finger with anticoagulants, bringing him back to health and baseball.

The following season, 1963, was Koufax's greatest. He was 13-3 by mid-July, including a no-hitter. He wound up the season at 25-5, striking out 306 batters, a figure topped by only three others since 1900. His eleven shutouts were a major-league record for a left-hander in one season, and his 311 innings pitched were the most by a National League left-hander since 1921. Koufax's earned-run average of 1.88 was the major league's best for the second year running. In the World Series against the New York Yankees, his two victories were crucial in helping the Dodgers win the championship. Koufax was unanimously named Cy Young Award winner as the best pitcher in the majors that year. He also won the National League's Most Valuable Player award.

In 1964 Koufax posted a 19-5 record, with an earned-run average of 1.74, before an arm ailment sidelined him at the end of August. On June 4th of that year, he pitched his third no-hitter, tying the major league record.

In 1965, despite arthritis in his elbow, Koufax won twenty-six games and struck out 382 batters to break Bob Feller's major-league record of 348. On September 9th, Koufax

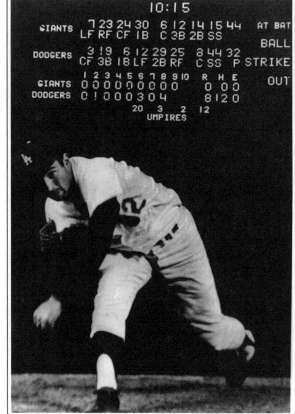

1963 game, Sandy Koufax's final pitch in his second of four career no-hitters.

pitched a perfect game against the Chicago Cubs, the fourth no-hitter of his career. He again won the Cy Young Award.

A host of stories, many of them simply not accurate, have developed surrounding Sandy Koufax's relationship to his Jewish faith. One that appears to be true is that the Dodgers took the Jewish High Holy Days into consideration so that Koufax could pitch as much as possible during September and October every year. Another, which Koufax himself denies, has it that because of Koufax, the Dodger clubhouse was stocked with bagels, lox, and chopped chicken liver, all traditional Jewish foods.

One incident that Koufax confirmed took place in October 1965, when the Dodgers and Minnesota Twins were playing in the World Series. The opening game fell on Yom Kippur, the holiest day of the Jewish Year, and Koufax was not at the ballpark. The Dodgers lost that game. The following morning the St. Paul *Pioneer Press* carried a sports column containing a few veiled and uncomplimentary references to Koufax's unwillingness to pitch the opening game of the Series. The column concluded, "The Twins love matzo balls on Thursdays." The Yom Kippur game was played on a Thursday.

"I couldn't believe it," Koufax responded. "I thought that kind of thing went out with dialect comics." He pitched the second game later that day and the Dodgers lost. But he pitched the seventh and deciding game, which the Dodgers won, capturing the World Series title.

In 1966 Koufax earned the highest salary paid a baseball player at that time: $135,000. His doctor wanted Koufax to quit at the start of that year because of his continuing injuries, but Koufax persevered and finished the season with an impressive 27-9 record, including winning the game that clinched the pennant for the Dodgers. He did so after only two days' rest. He turned in the third lowest earned-run average (1.73) of any major-league pitcher and won the Cy Young Award for an unprecedented third time. The Dodgers lost four straight in that year's World Series, and after that Koufax announced his retirement.

Koufax did brief stints as a television commentator and as an electrical appliance salesman, but he returned to the Dodgers in 1979 as a pitching instructor. He served in that capacity for eleven years, resigning in 1990 at the age of fifty-five.

In 1989 the Stage Deli, a Manhattan eatery famed for its Jewish specialties, took a poll to decide who should be on the all-time Jewish All-Star baseball team. Not surprisingly, Koufax received the most votes.

Sandy Koufax is married to actor Richard Widmark's daughter, Anne. He is a member of the Jewish Sports Hall of Fame in Israel and the Baseball Hall of Fame in Cooperstown, New York.

Koufax has spent many springs at the Los Angeles Dodgers' training camp in Vero Beach, Florida, tutoring the Dodger pitching staff.

In March 1998 the sixty-two-year-old Koufax showed up at the New York Mets' pre-season training at Port St. Lucie, Florida. A friend who was a pitching coach for the Mets had invited him for the day. Koufax now makes his home in Vero Beach, Florida, 30 miles from the Mets camp.

The Hall-of-Famer talked about how a pitcher had to establish himself early in the game; how he could not be afraid to pitch around an opponent's best hitter; how he had to learn to pitch away; and how he had to learn not to be afraid to fail.

Koufax told the Mets' pitchers to go out and throw every day with the idea of pitching a perfect game, and if it's no longer perfect, think about throwing a one-hitter and then a two-hitter and a three-hitter. "Fight for every out you can," Koufax told them.

Ordinarily shunning publicity, Koufax told stories to the pitchers that day of how he pitched around Hank Aaron and how he struck out Mickey Mantle in the 1963 World Series.

In the fall of 2002, *Sandy Koufax: A Lefty's Legacy*, by former *Washington Post* sports and feature writer Jane Leavy, was published and fast became a bestseller. For this well-researched work, Leavy interviewed hundreds of Koufax's teammates, rivals, fans, and childhood pals.

During spring training of 2004, Koufax met with pitchers for the Florida Marlins, who peppered him with questions about their favorite subject: pitching. Koufax noted that there are three main differences between pitchers of his era and those of the first decade of the twenty-first century. Today's pitchers, he said, are bigger and stronger, and some use a split-finger fastball.

RALPH LAUREN

Preeminent American Fashion Designer

Born October 14, 1939, in the Bronx, New York. American fashion designer. Ralph Lauren began his career designing men's ties, later branching out into a wide range of menswear items as well as fashions for women. Lauren built a nearly four-billion-dollar fashion empire that extends beyond clothing into perfume, shoes, and luggage. What separates Lauren from other designers is his ability to create products that exude an aura of old money and good breeding. His classic designs came to define the American well-heeled look in the 1980s.

R ALPH LAUREN, the youngest of four children, was born Ralph Lifshitz in the Bronx in 1939. In 1955 he and his two brothers, Jerome and Leonard, eagerly changed their surname to Lauren in response to constant teasing and abuse from their schoolmates.

Lauren has long resented the accusation that he changed his name to run away from his Judaism. "It's totally untrue. If my name had been Levine or Schwartz, it would never have been changed," Lauren said. "The real reason was that it had the word *shit* in it. That was a very difficult name to grow up with." He chose the name Lauren because it sounded "nice."

Ralph Lauren, several of whose uncles were cantors, grew up in an observant Jewish home in which the dietary laws were kept. He was given a yeshiva education through the elementary grades.

As a youngster, Lauren was interested in sports and addicted both to the movies and to F. Scott Fitzgerald's novels. In the seventh grade, he developed an interest in clothes. "My friends were the hoods wearing motorcycle jackets," he recalled in 1978, "but I was wearing tweed bermudas and button-down shirts."

Ralph Lauren

176

While a student at DeWitt Clinton High School in the Bronx, Lauren worked part-time as a stock boy at Alexander's department store. He spent a good deal of his fifty-dollars-a-week salary on clothes; he would save for weeks to purchase a Brooks Brothers suit. He was known as the only kid in the neighborhood who dressed nicely. Lauren became a full-time salesman at Alexander's after high school. He began taking night-school business courses at the City College of New York, but dropped out of the program within a few months because he found it boring.

Following service in the United States Army, Ralph Lauren became an assistant buyer for Allied Stores. He tried to get started on a career in designing by applying to Brooks Brothers and other menswear manufacturers, but with no portfolio and no sketches, he got nowhere.

In 1967 Lauren was hired by Beau Brummell Ties, Inc. Taking a daring approach, he designed ties four or five inches wider than the standard three-inch width. In his first year, 1967, sales of the controversial wide, bright ties reached half a million dollars. Lauren soon formed his own tie manufacturing company, which he called Polo.

Since wider ties made a larger knot, in 1968 Lauren started to design shirts with larger collars, followed by suit jackets with wider lapels. He began to add shirts, suits, knitwear, coats, shoes, and luggage to his Polo line.

For his fall 1970 major menswear collection, Lauren designed an unorthodox dinner suit that was comprised of a jacket with wide lapels, a white textured shirt, and red-and-black checked trousers, which created a stir and made everyone take notice. In response to such interesting designs, which were gaining a following, Bloomingdale's in New York City opened a special shop to showcase Lauren's clothes. He also won the 1970 Coty Menswear Award.

Lauren launched a women's line in 1971 and presented his first complete women's collection the next year. It featured small-collared, man-tailored shirts in soft cotton and handkerchief linen. "I didn't think it was necessary for a woman to dress like a vamp, like Jean Harlow or Marilyn Monroe, to look attractive," Lauren explained. "Clothing represents lifestyle, it represents a better life. It sort of formulates your life. If you were watching a Western movie as a kid and you said, 'I want to be there in the West,' then when you wore those clothes, you were there, you became a cowboy. That's why we buy clothes, not just because of a pretty color that we spot."

In 1973 Lauren introduced shawl-collared, Shaker-knit sweaters in black or white, meant to be a substitute for the standard dinner jacket; for informal wear, he designed a casual shirt-jacket to replace the usual blazer. In 1974 he designed the clothes worn by Robert Redford, Bruce Dern, and Sam Waterston in the film *The Great Gatsby*. Lauren, an Anglophile, believed that the ideal way for men to dress was to look like Englishmen in the country.

During the mid-1970s, Lauren's collections for women focused on conservatively cut, well-tailored, interchangeable separates, including a trim white wool turtleneck sweater and a trouser-top-waisted taupe-colored corduroy skirt. *Vogue* magazine opined that Lauren's 1976 collection was his best. "All the things he has always stood for—great fabrics (the best tweeds and Shetlands in the world!); great cutting and tailoring (he can set a small, perfect, feminine shoulder in a sports jacket and still leave room for a sweater); great country/sportswear dressing right across the board—this year they've all come together in the best Ralph Lauren collection ever."

In May 1979, Lauren shared the first Coty group award with fellow designers Geoffrey Beene,

Ralph Lauren

Calvin Klein, and Halston. Entering the new Coty Hall of Fame, they were cited for their roles in developing a purely American look that helped make New York City competitive with Paris as a fashion capital.

Lauren married Ricky (Low-Beer), a former schoolteacher, in 1964; they have two sons, Andrew, born in 1970, and David, born in 1972, and a daughter, Dylan, born in 1975.

He owns elegant homes in Manhattan, Colorado, Jamaica (West Indies), and Westchester County (New York), and maintains a jet for his personal use.

Lauren has built the largest private empire in American fashion. As of March 1994, Polo Ralph Lauren, with its three thousand employees, had worldwide retail sales for all products of $3.9 billion. There are 130 Polo Ralph Lauren stores, fifty-five in the United States and another seventy-five abroad. In April 1986, Lauren opened his flagship store in the former Rhinelander Mansion on Madison Avenue and 72nd Street in New York. The company was privately held, with Ralph Lauren holding ninety percent ownership, until August 1994, when the investment bank of Goldman Sachs purchased twenty-eight percent of the company.

Lauren was the first to put his company logo on products such as perfume, hosiery, shoes, and luggage. Other designers soon adopted this method of marketing. He was one of the first designers with enough clout to compete with department stores by opening his own retail stores.

"The fashion of the nineties is about health," he says. "And when I say health, I don't mean doctors. I mean body-consciousness, being conscious of eating the right foods, throwing away the junk foods, feeling good on the inside, looking it on the outside."

Lauren has this to say about his own Jewishness in the 1990s. "It is still strongly rooted inside me," he observed, adding that he still attends synagogue on the holidays. "There is a cultural observance, a belief in God, and a connection."

Both of Lauren's parents died in 1994, events that caused Lauren to turn to his rabbi "to try to understand this Jewish religion that I'm connected to a little more."

In the early summer of 1997, Lauren took his company, Polo Ralph Lauren, public. By 2002 Lauren had become the world's best-selling fashion designer; retail customers were spending over $10 million a year on products bearing his name. He was pushing hard to penetrate the European market, planning to invest more than $1 billion on expansion there over the next five years.

In 2001 Polo Ralph Lauren reported about $2.4 billion in revenue. The second most popular designer, Giorgio Armani, reported about half that. Two-thirds of Lauren's sales originated in the U.S., only a quarter of which were to the female sector.

HERBERT LEHMAN

American Liberal Political Leader

Born March 28, 1878, in New York City; died December 3, 1963. American politician and banker. Herbert Lehman was a leading figure among American liberals. A champion of social legislation and a highly successful vote-getter, Lehman was elected to four consecutive terms as Governor of New York. He also served as a United States Senator for eight years. President Franklin Roosevelt called him "that good right arm of mine."

HERBERT LEHMAN was born in East New York, the youngest of the eight children of Mayer Lehman and Babette (Newgass) Lehman. In 1849 his father had emigrated from Germany to Montgomery, Alabama, then later settled in New York. Lehman's father and uncles made a fortune in a cotton-brokerage business that later evolved into the great investment banking house of Lehman Brothers. Lehman's mother was an ardent advocate of women's suffrage.

As a child, Lehman went with his father to see the free ward of Mount Sinai Hospital because the elder Lehman wanted to impress upon his son the obligations of wealth and the importance of a liberal government that supported access to social services for the disenfranchised. This early education and value system had a lasting effect on Lehman and influenced his political ideas throughout his career.

Lehman received his secondary education at Dr. Julius Sachs' School for Boys, a private school on the West Side of New York City, which had a predominantly Jewish student body. In 1895 he enrolled in Williams College. Though shy, he was chosen president of his class one year. Lehman also managed the track and football teams and was a member of the debating team. He graduated from Williams in 1899. He then served as a volunteer worker at the Henry Street Settlement in New York City. That year, he entered the textile manufacturing business. In 1908 he joined the family investment banking house as a partner.

Two years later, Lehman married Edith Luise Altschul, daughter of a San Francisco banker. They adopted three children. The Lehmans' son Peter was killed while in military service during World War II.

Herbert Lehman's interest in politics started in 1910 and in that year he was chosen as a delegate to the Democratic party convention from his Assembly district.

When World War I broke out, Lehman was turned down for infantry officer training since he was ten years over the age limit. Instead, still wanting to help in the war effort, he worked for several months in the office of Assistant Secretary of the Navy Franklin D. Roosevelt.

Courtesy of Lehman College

Herbert Lehman

Lehman then was commissioned a captain of the United States Army. He was promoted to colonel by war's end, at which time he was delegated to be in charge of procurement and transportation for the general staff. He was awarded the distinguished service medal, the highest award for noncombatant service.

In 1914 Lehman cofounded a popular social movement that became known as the American Joint Distribution Committee. He returned to Lehman Brothers after the war, and from 1924 to 1927 he served on a mediation committee in the garment industry that helped to resolve many labor disputes.

New York Governor Alfred E. Smith appointed Lehman chairman of a citizens' committee on finances for New York City in 1926. In that capacity, Lehman wrote a comprehensive report on the city's financial status. That same year, he also managed Smith's reelection campaign.

In his earlier days, Lehman had promised himself that when he reached fifty he would retire, as long as he could afford such a step. A millionaire many times over when he did reach that age, Lehman changed his mind, now suggesting that "fifty was just the beginning."

In 1928, at the age of fifty, the stocky, square-jawed Lehman quit his high-salaried job as senior partner at Lehman Brothers to run for Lieutenant Governor of New York. "He liked the process of negotiating a complicated arrangement," a fellow Lehman partner recalled, "but he was not heart and soul a businessman." Heading the slate as the candidate for governor was Franklin D. Roosevelt. Lehman served as Al Smith's financial chairman in his run for the United States presidency. In the election, Smith lost New York and the presidential election, but the Roosevelt-Lehman slate was triumphant.

In 1930 Roosevelt and Lehman were reelected, FDR calling Lehman "my good right arm." Lehman assisted the governor with financial and budgetary issues, specifically attempting to find ways to make the state's administration agencies and social services more efficient. Lehman was especially active in hospital and prison reform and on labor issues.

Lehman was elected governor of New York in 1932, going on to serve four consecutive terms. One of his greatest achievements in Albany was converting a state budget deficit of $106 million to an $80 million surplus by the time he left office. Because his public persona was serious and unemotional, Lehman did not seem like a politician. His great asset was his sincerity. So liberal was the Lehman administration that it was known as the "Little New Deal" in a reference to Lehman's alignment with FDR. He himself was dubbed "silent dynamite."

As governor, Lehman introduced a comprehensive program of liberal legislation and obtained legislative passage of statutes that expanded low-cost housing, improved unemployment insurance benefits, and increased the minimum wage.

Legendary stories of Lehman's humane character abounded. Once, when he felt that his name in a prospectus had encouraged stockholders to invest in a business that failed, he paid them off himself. On another occasion, a bird flew into a wall of glass at his Westchester house and broke its neck; he took the glass out and built a solid wall. Another time at an Albany hotel, he took a heavy pile of laundry from the arms of an elderly chambermaid and carried it himself to the basement.

In 1942, a few weeks before his fourth term as governor was to end, Lehman resigned in order to accept an FDR appointment in the State Department, directing the distribution of American food, clothing, and medicine to war-torn populations during World War II. The following year, Lehman was chosen by the forty-four nations comprising the new United Nations Relief and Rehabilitation Administration (UNRRA) to be its first director-general.

Stepping down from that post in 1946, Lehman began dealing with the plight of Jewish refugees who wanted to establish a home in Palestine. Lehman favored free Jewish immigration to Palestine and, once the state of Israel was established in 1948, he became one of its strong supporters. Later, in 1958, he chaired the committee to celebrate Israel's tenth anniversary. Lehman was a highly successful fund-raiser for the Federation of Jewish Philanthropies, the United Jewish Appeal, and other charities. He helped organize the Joint Distribution Committee, the Palestine Loan Bank, and Palestine Ecomonic Corporation.

In 1946 Lehman sought the United States Senate seat from New York, running against Irving M. Ives, the former majority leader of the State Assembly. Lehman was unsuccessful in his bid, the only time in nine election campaigns that he would suffer defeat.

In 1949 Lehman won the race to fill the unexpired term (just fourteen months) of New York's Senator Robert F. Wagner, a Democrat who had resigned from the Senate because of ill health, defeating the Republican party candidate, John Foster Dulles. Lehman was elected to a full six-year term in 1950. He was a strong backer of the Fair Deal program, the domestic plan that President Harry Truman put before Congress to deal with employment, education, health care, agriculture, and civil-rights issues of the era. (Congress, however, rejected most of the Fair Deal.)

Known as the "conscience of the Senate," in the early 1950s Lehman was one of a few senators willing to dispute the witch-hunting tactics of Senator Joseph McCarthy. Lehman clashed sharply at times with McCarthy on the Senate floor.

Just before his second term as senator ended in 1956, Lehman, who was seventy-eight years old, announced he would not seek reelection. In 1963 he suffered a fatal heart attack. He was eighty-five years old and was about to leave his New York apartment to travel to Washington, D.C. There he was to receive the Presidential Medal of Freedom, the nation's highest peacetime award.

Lehman was known as a financier who combined his personal fortune and political power to gain reforms, to guarantee individual freedoms through legislative action, and to provide succor to the poor and needy. His commitment to his fellow man and dedication to making his country a better place for everyone are legendary and created the legacy of good works for which he is remembered.

WALTER LIPPMANN

Dean of American Journalists

Born September 23, 1889, in New York City; died December 14, 1974. American journalist and political analyst. The most respected American journalist of the twentieth century, Walter Lippmann was best known for his column "Today and Tomorrow," which appeared first in the New York *Herald Tribune* in 1931, and eventually in syndicated form in over 250 newspapers in twenty-five countries. Lippmann won the Pulitzer Prize for Journalism in both 1958 and 1962.

WALTER LIPPMANN was the only child of Jacob and Daisy (Baum) Lippmann, both of German extraction. His grandfather, Louis Lippmann, had moved from Germany to New York City in 1848. Young Lippmann grew up in a Jewish neighborhood, although his parents endeavored to live the life of assimilated Jews.

His father, a wealthy clothing manufacturer and real-estate broker, was able to nourish his son's obvious intellectual talents, which he exhibited even in childhood. To broaden the youngster's horizons, Walter was frequently taken on vacations abroad by his parents where he was exposed to European art, literature, and music.

At the age of seven, Lippmann was enrolled in Dr. Julius Sachs' School for Boys. Over the next decade, he won prizes for academic excellence and also wrote articles for student journals. Lippmann entered Harvard University in 1906, and although he completed his degree *cum laude* in three years, he waited to graduate with his class in 1910. While at Harvard, Lippmann studied philosophy, economics, and political science, and met his intellectual hero, the philosopher William James. In his senior year, Lippmann

Walter Lippmann

Associated Press

assisted George Santayana in the teaching of a course in the history of philosophy. He served as president of the Harvard Socialist Club, devoting many hours to discussions on social and economic problems.

In 1910 Lippmann briefly worked as a reporter for the weekly Boston *Common*. Then, for one year, he worked for Lincoln Steffens, the American muckraking journalist, helping to prepare articles for *Everybody's Magazine*, which was dedicated to exposing corruption in government and big business. Lippmann became editor of the magazine in 1911. Trying to put some of his ideas into practice, Lippmann served as executive secretary to Rev. George R. Lunn, the Socialist mayor of Schenectady, New York, in 1912.

In 1913 Lippmann published his first book, *A Preface to Politics*, which focused on the faults of the modern industrial system and

Walter Lippmann

the need for reform. Whereas liberals liked the book, socialists gave it only qualified approval.

A year later, Lippmann was one of the founders (the other was Herbert Croly) of the Liberal weekly *The New Republic* and was chosen to be its associate editor. While often agreeing with the policies of President Woodrow Wilson, the publication, Lippmann insisted, was not intended to be a mouthpiece for the administration. That same year, 1914, Lippmann wrote his book *Drift and Mastery*, in which he found great fault with the entire socialist movement, especially with Marxism. By the time he wrote *The Good Society* in 1917, Lippmann had rejected socialism altogether.

Lippmann married Faye Abertson on May 24, 1917. They were eventually divorced, and in 1938 he married Helen Byrne Armstrong. Lippmann had no children.

While Lippmann did not conceal the fact that he was Jewish, he did not discuss his own Jewishness, nor would he join Jewish organizations or even accept awards from them. He was sometimes harsh on his Jewish brethren, blaming some, particularly those who were conspicuous and ostentatious, for encouraging anti-Semitism. He was also bothered by the Zionist argument that American Jews, himself included, should feel an allegiance to a Jewish state.

In 1917, after the United States had finally entered World War I, Lippmann was appointed assistant to Secretary of War Newton D. Baker. Soon after, Lippmann began working for a research organization under Colonel Edward M. House, advisor to President Wilson, that was mandated to collect ethnic, political, and geographical information for use at the expected post-war peace conference.

Lippmann took on several other wartime assignments, including propaganda work in Europe. He also attended the Versailles Peace Conference as a member of the American Commission to Negotiate Peace. Returning to New York in March 1919, Lippmann resumed working for *The New Republic*, although he soon left the magazine to write a book.

In 1921 Lippmann accepted an offer to join the editorial staff of the *New York World*, a crusading daily newspaper that had a reputation for attacking corruption, poverty, and injustice. A year later, his book *Public Opinion* was published; it examined the difficulties in informing citizens of the complex issues that faced contemporary society. From 1923 to 1929, Lippmann directed the *World*'s editorial page. Starting in 1929, he edited the newspaper until it ceased publication in February 1931.

While at the *New York World*, Lippmann often used its pages to criticize the Republican Harding, Coolidge, and Hoover administrations. It surprised those who followed his editorials when he joined the staff of the New York *Herald Tribune*, a mouthpiece for the Republican party. Lippmann's first column appeared on September 8, 1931, and the newspaper promised readers that Lippmann would be independent, that he would "write freely . . . expressing whatever opinions he holds." Lippmann was allowed great editorial freedom, which he utilized.

The column, called "Today and Tomorrow," was at first published four times a week, then later cut back to three times weekly. By the early 1960s, the column, appearing twice a week, was syndicated in over 250 newspapers in twenty-five countries. Lippmann was awarded the Pulitzer Prize twice, in 1958 and 1962. In awarding him his first Pulitzer Prize, the judges commended Lippmann for "the wisdom, perception, and high sense of responsibility with which he has commented for many years on national and international affairs." Lippmann's second Pulitzer was also awarded to him for his highly regarded contributions to journalism. According to historians, Lippmann's columns had a direct influence on American foreign and domestic policy.

Analyzing world affairs in a calm, serious, sometimes scholarly manner, Lippmann avoided scoops, forecasts, denunciation, and gossip. His political philosophy, having shifted from socialism to liberalism, now shifted even further right, to neoconservatism. Each winter season, Lippmann would set out for a different part of the world. Heads of foreign governments, with whom he met regularly, prepared for his visits with care.

During World War II, in both his column and in his books *U.S. Foreign Policy: Shield of the Republic* (1943) and *U.S. War Aims* (1944), Lippmann argued forcefully that the United States should not adopt a policy of isolation during the post-war period. "He was as much as any one other single person the original architect of the Atlantic Alliance," wrote Joseph C. Harsch in the New York *Herald Tribune* on March 19, 1961.

In July 1960, Lippmann agreed to do a series of programs for *CBS Reports* in which he was interviewed for one hour for each installment. In these interviews, which were well received, Lippmann offered his impressions of world leaders and many other subjects. In 1962 he won the prestigious George Foster Peabody Award for having done "the most to promote international understanding during 1961."

For many years Lippmann insisted that controversies arising from the Cold War should be resolved through diplomatic means, not combat. In a 1961 television interview, Lippmann noted, "I don't think old men ought to promote wars for young men to fight."

Toward the end of his career, Lippmann wrote a regular column for *Newsweek* magazine. He retired in 1967 and died at the age of eighty-five in 1974.

The late James Reston, of the *New York Times*, wrote of Lippmann: "He has given my generation of newspapermen a wider vision of our duty. He has shown us how to put the event of the day in its proper relationship to the history of yesterday and the dream of tomorrow."

NORMAN MAILER

Enfant Terrible *of American Letters*

Born January 31, 1923, in Long Branch, New Jersey. American novelist. A controversial figure in twentieth-century American literature, Norman Mailer became instantly famous when his bestselling World War II novel *The Naked and the Dead* was published in 1948. His mistrust of authoritarian tendencies within the United States made him a patron saint of the burgeoning hippie movement of the 1960s. Mailer's book *Armies of the Night* (1968), a personal account of the four-day antiwar protest in Washington, D.C., in 1967, during which Mailer was arrested, won a Pulitzer Prize. Considered a brilliant though erratic writer, Mailer has been one of the dominant literary figures of post-World War II America.

NORMAN MAILER was born in Long Branch, New Jersey, in 1923. His father, Isaac Barnett Mailer, was a struggling accountant who had immigrated to America from South Africa via England. His mother, Fanny (Schneider) Mailer, was the daughter of Chaim Yehudah Schneider, the unofficial rabbi of Long Branch, New Jersey. Mailer once said of his mother: "She didn't care what [anyone] ended up doing—if he was famous and Jewish, that was good enough for her." Mailer's father thought his son's genius came from exposure to Rabbi Schneider.

The Mailer family moved from New Jersey to the Eastern Parkway section of Brooklyn when Mailer was four years old. He began writing when he was nine. At his mother's suggestion, Mailer wrote a story called "An Invasion of Mars." Writing a chapter a day, he filled two notebooks with the tale, but spent most of his leisure time building model airplanes. An excellent student both at P.S. 161 and Boys High School in Brooklyn, he hoped to become an aeronautical engineer.

Norman Mailer

Mailer had his bar mitzvah at Congregation Sharei Zedek in Brooklyn. In his speech, which revolved about the philosopher Baruch Spinoza, Mailer also expressed a wish to emulate "great Jews like Moses Maimonides and Karl Marx."

In 1939, at the age of sixteen, Mailer began his freshman year as an engineering student at Harvard University. The next year he wrote a number of short stories. One of them, "The Greatest Thing in the World," won *Story* magazine's college contest for 1941. During the summer of 1942, Mailer worked at a state mental hospital in Boston. Drawing upon that experience, Mailer wrote a novel called *A Transit to Narcissus* that was never published. Mailer described it as "romantic, morbid, twisted, and heavily tortured."

Despite his bar mitzvah, Norman took little interest in Judaism. During his childhood he described himself as an atheist and thought it a bit unpleasant to be Jewish. He was not ashamed of his Jewish heritage; he simply did not want to make it a major part of his life or be burdened by it. "I am not a typical Jew," he told one interviewer, admitting that he had spent his childhood "rejecting Jewishness at a great rate." Rarely thought of as a Jewish-American writer, he used specifically Jewish characters only in his first novel, *The Naked and the Dead*.

Mailer was awarded his degree in engineering from Harvard in 1943. While at the college, he had encountered some mild anti-Semitism. He acknowledged later that it "never occurred to us [Jews] that we were in an incredibly subtle ghetto."

After graduation, Mailer was inducted into the United States Army, serving as an infantry-man in the Philippines until the end of World War II. After the war, he served as a part of the United States occupation forces in Japan. Discharged in 1946, Mailer settled in New York with his wife, Beatrice Silverman, whom he had married two years earlier. He spent the next fifteen months writing *The Naked and the Dead*, which was published in 1948. Brock Bower, writing in *Life* magazine, noted that Mailer "made the GI a kind of holy figure and the GI's mother tongue (including obscenities) a new vulgate in American letters." The book sold almost two hundred thousand copies in its first year of publication.

Mailer flirted with communism in the late 1940s, then wrote *Barbary Shore* in 1951, a book that expressed his disillusionment with communism and his dismay that the United States government was becoming, in his view, more authoritarian. The book received negative reviews.

In 1951 Mailer left his first wife, with whom he had one daughter. He moved to the Greenwich Village area of New York City and helped found a weekly alternative newspaper, *The Village Voice*. In 1954 he married Adele Morales. They had two daughters.

Around that time, Mailer expounded his philosophy of "hip," or "American existentialism," in an essay entitled "The White Negro." He described the "hipster" as someone who understood that the only way to cope with life's woes—the threat of atomic warfare, the heavy hand of government, or the tendency toward conformity—was "to accept the terms of death, to live with death as immediate danger, to divorce oneself from society, to exist without roots, to set out on that uncharted journey into the rebellious imperative of the self."

In 1955 Mailer wrote *An American Dream*, which appeared in serial form in *Esquire* magazine. The novel covers two wild, violent, sex-ridden days in the life of Stephen Rojack, a war hero and former Congressman who is consumed by his own animal instincts. Critics disagreed about the book, some calling it "dreadful," others proclaiming it "powerful" and "electric."

Mailer spent four years writing his third novel, *The Deer Park* (1955), which was at first snubbed by critics but eventually considered one of his finest. Dealing with sex and drugs in Hollywood, its main character is Eital, a hip film director who is driven to psychopathic extremes.

This was the beginning of a bad period for Mailer. The critics' tepid reaction to *The Deer Park* aroused his anger, until one night he exploded. Toward the end of an all-night party at his Manhattan apartment on November 19, 1960, Mailer stabbed his wife, Adele, with a penknife, seriously wounding her. The once gentle, shy, quiet Mailer was arrested and given a suspended sentence when Adele refused to press charges. She made a complete recovery.

During the early 1960s, Mailer wrote monthly columns under the title "The Big Bite," for *Esquire* magazine. The best-known of his columns was "Superman Comes to Supermarket," a report on the 1960 Democratic National Convention portraying John F. Kennedy as Superman. Over the next three years, Mailer wrote numerous "open letters" to JFK in his columns, assailing the new president for not living up to his potential. These articles were collected in two books, *Advertisements for Myself* (1959) and *The Presidential Papers* (1963), both of which established Mailer as one of the best essayists in America.

In 1962 Mailer divorced Adele. He was married briefly that year to Lady Jean Campbell, with whom he had one daughter. In 1963 he married Beverly Bentley, an actress. They had two sons and were divorced in 1979. In November 1980 Mailer married singer Carol Stevens in order to "legitimize" (his phrase) their nine-year-old daughter Maggie. Immediately divorcing Stevens, Mailer married Norris Church, an art teacher, to "legitimize" their two-and-a-half-year-old son John Buffalo.

In 1967 Mailer wrote a stream-of-consciousness novel called *Why Are We in Vietnam?* Numerous critics assailed him for writing a novel that was, in fact, not about Vietnam. The next year, Mailer wrote *Armies of the Night*, a personal account of the four-day 1967 antiwar protest in Washington, D.C., during which he was arrested. The book won the Pulitzer Prize as well as the Polk and National Book Awards for 1968.

Reviewers praised Mailer's personalized reporting of the presidential nominating conventions of 1968, which appeared in his book published that same year, *Miami and the Siege of Chicago*. It was nominated for the National Book Award.

In 1970 Mailer wrote *A Fire on the Moon*, the story of the landing of the first man on the moon; in 1973 he published a biography of Marilyn Monroe called *Marilyn*. *The Executioner's Song*, published in 1979, blurred the boundaries between fiction and nonfiction. Described as a work of fiction, the book was largely a factual account of the life and death of condemned murderer Gary Gilmore.

In 1986 his long-awaited "big book," *Ancient Evenings*, about Egypt 2,300 years ago, appeared. Some reviews were quite respectful and praiseworthy, others were mixed; some were completely negative. Mailer's novel about the CIA, *Harlot's Ghost*, was published in 1991. In 1995 *Oswald's Tale* appeared. It is a nonfiction account of the life of Lee Harvey Oswald, the man believed to have killed President John F. Kennedy on November 22, 1963. In 1997 Mailer's *Gospel According to the Son*, a first-person account of the life of Christ, appeared to negative critical response.

In 2002, at the age of 79, Mailer felt he no longer had much to say about America, acknowledging that his more recent novels showed that he had lost touch with the country. But he would not give up, he said, adding that he was working on a secret novel, writing in longhand every day.

Asked if he had ever come close to writing the Great American Novel, Mailer suggested early in 2002 that three of his books had come reasonably close: *The Naked and the Dead*, *The Executioner's Song*, and *Harlot's Ghost*.

MOSES MAIMONIDES

Distinguished Jewish Thinker of the Middle Ages

Born 1135 in Cordova, Spain; died 1204. Jewish scholar. Known to Jews as Moses (Moshe) ben Maimon and more popularly by the Greek name Maimonides ("son of Maimon") and by the Hebrew acronym Rambam, he was one of the most influential figures in Jewish history and the greatest Jewish thinker of the Middle Ages. To Jews, he is famous for his *Mishneh Torah*; to non-Jews, for his philosophical works, the most important of which is his *Guide of the Perplexed*. A physician and linguist, Maimonides was also an astronomer and Talmudist. His nonreligious works were studied more by Moslems and Christians than by Jews.

MOSES MAIMONIDES, born in Cordova, Spain, was the son of a well-known Talmudist, mathematician, and astronomer. When he was thirteen, a fanatical Islamic sect captured Cordova, and in order to escape the expected persecution, the boy's family wandered throughout Spain for the next ten years, finally settling in the town of Fez in Morocco.

A voracious reader, Maimonides boasted that he had read everything in print on the subject of astronomy. By age sixteen the brilliant student had already written a treatise on logical terminology. Much of his time was devoted to the study of theology and medicine.

Because Fez was ruled by Islamic zealots, Maimonides may have decided to keep a low profile as far as his Judaism was concerned. Some historians have even suggested that he may have posed as a Moslem for a while. In 1165, due to the growing danger of religious persecution in Fez, Maimonides' family sailed for Palestine, which was then governed by Christians. For several months the family lived in Acre, along the Mediterranean coast. They also visited Jerusalem and Hebron. Living conditions were too harsh for them to consider settling there permanently. Therefore, within two years the family traveled to Egypt, where Maimonides spent the rest of his life.

In Cairo, Maimonides, along with his brother David, began a business dealing in precious stones. But tragedy struck. While on a business trip, David drowned in the Indian Ocean and the family fortune in jewels that he was carrying was lost. Maimonides was shattered. Forsaking business, Maimonides studied to become a physician, and in 1170 was selected to serve the family of the viceroy of Egypt.

Maimonides took his medical career very seriously, and, in fact, it was his main claim to fame among non-Jews. He wrote extensively on diet, drugs, and medical treatments, and lectured on physiology and therapeutics. He was soon regarded as one of the world's leading doctors, with a special ability to treat psychosomatic patients.

From Maimonides' own writings one gains a vivid picture of his life at court, taking care of patients, devoting his Sabbaths to community activities in his role as leader of Egyptian Jewry. Somehow he also found time to pursue Judaic studies and to write a comprehensive code of Jewish law, as well as other works that were highly regarded for their wisdom and clarity. By the time of Maimonides' death in 1204, most of his commentary had been translated into Hebrew.

Maimonides

Maimonides believed that the Geonim, the heads of the Babylonian Jewish academies, were leading some Jews astray by giving complicated answers to legal and ritual issues. He felt that uneducated Jews needed a simple, thorough, and internally consistent code of Jewish law that covered all subjects pertaining to Jewish life. Maimonides' first important work was written in response to this concern over the Geonim's pronouncements: a commentary on the *Mishnah*, the basic rabbinic code. Written in Arabic, it was an introduction to the Talmud and was an attempt to articulate the basic principles and central legal teachings of the traditional Jewish law. Most of the work is a description of Jewish law as found in the *Mishnah*, but it also has three long introductions: one deals with the transmission of the oral law from Moses as handed down to the Rabbis; another is the first attempt at formulating a Jewish creed; the final one is an introduction to the *Sayings of the Fathers*.

Maimonides' codification, which he completed in 1178, was known as the *Mishneh Torah*, or *Repetition of the Law*. It was the first effort to organize the various laws of the Talmud into a logical code. Written in Hebrew, it embraces all Talmudic legislation. Maimonides chose the title *Mishneh Torah*, the "Second Torah," for his codification of the Talmud, as a reminder to readers that its authority still rested in the Five Books of Moses. The choice of this title also led many critics to accuse Maimonides of intending to have his code replace the Talmud as the primary legal authority.

Heinrich Graetz, the nineteenth-century scholar, found the Talmud to be like a "Daedalian maze in which one can hardly find one's way even with the thread of Ariadne." The *Mishneh Torah*, however, was, in Graetz's view, a "well-contrived grand plan with wings, halls, apartments, and chambers through which a stranger might pass without a guide. Only a mind accustomed to think clearly and systematically, and filled with a genius of orders could have planned and built a structure like this."

The major flaw in the *Mishneh Torah*, and one that Maimonides himself acknowledged, was the fact that he had not identified the sources of the final legal decisions that he provided. This meant that readers had to trust Maimonides. The debate over this omission became known as the "Maimonides Controversy." In spite of this contention, the book became and has remained a Jewish classic.

Maimonides's other major literary effort, *Guide of the Perplexed*, was written, in Arabic, between 1185 and 1190. The *Guide* is essentially an attempt to reconcile the Bible with the world of science, and is held to be the most important Jewish theological-philosophical tome produced during the Middle Ages. In it, Maimonides dealt with such weighty issues as the nature of God and His relationship to the world and mankind, the nature of prophesy, ethics, and free will, etc.

Maimonides' "Thirteen Articles of Faith" spells out what he considered to be a basic Jewish creed. Each Article of Faith begins with the words *ani ma'amin*, "I believe." One of these statements—expressing belief in the coming of the Messiah—was frequently chanted by inmates of Nazi concentration camps as a sign of their faith in God's goodness.

The Egyptian Jewish community gave Maimonides the title of *nagid*, or leader, and relied on him as their guide. So respectful were these Jews of Maimonides that they conferred the title on his descendants as well, some of whom remained leaders of the Jewish community in Egypt for several generations.

Jews throughout the world mourned Maimonides' death, in 1204, at the age of sixty-nine. Both Jews and Moslems mourned for three days in Fustat, the town near Cairo where Maimonides had lived. Maimonides had wanted to be buried in Palestine—the land of Israel—and a delegation of Egyptians accompanied the coffin there. The Egyptians, however, told the Jews there that Maimonides had left no specific instructions, which led to a bitter dispute. The Jews of Jerusalem and Hebron each felt that he should be buried in their respective cities. Finally, according to one legend, a compromise was reached: it was decided that a camel would carry the coffin and wander freely. Wherever the camel stopped to kneel, that would be the scholar's final resting place. The camel wandered for several days before coming to rest in Tiberias, and so Maimonides was buried there.

Maimonides' grave became a site of pilgrimage, a tradition that continues to this day. On his tombstone is written: "From Moses [of the Bible] to Moses [Maimonides], there never arose another like Moses."

GROUCHO MARX

Wisecracking American Comedian

Born October 2, 1890, in New York; died August 19, 1977. American comedian. Groucho Marx was the master of the irreverent wisecrack, the outright insult, the outrageous pun. He spent his early years in vaudeville, then performed on the Broadway stage. Later, along with his comedian brothers, Groucho Marx took Hollywood by storm, making such film classics as *The Cocoanuts* (1929), *Animal Crackers* (1930), and *Duck Soup* (1933). It was, however, as master of ceremonies of the radio and television quiz program *You Bet Your Life* that Groucho Marx reached the peak of his popularity.

GROUCHO MARX was the most famous of the Marx Brothers, the American theatrical comedy team that was a huge success on Broadway in the 1920s and in Hollywood in the late 1920s and early 1930s.

Groucho and his four brothers were the children of German immigrants. They were all born in New York. Leonard was known as Chico; Adolf was called Harpo; and Julius, because he was the most serious and short-tempered of the brothers, was nicknamed Groucho. It was said that for Groucho impudence was a way of life.

Two less famous brothers were part of the Marx Brothers act at times: Milton (known as Gummo) and Herbert (known as Zeppo).

Simon Marrix, their father, was from the French province of Alsace and immigrated to the United States in 1881. He changed his surname to Marx and found work as a tailor. Simon and his wife, Minna (Shoenberg), lived in poverty on New York's Upper East Side.

Marx and his brothers had little schooling. Groucho was known for his wisecracking by fellow truants and often got beaten up for his jokes when they were taken wrong. He dropped out of school after the eighth grade. At first he had plans of becoming a physician, but he abandoned the idea when he realized he was not educated enough without high school and college to be admitted to medical school.

Searching for a way to make money, the Marx brothers followed the example of their Uncle Al, who had gone into show business. Groucho Marx answered an ad that offered four dollars a week for a male singer in a vaudeville act, the Laron Trio. The act had a two-week booking in Colorado, but Laron disappeared afterwards with Marx's salary. Minna Marx had to send her son the train fare back to New York.

In 1908, when Marx was eighteen, all five Marx brothers were part of a vaudeville act known as "Six Musical Mascots." (Their mother was the sixth.) When Minna Marx left the

191

From right to left, Groucho, Zeppo, and Harpo.

act, the Marx Brothers became known as "The Nightingales." By encouraging her sons to be performers, Minna believed that she was keeping them from getting into trouble, perhaps the kind that could land them in jail. Playing in all sorts of American towns and cities, the Nightingales eventually reached New York's Palace Theater in 1918. One of the brothers, Milton, dropped out of the act that year; Zeppo dropped out in 1933.

The brothers performed their vaudeville routine four or five times a day as they gained momentum as an act. In June 1923, the brothers opened in Philadelphia in a revue called *I'll Say She Is*. They did the show on Broadway the following year. In December 1925, the newly renamed Marx Brothers opened in the stage version of *The Cocoanuts* in New York—they were a smash hit. The play, a satire about the Florida land boom, ran for 377 performances. Irving Berlin wrote the music and George S. Kaufman wrote the book for the show. In fact, Groucho Marx gave Kaufman much of the credit for his early success. "Kaufman molded me. He gave me the walk and the talk," he remarked.

The Marx Brothers, as they always did, spent a lot of time improvising on a given theme. Kaufman said that he could not recognize his own work when he saw the Marx Brothers perform it.

The Marx Brothers began making films in Hollywood for Paramount Studios in 1929, which was the beginning of the talking era. Their first film was *The Cocoanuts*, adapted from their

A scene from Cocoanuts *(1929).*

Broadway hit. The movies they appeared in made them famous; their wacky style of comedy revolved around sight gags and a verbal wit that viewers found very appealing. Virtually plotless, their productions offered them great license to be inventive. So popular were the Marx Brothers that they have been credited with giving the new medium of "talkies" a strong push in the entertainment field.

The Marx Brothers' second Broadway show, *Animal Crackers*, was staged in 1928. It was turned into their second film in 1930. There followed a lengthy list of Marx Brothers films, now synonymous with great film comedy: *Horsefeathers* (1932); *Monkey Business* (1933); *Duck Soup* (1933); *A Night at the Opera* (1935); and *A Day at the Races* (1937).

Groucho Marx and his brothers each created a distinctive personal style. Groucho smoked a cigar, was a fast talker, and made constant wisecracks. He wore a trademark swallowtail coat and greasepaint that accentuated his thick eyebrows and dark mustache. Known as the master of the insult, he was also something of a con man in his routines. Chico was an eccentric pianist and used an Italian accent to get laughs. Harpo, redheaded and a harpist who played his instrument on stage, acted mute as part of his routine, although in real life he was not. Zeppo was the act's straight man.

After 1937, the Marx Brothers made films at MGM for another six years, although with less success than in the past. Their later films were: *At the Circus* (1939); *Go West* (1940); *The Big Store* (1940); *A Night in Casablanca* (1946); and *Love Happy* (1949). Groucho Marx appeared in movies sporadically until 1968.

It is Groucho Marx's quiz show *You Bet Your Life* for which he is best remembered. The show was a moderate success on radio when it was broadcast in 1947 over the ABC network. The show later moved to CBS, then to NBC. It was developed as a television program in 1950 and in that broadcasting medium became a major triumph. For safety's sake, since Marx could be unpredictable in his jokes, the program was prerecorded for both radio and television; neither the network nor Groucho were willing to take the chance of his saying something that might offend the wrong people: sponsors, the public, the critics.

Although his popularity faded with the demise of *You Bet Your Life* in the early 1960s, Groucho Marx had by then become a household name. And, in fact, the Marx Brothers' films were popular all over again, especially with young people, in the late 1960s and early 1970s. The films actually acquired a cult status for a while.

Groucho Marx was the last surviving brother when he received an honorary Award in 1973 citing his "brilliant creativity." His quips have become famous. Some examples:

- On being told that he could not join a swimming club because he was Jewish: "My son's only half-Jewish. Would he be permitted to go into the water up to his knees?"
- As a doctor taking a pulse: "Either you're dead or my watch has stopped."
- "From the moment I picked up your book until the moment I put it down, I was convulsed with laughter. Some day I intend to read it."
- "Anyone can get old. All you have to do is live long enough."

His most famous quip had to do with the Bel Air Country Club in Los Angeles not accepting Jews as members. Groucho said: "I wouldn't want to belong to any club that would accept me as a member."

Groucho Marx was married three times: to Ruth Johnson (1920–1942); to Catherine Marvis Gorcey (1945–1951); and to Eden Hartford (1954–1960). He had three children—a son, Arthur, and a daughter, Miriam, from his first marriage; and a daughter, Melinda, from his second.

Marx wrote *Groucho and Me* (1959), an autobiography, and *Memoirs of a Mangy Lover* (1963). He also compiled a lengthy, unconventional series of letters into a book called *The Groucho Letters* (1967).

Groucho Marx, one of the great comedians of the twentieth century, who brought laughter to millions of people during his lifetime, died in 1977 at the age of eighty-seven.

LOUIS B. MAYER

Hollywood Mogul

Born in 1885 in Minsk, Russia; died October 29, 1957. American film executive. Louis B. Mayer made Metro-Goldwyn-Mayer the most prestigious of the major Hollywood studios of the 1920s. He understood that America wanted stars and so he gave them Greta Garbo, Jimmy Stewart, and many others. Mayer liked to make "decent, wholesome" pictures and America turned out to watch them in droves. After World War II, however, Mayer was forced to step back when other Hollywood producers promoted a postwar realism depicted on the screen in order to meet audience demand for "slice of life" films.

Louis B. Mayer was born in Minsk, Russia, in 1885. His original name was probably Lazar; he himself was not certain. At the age of two, he and his parents went to New Brunswick, Canada, where he spent part of his childhood as a junk peddler.

Mayer began his show business career at nineteen by running a film theater near Boston. For a while he had followed his father in the scrap-metal business. But in 1904, Mayer decided he wanted to work on his own. For the first few years, however, he had little success making a living.

Also in 1904, Mayer married Maggie Shenburg, daughter of a Boston cantor. They had two daughters.

In 1907 a friend involved in film exhibitions advised Mayer to look into acquiring theaters. Now twenty-two years old, Mayer purchased a burlesque house in Haverhill, Massachusetts, with a six-hundred-dollar down payment. He began showing a French film version of the Oberammergau Passion Play. His success grew and he soon owned all the theaters in Haverhill, a small city just outside Boston.

One success led to another and in a short time Mayer struck it rich by owning the New England distribution rights to D.W. Griffith's historic film *The Birth of a Nation*. He also became secretary of the Metro Pictures Corporation. In 1918 he set up his own Los Angeles-based studio, the Louis B. Mayer Pictures Corporation. Six years later, the mogul Marcus Loew, who by that time had gained control of Metro, merged Metro with Goldwyn Pictures. Louis Mayer was hired as studio chief of the new "MGM."

MGM became incredibly successful, thanks to Mayer's understanding of what the public wanted and the way he showcased his stars. In 1925 he produced the well-received film *The Merry Widow*; he turned Sam Goldwyn's production of *Ben Hur* (1927) into one of the most successful silent pictures. Mayer had other hits as well, including *The Good Earth* in 1923, the Andy Hardy series, and *Treasure Island* in 1950.

Mayer was a great champion of the "star system." He believed firmly that the public had a massive appetite for Hollywood stars and so his strategy was to try to get control of as many of these popular stars as possible. Among those he "discovered" were Greta Garbo, Greer Garson, Norma Shearer, Lon Chaney, Joan Crawford, and Jean Harlow. He also brought under his wing Lana Turner, Judy Garland, Jimmy Stewart, Fred Astaire, Gene Kelly, Spencer Tracy, and Mickey Rooney.

Mayer enjoyed films with children in them; he launched the careers of some of the most famous child stars of all time: Jackie Cooper, Mickey Rooney, Peter Lawford, Judy Garland, and Elizabeth Taylor. Among the brilliant production people he nurtured at the studio were Irving Thalberg and Dore Schary.

Mayer had a clear idea of what kind of movies brought out big audiences. America needed "decent, wholesome pictures," he once said. But his instincts were not always sound. Mayer saw little future for any actor with the protruding ears of Clark Gable; he opposed one of Gable's first great triumphs, *Mutiny on the Bounty* (1935), because he thought the public would never accept his looks or approve of a rebel as a hero. Mayer rejected a proposal to help finance Mickey Mouse on the ground that, as he told Walt Disney, "every woman is frightened of a mouse."

In 1937 Mayer was America's highest-paid executive. As president of Metro-Goldwyn-Mayer, he collected well over a million dollars in annual salary. From 1931 to 1936, Mayer was the president of the Association of Motion Picture Producers.

Louis Mayer did not read scripts or screen treatments, much less books; when a story was to be considered, it was acted out for him by an assistant named Kate Corbaley, who was paid to tell him stories just as his mother had done years earlier in New Brunswick. One afternoon in May 1936, Miss Corbaley told Louis Mayer a new story about a tempestuous Southern girl named Scarlett O'Hara. Mayer wisely nodded his head and said, "Let's ask Irving," meaning Irving Thalberg, MGM's frail and sickly but powerful production chief. Thalberg said to forget it, that no Civil War picture had ever made a dime. And so *Gone with the Wind* (1937) was not produced by MGM.

Although Hitler had been increasingly hostile to Jews in Germany, Louis Mayer continued to behave as if making money were more important than standing up to anti-Semitic tyrants. Concerned that MGM-owned theaters in Berlin might be boycotted by German audiences, he worried about what the Hitler regime would think of a movie he produced, *Three Comrades*, which was based on a novel by Erich Maria Remarque and set in Weimar Germany. There was no doubt that some actors were meant to play Nazi officials, and in an effort not to offend Hitler, Mayer invited an official from the German consulate in Los Angeles to a private screening. The official was not pleased with what he saw and Mayer promised him that he would make the appropriate changes. When producer Joseph Mankiewicz threatened to resign if any changes were made, Mayer decided to leave the movie as it was.

In 1941 Mayer called in director William Wyler to complain to him that the early rushes of the film *Mrs. Miniver* showed an anti-German bias. One scene in particular portrayed a downed German pilot as a Nazi fanatic. Mayer argued, "We're not at war with anybody," but Wyler asked Mayer if he knew what the Nazis were doing to Jews in Germany. By way of an answer,

Mayer said, "This is a big corporation. I'm responsible to my stockholders. We have theaters all over the world, including a couple in Berlin. We don't make hate pictures. We don't hate anybody. We're not at war." After Pearl Harbor, when Hitler actually did declare war on the United States, Mayer summoned Wyler and gave him permission to portray the downed German pilot as he saw fit. "You just go ahead. You do it the way you wanted."

Louis Mayer stepped down as head of production at MGM in 1948, forced out by board members who wanted postwar realism in their films. Mayer was unconvinced that this was what viewers were demanding. "I know what the audience wants," Mayer barked back. "Andy Hardy! Sentimentality! What's wrong with it? Love! Is it bad? It entertains. It brings the audience to the box office."

Louis Mayer was just five feet seven inches tall, but he had strong shoulders and a sharp temper and he could literally pack a wallop

Louis B. Mayer

American Jewish Archives, Cincinnati Campus, Hebrew Union College, Jewish Institute of Religion

when he thought it was necessary. Mayer set his desk on a platform so that visitors would hold him in respectful awe. Once, he physically assaulted Charlie Chaplin for speaking disrespectfully of Chaplin's own ex-wife. Another time, he punched out someone else who had made the statement that all women were whores. It was part of the folklore at MGM that the studio commissary had to serve chicken soup with real pieces of chicken in it for lunch every day, at thirty-five cents a bowl, in honor of Mayer's long-deceased mother.

Mayer died at the age of seventy-two in 1957. A rival producer made a bad joke at Mayer's funeral, mocking Mayer's formula for bringing crowds to movies and alluding to the strong emotions he aroused in his colleagues: "You give the people what they want, they'll turn out." There's no doubt that Louis B. Mayer, or "L.B." as he had come to be known, was a dominant influence in the burgeoning movie industry of the World War II era. His good instincts about the film industry and its audiences and his personal dynamism were legendary. *Life* magazine chose him as one of the hundred most important Americans of the twentieth century in its special Fall 1970 edition.

ERIC MENDELSOHN

Influential Twentieth-Century Architect

Born March 21, 1887, in Allenstein, East Prussia, (now Olszytn, Poland), Germany; died September 15, 1953. German architect. One of the founders of the Modern Movement of architecture, Eric Mendelsohn designed public, commercial, and private buildings, and had a major influence on many contemporary architects. Leaving his native Germany when Hitler rose to power in 1933, Mendelsohn built memorable structures in the United States, Europe, and Israel. Among them are the Albert Einstein Tower in Potsdam, Germany; the Hadassah-Rothschild University Hospital in Jerusalem; and synagogue-community centers in St. Louis, Baltimore, and Dallas.

ERIC MENDELSOHN was born in Allenstein, East Prussia, in 1887. His father was a merchant, his mother a milliner and a musician. From an early age, Mendelsohn aspired to become an architect.

Between 1907 and 1912, Mendelsohn attended the Technical University in Berlin and then the Technical University in Munich. He spent a year studying economics, and the next four, architecture. While in school, he met cellist Louise Maas. They were married in 1915 and had one daughter, Esther, born in 1916.

In 1912, when he was twenty-five years old, Mendelsohn began working as an architect. Almost immediately he became a leading figure in the architectural movement that was based on the notion that it is possible to combine beauty and utility in the design of public buildings. Mendelsohn was greatly impressed by the German expressionist movement in architecture, particularly the Blaue Reiter group.

Soon after World War I began, Mendelsohn enlisted in the German army and served on both the Eastern and Western fronts. With fighting raging around him, he continued to do architectural sketches. Mendelsohn created his designs with a soft pencil on tracing paper, some no more than an inch high. These miniature drawings of scale-model factories, railroad stations, and grain elevators for future construction in steel and concrete became known as the Mendelsohn World War I sketches and are among the most important building blocks of modern architecture.

"Look at my sketches," he once said, "for they offer the clue to everything that follows."

The most intriguing of all the designs, and the sketch that led to Eric Mendelsohn's first important commission, was the original concept for the Einstein Tower in Potsdam, Germany, which Mendelsohn was asked to supervise in 1919, at the age of thirty-two. The Tower was part of an astrophysical institute that was built during 1920 and 1921 in order to test Einstein's theory of relativity. The building brought Mendelsohn immediate fame and many more commissions. "It is pure romantic expressionism," wrote Ada Louise Huxtable in the *New York Times*, "and he never built anything quite like its plastic, sculptural fantasy again. (I have always thought of it as a kind of Art Nouveau illustration for the old woman who lived in a shoe.)" When Mendelsohn gave Albert Einstein a tour of the building, the brilliant physicist uttered only one word: "Organic."

Mendelsohn was guided in the field of architecture by the belief that the twentieth century was ushering in a whole new era that permitted a clean break with the past.

What was so remarkable was that Mendelsohn designed his buildings on the basis of the World War I sketches, despite the fact that he had no idea how the elastic tension of steel and concrete could be engineered to stand up and support them. The technology of tension structures, such as reinforced concrete hyperbolic paraboloids or steel cable construction, came later. And when it did exist, a half-century later, other architects were able to implement projects themselves based on Mendelsohn's ideas.

One of the 1914 "trench sketches" for an imagined railroad station demonstrates an uncanny resemblance to the late Eero Saarinen's TWA terminal at John F. Kennedy Airport in New York, designed in 1956. A 1917 sketch could well be the basis for Saarinen's first doodle for his famous Dulles Airport terminal near Washington, D.C. A "trench sketch" Mendelsohn made in 1915 and called "Grain Elevator" appears to foretell the Watergate building complex, built much later along the Potomac River in Washington, D.C., from a design by the late Italian architect Luigi Moretti.

Mendelsohn sought to combine purpose with design in the buildings he created in the 1920s and 1930s. One important effort was the Metal Workers' Union headquarters in Berlin. Mendelsohn also designed the Shocken German department stores, which employed an imaginative use of glass for maximum display of merchandise. The department stores were built in Nuremberg (1925), Stuttgart (1926), and Chemnitz (1928).

Eric Mendelsohn designed a Jewish cemetery at Konigsberg (which became Kalingrad, the Soviet Union) that was later destroyed by the Nazis. He also conceived the plans for the Universum Cinema in Berlin in the 1920s. It became a pioneer of the modern movie house and attracted widespread attention.

When Hitler rose to power in 1933, Mendelsohn fled to England, where he founded a partnership with fellow architect Serge Chermayeff. Mendelsohn's most important project in conjunction with Chermayeff was the De La Warr Entertainment Pavilion in Bexhill (1935). One English newspaper described it as "the last word in modern architecture." A British fascist newspaper, however, attacked the choice of Mendelsohn as architect for that project, saying the selection should not go to "aliens who have found it necessary to flee their native land."

In 1941, Mendelsohn traveled to the United States, and four years later he settled with his family in San Francisco, though he spent a good deal of time in later years in Palestine designing buildings.

Mendelsohn was thoroughly smitten with San Francisco and pledged, however facetiously, that he would rebuild the city so that everyone, no matter where they lived or worked in the city by the bay, would have a view. In 1946 he designed the Maimonides Health Center and

Eric Mendelsohn

Hebrew Nursing Home in that city. He also lectured at the University of California's School of Architecture.

Mendelsohn expressed his religious beliefs through his architecture, especially in the building of synagogues, which he called humankind's "reply to the unknown . . . the symbol of man's finite life within the infinite cosmos."

Mendelsohn began designing and constructing synagogue-community centers in cities across America—Cleveland, St. Louis, Baltimore, St. Paul, Grand Rapids, and Dallas. The one he designed for a Jewish congregation in Cleveland has a dramatic dome that is one hundred feet in diameter.

Paul Goldberger, architectural critic for the *New York Times*, wrote in 1988 that "Mendelsohn was a modernist, as surely and as absolutely as Mies or Gropius, but he had little interest in the harsh, puritanical rigidity of the International Style. His architecture was more lyrical, more rhythmic, and vastly more emotional: where Mies van der Rohe built in clean, abstract lines, Eric Mendelsohn made great, sweeping curves. He sought not to rationalize the world but to express its dynamism. To Mendelsohn, the reserve and the restraint of the International Style orthodoxy was far too limiting; he was eager to express the sense of a new world as rich, energetic, and full of movement."

Mendelsohn did a great deal of work in Palestine, although the heat of the Middle Eastern climate made the extensive use of glass, which the architect favored, impractical. The Jerusalem requirement that all buildings be made of local stone may have also hampered Mendelsohn in his creative ventures.

Rarely did Eric Mendelsohn design private houses, but in 1935 he designed a home in Rehovot for the first president of the state of Israel, Chaim Weizmann. In Jerusalem, in the same year, he created a home for Salman Shocken, a member of the well-known family that owned the department stores in Germany that Mendelsohn had designed during the 1920s. Mendelsohn's most impressive work, in many people's minds, was the design of the Hadassah-Rothschild University Hospital in Jerusalem (1937–38). A decade later, he designed the British government hospital in Haifa (1947–48).

Mendelsohn died in San Francisco in 1953 at the age of sixty-six, after a brief illness. Experts agree that Eric Mendelsohn was one of the foremost architects of the twentieth century. His designs have already had an enormous influence on later generations of architects, as they will undoubtedly continue to have on future ones.

MOSES MENDELSSOHN

German Philosopher

Born in Desau, Germany, September 26, 1729; died January 4, 1786. German philosopher. Moses Mendelssohn became the spiritual leader of German Jewry and was influential in bringing about Jewish emancipation in Germany. A philosopher and translator of the Bible, Mendelssohn defended Judaism aggressively, constantly asserting that someone could believe in the rationalist tenets of the Enlightenment and at the same time remain faithful to Judaism.

MOSES MENDELSSOHN was born in 1729 in Desau, Germany, the son of a Torah scribe. Because of a childhood disease, Mendelssohn was permanently disfigured by a curvature of the spine that affected his nervous system.

As a youngster, he studied with the local rabbi, David Frankel, until Frankel returned home to Berlin. When Mendelssohn was fourteen, he followed Rabbi Frankel there. As a Jew, Mendelssohn was forced to pay a fee to enter the city. It then took Mendelssohn twenty years to earn a residence permit to stay in Berlin. Jews without means were not allowed to remain in the city indefinitely. Pursuing his religious studies with Rabbi Frankel, Mendelssohn also studied languages, the sciences, and especially philosophy. He remained an observant Jew all his life.

Finding it difficult to earn a living, however, Mendessohn was always on the verge of having to leave Berlin. Fortunately his academic talents impressed some scholars who in turn introduced him to other learned people who could serve as his mentors. In 1750, at the age of twenty-one, Mendelssohn began tutoring the children of the owner of a silk factory. Four years later, Mendelssohn became the firm's bookkeeper; he eventually became a partner in the business. He remained a merchant all his life, even while he pursued his intellectual activities.

When Mendelssohn was twenty-five years old, he was introduced to Gotthold Ephraim Lessing, a liberal writer, dramatist, and the major figure of the German Enlightenment. Quickly becoming friends with Mendelssohn, Lessing predicted in one of his writings that Mendelssohn would become a "second Spinoza." With Lessing aiding him in writing in German, Mendelssohn prepared a defense of Lessing's drama, *Die Juden*. Lessing and Mendelssohn also collaborated in writing a piece on the English poet Alexander Pope. The hero of Lessing's *Nathan the Wise* was inspired by Mendelssohn.

Mendelssohn wrote more and more in German, his work appearing in leading literary journals. In time, those writings brought Mendelssohn to the attention of important scholars as well as the King of Prussia, Frederick II. Mendelssohn was, after all, unique, being the first Jew

Moses Mendelssohn

to publish in German. He was daring, too, once writing a piece criticizing the poetry of the Prussian king.

In 1763, Mendelssohn married Fromet Guggenheim of Hamburg. Their home was turned into a salon; Jews and non-Jews alike were welcomed. That same year, Mendelssohn won first prize from the Prussian Royal Academy of Sciences for a treatise on evidence in metaphysics, challenging philosopher Immanuel Kant. In the wake of that triumph, the King of Prussia rewarded Mendelssohn by making him a "privileged Jew." He passed word to his police that the Jewish scholar was exempt from the harassment routinely practiced against Jews.

It was the 1767 publication of Moses Mendelssohn's essay "Phaedon" that brought him fame. Dealing with the immortality of the soul, the essay was written in the form of a Platonic dialogue. Mendelssohn asserted that even though things perish, they do not cease to exist but rather are dissolved into their elements. The soul, which is one of these elements, in Mendelssohn's view, was neither weakened by age nor destroyed by death. To Mendelssohn, the soul had to be imperishable. "If our souls were mortal," he wrote, "reason would be a dream . . . . We would be like animals destined only to seek food and to perish."

Mendelssohn became known as the "German Socrates." His advice was sought. He was accepted at the learned societies which were the social centers for Berlin's intelligentsia.

Until he was forty years old, Mendelssohn was mainly interested in spreading German culture to Germans, to the world, and particularly to Jews. His goal was to prepare German Jews to enter German society, yet they spoke only Yiddish. To facilitate their participation in German society, he sought to make these Jews familiar with the German language. He translated the Pentateuch into German. In 1783 he completed a Hebrew commentary that was consistent with the mood of the Enlightenment. Mendelssohn's efforts marked a milestone in the field of Jewish education. At Mendelssohn's urging, a Jewish free school was started in Berlin.

In 1769 a Swiss clergyman, a Christian named Johann Kaspar Lavater, challenged Mendelssohn to prove that Judaism was a better religion than Christianity. Lavater's purpose was to convince Mendelssohn to convert to Christianity.

Grudgingly accepting the challenge, Mendelssohn published a reply, writing that "It is unbecoming for one of us to openly defy the other and thereby furnish diversion to the idle, scandal to the simple, and malicious exultation to the revilers of truth and virtue. Were we to analyze our aggregate stock of knowledge, we certainly shall concur in so many important truths that I venture to say few individuals of one and the same religious persuasion would more harmonize in thinking. A point here and there on which we might perhaps still divide might be adjourned for some ages longer, without detriment to the welfare of the human race.

What a world of bliss we would live in did all men adopt the true principles which the best among the Christians and the best among the Jews have in common."

Mendelssohn found his debate with Lavater unpleasant. "I wanted to refute the world's derogatory opinion of the Jew by righteous living, not by pamphleteering," he said.

Mendelssohn was a great defender of Judaism, but at the same time he subjected his religion to the test of the searching rationalism of the Enlightenment. He endeavored to prove that Judaism could withstand this test. He wrote, "Let every man who does not disturb the public welfare, who obeys the law, acts righteously toward you and his fellow men, be allowed to speak as he thinks, to pray to God after his own fashion or after that of his fathers, and to seek eternal salvation where he thinks he may find it.

"We have no doctrines that are contrary to reason. We added nothing to natural religion save commandments and statutes. But the fundamental tenets of our religion rest on the fountain of reason. They are in consonance with the results of free inquiry, without any conflict or contradiction."

Mendelssohn was always eager to help Jewish communities; he tried to use his influence to keep anti-Jewish measures from being carried out in Switzerland and Germany. To aid the Jews in Alsace, Mendelssohn convinced his friend Christian Wilhelm von Dohm to write a memorandum and submit it to the French government; it was a plea for Jewish emancipation called "On the Civil Improvement of the Jews."

Mendelssohn's best-known work on Jewish matters was *Jerusalem* (1783). In it, he pleaded for the separation of church and state, and argued that religion was a matter of individual spirit and conscience, and therefore people should not be coerced about it.

When he died in 1786 at the age of sixty, Mendelssohn was honored by Jews and non-Jews alike. While he did not live to see the Jewish Emancipation in Germany—the entry of Jews into German society and culture that occurred from 1871 to 1914—Mendelssohn was above all else the one German Jewish figure who, by his literary achievements and through his other efforts, helped pave the way for its arrival.

DANIEL MENDOZA

Father of Modern Boxing

Born July 5, 1764, in London, England; died September 3, 1836. English boxer. Daniel Mendoza was the most celebrated and colorful Jewish sportsman of his time. He revolutionized boxing in England, introducing the "Mendoza School" (or the "Jewish School"), with its science of footwork, sparring, new punches, and strategy, replacing the brutal slugging that had constituted boxing until then. Mendoza was England's sixteenth heavyweight champion, which was at the time also world champion. Mendoza claimed, with good reason, that he invented the modern sport of boxing. Because of his spectacular athletic skills, Mendoza did much to raise the status of Jews in English society.

DANIEL MENDOZA was born in 1764 to Jewish parents in Whitechapel, a section of London. He received a traditional Jewish education. Mendoza spent his life defending Judaism—frequently with his bare fists.

Following his bar mitzvah, having come of age, Mendoza wanted to become a glazier. Although he found a job with a glazier, he lost it when he fought his employer's son and beat him. He then found work in a fruit and vegetable shop. Later, he worked in a tea shop where, while he was defending the owner from a disgruntled client who appeared ready to settle the argument with his fists, young Mendoza's threatening pose attracted a crowd.

The famous boxer Richard Humphreys, known as the "Gentleman Boxer," witnessed the scene and offered himself as Daniel Mendoza's second in the fight. Word spread that young Mendoza had boxing talent, and the following Saturday he was matched against a professional fighter. Mendoza, who soon became known as "The Star of Israel," won the fight, for which he was paid five guineas.

Daniel Mendoza then became a salesman for a tobacconist, but he was forever getting into physical altercations. Always feeling that he was the injured party, Mendoza was prepared to battle brutality and injustice of any kind. Eventually he put this energy to professional use. Mendoza won his first professional fight in 1790, a match that won him the patronage of the Prince of Wales. Mendoza was the first boxer to earn this honor. He was proud of this commendation, as well as of his heritage, and he began billing himself as "Mendoza the Jew."

Having promised his wife that he would soon give up the ring, Mendoza stipulated only one condition: that he first fight with Richard Humphreys, who by now had become his archrival. Mendoza had been injured in earlier fights, and therefore had worked out a new style of defense, one that included a technique called sidestepping, a straight left, and special ways to protect himself. Some purists who thought boxing was all punches and no tactics criticized Mendoza for adopting this "cowardly" manner of retreating from his opponent rather than standing up in true British bulldog style and hammering away with his fists, but Mendoza stuck firmly with his innovative and more "brainy" approach.

Mendoza finally got his chance to fight Humphreys and to test his new boxing style. The fight was set for January 9, 1788, at Odiham in Hampshire. The Jews of England, eager for a champion and a hero, placed many large wagers on the contest. Humphreys beat Mendoza in just fifteen minutes (many fights of the period were recorded this way), and Mendoza's Jewish fans despaired of having their triumph.

Humphreys' patron, Mr. Bradyl, received a message from the victor: "Sir, I have DONE the Jew, and am in good health. Signed. Richard Humphreys."

A second fight between the two rivals was organized for May 6, 1789, at Stilton. Mendoza's training quarters were at the Essex

Daniel Mendoza

Ring Magazine

home of Sir Thomas A. Price. Determined to achieve victory this time, Mendoza triumphed in this second fight, which was attended by nearly three thousand spectators. England had a new hero. Daniel Mendoza's name was added to the scripts of many plays, songs were written about him, and he could fill a theater for boxing exhibitions that earned him fifty pounds, a large sum for the time. Eventually, Mendoza appeared three times a week in theaters. The two famous fighters—Mendoza and Humphreys—fought a third time at Doncaster on September 29, 1790. By now convinced that he was the far better boxer, Mendoza's self-confidence helped him win easily.

In the early 1790s, fighting was so highly regarded that Daniel Mendoza opened a small theater at the Lyceum on the Strand in London in order to hold public exhibitions of sparring and to teach interested dandies of London society how to box.

When he defeated Bill Warr on Bexley Common on November 12, 1794, Mendoza became the English heavyweight champion. He held that title until his defeat, on April 15, 1795, at the hands of John Johnson. The latter won by grabbing Mendoza's shoulder-length hair and battering the champion boxer senseless in the ninth round.

Mendoza kept on fighting. On March 21, 1806, he fought Harry Lee at Grimsted Green in Kent. In the fifty-third round, Mendoza was declared the winner. On July 4, 1820, Mendoza met Tom Owen at Barnstead Downs; the fifty-six-year-old Mendoza lost when the younger man was declared the winner in the twelfth round. A poet (signed only W.W.) lamented

Mendoza's fading glory in the pages of an Edinburgh, Scotland, magazine on October 8, 1820: "Is this Mendoza?—this the Jew of whom my fancy cherished so beautiful a waking dream, a vision which has perished?"

Daniel Mendoza stood just five feet seven inches tall; he weighed 160 pounds. Despite his medium build, however, he had an enormous chest, which gave him unexpected power. He always fought larger men. Commenting in a speech he gave in 1820 on his new technique to combat fighters bigger in stature than he was, he said: "I think I have a right to call myself the father of the science, for it is well known that prizefighting lay dormant for several years. It was myself and Humphreys who revived it in our three contests for supremacy, and the science of pugilism has been patronized ever since."

During his boxing career, Daniel Mendoza became a wealthy man, but his generous nature landed him in debt. He served time in debtors' prison after his boxing career ended in 1820. Upon his release, Mendoza did some teaching and theatrical touring, and had a series of jobs as a recruiting sergeant, caterer, process server, and pubkeeper. Just prior to his death, he was managing an inn. He died a poor man at the age of seventy-two. His wife and their eleven children survived him.

Daniel Mendoza is considered the father of modern "scientific" boxing in large measure because of the defensive moves he devised that enabled him to fight much heavier opponents. He was the first boxer to receive royal patronage; that acceptance by royalty helped also to elevate the position of the Jew in general in English society.

In 1812 Pierce Egan, the author of *Boxiana*, a study of boxing of that period, noted that Daniel Mendoza was not "the Jew that Shakespeare drew, yet he was that Jew." And then Egan added, "In spite of his prejudice, he [the Christian] was compelled to exclaim—Mendoza was a pugilist of no ordinary merit."

Mendoza's life story and his view on his chosen profession are recorded in two books. He wrote *The Art of Boxing* in 1789 and *The Memoirs of Daniel Mendoza* in 1816. In 1965 Daniel Mendoza was one of the inaugural group chosen for the Boxing Hall of Fame in the United States. He was also named a member of the Jewish Sports Hall of Fame in Israel. His accomplishments and the style he brought to the act of boxing are memorable and have inspired contemporary fighters to use similar moves. He proved that bulk and a strong punch aren't the whole boxing game.

YEHUDI MENUHIN

Outstanding Violinist

Born April 22, 1916, in New York City; died March 12, 1999. American violinist. A child prodigy as a violinist, Yehudi Menuhin had millions of admirers around the world from a very young age. His career began to soar when he was eleven years old and astonished a Carnegie Hall audience with his command of the violin. He undertook a round-the-world concert tour as a teenager, took two years off to rethink his career, and then returned to concert playing, becoming the dominant violinist of his era.

BORN IN NEW YORK CITY IN 1916, Yehudi Menuhin was the oldest child of Moshe and Marutha (Sher) Menuhin, both of whom had been born in Russia. Moshe Menuhin had grown up in Palestine and was a Hebrew teacher in New York. Yehudi Menuhin was descended from a long line of Hasidic rabbis.

When Menuhin was nine months old, the family moved to San Francisco, where Moshe Menuhin became superintendent of the Jewish Education Society. Two daughters, Hephzibah and Yaltah, were born while the Menuhins lived in California.

Unable to afford a babysitter, Menuhin's parents often took their son to concerts with them, exposing him to music from an early age. When he was three years old, Menuhin seemed overly quiet and introverted. To help him become interested in an activity that might draw him out, Menuhin's parents gave him a toy violin.

Accustomed by then to good orchestral sounds, Menuhin was so distressed by the poor quality of the sound of the toy violin that his parents immediately took it away and replaced it with a real one. Menuhin took to the instrument immediately.

When he was five years old, Menuhin took violin lessons from Sigmund Anker, a specialist in the teaching of child prodigies. Two years later, at the age of seven, Menuhin began to study under Louis Persinger, who was the concertmaster of the San Francisco Symphony Orchestra and leader of the Persinger String Quartet. Menuhin's first public performance, with the San Francisco orchestra, came soon after that.

Menuhin's childhood was different from that of most other children of the day. He was educated at home. His father taught him mathematics, history, and Hebrew; his mother taught him French, German, Italian, and Spanish.

When Menuhin was ten years old, the family traveled to Europe through the benevolence of a San Francisco attorney and philanthropist, Sidney Ehgram, who became Menuhin's patron. Menuhin studied in Paris with the Romanian violinist Georges Enesco. He made his

Yehudi Menuhin

Paris debut in 1927 with the Lamoureux Orchestra, playing three major violin concertos.

Soon after, having returned to the United States, Menuhin made a historic appearance on November 25, 1927, with the New York Symphony under the direction of Fritz Bosch. Electrifying the Carnegie Hall audience with his performance of Beethoven's Violin Concerto in D, Yehudi Menuhin was on his way to becoming one of the finest musicians of the twentieth century. "It seems ridiculous to say that he showed a mature conception of Beethoven's concerto," Olin Downes wrote in the *New York Times*, "but that is the fact. When the boy touched the strings it was evident that an exceptional musical intelligence and sensibility were behind the performance." A few weeks later, police had to keep an overflow crowd under control when Menuhin performed a solo recital at Carnegie Hall.

Menuhin visited Europe often in the next few years, performing with some of the world's most important conductors. On April 12, 1929, for example, he performed with the Berlin Philharmonic, playing concertos by Bach, Beethoven, and Brahms, later repeating the program in Dresden and Paris. He made his London debut on November 4 of that year, playing the Brahms Concerto with the London Symphony in Queen's Hall.

Menuhin and his sister, Hephzibah, who was a wonderful pianist, started to give violin and piano recitals together. In 1932 they won the national Prix du Disque in France for their first joint recording.

In 1934 Menuhin began his first around-the-world concert tour, visiting sixty-three cities and performing 110 engagements in thirteen countries, including Australia and New Zealand. Completing the tour in 1935 at the age of 19, he withdrew to his family's estate in the hills near Los Gatos, California, where he spent the next two years resting and going through a process of self-examination.

While a gifted violinist, Yehudi Menuhin had no training in the technical basis of violin playing, which most students routinely learn. Instead, he relied on his instincts. During his two-year respite from recording, concerts, and touring, Menuhin tried to fill the gaps in his knowledge of the instrument.

Menuhin sensed that he was taking a chance on damaging his career with this extended sabbatical, but thought it well worth it. "Even at the risk of losing all the golden eggs of the future, I had to find out what made the goose lay those eggs. I wanted to know exactly in what way the smallest articulation of the fingers had to move, what sensation they had to evoke in

Yehudi Menuhin

the mind and in the subconscious, what feeling of ease, of balance, of facility, of strength was involved in each section and each subdivision of the intricate and complicated technique of the violin."

Resuming his performing in 1937, Menuhin could tell that the time away from the stage had been worthwhile. Over the next four years, he appeared as a soloist with the great symphony conductors of the world, including Toscanini and Stokowski. In one of his first concerts after ending his "retirement," on December 6, 1937, Menuhin introduced a violin concerto by German composer Robert Schumann, a widely heralded "lost" composition, to his Carnegie Hall audience.

Yehudi Menuhin gave more than five hundred concerts during World War II, many of them for the American troops overseas. He was the first well-known American artist to play in the liberated cities of Paris, Brussels, Antwerp, Bucharest, and Budapest. The Soviet government invited him to become the first American artist to play in Moscow when the fighting ended. Later, in 1951, he toured the Soviet Union and Eastern Europe as well as Japan; he toured India in 1952.

Menuhin was aptly called "America's best ambassador" by former Deputy Under Secretary of State Robert D. Murphy. He helped arrange the first major cultural exchange between the United States and the then Soviet Union since the initiation of the Cold War. After a Soviet pianist and violinist played in the United States in the fall of 1955, Menuhin played in Moscow in May 1956 in a reciprocal engagement.

Tickets were in such great demand for the two concerts Menuhin gave in Warsaw in April 1957 that the final rehearsal was thrown open to the public.

Throughout his career, Menuhin broadened his repertoire by reviving neglected scores. In 1956 he began a small, informal musical festival at Gstaad, Switzerland, in the church of Saanen. In 1959 he became director of the Bath Festival in England. "I like to think of my festivals as an evening at home consisting of people congenial to one another, musicians, and audiences," he wrote in the *New York Times* in 1960. In 1969, as part of his musical festival at Windsor, Queen Elizabeth made the unprecedented gesture of permitting two rooms at Windsor Castle to be used for Menuhin's performances.

Menuhin married twice, the first time in May 1938 to Nola Ruby Nicholas, the daughter of an Australian industrialist. They had a son and daughter, and were divorced in 1947. In October 1947 Menuhin married Diana Goluld, a ballerina and actress, the daughter of a British Foreign Office official. They had two sons.

Besides his estate in Los Gatos and his chalet in Gstaad, Menuhin owned a seventeenth-century home in London's Highgate district and a house on the Greek island of Mykonos.

In a letter to the authors on March 13, 1995, Menuhin wrote that his Jewishness was more "the result of background—specifically Hasidic—than of any indoctrination. The people who persuaded me most to feel a degree of Jewishness are, of course, Hitler and company and the other persecutors, though on the positive side there is a very real acknowledgment of a certain conditioning for abstract thought, which I have always had."

Menuhin was an advocate of yoga, which he practiced on a regular basis. In a 1963 BBC-TV program called "Yehudi Menuhin and His Guru," Menuhin talked about the value of yoga as a physical and mental discipline, suggesting that yoga relaxed him. Describing his yoga exercises, Menuhin said that he stood on his head for fifteen to twenty minutes a day to "irrigate" his brain.

In October 1997 Menuhin gave concerts on his third tour of China. In Beijing he played with the China National Symphony Orchestra.

Yehudi Menuhin played publicly for over seventy years, and his name was synonymous with the finest in violin performances of the twentieth century. He died while on tour in Berlin on March 12, 1999, a month short of his eighty-third birthday.

ARTHUR MILLER

Outstanding American Dramatist

Born October 17, 1915, in New York City. American playwright. Arthur
Miller is recognized as one of America's most significant dramatists, rivaling Eugene O'Neill and Tennessee Williams. His theatrical breakthrough
occurred in 1947 when his second play, the award-winning *All My Sons*,
was produced. Miller is also well known for two other classics of the modern theater, *Death of a Salesman* (1949) and *The Crucible* (1953). His play
Broken Glass was produced in 1994 and became a hit on the London stage.

ARTHUR MILLER was born in Harlem, New York City, the middle of three children. His
father, Isadore, was an immigrant from Austria-Hungary; his mother, Augusta (Barnett)
Miller, was a public school teacher.

Miller attended P.S. 29 in Harlem and, after the family moved to Brooklyn in 1928, James
Madison and Abraham Lincoln high schools, graduating from the latter in 1932. During his
high school years, sports interested Miller more than literature, although his literary interests
developed, he says, after he read Dostoevski's *The Brothers Karamazov*. Miller worked in an
auto parts warehouse for two years after high school, in order to save tuition money. He entered college in 1934.

Although he was barely conscious of being Jewish as a child, Arthur Miller credits his parents' reverence for family values, based on their Jewish tradition, with shaping his outlook on
life. Their beliefs, he said, made it impossible for him to write "a totally nihilistic work."

Miller studied playwriting while a student at the University of Michigan, from which he
graduated in 1938. While in college, he wrote a few plays that were never published. He married Mary Grace Slattery in 1940. They had two children, Jane and Robert, and were divorced
in 1956.

After graduation, Miller worked briefly with the Federal Theater Project, but the project
ended before any of his work was produced. His play *The Man Who Had All the Luck* (1944), his
first to be produced on Broadway, had a mediocre debut in New York—it closed after only four
performances. The play was about a man frustrated by the role blind fate had played in his life.
Miller sought, through the play, to deal with the question of whether there is predetermination
or free will in life.

The following year, 1945, the producers of a film called *The Story of G.I. Joe* assigned Miller
to tour United States Army camps in order to gather material for their film. Although relatively little of Miller's research showed up in the film, Miller published a journal, *Situation
Normal*, that same year, which described his visits to the army camps.

Miller's theatrical breakthrough occurred in 1947 with the production of his play *All My Sons*, which tells the story of a man who sells defective airplane parts to the United States Army, an act that results in the deaths of twenty-one people. The man, however, blames his business partner rather than take responsibility himself. The protagonist's favored son, a flyer believed dead at first, discovers his father's duplicity, which ultimately drives the father to suicide. In this play, Miller wanted to portray the conflict that people face between public and private morality. *All My Sons* won the New York Drama Critics Circle Award and gathered many favorable reviews.

Miller's next, and probably his most important work, was *Death of a Salesman*, for which he won the 1949 Pulitzer Prize and a second Drama Critics Circle Award. The play considers the plight of a common man and elevates him to a character of heroic dimensions. The protagonist, Willy Loman, barters his soul for the capitalist dream of wealth and success, then watches in helplessness as the dream turns bad. Loman is driven to suicide when he is finally coerced by his elder son to confront himself.

Critics have been unable to agree on whether Loman is a tragic hero or pathetic victim. But they do agree that *Salesman* is one of the most significant American dramas ever staged. It is Miller's most popular play; more than three million copies of the play have been sold and it has been performed on countless stages.

Miller dealt with a wide variety of issues, including the relationship between fathers and sons, and sin and punishment. *New York Times* drama critic Mel Gussow wrote that in play after play, Miller "holds man responsible for his—and for his neighbor's—actions. Each work is a drama of accountability."

Miller did not depict Jewish characters very often. He has said that he feared giving a Jewish character even a small defect, as it could be used to intensify anti-Semitism, and he did not want such an occurrence to be a result of his creative work.

Drawing an obvious parallel between the 1692 Salem witch trials and the witch hunts of the early 1950s carried out by United States Senator Joseph McCarthy, Arthur Miller wrote *The Crucible* (1953). The play deals with the witch trials in Puritan New England, yet the references in the play are clearly to contemporary anticommunist hysteria.

Arthur Miller was subpoenaed to testify before the House Un-American Activities Committee in June 1956. This was a time when the press was closely following Miller's recent marriage to Marilyn Monroe. Spyros Skouras, who held the actress's contract at Twentieth Century Fox, feared that unless Miller was forthcoming in his appearance before the Committee, Marilyn Monroe's acting career would suffer; Skouras therefore tried to persuade Miller to cooperate with the Committee by divulging the names of those Americans whom Miller knew to have Communist leanings, but the playwright refused.

Arthur Miller was convicted of contempt in 1957 for refusing to implicate others before the Committee, but he was acquitted on appeal the following year.

Miller's play *A View from the Bridge*, produced in 1955, is the story of repressed incest and fear of homosexuality. It is set among Sicilian immigrants in Brooklyn and won Miller a third Drama Critics Circle Award. Other Miller plays include *A Memory of Two Mondays* (1955) and *Incident at Vichy* (1964). The latter portrayed the confrontation between a Nazi officer and suspects awaiting interrogation as they look into the meaning of idealism and moral responsibility. *The Price*, another Miller drama, was produced in 1968; *The Creation of the World and Other Business* was staged in 1972. When that play flopped, Miller stopped writing plays for the rest of the 1970s.

Miller did return to playwriting eventually with these productions: *Playing for Time* (1981); *The Archbishop's Ceiling* (1986); and *The Ride Down Mt. Morgan* (1991).

Miller's early plays (from the 1950s and 1960s) concentrated on the individual in relation to the outside world, and the importance of self-knowledge as a way of coming to terms with reality. In his later plays, Miller stressed relationships between individuals.

Miller has occasionally written screenplays. His screenplay for *The Misfits* (1961) was intended as a vehicle for his wife, Marilyn Monroe, whom he married in 1956 and divorced four years later. Miller's play *After the Fall* examined the playwright's unhappy relationship with Monroe. The main character, Maggie, modeled after Monroe, goes from switchboard operator to famous singer.

In his plays *Incident at Vichy* and *Playing for Time* (1980), and in an early novel he wrote in 1945, *Focus* (1945), Miller explores anti-Semitism, the Holocaust, and the relationship between public and private acts of cruelty. In a 1966 interview in the *Paris Review*, he said: "There is tragedy in the world, but the world must continue. The Jews can't afford to revel too much in the tragic because it might overwhelm them. I have, so to speak, a psychic investment in the continuity of life." His autobiography, *Timebends*, was published in 1987.

Miller's play *Broken Glass* was staged in 1994. He wrote it after sensing the public's indifference to events in Rwanda, Bosnia, and Haiti. The play tells the story of a woman in Brooklyn who is stricken by paralysis when she reads newspaper accounts of Jewish persecution by the Nazis in 1938.

"I used Kristallnacht as a metaphor," Miller said, "because I see the Holocaust as a huge turning point in man's inhumanity to man. Technology was used to become a tool for death instead of liberation, and this happened in a cultured society." The play had mixed reviews in New York but has been a huge success in London, winning England's Olivier Award in 1995 for best play.

Miller lives in Connecticut with his third wife, the photojournalist Inge Morath. In December 1994, nearing his eightieth birthday, Miller was busy writing yet another play. He would not reveal the subject. But it would be a surprise if it wasn't one that is thought-provoking, relevant to the world today, and quite possibly controversial, with memorable lead characters. In 1996 the movie version of Miller's *The Crucible*, was screened; his screenplay was nominated for an Academy Award.

Arthur Miller is without doubt one of the leading American playwrights of the twentieth century. He is the product of a once well-off family that had to endure poverty when the Depression ruined Miller's father's business as a women's coat manufacturer. From his personal experiences, young Miller learned how difficult hard times could be, and those experiences found their way into some of his plays. As he has grown and matured as a dramatist, he has tackled many difficult subjects involving human relationships and the meaning of life.

In October 1999, accepting the prestigious Dorothy and Lillian Gish Prize, Miller said that what he has been trying to do for fifty years was "part the curtain on what we deny." The theater's purpose is, he said, "to discover what we are desperately trying to suppress." Miller said that even at age eighty-three he was writing every day, busily working on a new play.

In October 2000, Miller published *Echoes Down the Corridor*, a collection of essays on travel, politics, and education.

AMEDEO MODIGLIANI

Archetypal Twentieth-Century Artist

Born July 12, 1884, in Livorno, Italy; died January 24, 1920. Italian painter and sculptor. Amedeo Modigliani's singular sculptures and distinctive portraits of elongated, sensual nudes are unmistakable originals. He was a classic example of the struggling, poor artist whose work is more fully recognized after his premature death. About 1916, just four years before he died, he began sculpting the elongated figures that have become known as classic Modiglianis.

AMEDEO MODIGLIANI was born in the provincial Italian port city of Livorno, where his father owned a small business. His mother claimed to be a descendant of the Jewish philosopher Baruch Spinoza. Forced to abandon his formal education, perhaps the result of a drug problem, Modigliani began studying art in Livorno with Guglielmo Michele, who trained his student in the basics of art and art history.

From 1903 to 1905, Modigliani's uncle paid for his art classes. When, in 1905, the uncle died, leaving the young artist without personal resources, Amedeo was forced to leave Livorno after friends laughed at his sculptures and showed no appreciation for his paintings. He was twenty-one years old when

Amedeo Modigliani

he moved to Paris, hoping to make a living as an artist there. His mother sent him whatever money she could manage.

Modigliani did have some luck in Paris. In 1906 he settled and established himself in the Montparnasse district with other Jewish immigrant artists such as Chagall, Lipchitz, Soutine, Zadkine, and Delaunay. As an artist, Modigliani was greatly influenced by the works of French artists of the era—Cézanne, Gaugin, and Toulouse-Lautrec—but the flat, facial planes and abstract, African-style forms that became part of his sculptural style were his own creation.

Modigliani arrived in Paris the year that Captain Alfred Dreyfus was acquitted of treason, and anti-Semitism was rampant in the city. Seemingly unintimidated by the Parisians' anti-Semitic sentiments, when he sketched patrons in cafes to earn a few francs, he signed them "Modigliani—Jew."

Modigliani took Chaim Soutine, another noted young painter of the day, under his wing and introduced him to gallery owners and others in the art world; it was largely due to Modigliani that Soutine's work became known.

Modigliani created his art despite poverty, a tendency to drink too much alcohol, and various illnesses. Modigliani was so poor that he often was compelled to paint on both sides of his canvases. Yet he managed to produce, during his brief career, over twenty sculptures, five hundred paintings, and thousands of watercolors and drawings.

Modigliani frequently painted single figures with backgrounds that were not sharply defined. He also did portraits of his artist friends as well as the two women in his life. These women were the English poet Beatrice Hastings, with whom he lived from 1914 to 1916, and, later, Jeanne Hebuterné, whom he married.

In 1918 Modigliani fell in love with Hebuterné, a nineteen year-old art student. A year later, they had a daughter, whose name was also Jeanne. The daughter, as an adult, wrote a highly regarded biography of her father.

Between 1909 and 1914, Modigliani worked mainly as a sculptor, beginning his efforts in wood, using railroad ties from the building sites of the Paris subway. After moving to La Cité Falguière, he began to use limestone, which he also found at construction sites. Sometimes the laborers gave him stones at no cost; at other times he journeyed to the sites at night and helped himself. The dust from his wood and stone carvings affected his lungs adversely, accounting for some of his ill health as a young man.

When construction in France virtually stopped with the onset of World War I, Modigliani could no longer sculpt because these building sites were his only source of the stone he could not afford to purchase. The little money that his mother had been sending him had stopped coming. He had sold none of his sculptures, so he began painting again as well as continuing his sketching at cafes. At one establishment, La Rotonde, he was given food and drinks in exchange for his paintings.

Between 1909 and 1914, Modigliani produced hundreds of drawings for sculptures as well as lifelike drawings of subjects he found in many different places. But his health deteriorated over time. He drank alcohol to excess. He often erupted in violent outbursts, occasionally even assaulting friends. Beatrice Hastings, whom he attacked during the time they lived together, described Modigliani as an "*enfant*, sometimes terrible, but always forgiven."

Modigliani painted Beatrice's portrait more than a dozen times. Sometimes he won commissions to paint others, but he was never well paid. He painted the sculptor Jacques Lipchitz and his wife. For each sitting, he asked for ten francs and brandy in payment.

The elongated figures that have become known as classic Modiglianis were first executed by the artist in 1916. These figures usually face the viewer, with their heads tilted to one side. Modigliani often used the prostitutes of the Left Bank of Paris as models. Although he pitied them, he never made them look pretty in his paintings. Their hands dangle limply on their laps, their heads are bowed, their eyes are listless, as if the painter caught them at their most difficult moments. Their distinctively shaped heads are connected by long, thin necks to the larger, oval shapes of their rounded shoulders.

Modigliani was a wonderful draftsman with a great sense of color. When he painted his famous sensuous nudes, he used vivid ocher, orange, and other earthy colors. He was able to create iridescent tones by covering thin layers of color with numerous coats of varnish.

In 1916, after painting the series of reclining nudes that is among his best work, Modigliani asked the Polish poet Leopold Zborowski to be his dealer. Zborowski arranged for the paintings to be exhibited at the Berthe Weill Gallery. In doing so, Zborowski ignored the sensibilities of certain well-connected members of conservative French circles, who convinced the police to take action against the exhibit before it even opened. The police descended upon it and removed the nudes, first from the gallery window, then from its walls.

Art critic Monica Bohm-Duchen wrote that, in opposition to the artist's turbulent life, "Modigliani's art is serenely sensual, although many of his portraits betray an inner melancholy. Relatively unaffected by the radical art movements of the day, Modigliani's paintings are strongly indebted to the Italian Renaissance for their classical simplicity of form. His use of color is deeply sensuous, and his nudes done in 1917 and 1918, while never prurient, are almost shockingly frank in their sexuality."

Zborowski's patronage allowed Modigliani to travel to Nice for two months after the gallery debacle. There he painted peasants, servants, children, and landscapes.

In November 1919 Modigliani began spitting up blood. There is an unconfirmed report that he sang the Mourners' Kaddish for himself at a friend's house after he began experiencing this symptom. Two months later, the still-young artist died. The day after his death, his wife, Jeanne Hebuterné, committed suicide by jumping out of a window on the fifth floor of her parents' home.

When Modigliani died of tuberculosis in 1920, he was thirty-six years old. It wasn't long before people discovered his works and recognized their worth. Museum curators and art collectors began to acquire his sculpture and paintings. In 1989 Sotheby's auctioned off a Modigliani portrait for over eight million dollars.

Modigliani's Jewishness never figured in his art. Yet he seemed to have been very proud of his origins and very sensitive to anti-Semitism. When the Italian dictator Benito Mussolini asked art experts to name the greatest contemporary Italian artist, they all asserted that it was Modigliani. Yet, because he was Jewish, the artist and his works were officially ignored by Mussolini, the leader of Modigliani's homeland.

A feature film entitled *Modigliani*, with Andy Garcia in the lead role, appeared in 2004. In the summer of 2004, New York's Jewish Museum mounted an acclaimed sold-out retrospective of the artist's life and work, the first major Modigliani exhibition since 1951.

MOSES

Founder of the Jewish Nation

> Born in Egypt in the thirteenth century B.C.E. Biblical hero. As lawgiver
> and prophet, Moses is the most majestic figure in the Bible. He formu-
> lated Judaism's basic religious code, which was anchored in monotheism
> and shaped by the covenant between God and Israel. Moses led the Chil-
> dren of Israel out of Egypt in what is known as the Exodus, the critical
> event leading to the emergence of the Jewish people.

THE BIBLE SPEAKS OF A NUMBER of great men and women who helped shape Jewish history
and culture, but none was as great as Moses (in Hebrew, Moshe), a leader who was so
central that the Pentateuch is called the Five Books of Moses. His magnificent achievement was the transformation of a group of slaves into a people with the potential of becoming
a "treasured possession," "a kingdom of priests." Moses gave the Jewish people the Torah, with
its laws of justice, holiness, and lovingkindness. He transformed God's words into a system of
beliefs and practices for future generations.

The only source for Moses' life is the Torah itself which, according to Jewish tradition, was
written completely by his hand (except for the last verses), with God dictating the words.

When Moses was born, the Israelites were slaves in Egypt; Egyptian persecution was at a
height. Moses' mother, Jochebed, and his father, Amram, were of the tribe of Levi. Moses had
an older sister and brother—Miriam and Aaron.

The Pharaoh of Egypt had ordered the Children of Israel to perform forced labor. In order
to reduce their numbers, he had also ordered the Hebrew midwives, Shiphrah and Puah, to
kill the Israelite boys at birth. When the plan failed, Pharaoh instructed that every newborn
Hebrew boy be thrown into the Nile River. Jochebed managed to save the infant Moses by
placing him in a wicker basket and hiding him in the bulrushes along the banks of the Nile.
Miriam was sent to keep an eye on him and ensure his safety.

One day, when coming to bathe in the Nile, Pharaoh's daughter came upon the child. She
adopted him as her son, calling him Moses, meaning, in Hebrew, "drawn out [of the water]."

Moses grew up in the royal court. One day he saw an Egyptian taskmaster beating an Israelite slave. Moses killed the taskmaster and fled the country, seeking refuge in the land of
Midian. There, Moses was welcomed into the household of Jethro, a Midianite priest. Jethro
gave Moses his daughter, Zipporah, as a wife, and Moses stayed in Midian for many years
tending his father-in-law's sheep.

One day, in the wilderness, Moses experienced a theophany. From within a bush that burned
but was not consumed by the fire, God appeared to Moses, ordering him to return to Egypt and

The Jewish Week

Moses

to lead his people to freedom. Reluctant at first, Moses stammered, not able to understand how he could become a spokesman for his people. When God agreed that Aaron would help him with his public speaking, Moses, now eighty years old, accepted the mission.

Returning to Egypt along with his brother, Moses confronted the king and insisted that the Israelites be freed. The Pharaoh said no. He would not even permit them to enter the desert briefly to worship their God. Indeed, he threatened to treat them even more harshly.

God then afflicted the Egyptians with ten plagues. After the tenth and most brutal plague, in which all firstborn Egyptians were killed, Pharaoh relented. No sooner had the Israelites left, however, than Pharaoh ordered his army to pursue them as they headed for the Red Sea. It appeared that the Israelites were in grave trouble with the sea in front of them and the Egyptians behind them. At the Lord's command, Moses stretched out his hand over the sea, and a strong east wind miraculously divided the waters so that the Children of Israel were able to cross in safety. As the Egyptians pursued them into the divide, the waters returned and the Egyptian soldiers were drowned.

A few weeks later, the Israelites, numbering six hundred thousand males, and their families, arrived at Mount Sinai. After three days, Moses scaled the mountain, remaining at the top for forty days. During that time, God presented him with the Ten Commandments, inscribed on two tablets of stone.

With Moses remaining on the mountain for so long, the people below began to despair, wondering if he would ever come down. They finally prevailed upon Aaron to make a golden calf whom they might worship. When Moses finally descended the mountain, he beheld a horrific scene: the Israelites were dancing around the idol. In his fury Moses threw the two tablets bearing the Commandments to the ground, smashing them to pieces.

The Israelites repented, and Moses asked God not to punish them. Moses then went up the mountain a second time, and there he received a second set of tablets.

The Children of Israel remained in the Sinai Desert for another forty years with Moses as their leader, staying most of the time at Kadesh Barnea. During this time, however, Moses faced a number of rebellions.

God had decreed that none of the Israelites who left Egypt would be able to enter the Promised Land; this order included Moses and Aaron. Moses was, however, allowed to approach the boundaries of the Promised Land and see it, from afar, from atop Mt. Nebo. When he died at age 120, his eyes were undimmed and his vigor unabated.

The Bible sums up the life of this great leader of the Jewish people: "There has not risen a prophet in Israel like unto Moses, whom the Lord knew face to face."

MOSES BEN NACHMAN

Leading Talmudist of the Middle Ages

Born 1194 in Gerona, Catalonia; died 1270. Medieval Talmudic scholar. Rabbi Moses ben Nachman, who was also known by the Greek name of Nahmanides as well as by the Hebrew acronym Ramban, was a leading commentator on the Bible and Talmud. In July 1263, when he was sixty-nine years old, Rabbi ben Nachman was compelled by King James of Aragon to defend Judaism in a public controversy involving a Jewish convert to Christianity. The debate, which occurred in Barcelona, lasted four days. Later, the Ramban immigrated to the Holy Land, where he helped improve Jewish life.

HIS REAL NAME WAS MOSES BEN NACHMAN. He was known, however, as the Ramban—an acronym of Rabbi Moses ben Nachman—and, on occasion, as Rabbenu Moses Gerondi or Yeroni after the town where he was born, Gerona, in Catalonia. He was also called Nahmanides by some. As a youth he was praised for his Talmudic scholarship. He became one of the major authors of Talmudic literature in the Middle Ages.

Moses ben Nachman was a man of many talents: philosopher, kabbalist, biblical scholar, poet, and physician. He became rabbi of Gerona. Because of his personality and scholarship, he was recognized as the spiritual leader of the entire Spanish Jewish community.

Ben Nachman earned an income by working as a physician. Sometimes even the king, James I of Aragon, sought his medical advice.

In July 1263, when he was sixty-nine years old and known far and wide as the Ramban, ben Nachman's life changed when King James compelled him to defend Judaism in a public controversy involving a Jewish convert to Christianity. The convert was Pablo Christiani, who had been involved in missionary work among the Jews. Christiani claimed that passages in the Talmud confirmed the truth of the Christian faith.

The dispute went on for four days in Barcelona, with the King, members of the court, and senior Church officials present. Because the King had given the Ramban total freedom to speak out, he did so, and his bluntness offended members of the Church.

At the debate, Pablo Christiani used various Talmudic legends to prove that the Messiah had already appeared and that he was both human and divine. Christiani argued further that Christ's death atoned for humanity's sins and rendered the Halachic commandments of Judaism no longer valid.

No, claimed the Ramban, Talmudic legends were not to be taken literally. Jews understood that they were allegories and not historical events. He thought it nonsense for Christians to believe that Jesus was the "prince of peace" since "from the time of Jesus until the present, the world has been filled with violence and injustice and the Christians have shed more blood than all other peoples."

The Christian representatives were taken off guard. They did not like the way the debate was progressing. At their insistence, the discussion was stopped and no formal conclusion was reached.

According to the Ramban's version, King James complimented Rabbi ben Nachman: "I have never seen a man defend a wrong cause so well." A week later, the Ramban attended the synagogue in Barcelona. A Christian friar gave the sermon, which urged Jews to convert. Then the King got up and spoke, although what he said is not recorded. His very presence in the synagogue, however, was an unprecedented event in the Middle Ages. Finally, it was the Ramban's turn to speak. The King was so impressed with the way the Ramban articulated his defense of Judaism that he gave him a gift of three hundred dinars. The Ramban then returned to Gerona.

The Church, however, did not let the matter rest. In 1265 the Dominicans began proceedings against the Ramban in the court of the Inquisition by charging him with blaspheming Jesus. The King suggested that the Ramban be banished for two years and that his version of the dispute of 1263 be burned. The Dominican friars would not accept this settlement. So the Ramban left Spain and immigrated to the Holy Land. He arrived there in the summer of 1267.

Some fifty of ben Nachman's literary works are extant. (There are other works that have been attributed to him, but it has not been possible to confirm that he penned them.) Most of these works are commentaries on the Talmud and Halacha. His Halachic commentaries are considered among the masterpieces of rabbinic literature. He also wrote books; their subject matter was mainly an effort to educate people. One book was devoted to the nature of the belief in redemption and called the *Sefer ha-Ge'ullah* (about 1263). He wrote numerous poems and prayers as well, including one that he composed upon his entry to Jerusalem.

When the Ramban first went to Jerusalem, he found the Jewish communities in disarray after the Crusades and the Tatar invasion. He reorganized the community and established a synagogue there. He wrote to his son Nahum, "We found a ruined building with a beautiful dome supported by marble columns and we took it for a synagogue as the city is ownerless and whoever wishes to take possession of some parts of the ruins may do so." (He had two other sons, Solomon and Joseph.) Ben Nachman's magnetic presence attracted Jews to Jerusalem. For centuries this synagogue was the only one in that city.

The Ramban moved to Acre in the northern part of the country in 1268, where he led the Jewish community and spent his final days until his death at the age of seventy-six. It is not known whether he is buried in Jerusalem, at the foot of Mount Carmel near Acre, or in Hebron.

Because of his writings on the Talmud, ben Nachman became a leading figure in the development of Talmudic study. He is best known for his Bible commentary. Most of his commentaries were written while he was living in Spain, but some were written later in *Eretz Yisrael*. Ben Nachman noted that the aim of his commentaries was "to appease the minds of the students, weary through exile and trouble, when they read the portion on Sabbaths and festivals."

Ben Nachman was especially interested in the sequence of the biblical passages and the meaning of the Bible's laws and narrative. His commentaries reflected his views on God, the Torah, and the world. He believed that the narratives of the Bible could serve as portents of the future, that the Bible's account of creation contained prophecies about the crucial events of the next six thousand years.

The Ramban also felt free to criticize the behavior of biblical figures. For example, he argued that Abraham "unintentionally committed a great sin" when, upon arriving in Egypt and fearing for his life, he said that Sarah was his sister. In so doing, Abraham exposed his wife to moral corruption, the Ramban contended; Abraham should have exhibited faith that God would save both him and Sarah.

Ben Nachman also argued that there was a reason behind every commandment. He claimed that the commandments are all for the good of mankind—whether by keeping people from harm, removing evil beliefs and habits, teaching mercy and goodness, or recalling the miracles of God. While the Ramban explained some of the dietary regulations as important for health reasons, he interpreted others as designed to keep the Jewish people from eating foods that could dull the mind or harden the heart. Although at times he offered mystical interpretations of biblical texts, ben Nachman also held the traditional belief that God dictated the entire Torah to Moses.

The Ramban offered encouragement and comfort to the Jewish people. Regarding the song of *Ha'azinu* (Deuteronomy 32), the Ramban wrote in a commentary: "And behold there is nothing conditional in this song. It is a charter testifying that we shall have to suffer heavily for our sins, but that, nevertheless, God will not destroy us, being reconciled to us (though we shall have no merits) and forgiving our sins for his name's sake alone . . . ."

ADOLPH OCHS

Founder of the New York Times

Born March 12, 1858, in Cincinnati, Ohio; died April 8, 1935. American newspaper publisher. In opposition to the "yellow journalism" practiced routinely in the late nineteenth century, publisher Adolph Ochs worked to raise the newspaper profession's standards and changed the face of American journalism. As publisher of the *New York Times* for thirty-nine years, he not only increased the newspaper's circulation but also gave its news pages a reputation for integrity and objectivity.

A DOLPH OCHS'S FATHER, Julius, was a Jewish immigrant from Bavaria who arrived in Cincinnati in 1845—his son Adolph Simon was born there in 1858. The family moved to Knoxville, Tennessee, where Julius Ochs was a leader of the Jewish community and served as a volunteer rabbi for twenty-five years. Julius's two other sons became newspaper publishers and editors.

Ochs had newsprint in his blood from an early age. He left school at the age of eleven and began working as an office boy for the Knoxville *Chronicle*. When he was fourteen, he began learning more about the newspaper business by working in the composing room of another smaller newspaper in Tennessee, the Knoxville *Tribune*. By the age of seventeen, Ochs had moved up to a job as a compositor at the Louisville *Courier-Journal*.

Moving to Chattanooga in 1877, when he was nineteen years old, Ochs made a major move up the career ladder. There he was the editor of the Chattanooga *Dispatch* until it went out of business the following year.

Having seen the inside of a newspaper, Ochs wanted to own one. That same year, he paid $6,750 to purchase a failing newspaper, the Chattanooga *Times*. Ochs soon built it into one of the great newspapers of the South.

Ochs's experience with the Tennessee newspaper convinced him that he was ready to purchase more newspapers. In 1896, the *New York Times* seemed to be collapsing. It had once been a flourishing, well-regarded newspaper, but its daily paid circulation was down to nine thousand, less than the newspaper had when it was ten days old in 1851.

To purchase the newspaper, Ochs borrowed $75,000 and agreed to a deal whereby he would assume the controlling interest if he could show a profit for three straight years. He persuaded the remaining stockholders of the old *Times* to reinvest in his new company.

Ochs bucked the popular trend in journalism toward sensationalism, known as "yellow journalism," and tried to appeal to the intelligence of readers by offering them thorough, unbiased news coverage they could trust. He insisted that editorial opinion had to be subordinate to

Adolph Ochs

news and that news reporting had to be objective. He refused to accept fraudulent or improper advertising, nor did he permit the practice, which was routine at the time, of allowing advertisers to dictate the editorial policy of the newspaper.

Ochs also sought to expand the *New York Times*'s physical plant. He built more production facilities and introduced rotogravure printing to create a better looking publication. He also began producing a separate book review section; today it is still both popular and highly regarded. Ochs wanted the paper to be serious, so there were no comics, no cartoons, no screaming headlines designed to make someone say "Gee whiz" and dig in his pocket to buy the paper and read about a scandal.

Ochs's credo, as he announced on the editorial page the day he took over the newspaper, was "to give the news impartially, without fear or favor, regardless of party, sect, or interest involved . . . ." This belief was displayed in different places around the building that housed the newspaper as well as, later, in the *Times*'s bureaus that were established in various parts of the world. It was Ochs who came up with the famous phrase that, to this day, is printed on the front page of every issue of the newspaper: "All the News That's Fit To Print." This meant that certain news, by virtue of its sensational nature, is not deemed by the editors to be suitable for its pages and thus, in order for the newspaper to maintain its high journalistic standards, this information would not be printed.

In 1898 Ochs reduced the price of the *Times* from three cents to one penny to compete with the newspapers that practiced the yellow journalism that sold publications. With that one step, Ochs tripled his circulation. In the thirty-nine years Ochs was publisher of the newspaper, he helped build its circulation from 9,000 to 466,000 daily and 730,000 on Sunday.

While developing the *New York Times*, Ochs continued to control the Chattanooga *Times*. In 1902 he purchased the *Times* and the *Ledger* of Philadelphia, merged them, and made his brother George the editor. When the company was sold in 1913, George remained as editor for two more years and then became editor of *Current History*, a monthly magazine published by the *New York Times*.

During World War I, George anglicized his Germanic-sounding family name of Ochs to Oakes. His son, John B. Oakes, took charge of the editorial page of the *New York Times* in 1961 and oversaw it until 1977. Milton B. Ochs, the youngest of the three brothers, became vice-president of The New York Times Company.

During the years before the United States entered World War I, Ochs did not want the *Times* to be thought of as either pro-British or pro-German. It had been accused of being both. Ochs also had to deal with the fact that the newspaper was owned by Jews. He did not want the paper to be identified as a "Jewish paper." His wife, Effie, was the daughter of Rabbi Isaac M. Wise of Cincinnati, one of the major figures of American Reform Judaism. Ochs often seemed proud to be Jewish, but at times appeared uncomfortable being among his fellow Jews. When Ochs attended a dinner at Delmonico's during his first months as the *Times*'s new owner, he was uneasy about the fact that "the party was made up of the *crème de la crème* of New York Jewish culture and refinement . . . not a coarse joke, nothing boisterous, not too much drinking—nothing that would not have taken place in the very best society."

To Ochs, it was important to convince others that he believed Judaism to be a religion, not a national identity. Once he specifically ordered his city editor not to give "too much space" to the activities of the American Jewish Committee (AJC), which was assisting European Jews caught in the war zone.

"The AJC activists," he told an editor, "work to preserve the characteristics and traditions of the Jew, making him a man apart from other men. I am interested in the Jewish religion—I want that preserved—but that's as far as I want to go." He stuck to his views. In 1925, he declared, "Religion is all I stand for as a Jew."

Jewish groups assailed Ochs's newspaper for its policies on the immigration of Eastern European Jews to the United States and its editorials against the Zionist idea of a national homeland for the Jews. Ochs's unwillingness to embrace the Jewish national movement was echoed in editorials long after his death when the *Times*, under the leadership of his son-in-law, Arthur Hays Sulzberger, remained opposed to Zionism.

When Ochs died in 1935 at the age of seventy-seven, the *New York Times*'s daily circulation was 466,000. Ochs's high standards of journalism continue to influence generations of *Times* editors and writers and to set a tone for American journalism that implies credibility. The *New York Times* is considered the "newspaper of record." Many people find it the best source of factual information available in newspaper form.

J. ROBERT OPPENHEIMER

Disillusioned Father of the Atomic Bomb

Born April 22, 1904, in New York City; died February 18, 1967. American physicist. Admired for his intellect and adored by students, J. Robert Oppenheimer directed the ultra-secret Manhattan Project, in which the first atomic bombs were created during World War II. After the war, however, Oppenheimer opposed plans to build the far more powerful hydrogen bomb. For that position, and because of his rumored association with pre-War leftist causes, his security clearance was revoked in 1953. Ten years later, however, Presidents Kennedy and Johnson honored Oppenheimer's contribution to science, thus reviving Oppenheimer's status as a renowned physicist.

JULIUS ROBERT OPPENHEIMER was born in New York City in 1904, the eldest son of a wealthy, liberal Jewish family. His father, Julius, had emigrated from Germany in 1888 and had a successful textile importing business. His mother, Ella (Freedman) Oppenheimer, was a painter from Baltimore. She died when Oppenheimer was nine years old.

Oppenheimer attended the Ethical Culture School and was a brilliant student. Mathematics and chemistry interested him from an early age. By age eleven he possessed an impressive rock collection and had become the youngest member of the New York Mineralogical Society.

Oppenheimer completed his undergraduate studies at Harvard University in three years, graduating *summa cum laude* in 1926. His interest in atomic physics led him to study abroad at two centers of atomic research: Cambridge University, in 1925 and 1926, where he worked under the famous scientist Ernest Rutherford, and at the University of Gottingen, in 1926 and 1927, where he studied with Max Born. He earned his doctorate at the latter school in 1927 after submitting a thesis on quantum theory. He subsequently completed two years of postdoctoral study, first as a National Research Fellow at Harvard and the California Institute of Technology in 1927 and 1928; then abroad in 1928 and 1929 at the University of Leiden (Netherlands) and the Technische Hochschule in Zurich.

Returning to the United States in the spring of 1929, Oppenheimer had offers to teach at ten American universities. He accepted posts on the faculty of the University of California at Berkeley and the California Institute of Technology. He maintained connections with both schools until 1947.

Oppenheimer was considered a wonderful teacher; his intellectual life went beyond physics. At the age of thirty, he taught himself his eighth language, Sanskrit, so that he could study

Hindu scriptures in the original. He owned no telephone, never listened to a radio, read no newspapers.

At Berkeley, Oppenheimer created the largest graduate and postdoctoral theoretical physics department in the United States. His students were so devoted to him that when Oppenheimer left Berkeley to teach at the California Institute of Technology, his students followed him to repeat his courses there.

Oppenheimer was not politically involved during the 1920s. He did not vote until the 1936 elections. He became more interested in society in general, however, after hearing reports of the mistreatment of German Jews, some of whom were his relatives, and of the deprivations suffered by fellow Americans during the Great Depression.

During the late 1930s, Oppenheimer came into contact with numerous members of the political left. He worked for and contributed to leftist causes, both in America and abroad, including the Loyalist cause in Spain.

Oppenheimer's research in physics concerned the study of the electron-atom collision processes, cosmic ray showers, and quan-

J. Robert Oppenheimer

AP/Wide World Photos

tum electrodynamics. He participated in the development of what came to be called the Oppenheimer-Phillips reaction, which helped others gain new knowledge about the structure of the nucleus of the atom.

He first became involved with the government's atomic energy program in 1941. In the summer of 1942, Oppenheimer directed a small number of scientists at Berkeley who were considering the theoretical aspects of atom-bomb production. He concluded that the separate laboratories in the United States, England, and Canada where scientists had been working on the problem should be united under one roof.

Oppenheimer suggested the New Mexican desert as the site for the new laboratory, since he had spent numerous pleasant vacations there and it was remote and thus safer for the surrounding population when the atom bomb was tested. So influential was he with the officials responsible for the program that his suggestion was quickly accepted.

In 1943, during World War II, Oppenheimer was appointed director of the Manhattan Project, based at Los Alamos, New Mexico, the Allied effort to produce an atomic bomb. Oppy, as he was affectionately known by students and other scientists, recruited many of his former graduate students to work with him. The hardest part was convincing scientists to commit themselves to the highly secret project for the duration of the war. His "intellectual sex appeal," as one recruit called it, did the trick, however.

On July 16, 1945, from five miles away in the control room, Oppenheimer witnessed the first atomic bomb explosion, the successful conclusion of his work. Immediately, the following lines from the sacred Hindu poem the *Bhagavad-Gita* came into his mind:

If the radiance of a thousand suns
Were to burst at once into the sky
That would be the splendor of the Mighty One.
I am become Death
The destroyer of worlds.

That the poem came to Oppenheimer's mind may have been an early indication of the misgivings he would later have about the military use of nuclear weapons.

Oppenheimer's scientific genius and inspirational leadership of the complex project was considered a key to the development of this powerful bomb. In 1946, Oppenheimer received the Presidential Medal of Merit in recognition of his contribution to science.

Following World War II, Oppenheimer returned to the California Institute of Technology. In 1947, however, he moved to Princeton University, where he became the head of the Institute of Advanced Studies. From 1946 to 1952 he was chairman of the General Advisory Committee to the Atomic Energy Commission (AEC).

Oppenheimer's objection to the hydrogen bomb was based on his concern that it might be used against the Russians as the Cold War took hold of American politics. In a letter to James B. Conant, a fellow member of the General Advisory Committee, Oppenheimer noted that the technical problems of producing the new bomb were not his main concern. Rather, he noted, "what does worry me is that this thing appears to have caught the imagination both of the Congressional and of the military people, as the answer to the problem posed by the Russian advance. It would be folly to oppose the exploration of this weapon. We have always known it had to be done; and it does have to be done . . . . But that we become committed to it as the way to save the country and the peace, appears to me full of dangers."

McCarthyism was a powerful, if insidious, force on the American scene in the early 1950s, and the inflammatory atmosphere it generated in the nation worked against Oppenheimer. His contacts with leftists in the 1930s became suspect. A letter written in December 1953 accusing Oppenheimer of being a Soviet agent was taken seriously by members of Congress. The charges against him focused on what were viewed as his Communist links in the late 1930s and early 1940s, and he was accused of opposing the hydrogen bomb program for subversive reasons.

The Atomic Energy Commission reviewed Oppenheimer's case twice; he was accused of hampering the development of the hydrogen bomb and of associating with Communists. These allegations of disloyalty led to Oppenheimer's security clearance being revoked in December 1953. His dismissal from the Atomic Energy Commission made him a symbol of the victimization that seemed to characterize the McCarthy era. When his case was reviewed, the Atomic Energy Commission dropped the charge of hampering the hydrogen bomb development, but would not set aside the allegation that he had associated with Communists.

By the early 1960s, the atmosphere in Washington had changed. The passage of time had led many to conclude that McCarthyism had needlessly destroyed reputations, Oppenheimer's among them. In the first public step toward the restoration of Oppenheimer's reputation, President John F. Kennedy invited him to a White House dinner in April 1962.

In late 1963 President Lyndon Johnson presented Oppenheimer with the Atomic Energy Commission's highest honor, the $50,000 Fermi Award. Oppenheimer continued to direct the Institute for Advanced Study at Princeton until he retired in 1966. He died at the age of sixty-three.

Life magazine, in a special Fall 1970 edition, named him one of the top one hundred Americans of the twentieth century.

AMOS OZ

Renowned Israeli Writer

Born May 4, 1939, in Jerusalem. Israeli writer. Amos Oz is Israel's best known and most successful writer. A native-born Israeli, Oz is credited with providing the most sensitive portrait of his country in his books. Oz was a member of Kibbutz Hulda from 1954 until 1985, then moved to the Israeli desert town of Arad. Among his best-known novels are *My Michael* (1968), *The Hill of Evil Counsel* (1976), and *In the Land of Israel* (1983).

AMOS OZ WAS BORN Amos Klausner in Jerusalem in 1939 and came from a family of enthusiastic Zionists. His grandfather, Alexander Klausner, fled from Odessa, Russia, soon after the 1917 Russian Revolution, and settled in Vilna, Poland, with his wife and two sons; Alexander moved on to Jerusalem in 1933. One son, Amos's father, Yehudah Arieh Klausner, married the former Fania Mussman, daughter of a Polish miller. Oz grew up in a house filled with books.

"What was Jewish about the house," Oz said, "was the terrible sense of insecurity and fear, the knowledge that anything could happen at any moment, that even when Hitler was dead, he's not dead."

Though Yehudah Klausner knew fifteen languages, Oz learned only Hebrew as a child growing up in Kerem Avraham, a Jerusalem suburb. He studied at the Takhemoni Orthodox Boys School.

Oz always wanted to write. When he was five years old, he learned the alphabet and his father taught him how to type with one finger. "The first thing I printed was my name and the subtitle: writer," Oz said.

Fania Klausner committed suicide in 1952 when Amos was thirteen years old. Her death had a profound impact on him and on his later novels.

"A lot of what I wrote," Oz said, "was an attempt to decipher why she killed herself and perhaps to resume the conversation with her which was so abruptly interrupted even before it began." His mother's suicide, Oz said, "made me change direction. I had been a chauvinistic, nationalistic poet. I became immensely curious about people, women, families."

Oz adopted the name Oz, which means "strength" in Hebrew, as a teenager. Two years after his mother's death, though only fifteen years old, Oz left home to join Kibbutz Hulda, midway between Jerusalem and Tel Aviv.

Oz married Nily Zuckerman in 1960; they have three children—Fania, Gaia, and Daniel. That same year, after three years in the Israeli army, Oz was sent by the kibbutz to study literature and philosophy at Jerusalem's Hebrew University. After earning his B.A. in 1963, Oz returned to the kibbutz to teach, share in kibbutz duties, and write. All of his literary earnings were turned over to Hulda, in keeping with the kibbutz rule that members had to contribute outside income to the kibbutz.

Oz's collection of short stories *Where the Jackals Howl* (Hebrew, 1965; English, 1981) depicts the landscape and atmosphere of kibbutz life. The jackal symbolizes the dark, hidden world that poses a threat to the calm and stability of daily life of the civilized world. His first novel, *Elsewhere, Perhaps* (Hebrew, 1966; English, 1973), concerns an older generation of Russian and German Jewish refugees who, motivated by optimistic idealism, settles a fictitious mountain kibbutz. The main theme of the book is the fragility of civilized societies.

In 1966 Oz was awarded the prestigious Holon Prize. By 1967, during the Six-Day War, Oz was serving his country with Israeli armored divisions as they advanced across the Sinai Desert to the Suez Canal. Israel's occupation of Arab territories after the war and the troubled moral ambiguities attending that occupation brought Oz's writings to a new level of seriousness.

Amos Oz

State of Israel Government Press Office

Oz's second novel, *My Michael* (Hebrew, 1968; English, 1972), is his best-known work. The book was an unprecedented bestseller in Israel. The *New York Times* called *My Michael* "one of the most accomplished foreign novels to appear here in the last few years."

In 1969 Oz was a visiting fellow at St. Cross College, Oxford University, where he received a master's degree the following year. That year also saw the publication of his *Unto Death* (Hebrew, 1970; English, 1975). It contained two novellas on the theme of paranoid hatred. Oz said that in these, as well as other works, he wrote "about the haunting shadows, about yearnings, fears, hatreds, nightmares, messianic aspirations, longings for the absolute. I wrote to explore in words whence and why my family had come, and what we had hoped to find here and what we actually found."

Oz has said that the family is the most important element in his writing. Endlessly fascinated by this institution, he believes it has no business existing, as it has been rejected by so many people. "So many ideologies and religions have tried to demolish the family, yet it seems to be alive and kicking," he said.

Oz's third novel, *Touch the Water, Touch the Wind*, was published in Hebrew in 1973; in English, a year later. Meanwhile, during the Israeli-Arab war that occurred at that time, Oz served with the Israeli tank corps on the Golan Heights.

Oz also wrote nonfiction. *In the Land of Israel* (1983) is an impressionistic report on life in Israel, especially its politics, based on Oz's interviews with Israelis.

Oz, a long-time political activist, has been identified with the political left and in July 1967, soon after the Six-Day War, he was among the first to advocate a two-state (one Israeli, one

Arab) solution to the political conflict, believing that the land belonged to the Arabs as well as the Israelis. "I'm a political guerrilla," Oz said, "not a regular solider. Whenever anything makes me angry, I emerge out of the bush, and tell the government what to do, not that they ever listen."

Oz's daily routine rarely varies. He rises by 5:30 a.m. and immediately takes a thirty-minute walk in the desert, "which starts just three minutes from here," near his home in Arad. "The walk helps to knock things into proportion. When a politician says never and forever, you know in the desert the stones are laughing. In the Middle East, never is between six months and three years."

By 7:30 a.m. Oz is in his cellar study at home, standing over a writing stand where he composes in longhand, unable to sit for long stretches because of a bad back. The phone is disconnected. When the words don't flow, Oz feels guilty: "At the kibbutz I saw people milking cows or plowing the fields, and I knew all I had done that day was to write three sentences of which I had scratched out two."

To sharpen dialogue, Oz walks around Arad and talks to himself, getting odd looks from passers-by. But he is not deterred: "I need to have everything in my ears, like music. Only after that do I put it on paper." After lunch, Oz returns to his desk, evaluating his writing, sometimes discarding what he has written, or filling the margins with question marks.

Commenting, in 1994, on what being Jewish meant to him, Oz suggested that Jewishness is a set of "sensibilities," a collection of traits that can be present in both Jew and non-Jew, but seem to be more present in Jews. Jewishness could not, should not, he said, be defined in religious or cultural or racial terms. Every Friday night, Oz and his family light candles and read a chapter from the Bible, but not necessarily the portion of the week. Oz stays away from synagogue, explaining, "I have no attraction to ritual."

In 1987 Oz's book *Black Box* was published. Oz said that he was most proud of this novel for its "technical sophistication." "In *Black Box*, I reached a clean tune. It's a good performance technically." Two years later, another novel, *To Know a Woman*, was published, followed by *Fima* (1992) and *Don't Pronounce It Night* (1994).

In 1989 Oz received France's top literary award, the Paris Prize, for the best foreign novel of that year (*Black Box*). In 1992 he was awarded the German Publishers Association's international peace prize.

Amos Oz is a teacher of Modern Israeli Literature at Beersheba's Ben-Gurion University two days a week during the second semester of each year. For five months in late 1997, Oz taught Hebrew literature at Princeton University and promoted his nineteenth book, *Panther in the Basement*.

In March 1998, Oz was awarded the esteemed Israel Prize for his literary efforts. In October 2001, he published *The Same Sea*, which features both free and rhyming verse. *Publishers Weekly* described the book as "a meditation, a lamentation, a quest for meaning, a story of family love and of erotic longing, and a vibrantly poetic prose poem."

In March 2002, *The Jerusalem Post* paid tribute to Oz by saying that "long ago he transcended his position as merely this country's finest living novelist. His eloquent speeches at peace rallies, thoughtful public opinion pieces in leading newspapers here and abroad, and his capacity as unofficial advisor to some major political figures [most notably Shimon Peres] have elevated Oz to a position akin to his biblical namesake as a modern-day prophet of Israel's secular Left."

A Tale of Love and Darkness, an Amos Oz memoir cum family history, was published in 2004.

WILLIAM S. PALEY

Founder of CBS

> Born September 28, 1901, in Chicago, Illinois; died October 26, 1990. American television network founder. On his own, William S. Paley turned a small network of radio stations into a major communications empire. Transforming the failing CBS radio network into a competitive rival of David Sarnoff's NBC, Paley used his genius in mass-audience programming to build the $4.6-billion entertainment empire known as the CBS television network. For twenty-six years, CBS led the ratings due to such highly-popular sitcoms as *I Love Lucy*, *M*A*S*H*, and *All in the Family*. William Paley was also a pioneer in using radio as a news medium. Paley retired in 1983, but when CBS slipped to second place in the network ratings, he resumed the chairmanship at the age of eighty-six and remained in that post until his death.

WILLIAM PALEY WAS BORN IN THE JEWISH NEIGHBORHOOD of Chicago's West Side in 1901, the elder of the two children of Samuel and Goldie (Drell) Paley. He added the middle initial "S" to his name at age twelve, even though it did not stand for anything.

Paley's sister Blanche was born when he was four years old. She received more attention from their mother than he, according to Paley. Persuaded that his mother did not find him attractive, Paley developed an inferiority complex; he believed he was unappealing in some way. He did, however, develop a strong, positive relationship with his father. Paley spent his summers working for his father and his Uncle Jay in their Congress Cigar factory. Paley swept the floors, ran errands, and absorbed everything about the business.

Despite a mixed academic record at school, Paley displayed an enthusiasm for reading. He also had a good ear for music and had begun violin lessons. After he attended a Mischa Elman concert, Paley decided to become a violinist, but his violin teacher refused to continue to teach him, saying that the boy lacked the proper talent. Undeterred from his interest in music, Paley learned how to play piano, but soon tired of that musical instrument.

At age sixteen, Bill was sent to the Western Military Academy in Alton, Illinois, to complete his higher education. He earned two years of high school credit in a single year. In 1918 he was admitted to the University of Chicago when he was only seventeen years old. With the United States at war, Paley wanted to enlist, but his father talked him out of it.

Labor difficulties prompted Sam and Jay to open a branch factory in Philadelphia for their Congress Cigar Company in 1919. Eventually Sam Paley moved the family to Philadelphia when it became clear that the branch factory was fast becoming the cigar operation's main plant.

When Paley's grandfather died suddenly, Sam Paley rushed back to Chicago, leaving his son to manage the new factory. A month later, after his father returned to Philadelphia, Paley entered the University of Pennsylvania's Wharton School of Business, from which he graduated in the spring of 1922. Paley then went to work full time at the cigar factory, becoming vice-president and advertising manager.

In the summer of 1925, Paley tested the new medium of radio as an advertising vehicle. He arranged for La Palina cigars, the pride and joy of the Paley business, to be advertised over WCAU, a local Philadelphia radio station, by sponsoring a one-hour program called the "La Palina Hour." The elder Paley expressed grave doubts at first, but eventually was won over to radio's advertising potential.

Sensing the great possibilities radio offered, Bill Paley in 1928 bought into the United Independent Broadcasters, Inc., which until then had not been a great success. His initial investment was $400,000. At this point the network owned twelve radio stations in the Northeast. Paley, as president, renamed the chain the Columbia Broadcasting System, Inc., and expanded it to the West Coast market. Paley's original investment grew to $350 million by the time of his death in 1990.

Soon Paley had some sixty radio stations that were utilizing network programming, making CBS radio a coast-to-coast network. Paley's skill was for recruiting talent audiences loved, including Fred Allen, George Burns and Gracie Allen, Jack Benny, and Bing Crosby.

Bill Paley also proved an innovative programmer. In 1931 he organized live broadcasts of the New York Philharmonic Symphony Society concerts. The network soon began providing newscasts as well. Live drama, presented by Norman Corwin and called *The Columbia Workshop*, debuted in 1936.

By the late 1930s, CBS was moving into shortwave broadcasting that could provide programs from overseas. In 1938 the network broadcast the famous abdication speech of King Edward VIII. It also transmitted some of the first in-depth field reports ever carried by radio when the Nazis invaded different areas of Europe during the early phases of World War II. At Paley's initiative, CBS also ventured beyond the radio business. For example, it built Columbia Records into one of the greatest forces in the recorded music industry.

The writer of a 1935 *Fortune* magazine article noted that "Mr. Paley as a businessman is a theme that practically brings tears to the eyes of his directors—never in all their lives, they say, have they been associated with anybody as clever at business. Not only is he a master advertiser and feeler of the public pulse, but these gentlemen say he is the greatest organizer, the best executive, the quickest thinker, the coolest negotiator they have ever seen."

Paley married Dorothy Hart Hearst, the daughter of a Los Angeles insurance executive in 1932; they had one son and one daughter. Their marriage ended in divorce in July 1947. That same month, Paley married Barbara "Babs" (Cushing) Mortimer, with whom he had another son, William, and a daughter, Kate.

During World War II, Paley was stationed in London as a colonel, and was deputy chief of the Psychological Warfare Division of the Allied Command in Europe. At war's end he returned to the United States and once again presided over CBS, developing it into one of the great national television networks. Paley revolutionized the television industry by taking control of programming, moving it away from advertising agencies and giving it to the network executives to determine. He built studios on both coasts and produced situation comedies and game shows, all to lure audiences through innovative entertainment in this new medium.

Paley built CBS television into a $4.6-billion entertainment empire. By the mid-1960s, CBS led NBC and ABC in the national ratings, remaining in the top spot for twenty-six years. This was due in large part to the success of such highly popular sitcoms as *I Love Lucy*, *M*A*S*H**, and *All in the Family*, testimony to Paley's excellent instincts about what audiences liked.

In 1979 Paley wrote his memoirs, which were entitled *As It Happened: A Memoir*. Four years later, at the age of seventy-eight, Paley retired, but in later years, when CBS slipped to second place in the network ratings, he resumed the chairmanship despite his age.

Although it was the entertainment side of CBS that was most lucrative, Paley understood from the start how important it also was to offer good news coverage. In the early 1930s he pioneered high-quality, in-depth news shows. His star anchorman was Edward R. Murrow who, together with other CBS news correspondents, first essentially built and developed radio and later television news. CBS, not coincidentally, has been home to the highly respected news anchor, Walter Cronkite, and to *Sixty Minutes*, the pioneering news-magazine program.

Paley was also a co-chairman of the *International Herald Tribune* and a president of the Museum of Modern Art. His hobby was collecting French post-Impressionist art.

Upon Paley's death in 1990 at the age of eighty-nine, the *New York Times* called him "a twentieth-century visionary with the ambitions of a nineteenth-century robber baron." Certainly Paley was the vigorous and visionary mind behind modern-day broadcasting in all its many forms.

He was still CBS chairman at the time of his death.

CAMILLE PISSARRO

Renowned Impressionist Painter

Born July 10, 1830, on St. Thomas, the Virgin Islands; died November 13, 1903. French impressionist painter. With his long, flowing white beard, Camille Pissarro looked like a biblical character. Pissarro became one of the key figures in the Impressionist group of painters. He was an important father figure to younger artists such as Paul Cézanne and Paul Gauguin, and was considered the most original landscape artist of his era. Though thought of as the most important Jewish artist of the nineteenth century, Pissarro never painted a Jewish subject.

JACOB ABRAHAM CAMILLE PISSARRO was born on St. Thomas in the Danish-held Virgin Islands in 1830. His family was Sephardic and had migrated there from Bordeaux, France. Pissarro's father, Frederic, originally arrived on the island to serve as the executor of his uncle's estate. A year later, when Frederic wanted to marry his widowed aunt, the synagogue refused permission because they were related. The Danish authorities, however, recognized the marriage as valid and allowed it to occur. Eventually the synagogue recognized the marriage as well, but it was after the couple had registered the birth of their four sons in the congregation.

Camille Pissarro was the third of the four sons. In 1841, at the age of eleven, he was sent to a boarding school on the outskirts of Paris where he learned French, Latin grammar, the sciences, and, probably most importantly, drawing. School outings to Paris gave him a chance to visit the Louvre, the famous French art museum.

In the summer of 1847, Camille returned to St. Thomas to work as a clerk in his father's general store. He wanted to become an artist, however, and so he and a close friend, a Danish painter named Fritz George Melbye,

Pissarro Museum, Pontoise, France

Camille Pissarro

ran away in 1852 to Caracas, Venezuela. Undertaking sketching expeditions to the country-side, Pissarro exhibited his resulting art works in a Caracas studio. Two years later, due to pressure from his father, Pissarro returned to St. Thomas to help in the family business. In return, his father promised to support his career as an artist.

A year later, however, in 1855, Pissarro left for Paris and never returned to the West Indies. Soon after, his parents moved to Paris as well. In 1860 Pissarro fell in love with Julie Vellay, a servant in his parents' home. She was of Catholic peasant stock. He asked his parents for permission to marry her, but they refused. The couple remained together anyway, moving to Pontoise, northwest of Paris, where Pissarro began painting seriously.

In Pontoise, France, where they had a home for ten years, Julie Pissarro tended a vegetable garden to help them survive. She also raised rabbits and chickens in order to feed the family.

When one of Pissarro's paintings was accepted for exhibition at the Salon of 1859, his family decided to extend him some financial aid. He was introduced to the artist J.B.C. Corot, who encouraged him and allowed him to list himself in the Salon catalogue as the "pupil of Corot." Pissarro was influenced by several more established artists, including Gustave Courbet.

In 1865 Pissarro was deeply moved by the paintings of Edouard Manet, which affected his own work. Three years later, Pissarro was hired to paint landscapes on window shades, a job he was evidently forced to take in order to earn a living. Pissarro painted them out-of-doors at Pontoise, where he was able to explore the effect of the light on colors and contours, a phe-nomenon that fascinated him.

Pissarro had wanted to fight for the French in the Franco-Prussian War of 1870, but his mother argued persuasively against it. In that year, he, Julie, and their son Lucien went to England with funds supplied to them by Pissarro's mother, his ardor for soldiering having cooled.

When they returned to France in 1871, they found that their house in Pontoise had been devastated by Prussian troops. Fifteen years of paintings were destroyed as well as numerous paintings by Claude Monet which had been left with Pissarro for safekeeping. Despite this tragedy, the Pissarros stayed in Pontoise for ten more years.

In 1872 Paul Cézanne and his family came to live near Pissarro. Pissarro had encouraged Cézanne to paint outdoors and to paint what he saw. Often the two would go out together looking for a "motif."

When their paintings were not accepted for exhibition in the Salon, Pissarro, Claude Monet, and Alfred Sisley organized an exhibit with thirty nonconformist artists like themselves, in-cluding Edgar Degas and Cézanne. They called themselves the Société Anonyme des Artistes, Peintres, Sculpteurs et Graveurs. (Anonymous Society of Artists, Painters, Sculptors and En-gravers.) But when one critic sharply condemned Monet's painting "An Impression: The Ris-ing Sun," the group was dubbed the "Impressionists."

These first Impressionists had eight group shows and Pissarro exhibited in all of them. The public and press were not very kind to him, but it was he who held the group together. In 1886, however, its prime mover, Monet, as well as Cézanne and Auguste Renoir, also part of the group, lost interest.

After much difficulty trying to sell his paintings, Pissarro found a dealer in 1878—A. Portier—who began to find buyers for them.

During the 1880s, Pissarro became friendly with Georges Seurat, another French painter. Pissarro experimented with Seurat's pointillist technique for several years, creating paintings through the "divisionist" method of applying hundreds of thousands of little dots of primary colors to the canvas. The technique required waiting until each color was dry before adding the next, which meant that Pissarro produced fewer paintings than when he used the Impressionist technique.

Today Pissarro is largely known for his Impressionist landscapes and cityscapes. He believed that he saw nature objectively, but art critics have noted that, in fact, he painted nature subjectively, rendering it in well-constructed architectural formats, using his senses and his keen mind to develop his paintings. One can elicit from his canvases a feeling that he sought order and organization. If his works seem uneven, the blame can be put on his need to paint volume enough to prevent his family from starving.

Pissarro did not observe any Jewish holidays. He held socialist-anarchist beliefs and thought of himself as a citizen of the world. But the Dreyfus case, which occurred during his adulthood, shocked him, not so much as a Jew, but as someone with progressive political ideals. His sympathy for Dreyfus cost him the friendship of some of his closest artist friends, including Cézanne and Renoir. Degas never spoke to Pissarro after the case. It was felt that some of the violent attacks against Pissarro's art were based not on artistic criticism but on latent anti-Semitism.

Although he is considered the most important Jewish artist of the nineteenth century, Pissarro never painted a Jewish subject. He seemed to have little consciousness of his Jewishness except for the Dreyfus Affair, which moved him very deeply. Some analysts, however, have found his Jewishness expressed in his left-wing ideals and his strong humanitarian stance, which was expressed in his many paintings of rural, noble peasants working in the fields.

Each of Pissarro's sons—Lucien, George, Felix, Ludovic-Rudolphe, and Paul-Emile—was a gifted artist. Only one, however, Lucien Pissarro, achieved some degree of fame for his Impressionist landscapes and his woodcuts. Pissarro had three daughters as well.

With his flowing white beard, Pissarro had what some described as a biblical appearance. Indeed, when his friends at the Café des Nouvelles Athenes saw him, they shouted, "Here comes Moses bearing the Tablets of the Law."

In his later years Pissarro developed an incurable eye problem. He wore a bandage over his eye for lengthy periods of time and began working indoors. He painted the views from hotels in Paris, Rouen, and Le Havre from his window. Despite his visual difficulties, Pissarro produced 160 paintings in the last three years of his life. He sold two of them to the Louvre.

When Henri Matisse asked Pissarro what an Impressionist was, Pissarro answered that an Impressionist was someone who never did the same painting twice.

Camille Pissarro died on November 13, 1903, at the age of seventy-three. His influence on the art world has extended into the twenty-first century.

OTTO PREMINGER

Controversial Hollywood Film Director

Born December 5, 1906, in Vienna, Austria; died April 23, 1986. American film director and producer. Among Otto Preminger's best known films are *Laura* (1944), *The Moon Is Blue* (1953), and *The Man with the Golden Arm* (1955). Preminger had a reputation for defying Hollywood taboos, particularly in his use of explicit language, which by current Hollywood standards now seems tame. Notorious for temper tantrums, Preminger made life on a movie set difficult for actors. Nevertheless, he is regarded as one of Hollywood's finest directors.

OTTO PREMINGER WAS BORN IN 1906 in Vienna, Austria. His father was the first Jew to be appointed chief prosecutor of the Austrian Empire, a remarkable achievement in the midst of so much anti-Semitism. Preminger followed in his father's footsteps and studied law, earning a doctorate in the field. He decided, however, to follow his preference for the theater. He wanted to become an actor and director.

By 1928 Preminger, though only twenty-two years old, was working as an aide to the great theater director Max Reinhardt in Reinhardt's Josefstadt Theater in Vienna. In 1933 he succeeded Reinhardt as the Josefstadt's director.

As his career took off, Preminger pursued other opportunities. To become director of Vienna's State Theater, however, he would have had to convert to Catholicism—he refused. Instead, he accepted an offer from Joseph Schenck, founder and chairman of Twentieth Century Fox, and departed for the United States in 1935. He was just twenty-nine years old.

Otto Preminger was thought to be very bright, ambitious, and assertive. Upon his arrival in Hollywood, he was taken by chauffeured limousine to a suite at the Beverly Wilshire Hotel, where flowers and champagne awaited him. Schenck then threw a big party for the new man in Hollywood.

Darryl Zanuck, then running the Fox studio, told Preminger to spend his first weeks watching other directors and observing how films are made. Not interested in wasting his time too much in the learning process, Preminger quickly announced he was ready to begin.

Preminger was given a stalled film to direct called *Under Your Spell*, starring Lawrence Tibbett, a Metropolitan Opera baritone. Preminger turned this "disaster" into a reasonable success. Pleasantly surprised, Darryl Zanuck showered his find with a new contract, a raise, fresh assignments, and best of all, invitations to dinner at Zanuck's home.

Zanuck turned over to Preminger one of the studio's biggest projects, a movie that was to be

Otto Preminger

based on the Robert Louis Stevenson novel *Kidnapped*. Preminger's reaction was quite negative—he had never heard of the Stevenson novel, never been to Scotland, where the film was to be made, and had no interest in doing the movie. Starting off with such a bad attitude, it was no wonder that Preminger got on Zanuck's wrong side almost immediately. Zanuck accused Preminger of altering the script, something no director working for Zanuck was permitted to do. Preminger denied that he had changed the script. But Zanuck snatched the project from him anyway and ceased asking Preminger to make movies.

Otto Preminger remained under contract to Zanuck's studio, however. The director sat in his office and waited for an assignment—in vain. One day he found that his name had been removed from the door and the lock changed. Still hoping to be paid, Preminger also wanted to work. Although Preminger hired an agent to find him projects at some other studio, because no one wanted to offend Darryl Zanuck, Preminger was squeezed out of work everywhere in Hollywood.

When his contract did expire in the late 1930s, Preminger went to New York and found several plays to direct. One was Claire Booth Luce's *Margin of Error*. When the German playing the villainous Nazi consul in the play returned to Germany in the midst of rehearsal, Mrs. Luce proposed that Preminger, a Jew, replace him. The timing seemed awkward—it was 1939, the Nazis were acting harshly toward Jews, and here was a Jew about to play a Nazi on the Broadway stage!

Preminger was a hit in the role and Twentieth Century Fox wanted to film the play (Zanuck was overseas with the American troops), hoping that Preminger would play the same role in the film. Preminger asked to direct the movie as well, but was turned down. He then offered to direct without pay. Fox reluctantly agreed and, as a result, when Zanuck returned to the studio in 1943, he discovered Preminger, whom he thought he had exiled from Hollywood, back under contract at his studio.

The film that gave Preminger his first real luster as an important Hollywood film director was *Laura*, which he directed in 1944. In time, Preminger became one of Hollywood's most controversial and significant film directors. He was notorious for the temper tantrums he threw on movie sets, making life for movie actors unpleasant and difficult.

Preminger also established a reputation for breaking film taboos. It was based largely on three films from the 1950s. One was the United Artists film *The Moon Is Blue* (1952). It was released without the usual Production Code seal of approval because it used language that was not considered acceptable for the movies, including such words as "pregnant" and "virgin."

The film led to a Supreme Court decision that prohibited local censors from stopping the distribution of films.

The second controversial film was *The Man With the Golden Arm* (1956). This movie broke more taboos by dealing openly with the problem of heroin addiction. The third film was *Anatomy of a Murder* (1959), which featured the same kind of explicitness in discussing the issue of rape.

In the late 1950s, Preminger was looking around in the office of his brother Ingo, who was agent to Leon Uris, author of the bestselling novel *Exodus*. Dore Schary of MGM had commissioned Uris to write the novel, then bought the movie rights for $75,000. No movie had been made, however. In his brother's office, Preminger unearthed "an untidy pile of cardboard boxes filled with manuscript pages."

Preminger spotted an opportunity, phoned the president of MGM, Joseph Vogel, who had fired Dore Schary two years earlier, and told him that, he, Preminger, was prepared to save MGM a lot of money. "You own a book by Leon Uris about the exodus of the Jews to Israel, but you'll never produce it. I'm here to take it off your hands." Vogel said he still hoped to produce it. "If you make it, the Arab countries will close all MGM theaters and ban all MGM films," Preminger told him. "*You* can't afford an Arab boycott, but I can."

A week later, Preminger bought the movie rights to *Exodus* for $75,000, then went to Arthur Krim of United Artists and raised $3.5 million to produce the film. For the screenplay, he took the courageous step of commissioning Dalton Trumbo, who had been blacklisted as part of Senator Joseph McCarthy's Communist witchhunt of the early 1950s. Preminger's film *Exodus*, which is considered a classic and featured an all-star cast, appeared in 1960.

Preminger also made successful movie versions of the musicals *Carmen Jones* (1954) and *Porgy and Bess* (1959).

Otto Preminger made more films in the 1960s, but they were not as highly regarded as his earlier movies. Among them were *Advise and Consent* (1962), based on the Allen Drury novel about Washington politics, and *Bunny Lake Is Missing* (1965). Several of his films were assailed by the Roman Catholic League of Decency, but Preminger was still decorated by the Vatican for his 1963 film *The Cardinal*. He made his final film, *The Human Factor*, in 1980. He died in 1986 at the age of seventy-nine.

ISADOR ISAAC RABI

Winner of the 1944 Nobel Prize for Physics

Born July 29, 1898, in Rymanow, Austria; died January 11, 1988. American physicist. Isador Rabi was one of a small group of scientists who helped the United States become the first country to produce an atomic weapon. He served as a discreet but influential voice of the international scientific community during the 1950s, opposing the construction of a thermonuclear superbomb. Rabi won the 1944 Nobel Prize for developing a method of measuring magnetic properties of atoms, molecules, and nuclei. Rabi's efforts made possible the precise measurements that were necessary to develop the laser, the atomic clock, and the diagnostic scanning of the human body through the use of nuclear magnetic resonance.

ISADOR RABI WAS BORN into an Orthodox Jewish family in Austria. His father, David, was in the grocery business. His mother was Scheindl (Teig) Rabi. In 1900 they immigrated to the United States when Rabi was one year old. The family settled on the Lower East Side of New York, and Rabi's parents opened a small grocery store in Brooklyn. Rabi's parents were concerned about both his secular and Jewish education. Upon returning from school to his parents' rooms in the back of the store, his mother would ask: "Did you ask any good questions today?"

Active socially in his neighborhood as a youngster, Rabi organized the local boys into discussion groups. He taught them how to play chess and how to construct a wireless radio. He read constantly, eager to go beyond his traditional Jewish background and explore the secular world as well.

Rabi attended the Manual Training High School, where most of the students were not Jewish. "I turned away from the Old World," he said. "I realized I had to be an American, not a Jewish American." After his family moved to the Brownsville section of Brooklyn, Rabi began to explore the local branch of the Brooklyn Public Library and read a great deal of American colonial history. He began alphabetically with a book on astronomy, eager to find scientific rather than theological explanations for the universe. He offered an explanation of "How the Electric Light Bulb Works" for his bar mitzvah speech.

In 1915 Rabi entered Cornell University, where he majored in chemistry and graduated in three years. In 1923 he returned to Cornell, where he did graduate work in physical chemistry. However, he realized that his real love was physics. Rabi kept up his voracious reading at the public library. Once he attended a lecture given by Albert Einstein at New York City College. As was his habit, Rabi shared his knowledge by giving a lecture on Einstein's theory of relativity to a neighborhood study group.

Rabi married Helen Newmark, of New York City, on August 17, 1926. They had two daughters, Nancy and Margaret.

In order to meet his expenses, Rabi became a tutor in physics at City College in New York. In 1927 he received his doctorate from Columbia University. His doctoral thesis was on the magnetic properties of crystals.

While at Columbia, Rabi won fellowships to a number of European universities. For the next two years, he studied theory with Wolfgang Pauli. He also worked with Otto Stern on the Stern-Gerlach experiments for measuring the magnetic characteristics of the atom. Rabi became fascinated by the new field of molecular beams, particularly as it related to the measurement of atomic magnetism.

In 1929 Rabi was asked to take a position as a lecturer in Columbia University's physics department. He shifted between teaching and doing research in nuclear physics, quantum mechanics, and magnetism. In 1930 he started a series of experiments on the magnetic properties of atomic nuclei. He tried to determine the precise nature of the forces that held together the protons within the nucleus of an atom, overcoming the mutual repulsion that had to exist within them, because all were positively charged. He theorized that this information would reveal the magnetic and electrical properties of the atom. He spent the next fifteen years engaged in this research.

In 1937 Rabi was appointed professor of physics at Columbia University. From 1938 to 1939 he was a member of the Institute for Advanced Study in Princeton, New Jersey.

Otto Stern won the Nobel Prize in physics in 1943 for discovering the molecular beam that holds the different parts of the molecule together. Rabi took this research further, determining the spectrum of the wavelength of those beams; this was a process ten thousand times more sensitive than determining the light spectrum.

Soon after World War II began in Europe, Rabi divided his time between teaching at Columbia and working on a secret project at Massachusetts Institute of Technology (MIT) in Cambridge, Massachusetts, which led to the development of military radar. At MIT Rabi became associate director of the radiation lab and investigated the nature of bonds in the atom. He was also a senior adviser on the Manhattan Project, through which the atomic bomb was developed.

Present when the first atomic bomb was tested in the New Mexico desert, where the Manhattan Project was headquartered, Rabi wrote: "The Atomic Age came at about five-thirty in the morning of July 16, 1945. It was a sight that I have attempted from time to time to describe. I never felt successful in doing it. One has to go back to the Bible, to witnesses of the ancient miracles, to get some impression of the tremendous emotional experience it produced . . . ."

Rabi was given the Nobel Prize in 1944 for his resonance method of recording the magnetic properties of atomic nuclei. Rabi's work made possible the precise measurements that were needed to develop the atomic clock, the laser, and the diagnostic scanning of the human body by nuclear magnetic resonance. Because it was wartime, he did not deliver the traditional Nobel Prize lecture in Stockholm—he was too involved in work he was doing for the American military. During the remainder of World War II, Rabi was a civilian investigator for the United States Government Office of Scientific Research and Development.

In 1945 the defense department awarded Isador Rabi the Medal of Merit for "exceptional meritorious conduct in the performance of outstanding service to the United States, from November 1940 to December 1945, as consultant to many key defense organizations . . . ."

Rabi continued to lecture at Columbia University, where he was made a full professor in 1950. Beginning in 1953 he served as chairman of the general advisory committee of the Atomic Energy Commission. Rabi was fearful of the misuse of atomic energy and actively sought to use his influence to reduce its easy accessibility and potential for destruction. Others on the committee had the main goal of increasing the American atomic arsenal. Rabi, however, preferred finding peaceful uses for atomic energy. A crash program for building a thermonuclear super-bomb came up among the scientists. Only Rabi and fellow scientist Enrico Fermi were opposed to building such a weapon.

Rabi took part in the national effort to build a cyclotron, which accelerates protons to high energies; in spinning, the particles generate a magnetic field, which Rabi explored and measured. He also worked at the Brookhaven National Laboratory for Atomic Research. In the early 1950s, he helped to set up the European Center for Nuclear Research, which brought eleven European nations under one umbrella organization in the field of high-energy physics.

Rabi served as science adviser to United States President Dwight Eisenhower. He took a strong interest in the development of important scientific institutions in Israel, particularly the Technion in Haifa and the Weizmann Institute in Rehovot. He visited Israel a number of times and served as a mentor to other scientists who were engaged in different phases of scientific development in that country.

Rabi died on January 11, 1988, at the age of eighty-nine. He was a pioneer in exploring the atom and a crucial force in twentieth-century physics. The critical medical diagnostic tool of magnetic resonance imaging (MRI) can be traced to his early scientific discoveries.

YITZHAK RABIN

Israel's Soldier for Peace

Born March 1, 1922, in Jerusalem; died November 4, 1995. Israeli political and military leader. A soldier for twenty-seven years, Yitzhak Rabin became chief of staff of the Israel Defense Forces in the early 1960s. Later in his career, he served as prime minister in the 1970s, defense minister in the 1980s, and prime minister for a second time in June 1992. As prime minister, Rabin broke a long-standing Israeli taboo against negotiating with the Palestine Liberation Organization (PLO) and its chairman, Yassir Arafat. He also engineered a peace accord with the Palestinians and a peace treaty with Jordan. For his peace efforts, Rabin, in October 1994, was a co-recipient of the Nobel Peace Prize, along with Israeli Foreign Minister Shimon Peres and Yassir Arafat.

YITZHAK RABIN'S PARENTS were born in Russia and grew up under the uncertain and frequently violent czarist rule of the late nineteenth century. Rabin's father, Nehemiah Robichov, was born in 1886 in Sidrovitch, Russia, and reached Palestine in 1917 to fight in the British-sponsored Jewish Legion against Turkish rule. There he met and married Rabin's mother, the Russian-born Rosa Cohen.

Yitzhak Rabin was born in Jerusalem on March 1, 1922, and although he showed signs of wanting to become a farmer, the festering Arab-Israeli conflict forced him during his youth and much of his adult career into soldiering, which eventually led to his political leadership. Rabin's younger sister, Rachel, was born in 1925. With his strong build, high forehead, wavy black hair, and penetrating eyes, Rabin physically resembled his father. He also inherited his father's quiet, serious manner, and deep voice. His mother, who was constantly engaged in political activities that kept her away from the house, served as a model of the ideal public servant, and despite her frequent absences from home, Rabin was deeply attached to her. She died when he was fifteen years old.

Rabin attended the prestigious Kadourie Agricultural High School in the Galilee in 1937 and two years later enlisted in the Haganah, the pre-state Jewish defense force. In 1941 he was mobilized into the Haganah's full-time mobile strike force, the Palmach.

Rabin met his future wife Leah in 1944 when both were in the army; they were married on August 23, 1948. They had two children—a son, Yuval, and a daughter, Dalia.

During Israel's 1948 War of Independence, as commander of the Har-El Brigade, Rabin was responsible for opening the road to Jerusalem, then under siege; by war's end he was deputy commander of the Palmach. Rising through the ranks during the 1950s and early 1960s, he became chief of operations in 1959 and five years later, at age forty-one, chief of staff.

State of Israel Government Press Office

Yitzhak Rabin shakes hands with PLO Chairman Yassir Arafat at the September 13, 1993 White House ceremony marking the signing of the Israeli-PLO Declaration of Principles. U.S. President Bill Clinton looks on.

On the eve of the 1967 Six-Day War, as Israel inched closer to battle with Egypt, the burden of decision making fell on Rabin's shoulders. One night in late May he returned home, in his own words, in a "state of mental and physical exhaustion." His critics described his absence from work over the next few days, while he tried to recoup, as a nervous breakdown. Rabin himself never admitted that he had suffered an actual breakdown. In any case, despite this setback, from which he recovered in a short time, Rabin led his country to a spectacular victory in the war.

Although Moshe Dayan has been generally regarded as the hero of the 1967 war, many believed that Rabin deserved that credit. It was Rabin who molded the Israel Defense Forces (IDF) into an aggressive, unbeatable fighting force. Following that war, Rabin took on his country's toughest diplomatic posting as Israeli ambassador in Washington. The assignment was all the more challenging because of his halting English, but he was able to overcome this difficulty and handle his duties well, gaining international respect.

Returning to Israel in 1973, Rabin became the nation's first sabra (native-born) prime minister in June of 1974, his first of two terms as Israeli leader. Rabin's supreme diplomatic feat occurred in September 1975 when he successfully negotiated the Israel-Egypt interim peace agreement, which required a partial Israeli troop pullback in the Sinai. Rabin's most dramatic accomplishment was the successful Israeli rescue on July 4, 1976, of hostages aboard an Air France jet hijacked by Palestinian terrorists and taken to Entebbe, Uganda.

Disaster struck Rabin a few months before the planned Israeli election of May 1977, when it

Yitzhak Rabin signs the Agreement on the Gaza Strip and the Jericho Area, in Cairo, May 4, 1994.

was revealed that his wife, Leah, had a dollar account at a bank in Washington, D.C., in violation of the law that prohibited Israelis from holding such accounts overseas. On April 7, Rabin announced his departure from office and his renunciation of his party's nomination for a second term as prime minister. He spent the next few years as a Labor party backbencher, staying on the sidelines, writing his memoirs, hoping eventually to be rehabilitated politically.

Still immensely popular with the Israeli populace, Rabin returned to a leadership position in September 1984 as defense minister in the National Unity Government headed by his archrival, Shimon Peres. He presided over Israel's withdrawal of troops from Lebanon following the IDF's three-year occupation of Lebanon, which had grown out of the controversial 1982 war there. He also directed Israel's military response to the Palestinian intifada, the uprising that erupted in December 1987 in the Israeli-occupied West Bank and Gaza Strip.

In the early 1990s, Rabin sought the prime minister's position again. He had a unique advantage. Only Rabin combined a reputation for toughness with a genuine conviction that peacemaking with the Arabs was essential. This new Rabin-Peres contest for Labor party leadership occurred on February 19, 1992. Rabin won by a slim margin, but because of it, he could call his political rehabilitation complete. He had campaigned on a promise to accelerate the sluggish peace process with the Arabs. He also pledged to improve Israel's internal security. These were matters of great importance to Israel.

In the elections, Rabin scored an impressive victory on June 23, 1992, over Yitzhak Shamir's Likud party, and thus became Israel's new prime minister. To prepare Israelis for peace with Syria, Lebanon, Jordan, and the Palestinians, Rabin sought to convince his people that the world was not entirely against them. In remarks made to the Knesset on July 13, when presenting his new government, he also made a special, impassioned plea to the Palestinian Arabs.

"You have failed in the war against us," he told them. "One hundred years of your bloodshed and terror against us have brought you only suffering, humiliation, bereavement, and pain. You have lost thousands of your sons and daughters, and you are losing ground all the time. Your leaders have led you through lies and deceits. They have missed every opportunity."

Rabin remained convinced that the best opportunity for peace lay with the Palestinians, not with the Syrians. To that end, he gave his stamp of approval to secret negotiations with Yassir Arafat's Palestine Liberation Organization in Oslo, Norway. Those talks, which culminated in the Israeli-PLO accord signed on September 13, 1993, in Washington, D.C., called for Palestinian autonomy in the Gaza Strip and in the West Bank town of Jericho. Rabin's handshake with Arafat on the White House lawn that day became a symbol of how formidable enemies could successfully embark on reconciliation.

The following July, in 1994, Rabin met with Jordan's King Hussein for the first time publicly, also on the White House lawn, where the two leaders signed the Washington Declaration pledging nonbelligerency between their two countries. Rabin and Hussein had met on earlier occasions, but always in secret.

On October 14, 1994, Rabin, along with Israeli Foreign Minister Shimon Peres and PLO Chairman Yassir Arafat, was named a corecipient of the Nobel Peace Prize. "The work is not yet finished," said Rabin, in response to receiving the prestigious award,"[It] is a prize for the future." Twelve days later, Rabin and Hussein signed the Israel-Jordan peace treaty in the presence of American President Bill Clinton at a site on the Israeli-Jordanian border.

In an interview in the *Jerusalem Post* on September 5, 1994, Rabin was asked how he felt about being Jewish. "I am Jewish," he replied, "in the way that I understand the meaning of Judaism. It is a combination of people, values, history, and tradition. I was born Jewish. I took it for granted and never questioned it."

Rabin called himself a member of the "generation of the 1940s." He described that era as the most important decade since the destruction of the Second Temple because it was the time of both the Holocaust and the creation of the state of Israel. "For me these were the two most important events." he said. "Let's not forget them." For both Jews and non-Jews, Rabin's peace-directed attitudes and clear thinking have made the world a safer and, perhaps for now, saner place.

Yitzhak Rabin was assassinated on November 4, 1995, as he left a peace rally in Tel Aviv. The self-confessed assassin, a twenty-five-year-old law student named Yigal Amir, shot Rabin at close range and was captured on the spot. Amir carried out the deed, he said, in order to halt the peace process. Rabin was seventy-three years old at the time of his death.

Years after Yitzhak Rabin's death, prospects for peaceful coexistence in the Middle East remained remote. In the fall of 2000, Palestinians launched what they called a second Intifada, or uprising, thereby further heightening tensions and polarizing the two sides. When Palestinian leader Yassir Arafat died in November 2004, hope arose that the previous four years of Israeli-Palestinian violence might wane and lead to a more peaceful future.

RASHI

Outstanding Commentator on Bible and Talmud

Born 1040 in Troyes, France; died 1105. Commentator on the Bible and the Talmud. Rabbi Shlomo Ben Isaac, known as Rashi, lived in northern France and developed a school of disciples and descendants, known as the *Tosafists* (the Supplementers). So crucial are Rashi's thoughts for biblical study that his commentaries seem almost an integral part of the actual text; they are read by most students. Rashi wrote a comprehensive commentary on both the Bible and the Babylonian Talmud. Rashi's commentary, when translated into Latin, made the Bible more accessible to Christian scholars.

SHLOMO BEN ISAAC WAS BORN in Troyes, France, in 1040. Few details exist about his childhood. He became known by the acronym "Rashi." Rashi was a descendant on his mother's side of a long line of scholars, dating back to the Talmudic sage Rabbi Yohanan the Sandalmaker. Rashi's father was a scholar and was quoted in his son's writing.

Rashi's education focused on the basics: Bible, Talmud, and Midrash, plus studying those words of grammar and lexicography that were available in Hebrew.

One legend has it that Rashi's father cast a precious gem into the sea rather than surrender it to Christians who wanted it for idolatrous purposes. Another has it that a Heavenly voice foretold to him that a son would be born and would enlighten the world with his brilliance. Yet another legend related that, while pregnant, Rashi's mother had been threatened by a stranger as she walked down a narrow street. Pressing herself against a wall, Rashi's mother was rescued when a niche formed that hid her from the attacker.

Before the Crusades, which began near the end of Rashi's life, Jews in the Champagne district lived much like their Christian neighbors, speaking French and mixing freely with their non-Jewish fellow citizens. This is the atmosphere in which Rashi grew and matured.

Medallion with a likeness of Rashi

Rashi was educated at Worms, then studied in Mainz before finally returning to Troyes. There he founded his own Talmudic academy around the year 1100, attracting many students. But Rashi's most prized pupils were his relatives. He was married when he was sixteen years old; he and his wife had three daughters. All three daughters married important religious scholars.

Though Rashi was only twenty-five years old at the time, he was appointed the religious judge of the community. Students came from far and wide to study with him. Like the rabbis of earlier times, Rashi earned his living from a secular trade—he was a wine merchant and owner of several vineyards. It is no surprise that Rashi's commentaries are replete with details of medieval commerce, technology, law, and social custom.

Bible commentary prior to Rashi was dominated by Rabbi Moses, the Midrashist of Narbonne. Rashi often cited him. Before Rashi's commentaries, the Talmud, written in Aramaic, was thought to be too convoluted to influence large audiences. Rashi's studies, however, won wide acceptance because they explained what the various words of a phrase in the Bible meant; he was concise, lucid, and, in his thoughts and explanations, balanced.

Rashi immersed himself in Jewish law; he introduced each general topic that was to be discussed and then explained it, one phrase after the other, giving the meaning, context, and relevance of the text. For example, in the biblical sentence, "And thou shalt love the Lord thy God with all thy heart," Rashi explained the phrase "And thou shalt love" this way: People should perform God's commandments out of love, not fear.

In contrast with other medieval commentaries, Rashi's explanations of the Bible did not go into lengthy theological or philosophical digressions. Because of his commentary, the Babylonian Talmud became the accepted authority and guide in Jewish life, while the parallel Jerusalem Talmud, which lacked the kind of commentary that Rashi provided, soon fell into disuse.

Rashi was more of an innovator in his Talmudic commentaries than in his Bible explanations. In his discussions of the Talmud, he carefully established the correct reading of disputed texts and wrote original interpretations of legal issues. Rashi preferred to base his commentaries on the standard Midrash collections, but not by simply parroting what the rabbis had said; he paraphrased his sources, seeking also to establish a consistency of style in his work.

Rashi's commentaries suggest that the biblical text must never divorce itself from the plain, factual, historic, realistic sense—the *peshat*. He was not against more symbolic interpretations of the text—called the *derash*—but he would only use the *derash* after being satisfied that he had adequately explained the ordinary meaning. Rashi once wrote, "As for me, I am only concerned with the literal meaning of the Scriptures and with such *aggadot* [the part of rabbinic teaching not concerned with religious law] as explain the biblical passages in a fitting manner."

Rashi's commentary on the opening verse of Genesis was important. He focused on the much disputed syntax of this section, concluding that the first words were not to be construed as "In the beginning, God created. . ." but instead, "When God began to create . . . ."

Seventy-five percent of Rashi's commentaries are based on rabbinic sources. His Bible and Talmud commentaries have appeared in every subsequent standard printing of the Bible next to the appropriate passage. Many of his interpretations were crucial in the determination of legal decisions of his day. Students of the Bible routinely read a sentence or two from the original text, then quickly perused Rashi's commentaries to find out what the master thought the text meant.

The typography used for Rashi's commentary is known as "Rashi script," but Rashi did not invent it. It was invented by Italian printers in order to distinguish between the commentary and text and is the typeface now used for most Hebrew language commentaries.

Rashi's commentary was translated into Latin and this helped make the Bible more accessible to Christian scholars. The first Hebrew-language book to be formally printed was a Bible with Rashi's commentary that appeared in Italy in 1475.

Rashi also wrote *responsa*, replies to inquiries on matters of Jewish law. Accepted as authoritative, they reflected the scholar's liberalism. For example, Rashi ruled that it was acceptable to interrupt the Grace After Meals to feed one's animals. He based this on the Scriptural injunction for a man to feed his animals before himself.

As for his legendary humility, Rashi once told a questioner: "I was asked this question before, but I realized that my answer then was

Rashi

wrong and I welcome the opportunity to correct my mistake." Unlike other commentators, he was willing to admit that he did not always understand the meaning of a certain text.

Rashi did not finish all of the commentaries; his work was completed by his sons-in-law and grandchildren, who formed the heart of the *Tosafists*, the key school of Talmudic scholarship and exposition over the next two hundred years. Their annotations are printed on pages of the Talmud opposite Rashi's commentary.

During Rashi's final years, Jews in France and Germany went through the turmoil of the First Crusade of 1095–1096. Troyes itself was untouched, but many other communities were totally destroyed. Rashi was dismayed by the massacres that were committed at the start of the First Crusade, in which he lost relatives and friends. Tradition has it that Rashi predicted that the expedition of Godfrey of Bouillon would be defeated; he correctly predicted that Godfrey would return to his native city with only three horses remaining from his entire army.

Rashi is reported to have died at the age of sixty-five while sitting at his desk writing the Hebrew word *tam* (pure) in his commentary to *Makkot* on the Hebrew calendar date of 29 Tammuz. His burial site is unknown. His scholarship, however, lives on, and influences Jews everywhere.

EDWARD G. ROBINSON

Hollywood Tough Guy

Born December 12, 1893, in Bucharest, Romania; died January 26, 1973. American actor. Before moving to Hollywood in 1929, Edward G. Robinson achieved stage success on Broadway. He became internationally famous for portraying tough guys in the movies, especially in *Little Caesar* (1931). Later in his career he played more sympathetic characters. Edward G. Robinson appeared in over 150 films.

EDWARD G. ROBINSON, whose birth name was Emanuel Goldenberg, was born in Romania in 1893. He was one of six sons born to Morris and Sarah (Guttman) Goldenberg. His parents took him from his native Bucharest to the United States in 1902.

Robinson's father was a building contractor in Romania, but after the family settled in New York City, he became a merchant. Robinson attended New York City public schools and graduated from Townsend Harris Hall High School in 1910. Later he was a student at the College of the City of New York and at Columbia University. He hoped to become a lawyer but was attracted to the theater, and eventually abandoned the idea of studying law. He was a wonderful debater and public speaker; acting seemed like a natural profession for him. He could read and converse in Yiddish and Hebrew.

In 1912 Robinson entered the American Academy of Dramatic Arts and studied there for a year. He began to sense that the name Goldenberg was "too long, too foreign . . . too Jewish." He considered changing it to Goldenhill, Goldenmount, or Montedore. But those surnames seemed too pretentious and contrived. About this time, he saw a play called *The Passerby* in which a butler announced, "Madame, a gentleman to see you—a Mr. Robinson." He told friends he planned to call himself Emanuel Robinson, but when

Edward G. Robinson

that received a lukewarm response, he named himself after the British King Edward VIII. He did not want to give up Goldenberg completely, so that became the "G" in Edward G. Robinson.

Robinson made his stage debut in 1913 as Sato in the play *Paid in Full*. After playing a few small roles following that, he took time out from his stage career to serve in the United States Navy during World War I. Then, in 1919, Robinson took the part of Steve in the play *First Is Last*. He had several roles in minor productions before the Theatre Guild commissioned him to play Louis in *Bianco* in 1922. Three years later, he played the emperor in the Guild's production of George Bernard Shaw's *Androcles and the Lion*.

In 1927 Robinson had a supporting role as a gangster in the movie *The Racket*. His handling of the part was called "a masterly creation of character" by *Theatre* magazine. As a result, Robinson began to receive offers from Hollywood. At first, he turned them down, convinced that he was not a good enough actor for the new medium.

Robinson eventually felt the lure of Hollywood, however, and he moved there to make such films as *The Night Ride* (1929), *They Knew What They Wanted*, (1929), and his most famous one, *Little Caesar* (1931). He refused to sign a long-term contract, and in 1930 he returned to the Broadway stage. What he tried on Broadway failed, while the movie *Little Caesar* became a big hit, so Robinson returned to California, deciding at that point to devote all his time to playing Hollywood roles. *Little Caesar* established the significance of the so-called "gangster" picture as a genre, and moviegoers were looking for more films of this nature. Robinson continued to play the tough guy in other Hollywood films: *Smart Money* (1932), *Five Star Final* (1932), and *The Last Gangster* (1937). Finally, in 1940, Robinson took on his first sympathetic character when he portrayed a scientist in *Dr. Ehrlich's Magic Bullet*.

In the early 1940s, Robinson's Hollywood roles became more varied. He was the insurance claims adjuster in pursuit of murderers in *Double Indemnity* (1944), an important part in a film that did well. Alton Cook, writing in the New York *World-Telegram*, gave Robinson praise for that role as "an elaborately detailed study of a grim sleuth."

During World War II, Robinson broadcast messages in German to Germany's anti-Nazi underground; he was the first Hollywood film star to appear in a show before the American troops in France after D-Day in June 1944. That same year, Robinson had another film triumph as a college professor in *The Woman in the Window*.

Having left Warner Brothers in the early 1940s, and not tied down by a contract, Robinson became a freelance actor, later forming his own motion-picture company, the Film Guild Corporation. Its first film, *The Red House*, was shown in 1947 and starred Robinson, but Film Guild went out of business with only this one movie to its credit. Robinson returned to independent acting.

Robinson played major roles in the films *Scarlet Street* (1946), *Night Has a Thousand Eyes* (1948), and *Key Largo* (1948). He was praised for his role as the father and businessman who used defective war material in the film adaptation of Arthur Miller's play *All My Sons*. The *New York Times* critic wrote that Robinson did "a superior job of showing the shades of personality in a little tough guy who has a softer side."

In 1949 Robinson was honored by the Cannes Film Festival for his acting in *House of Strangers*, a Twentieth-Century Fox film also starring Susan Hayward and Richard Conte. Wanda Hale of the New York *Daily News* thought Robinson's portrayal of the head of a banking house in New York's Little Italy was the best acting performance of his, at that point, twenty-year career.

In the late 1940s, Robinson's acting career was marred when he was nearly blacklisted.

On three occasions he testified before the House Un-American Activities Committee (HUAC), insisting each time that he had never been a Communist: "I may not have been as good a husband or father or friend as I should have been, but I know my Americanism is unblemished and fine and wonderful, and I am proud of it."

During his third appearance before the Committee, Robinson asserted that he had been duped by certain organizations to which he had belonged, later identified as Communist fronts. The Committee took no action against him. When he resumed his film career, however, he received fewer offers, and the parts were smaller. Robinson was never nominated for an Academy Award, although he won steady praise for his acting during his fifty-year career in the movies. His encounter with HUAC has been held partly responsible, even though his name was cleared.

Yigael Yadin presents Edward G. Robinson with the "Haganah Pin" during Robinson's 1950 visit to Israel.

State of Israel Government Press Office

Robinson's film career continued into the 1950s and 1960s. He had roles in *The Ten Commandments* (1956) and *The Prize* (1963). He returned to the stage at times, playing in *Darkness at Noon* (1951) and Paddy Chayefsky's *Middle of the Night* (1956) in which, according to film critics, he scored significant success.

Edward G. Robinson was a serious art collector, purchasing his first piece of art at an auction in 1913 for two dollars. Over the years he amassed one of America's best private art collections, valued at over three million dollars. Robinson also loved music and learned to play the harp. He could read and converse in French, Spanish, German, Italian, Russian, Yiddish, Hebrew, and his native Romanian. The actor was married three times, always to actresses: first to Frances Robinson, then Elaine M. Conte, and finally to Gladys Lloyd, with whom he had a son, Edward G. Robinson, Jr.

In 1972, when news that Robinson was mortally ill reached Hollywood, it was decided to present him with a prestigious Honorary Oscar marking his "greatness as a player, a patron of the arts, and a dedicated citizen . . . in sum, a Renaissance man." Robinson died a few short months before the 1973 Oscar ceremonies at which he was so honored.

The following year, his son and only child, Edward G. Robinson, Jr., died at the age of forty. Father and son had had a tumultuous relationship. In fact, Robinson had ejected his son from his home when the then nineteen-year-old eloped in 1952; he felt that his son was too young to get married.

Edward G. Robinson created unforgettable characters in his long and vibrant career. At the time of his death at the age of seventy-nine, he was in the process of writing his autobiography. Reviewing Robinson's Broadway career, R. Danan Skinner, critic for *Commonweal* magazine, wrote in 1933 that the actor had "dynamic instinct for creating character and illusion and dominating make-believe."

RICHARD RODGERS

Composer of Memorable Broadway Musicals

Born June 28, 1902, in New York City; died December 30, 1979. American composer and producer. Teamed with his equally talented librettists, whether it was Lorenz Hart between 1920 and 1942 or Oscar Hammerstein II from 1943 to 1959, Richard Rodgers helped to establish the American musical comedy as an indigenous theatrical form. Rodgers wrote the music for the Broadway classics *Pal Joey, Oklahoma!, Carousel, South Pacific, The King and I, Flower Drum Song, The Sound of Music,* and thirty-two other shows. He also wrote musical scores for television shows and Hollywood films. Rodgers won an Academy Award for Best Song in 1945 for "It Might As Well Be Spring" from the film *State Fair.*

RICHARD RODGERS WAS BORN in New York City in 1902. His mother, Mamie (Levy) Rodgers, was a wonderful pianist. His father, William Abraham Rodgers, was a physician as well as a baritone singer. The family held concerts in their New York apartment, preferring to perform songs from the most recent musicals and operettas of the day. These home concerts were Richard's introduction to the world of music.

At the age of four, Rodgers, without taking any lessons, could play melodies with one hand on the piano. He started to mimic popular melodies from *The Merry Widow* and *Mademoiselle Modiste.* Two years later, he was playing recognizable tunes with both hands. Rodgers became fascinated with the concept of the Broadway musical. As a teenager, he could be found every Saturday afternoon at a matinee. He was a particular admirer of Jerome Kern, whose musicals he went to see over and over again. Rodgers once said that "If you were at all sensitive to music, Kern had to be your idol. You had to worship Kern."

When Rodgers was fourteen years old, while at the Wigwam summer camp in Maine, he wrote his first song, called "Campfire Days." Back home in New York, he wrote "Auto Show Girl," his first copyrighted piece of music. Rodgers received great encouragement and practical assistance from both his father and his brother, Mortimer, who helped him when he began to write for the theater. Rodgers was only fifteen years old when he wrote the entire score for a musical called *One Minuet Please,* which was performed in the Grand Ballroom of New York's Plaza Hotel. Among its songs were "When They Rub Noses in Alaska" and "I'm a Vampire."

Rodgers paired himself with a number of librettists and produced some of the greatest musical comedy ever to hit Broadway. At the age of seventeen, he was introduced to Lorenz Milton Hart. In 1919 both men enrolled at Columbia University largely because the school put on a

International Musician

Richard Rodgers

variety show, which proved to be their first collaborative effort. Called *Fly with Me*, the play was a satire on undergraduate life and took place on a fictional island that was under Soviet control.

From 1920 to 1942, Rodgers and Hart were the most successful and prolific songwriting team in America. Among their musicals were *A Connecticut Yankee in King Arthur's Court*, *Simple Simon*, *America's Sweetheart*, and their more famous efforts, *Babes in Arms*, *Pal Joey*, and *The Boys from Syracuse*, a story adapted from William Shakespeare's *The Comedy of Errors*. Richard Watts, Jr., writing in the New York *Herald Tribune*, noted that "If you have been wondering all these years just what was wrong with *The Comedy of Errors*, it is now possible to tell you. It has been waiting for a score by Rodgers and Hart . . . ."

When Hart died in 1943, Rodgers, at the height of his composing talents, found Oscar Hammerstein II as Hart's replacement. Rodgers and Hammerstein collaborated on musicals for the next sixteen years.

In 1943 the team's very first show, *Oklahoma!*, broke new ground in the American musical field. The opening number, with a simple farm woman standing alone on stage hearing the first strains of "Oh, What a Beautiful Mornin'" from a rich baritone voice offstage, was quite different from the large production numbers that typically began Broadway musicals. Rodgers and Hammerstein musicals, as exemplified by *Oklahoma!*, incorporated dancing as an integral part of the musical's story. Audiences and critics loved it.

Rodgers married Dorothy Feiner on March 5, 1930. They had two daughters, Mary and Linda. Dorothy Rodgers noted that "People used to say to Dick, especially after *Oklahoma!*, 'You'll never write anything as good as that again.' I know they meant to be kind, but it hit home, and he used to worry about whether he was going to be able to write [another hit]. When he had gotten the first number done on a new show, he had an expression. He used to say the first olive was out of the jar."

In 1945 Rodgers and Hammerstein produced another spectacular hit in *Carousel*, adapted by Hammerstein from the Ferenc Molnar story *Liliom*. Of the nine Rodgers and Hammerstein shows, this was the composer's favorite because he felt that it had one of their best musical scores, including the songs "You'll Never Walk Alone," "June is Bustin' Out All Over," "If I Loved You," and "What's the Use of Wond'rin'?" That year Rodgers won an Oscar for the song "It Might As Well Be Spring" from the film *State Fair*.

In 1949 Rodgers and Hammerstein produced *South Pacific*, a musical play set on an exotic Pacific island that also proved controversial because of its handling of racism. The show was performed 1,925 times on Broadway. It also won a Pulitzer Prize.

The King and I opened in 1951. It tells the story of a widowed English teacher who takes a job teaching the children of the king of Siam. The plot revolves around the king's wish to become less of a barbarian and more civilized, and is based on the actual experiences of a woman who recorded them in her memoirs.

In 1959 *The Sound of Music*, also based on a true story, opened on Broadway with record-breaking advance ticket sales of over three million dollars. The musical told the story of the seven Von Trapp children and the romantic relationship between their widowed father and their governess, Maria. As with many of the team's Broadway hits, *The Sound of Music* became a Hollywood movie; it won the 1965 Oscar for Best Picture of the Year. Hammerstein's death in 1960 brought the Rodgers and Hammerstein partnership to an end, but Rodgers continued to bring music to Broadway. In his final years, Rodgers collaborated with lyricists Stephen Sondheim, Sheldon Harnick, and Martin Charnin.

Although it is difficult to choose from the long list of wonderful songs Rodgers composed over the years, some of his most enduring ones include: "Mountain Greenery," "Thou Swell," "Manhattan," "Isn't It Romantic?" "With a Song in My Heart," "I'm Gonna Wash that Man Right out of My Hair," "My Favorite Things," "The Lady Is a Tramp," "Bewitched, Bothered, and Bewildered," "Some Enchanted Evening," "There Is Nothing Like a Dame," "Oh, What a Beautiful Mornin'," "There's a Small Hotel," "People Will Say We're in Love," "My Funny Valentine," "This Can't Be Love," and "Where or When."

Richard Rodgers battled cancer off and on throughout his life. He died in 1979 at the age of seventy-seven. By the time of his death, he had written over a thousand songs, forty-five musical plays, twelve original films and television shows, two multi-part documentaries, and a ballet score. "He didn't have many close friends," his wife Dorothy noted once. "He was so absorbed in his work." Because of Richard Rodgers' prodigious talent, musical comedy became an indigenous theater form in America, influencing the genre for generations to come.

A.M. ROSENTHAL

Outstanding Editor of the New York Times

Born May 2, 1922, in Sault Ste. Marie, Ontario, Canada. American newspaper reporter and editor. A.M. Rosenthal began his career at the *New York Times* as the United Nations correspondent for eight years, then served abroad as a foreign correspondent for six years. In 1960 he won the Pulitzer Prize for his reporting from Poland. From 1969 to 1977, Rosenthal was managing editor of the *Times*. He was then named executive editor, serving in that capacity for the next ten years. Upon his retirement in 1986, Rosenthal became a twice-weekly columnist for the *Times*. He has been credited with saving the most famous newspaper in the world from financial trouble by changing the newspaper's format and expanding its contents.

ABRAHAM MICHAEL ROSENTHAL was born in 1922 in Canada to Russian-Jewish immigrants, Harry and Sarah (Dickstein) Rosenthal. His father was a fur trader in Russia, then a farmer in Canada before moving the family to the Bronx, New York, in 1926. Harry, who hoped his son would become a forester, died when the boy was thirteen.

Though Sarah Rosenthal kept a "pseudo-kosher" (Abe Rosenthal's phrase) home, Harry kept a low profile concerning Judaism because, as Abe Rosenthal recalled, "he despised everything that reminded him of Russia." Abe Rosenthal, however, always acknowledged that he was Jewish. "When you say my first name is Abraham, you're saying, 'Hello, I'm a Jew.' It was okay with me," he said.

The teenaged Rosenthal sympathized with the Socialists, but he turned into an avid anti-communist in 1939 with the signing of the Hitler-Stalin pact. It was the same year that he graduated from DeWitt Clinton High School in New York City.

Rosenthal entered the City College of New York in 1940. Three years later, he started his newspaper career as a part-time correspondent for the *New York Times*; his assignment was to cover news from his own college, from which he graduated in 1944. He then joined the newspaper as a staff reporter. From 1946 until 1954, Rosenthal was the *Times*'s United Nations correspondent. Canadian by birth, Rosenthal chose to become a naturalized American citizen in 1952, when he was twenty-nine years old.

His byline always appeared as A.M. Rosenthal, never as Abraham M. Rosenthal. "I've never seen my name in print," he remarked. "The name Abraham was somehow too much for the *Times*'s editors." The omission rankled him; he observed: "When I was born, my mother really did not cry out, 'Harry, let's call him A.M.'" (When he became the *Times*'s first Jewish managing editor in 1969, Rosenthal promised himself he would hire the first applicant for a reporter's job named Abraham. To his dismay, none showed up.)

For nine years, Rosenthal worked as an overseas correspondent, first in India (1957–1958); then Warsaw, Poland (1958–1959); and during 1960 and 1961, in Geneva, Switzerland; Vienna; the Congo; and Central Africa. In 1959 the Polish government expelled him for probing too deeply into the country's affairs. A year later, he won a Pulitzer Prize for his reporting from Poland. From 1961 to 1963, he filed reports from Tokyo.

Rosenthal won prizes given by the Overseas Press Club three times, once in 1956 for his reporting from India, and twice in 1966 for two large magazine pieces. In 1960 and 1965, Rosenthal won the George Polk Memorial Award for his journalism, and in 1966, the Page One Award from the Newspaper Guild of New York.

In 1963, at the age of 41, Rosenthal returned to New York to become the metropolitan editor of the *Times*, retaining that post for three years.

Rosenthal also wrote books. His 1964 book, *Thirty-Eight Witnesses*, told of the brutal Queens, New York, murder of a young woman named Kitty Genovese and the unfortunate reaction of those who were nearby at the time. Some thirty-eight witnesses, mainly her neighbors, heard her screams, and although many of them realized that she was being threatened, no one came forth to help her.

A year later, in 1965, Rosenthal and deputy managing editor Arthur Gelb wrote a book called *The Night the Lights Went Out*, which described the blackout that struck most of the East Coast on November 9, 1965. Rosenthal and Gelb also wrote *One More Victim* (1967), a biography of Daniel Burros, the prominent Ku Klux Klan leader who shot himself when the *New York Times* revealed in 1965 that he was Jewish.

In 1968 Rosenthal was appointed assistant managing editor of the *Times* and served in that post for a year. He was chosen managing editor in 1969, and in 1977 he was selected as the *Times's* executive editor.

Rosenthal's most remarkable achievement as the *Times's* executive editor was his 1971 decision to publish the controversial Pentagon Papers, despite strong pressure from *Times* officials and advisors not to do so. The Pentagon Papers were documents written by United States government officials to analyze the dimensions and implications of the Vietnam War. What the Papers in fact did was to portray with great specificity the hopelessness and bleak future of the American military effort in Vietnam.

The *Times* obtained a copy of these documents and began publishing them in the pages of the newspaper. When President Richard Nixon ordered that the publication of the Pentagon Papers be halted—exercising the doctrine of prior restraint for the first time in America—the newspaper went to the United States Supreme Court, which then voted against their suppression. The *Times* then resumed its publication of the reports.

Rosenthal's ascendancy to the editorship of the newspaper coincided with a growing perception among its readers that it was getting too stuffy in its news coverage and too liberal in its political leanings. The *Times's* executives realized that, unless corrective measures were taken soon, the paper might begin to lose readers—and money.

To lure more readers, Rosenthal decided that he had to adopt the paradoxical strategy of giving veteran readers the impression that the *Times* was still the great newspaper they had always known, while making changes that would give the paper a new look. The alterations

Courtesy of A.M. Rosenthal

A.M. Rosenthal

that he made were designed to make the newspaper more centrist in political matters and to attract the newly affluent suburban readers whose numbers were growing by leaps and bounds.

"Our readers buy us because we're straight," Rosenthal suggested, using the word straight as a synonym for fair, "but straight doesn't mean dull."

The *Times*'s makeover meant attempting to ensure that the newspaper was more engaging to read. Rosenthal made the reporting more straightforward, less trendy. He deemphasized the "why" in the reporter's formula of "who-what-where-when-why" on the grounds that the reporter could not really tell what motivated someone's actions; he was either guessing or editorializing.

Rosenthal sought to liven up the newspaper by adding new regular sections—sports on Mondays; science on Tuesdays; "living" on Wednesdays; "home" on Thursdays, and the New York City "weekend" on Fridays. So successful were these sections that they were soon copied by other newspapers around the country.

While Rosenthal was credited with saving the newspaper from premature death and possible bankruptcy after it had fallen into the doldrums, he did not escape a tongue-lashing from critics who felt that he was too tyrannical in his handling of employees. A 1988 book about Rosenthal called *Fit To Print: A.M. Rosenthal and his Times*, written by Joseph C. Goulden, described Rosenthal's ruling hand. The sentiment was echoed in an article in *Time* magazine that called Rosenthal's style "autocratic." To these charges Rosenthal responded that he had been attacked because he had been required to yank the *Times* out of its predicament as a dying newspaper. "I was the agent of change and people don't like change," he said.

Rosenthal married London-born Shirley Lord Anderson, a senior editor at *Vogue* magazine, in June 1987. An earlier marriage ended in divorce. Rosenthal has three sons from his first marriage.

Rosenthal retired from his post as executive editor in late 1986. He was made associate editor of the *Times*, writing a twice-weekly column called "On My Mind" that appeared on the op-ed page. Arthur Ochs Sulzberger, publisher of the newspaper, paid Rosenthal this tribute when he stepped down: he was "one of the titans of American journalistic history."

In the fall of 1994, Rosenthal successfully underwent open-heart surgery.

Rosenthal has left a legacy of a livelier "newspaper of record." Toward the end of 1999 he stopped writing for *The New York Times*, and shortly thereafter his column began to appear in the New York *Daily News*. In March 2004, in a farewell column in the *Daily News*, Rosenthal noted that he planned to devote himself to writing a book.

PHILIP ROTH

The Quintessential American-Jewish Writer

> Born March 19, 1933, in Newark, New Jersey. American novelist. Philip
> Roth's novels and short stories recount the frequently tormented struggle
> that American-Jewish men face over the conflicts between their Jewish
> heritage and the attraction of the dominant Christian-oriented Ameri-
> can culture. Roth's books are about young Jewish men in search of their
> identity and masculinity. His best-known works are *Goodbye, Columbus*
> (1959), *Portnoy's Complaint* (1967), and *Patrimony* (1991).

PHILIP ROTH WAS BORN in Newark, New Jersey, in 1933, to Herman Roth, an insurance
salesman, and Bess (Finkel) Roth, a homemaker.

Roth grew up in a Jewish neighborhood in Newark, and went to Weequahic High
School, which was predominantly Jewish. He had three years of after-school Hebrew school
from the ages of ten to thirteen. Roth constantly harbored fears that non-Jewish students from
rival schools would act out their anti-Semitic beliefs. He wrote in *The Facts*, an autobiographical account published in 1988, "I was never to be one of the few who stayed behind for a fight
but always among the many whose impulse is to run to avoid it. A boy in our neighborhood
might be expected to protect himself in a schoolyard confrontation with another boy his age
and size, but no stigma was attached to taking flight from a violent melee—by and large it was
considered both shameful and stupid for a bright Jewish child to get caught up in something so
dangerous to his physical safety, and so repugnant to Jewish instincts."

At the time Roth began his studies at Rutgers University in 1950, he also started writing
seriously. After a year, he transferred to Bucknell University in Pennsylvania, earning a B.A.
degree in 1954 and graduating *magna cum laude* and Phi Beta Kappa. In 1955 Roth received a
master's degree in English literature from the University of Chicago. He then entered a doctoral program there, but never completed the degree.

Roth taught English at the University of Chicago from 1955 to 1958, and at the same time
began writing with great frequency. His stories were published in the *Chicago Review*, *Paris
Review*, *Commentary*, *Esquire*, and the *New Yorker*.

When Roth was only twenty-six, his short-story collection *Goodbye, Columbus* was published, and it brought him national recognition. These stories offer a satirical, incisive look at
middle-class American Jewry. The title story, really a novella, tells of a summer romance between a young male Jewish librarian from Newark and a well-off Radcliffe undergraduate from
Short Hills, New Jersey, a middle-class Jewish suburb. Four of the other five stories also dealt
with Jewish characters.

The book won both the National Book Award for the best fiction of 1959 and the Daroff Award from the Jewish Book Council in 1960. Roth's satire on the Jewish community's materialism caused some critics to assail him for Jewish self-hatred. The book gave the American public a prototype for the "Jewish American Princess," which became a widely used epithet.

Roth won a Guggenheim fellowship for 1959 to 1960, and he used it to write his first novel, *Letting Go*, which was published in 1961. It tells the story of Gabe Wallach, an English instructor who moves from Chicago to New York, where he circulates among an academic Jewish crowd.

Roth's second novel, *When She Was Good*, appeared in 1967. Set in the Midwest, the book was Roth's attempt to prove that he could write about non-Jewish themes. This book, however, was not well received.

Roth's third novel, *Portnoy's Complaint*, published in 1967, became a bestseller. It recounted the sexual conquests of Alexander Portnoy, thirty-three years old and a successful young lawyer in Mayor John V. Lindsay's New York City administration. His romances are with non-Jewish women, a rebellion against his overbearing Jewish mother. He comes of age in the book by shedding his guilt (or at least he thinks he does), fighting back against his mother by revealing his sexual frustrations to his psychoanalyst.

Roth's use of comic, obscene, often cruel, language aroused great criticism of the book as, again, an example of Jewish self-hatred. It was seen as an attack on Jewish motherhood, with its lethal yet very humorous dissection of Sophie Portnoy as the archetypal Jewish mother, but Roth's vivid portrait has become a classic in American-Jewish literature.

Portnoy strengthened Roth's reputation as a writer, both in the United States and abroad. Some critics suggested that in writing the book Roth had invented a Jewish novel of manners. This was characteristic of the reaction to his work. Roth has become controversial both because he casts the struggles of American Jews in a sexual framework and because he satirizes a variety of American Jewish "types."

In 1971 Roth wrote *Our Gang*, a novel that parodied politics. A year later came *The Breast*, whose main character, David Kepesh, turns into a female breast and lives out a series of humorous adventures in his new incarnation.

The Great American Novel, published in 1973, was meant to use the sport of baseball to parody American society, but, largely because of its lengthy, complicated text, the book fell flat and did not do well.

The 1974 debut of Roth's character Nathan Zuckerman was as the protagonist of a novel entitled *My Life as a Man*. In 1977 the Roth character David Kepesh from *The Breast* made a comeback in *The Professor of Desire*. Zuckerman returned in the 1979 novel *The Ghost Writer*, for which Roth won the Pulitzer Prize. It was the first part of a trilogy and was followed by *Zuckerman Unbound* (1981) and *Anatomy Lesson* (1983). Another novel, *Epilogue: The Prague Orgy*, followed in 1985.

In 1987 Roth wrote *The Counterlife*, which describes Nathan Zuckerman's relationship with his brother Henry, along with his encounter with death, modern Israel, and contemporary Jewish issues. Roth wrote what he called "a novelist's autobiography" called *The Facts*, published in 1988. A year later came *Deceptions*, an account of the erotic affairs between an author named Philip and his fictitious female characters.

Films have been made from several Roth novels, including *Goodbye, Columbus* (1969) and *Portnoy's Complaint* (1972). In 1984 *The Ghost Writer* was made into a movie for television and starred Claire

Bloom, with whom Roth has had a close relationship for years. (Roth married Margaret Martinson in 1959; they separated in 1963. There were no children. She died in 1968.)

Patrimony (1991) recounts Roth's experience caring for his dying eighty-six-year-old father, who suffered from a terminal brain tumor. The book was *Time* magazine's choice as the best nonfiction book of 1991 and was hailed for its sensitive account of one of life's crucial events, told with clarity and literary elegance.

In 1993 Roth published *Operation Shylock: A Confession*. In this book, set in Israel, an impostor passes himself off as novelist Philip Roth, telling Israeli Jews that they must return to Europe in order to avoid a second Arab-organized Holocaust.

At their most basic, Roth's books are about young Jewish men in search of their identity and masculinity. Most of Roth's characters in his later works are intelligent, accomplished men, many of whom are smitten with non-Jewish women.

Philip Roth

The Jewish Week

Frequent themes in Philip Roth's books are the complex, often painful relationships of families, which the author tries to treat in a humorous vein. He writes of the relationships of sons and mothers, sons and fathers, and men with their wives and mistresses. He writes also of the guilt that a rebellious but loving son feels toward an ailing or industrious father as well as the struggle of men who want to control their own existence with the females in their lives who have other plans for them.

Roth's twenty-first book, *Sabbath's Theater*, published in 1995, earned the author a second National Book Award. The novel, said *Time* magazine, is about "an obnoxious hero, Mickey Sabbath, rampaging through a novel about facing death in a lonely old age." His next book, *American Pastoral*, which was published in 1997 and garnered the 1998 Pulitzer Prize, addresses the question: How is it that so decent a fellow as Seymour Levov could have raised a monster like Merry?

Roth won the PEN/Faulkner Award for his 2001 novel *The Human Stain*, the final volume in his postwar America trilogy. Coleman Silk, the central character, is an Athena College classics professor who has to retire due to a classroom comment that is misinterpreted as a racial slur. Roth deals with political correctness, race, identity, family, and the Vietnam War against the backdrop of former President Bill Clinton's impeachment proceedings.

In July 2002, Roth published a 160-page novella entitled *The Dying Animal*. The protagonist is again David Kepesh, of *The Breast* and *The Professor of Desire*, who is now a seventy-year-old cultural critic and lecturer at a New York college. Roth's 2004 best-seller, *The Plot Against America*, is based on the premise that Charles A. Lindbergh had defeated Franklin Roosevelt in the 1940 presidential election.

MAYER AMSCHEL ROTHSCHILD

Banker and Financier

Born February 23, 1743, in Frankfurt, Germany; died September 19, 1812. Founder of the House of Rothschild. Mayer Amschel Rothschild created a powerful banking kingdom, which his sons later expanded to London, Paris, Naples, and Vienna. The Rothschild family helped in large part to finance the founding of Belgium, the building of the Suez Canal, France's reparations to Germany after those two countries fought in 1870 and 1871, and Italy's independence.

T HE FAMILY NAME ROTHSCHILD comes from a *roth schild* or red shield that once hung in front of the house of Isaac Elhanan Rotschild, who in the 1560s acquired a house on the *Judengasse* (the main Jewish street) in Frankfurt. Rotschild died in 1585 in that city.

Mayer Amschel Rothschild

In the eighteenth century, a family named Schiff, and the Rothschilds, descended from Isaac Rotschild, shared a double house in the Frankfurt *Judengasse*; they hung house signs proclaiming *Zum Schiff* and *Zum Roten Schild* alongside each other. One of the Schiffs, deciding to move to London, sold the balance of the house to the first rich Rothschild, Mayer Amschel.

Until the birth of Mayer Amschel Rothschild in 1743, the son of Amschel Moses Rothschild, the Rothschilds were mostly undistinguished merchants. Rothschild attended a rabbinical school in Fürth. After his father's death, however, Rothschild was sent to Hanover, where he trained to become a banker. He also studied coins, medals, sculpture, and painting.

When his higher education was completed, Rothschild returned to Frankfurt and became a general trader, specializing in antiques and old coins. He was in the money-changing business as well.

In 1764, when he was twenty-one years old, Rothschild started doing business with Count William IX of Hesse-Kassel, who happened to be an avid coin collector. William was also heir to the largest fortune in Europe. Rothschild offered his merchandise to the imperial court of William IX. In 1769 Rothschild was appointed supplier of rare coins to the principality of Hesse-Hanau. As the informal court agent, Rothschild provided William IX with rare coins; he also printed his own coin catalogs for use in merchandising his coins to others.

In 1769 Mayer Amschel was given the official title of Court Agent. He was, according to Egan Corti, author of a 1928 book on the Rothschilds, "a tall, impressive-looking man of pronounced Hebraic type; his expression, if rather sly, was good-natured." Rothschild wore a wig, although as a Jew he was not permitted to have it powdered. He also wore a small, pointed black beard.

In 1770 Mayer Amschel Rothschild married Gudule (Schnapper) Rothschild and she bore him nineteen children; five boys and five girls survived. The Rothschilds had a rule that only their sons could enter the family business. The daughters and sons-in-law were excluded, a rule that was followed for succeeding generations.

When William IX became landgrave (a German count with a certain territorial jurisdiction) in 1785, Mayer Rothschild was one of just a dozen Jewish court agents who competed to do business with the ruler and who were also in a position to lend large amounts of money to other rulers. Gradually Rothschild increased his financial dealings with William, aided by his close connection to the landgrave's confidential financial advisor, C.F. Buderus, who later became Rothschild's silent partner.

Finding the radical ideas of the Enlightenment appealing, in 1792 Rothschild tried to start Phalanthropin, which was to be a Jewish school with a modern curriculum. He encountered too much resistance within the community, however, and he had to put off the effort.

That same year, Rothschild brought his two older sons, Amschel Mayer and Salomon Mayer, into partnership. The other boys, Nathan Mayer, Carl Mayer, and James Mayer, were brought in as partners as they reached maturity at age twenty-one. The five brothers were dubbed the "Frankfurt Five" and sent to the capitals of Europe to do business. Over the next two decades, they established the greatest international banking syndicate of the era. Amschel took over running the original bank in Frankfurt. Salomon opened the Rothschild bank in Vienna; Carl set up a bank in Naples. James settled in Paris in 1812 and acted as agent for Nathan, who was based in London.

By this time, Mayer Amschel Rothschild was one of Frankfurt's wealthiest citizens. When Frankfurt was invaded by France in 1792, once again the landgrave's fortune was in disarray. With the liberation of Frankfurt, it was left to Rothschild to put Landgrave William's finances back in order. As William's intermediary, the house of Rothschild won great respect. Honors were given to Rothschild, among them the German Order of Saint John, for his successful handling of William's financial affairs.

In 1800 Rothschild was appointed Imperial Crown Agent, a post that entitled him to bear arms and to benefit from certain tax exemptions. He also could move freely throughout the imperial domain. Soon Napoleon rose to power and William IX went into exile. The Rothschilds began providing the French leader, Napoleon, with loans.

Mayer Amschel Rothschild's biggest stoke of luck occurred after the Battle of Jena in 1806. It was then that William IX, while in exile, entrusted Nathan Rothschild who was headquartered in London, with the purchase of large amounts of British securities. Through incredibly adept speculation, Nathan Rothschild managed to build a fortune for the landgrave.

The senior Rothschild and his sons performed a valuable service for those who wished to do business in Europe discreetly. They became go-betweens, sending coded messages to different parts of the continent, transporting money in secret sections of coaches, concealing documents and bullion at their home in Frankfurt.

On September 16, 1812, Rothschild fasted on Yom Kippur, the holiest day of the Jewish calendar. He spent hours in the synagogue and, that evening, he felt severe pains. Despite discomfort, he wrote a new will. Rothschild sold to his five sons all his shares in the business, his securities, and other possessions, as well as his large stocks of wine, for the sum of 190,000 gulden, far below their true value. His sons became the exclusive owners of the business. Three days later, Mayer Amschel Rothschild, the founding father of the House of Rothschild, died at the age of sixty-nine.

Rothschild's last testament included the phrases: "I will and ordain that my daughters and sons-in-law and their heirs have no share in the trading business existing under the firm of Mayer Amschel Rothschild & Sons . . . [which] belongs to my sons exclusively. None of my daughters, sons-in-law, and their heirs is therefore entitled to demand sight of business transactions . . . . I would never be able to forgive any of my children, if contrary to these my paternal wishes, it should be allowed to happen that my sons were upset in the peaceful possession and prosecution of their business interests."

These words showed how little confidence Rothschild had in his daughters' choices of spouses. It went without saying that unmarried females of that time did not even bear consideration for inheriting any of the business.

Between World Wars I and II, the growth of other major banking concerns and the effects of high taxation curbed the relative significance of the House of Rothschild. Before and during World War II, the Nazis were eager to expropriate the assets of the Rothschilds, but by that time the Rothschilds had transferred their properties to holding companies in neutral or noncombatant countries.

After World War II, the Rothschilds exploited new post war opportunities created in the field of merchant banking. They built modern offices, ran unit trusts, and acquired major interests in Canada. They invested in the growing industry of films and television.

In January 1994 descendants of the Rothschild family marked the 250th birthday of the founder of the Rothschild banking empire. Nathaniel Charles Jacob Rothschild, whose title is the fourth Baron Rothschild, and other descendants of Mayer Amschel Rothschild gathered at his grave at an old Jewish cemetery in Frankfurt to pay tribute to him and honor the memory of his great business acumen.

JONAS SALK

Developer of the First Effective Polio Vaccine

Born October 28, 1914, in New York City; died June 23, 1995. American epidemiologist. Jonas Salk developed the first vaccine that was effective against polio. He was honored the world over for his work in eliminating this dreaded disease, but science's highest honor, the Nobel Prize, eluded him. He founded the Salk Institute, where research is now being conducted to develop a vaccine to prevent AIDS.

JONAS SALK'S PARENTS, Dora Press and Daniel Salk, met in New York City and were married in 1912. Dora, who had emigrated from Minsk, was an observant Jew with little formal education. Daniel was a native New Yorker; he designed ladies' scarves and blouses for a living. The family lived in the Bronx, where Salk went to grade school and then to the Townsend Harris High School for especially promising students.

Courtesy of Jonas Salk

Jonas Salk

The Salks had three sons. Jonas was the eldest and the most observant Jew. "My brothers called me the 'little rabbi,'" he said. He attended Hebrew School from the age of eight, laying *tefillin* daily, and going to synagogue on his own until the end of high school. Salk was aware of anti-Semitism as a youngster: "There was a school at the end of the street and some children would throw stones or make nasty remarks."

Salk's mother would have been pleased had he become a schoolteacher or rabbi. Salk, however, "became interested in the laws of nature," he recalled. "I was impressed early in life by tragedies in life, to say nothing of what had happened to our forebears." These thoughts compelled him to do something positive for humanity as a whole.

Salk completed his undergraduate studies at City College of New York in 1934 and then studied medicine at New York University. He felt he would go into research rather than practice although, he noted, "My mother would have loved it if I had had an office on Park Avenue."

At the end of his first year of medical school, Salk took a year's leave of absence to do research in chemistry. He was awarded his medical degree in 1939, did a two-year internship at Mt. Sinai Hospital in New York, and then embarked on a research career.

Salk won a research fellowship to the University of Michigan, where he gained firsthand experience in viral immunization with Dr. Thomas Francis, Jr., who was developing an influenza vaccine using inactivated influenza virus. During World War II, Salk served as a member of the United States Army Influenza Commission.

Salk married social worker Donna Lindsay on June 8, 1939. They had three sons, but were divorced in 1969. On June 29, 1970, Salk married Françoise Gilot, a French painter and writer who had shared her life with Picasso in the late 1940s and early 1950s. Salk and Gilot had no children.

After World War II, Salk moved to the University of Pittsburgh's school of medicine, becoming research professor of bacteriology in 1949. He was named professor of preventive medicine in 1954, and was professor of experimental medicine from 1957 to 1963.

At the University of Pittsburgh, Salk researched poliomyelitis (infantile paralysis), a viral disease that causes a flu-like illness which can enter the nervous system and cause paralysis and death. It is transmitted by contact with infected individuals and primarily affects children. At the time Salk began working on the disease, there were yearly epidemics that caused fear and panic. Albert Sabin's vaccine was developed later and came into use in the 1960s. Though Salk's and Sabin's vaccines have largely wiped out polio, no one actually knows exactly how it is transmitted, or why its normal, mild, flu-like course sometimes leads to the paralytic phase for which polio is best-known and most feared.

Salk's basic work established that there are three types of polio virus, each requiring separate immunization. The real breakthrough that influenced Salk in creating his polio vaccine was the pathbreaking work of Dr. John F. Enders, who received the Nobel Prize in 1954 for successfully growing polio virus in test tubes rather than in living monkeys. This permitted safe and rapid production of virus for research and vaccine production.

In trying to develop a polio vaccine from killed viruses, Salk challenged medical orthodoxy which held that only vaccines made of living viruses can provide effective, enduring immunity. Salk believed that immunity could be provided safely and effectively with a vaccine made from inactivated virus. In 1952 he successfully tested a killed-virus vaccine at the Watson Home for Crippled Children in Leetsdale, Pennsylvania. On January 23, 1953, Salk reported his favorable results to a group of scientists meeting in Hershey, Pennsylvania. A year later, aided by National Foundation for Infantile Paralysis grants, Salk and Dr. Thomas Francis, Jr., conducted field trials on 388,800 children to assess the effectiveness of the new vaccine.

On April 12, 1955, some 150 journalists arrived at the University of Michigan to learn of Salk's results. The vaccine was found to be safe and effective. Salk had found a way to end the scourge that, since the turn of the century, had killed or disabled perhaps a million Americans.

The success of his vaccine made Salk an international hero. New York City wanted to give him a ticker-tape parade. A manufacturer asked him to endorse a line of pajamas emblazoned with, "Thank You, Dr. Salk." He declined both honors. Over the years, however, streets, schools, hospitals, and babies were named after him. He was offered flowers, candy, large checks, job opportunities, and honorary degrees. He was awarded the Presidential Citation and the Congressional Medal for Distinguished Achievement.

The honors that came Salk's way were somewhat marred by a long-standing controversy with scientist Albert Sabin, who developed a live-virus polio vaccine that could be swallowed in a sugar cube. Many contended that the Sabin vaccine, licensed in 1961, was an improvement over Salk's because the Sabin vaccine was made from a living virus, which was felt to give superior, longer-lasting immunity and could be administered orally.

In an interview at his Salk institute in November 1994, Salk said, "I had no bitterness. Sabin did. He was determined to seek a cure for polio his way. It became like a holy war. In 1960, he said to me in Copenhagen that he was determined to eliminate the 'killed' vaccine. I said, 'Albert, more power to you.'" In 1985 Salk and Sabin appeared

Jonas Salk

together in Washington, D.C., and Sabin, pounding his fist on the table, said there was no need for two polio vaccines. Salk recalled that "then they turned to me. I smiled and said, 'About that, Dr. Sabin and I are in agreement.'"

In 1961 Salk served as an expert on virus diseases for the World Health Organization. In 1963 he founded and directed the Salk Institute for Biological Studies, located in La Jolla, California.

At La Jolla, starting in 1986 and working with colleagues across the country, Salk attempted to develop an AIDS vaccine. He worked diligently on it. "I haven't been able to stop. You fail only if you stop too soon," he said. In November 1994, he said that he had made "enormous progress."

Salk encountered obstacles in his path. However, he reacted to these challenges philosophically, saying, "I was very mindful that some doors were closed to me, which resulted in some doors being opened." When Salk applied to work on rheumatic diseases as a young researcher, his application was turned down. A door closed on him, so he turned to research in influenza.

Salk believed that his Jewish ancestry played a definitive role in influencing his career and life: "The process of natural selection undoubtedly resulted in a stock that has been passed on to its successors. It gave me whatever qualities were necessary to survive and to evolve. So I've seen adversity as an advantage. Jews have developed an innate wisdom about how to manage to continue to thrive and strive. I could see that in the way my mother brought up her children. What she wanted more than anything else was for us to go beyond her status."

For over thirty years, Salk made written observations about the nature of reality, consciousness, and the human condition. He accumulated more than twelve thousand pages of notes and published three books on the subject. He believed that what he was documenting in writing was the expression of the evolutionary process moving toward the betterment of human existence.

Salk died before he could finish this project. He was eighty years old when he suffered a fatal heart attack in 1995; he was engaged at the time in research into the AIDS virus and ways to prevent it.

All three of Salks's sons are physicians: Peter, born in 1944; Darrell, born in 1947; and Jonathan, born in 1950.

Discovering the vaccine that virtually wiped out polio a few decades ago, Jonas Salk became one of the great medical heroes of the era. *Life* magazine chose him as one of its hundred most important Americans in its special Fall 1970 edition. Salk's name will always be associated with saving people from one of the most dreaded diseases of the century.

DAVID SARNOFF

Broadcasting Pioneer and Executive

Born February 27, 1891, in Uzlian, Russia; died December 12, 1971. American broadcaster. Dominating the electronic communications industry for more than fifty years, David Sarnoff founded the first broadcast network, NBC, in 1926. As head of the RCA Corporation, he was a pioneer in the development of radio, early television, and color television. During the late 1920s, Sarnoff presided over RCA's acquisition of the Victor Talking Machine Company, forming RCA Victor, a leading name in electronics. Sarnoff was president of RCA from 1930 to 1947, chief executive officer from 1947 to 1966, and board chairman from 1947 until his death.

DAVID SARNOFF, the eldest of five children, was born in 1891 in Uzlian, a small Jewish community close to the Russian city of Minsk. His father, Abraham Sarnoff, an itinerant trader, hoped that his first-born would follow in his footsteps and become a trader. His mother, the former Lena Privin, wanted him to become a scholar.

When Abraham Sarnoff left Russia for the United States in 1895, Lena sent David, aged four, to study with her uncle, a rabbi. During the next five years David studied the Talmud at fifteen-hour stretches. He memorized two thousand words a day.

When, in the summer of 1900, Abraham Sarnoff's health deteriorated, he sent for his family. Young Sarnoff, now nine, his mother, and two younger brothers arrived in the United States via steerage to Montreal and then train to Albany, New York. Two days later, David was peddling newspapers in the streets on New York's Lower East Side to help support the family. He also ran errands for a butcher and sang in a synagogue choir on Jewish holidays.

Sarnoff's father died in 1906. This left fifteen-year-old David in charge of supporting the family, so he dropped out of school. He became a messenger for the Commercial Cable Company. The new wireless communications intrigued him. He used his small savings to purchase a simple telegraph key and soon mastered the Morse Code. Six months later, in September 1906, Sarnoff began working as an operator for the Marconi Wireless Telegraph Company of America.

At age seventeen, in 1908, Sarnoff was sent as a junior operator to the Marconi station at Siasconset on Nantucket Island, off the Massachusetts coast. He hardly minded that it was a lonely outpost because the pay was good (sixty dollars a month) and he had the opportunity to read technical books in the station's large library.

Back in New York, Sarnoff acquired instant fame on the night of April 14, 1912, while

David Sarnoff

working on his own. He was the twenty-one-year-old manager of an experimental wireless station on the roof of Wanamaker's New York department store when he suddenly picked up the message "S.S. *Titanic* ran into iceberg, sinking fast." For the next seventy-two hours, without sleep and practically without eating, he received and gave out news of the disaster and the names of survivors. The tragedy claimed the lives of 1,517 people. "The *Titanic* disaster," Sarnoff later noted, "brought radio to the front, and incidentally me." David Sarnoff's name was now known around the country.

The Marconi Company rewarded Sarnoff by appointing him a radio inspector. In 1913 he became chief inspector and a year later was promoted to contract manager. As he rose in rank during those war years, Sarnoff combined his technical knowledge with marketing skills.

In 1915 he advised the company to sell radios as a household utility in much the same way pianos or phonographs had been sold. More specifically, Sarnoff proposed that the company sell a "radio music box" that would send music over the air. The music could then be picked up by a simple radio programmed for different wavelengths that could be changed by pressing a button. Sarnoff was in fact thinking of a device that was the forerunner of the modern radio receiving set.

Sarnoff married Parisian-born Lizette Hermant on July 4, 1917, and they had three sons: Robert, Edward, and Thomas.

In 1919 the newly formed Radio Corporation of America (RCA), headed by Owen D. Young, absorbed American-Marconi, and Sarnoff became its commercial manager. RCA accepted Sarnoff's 1915 plan to make radio a household utility. RCA, however, was willing to invest only two thousand dollars in the project. To demonstrate his radio plan, Sarnoff borrowed a Navy transmitter and helped provide a blow-by-blow broadcast of the 1921 Jack Dempsey-Georges Carpentier world heavyweight championship fight. Some two hundred thousand amateur wireless operators heard the fight, and Sarnoff's broadcast caused much excitement. As a result, RCA began making receiving sets. On September 8, 1922, Sarnoff was elected vice president of the company. By 1925 sales of RCA's radio sets had risen to $83 million.

Sarnoff believed in the concept of quality programs for his radio listeners. He invited talented musicians and educators to give advice about the new medium and to help organize entertainment and educational programs.

In 1926 Sarnoff founded the National Broadcasting Company (NBC) as an RCA subsidiary in order to expand further the market for radio sets. Sarnoff was convinced that coast-to-coast radio broadcasting was practical and would help sell more radios. NBC represented a new concept in broadcasting, a central broadcasting organization that fed radio programs to interconnected radio stations. It was the beginning of nationwide radio and, later television networks.

During the late 1920s Sarnoff negotiated RCA's acquisition of the Victor Talking Machine Company, which had a familiar trademark: "His Master's Voice." Sarnoff also originated the idea of the combination radio and phonograph cabinet to house the units and make them more pleasant to look at so that people would want them in their homes.

In 1930 Sarnoff was elected president of RCA. The corporation nearly collapsed, however, at the time of the 1932 stock market setback.

During the 1930s, RCA's research arm experimented with television. In April 1939, during the dedication ceremonies at the New York World's Fair, Sarnoff pioneered public television broadcasting in the United States when he himself appeared on camera, noting with assurance, "Now we add sight to sound—this miracle of engineering skill brings the world to the home." He was right. Television became part of the everyday world. In 1942 Sarnoff became RCA's board chairman and chief executive officer.

With the start of World War II, Sarnoff became a colonel in the United States Army. He was on active duty from March 1944 to the war's end in May 1945, serving as a communications consultant in the Pentagon and at General Dwight D. Eisenhower's headquarters in Europe. In 1944, promoted to brigadier general, Sarnoff used his expertise in communications to contribute to the Allied victory. Back home, RCA was producing radar and signaling systems for the Army.

In the late 1940s, Sarnoff was instrumental in making television a success, showing that it could become an inexpensive way to provide entertainment and information to large numbers of Americans. Around that time, scientists had been working at RCA's David Sarnoff Research Center in Princeton, New Jersey, to develop a color television system that could receive both black and white and color pictures. Although Sarnoff encountered stiff opposition within RCA, he insisted on promoting the idea of color television and was eventually vindicated. Americans moved easily from black and white to color once the new form of television was made available to the public.

Sarnoff was active in Jewish affairs. He was the first honorary fellow of the Weizmann Institute of Science in Rehovot, Israel, and was a member of the board of the Jewish Theological Seminary in New York City. He seemed proud of his Jewish heritage. In an interview he gave to the *Jewish Journal* on March 24, 1960, Sarnoff said, "The essential Jewish identity is worth preserving because it is an influence that conditions the formation of a better type of human being. Jewish ethics, morality, and wisdom are constructive influences."

Sarnoff admonished his fellow Jews to be above reproach since non-Jews tended to accuse all Jews of corruption when spotting but one corrupt Jew. "Every individual Jew must therefore assume responsibility for the honor of the entire Jewish people, and realize clearly that improper conduct on his part may be damaging to all Jews by encouraging anti-Semitism."

For over fifty years, David Sarnoff dominated the electronic communications industry. He built RCA into one of the fifteen largest American firms. His name was virtually synonymous with the entire field of modern radio and television. In 1966 he retired as RCA's chief executive officer, but stayed on as board chairman until his death in 1971 at the age of eighty.

JACOB SCHIFF

American Industrial Financier

> Born January 10, 1847, in Frankfurt, Germany; died September 25, 1920. American financier and philanthropist. The leading American Jewish figure of the late nineteenth and early twentieth century, Jacob Schiff used his position as head of one of America's largest investment banks, Kuhn, Loeb and Co., to promote the development and expansion of industrialization, especially by helping finance the railroads. Schiff was a leading philanthropist when it came to Jewish causes and campaigned assiduously against the czarist regime's policies of anti-Semitism.

JACOB SCHIFF WAS BORN in 1847 in Frankfurt, Germany. His family included wealthy bankers, scholarly figures, and rabbis, and dated back to the fourteenth century. Schiff actually contended that he was a descendant of King Solomon as well as of David and Bathsheba. His education was both secular and religious. He studied at the Israelitische Religionsgesellschaft.

Schiff had personality quirks as a child. He was restless, unpredictable, quick to anger, and capable of violent outbursts. Only five feet two inches tall as an adult, he had a gruff temper that made him seem larger in stature than he really was. Stephen Birmingham, writing in *Our Crowd* (1967), notes that Schiff could be "exquisitely poised and logical and patient, and he could also be irrational and arbitrary and petty and demanding." Schiff was a fanatic about physical fitness, always walking and bicycling to keep himself healthy.

In 1863, at the age of sixteen, Jacob began working with his father, Moses, at the Frankfurt stock exchange. Moses Schiff was associated with the Rothschild banking firm. Two years later, Jacob Schiff moved to New York. In 1867 he formed his own brokerage firm, Budge, Schiff and Co., joining forces with two men from Frankfurt. The partnership papers were prepared for signatures. At the last moment, however, someone realized that Schiff, who was only twenty years old, was too young to sign legally. The partnership was dissolved, partly because Schiff had signed illegally and partly due to his domineering and difficult personality. Although it was something of a demotion, Schiff accepted a job briefly as manager of the Deutsche Bank in Hamburg. But he became restless and dissatisfied; commercial banking bored him. Returning to New York in 1863 at the age of twenty-six, he joined the six year-old firm of Kuhn, Loeb and Co.

There Schiff, though only a junior partner, specialized in railroad management and financing. He decided to become an expert on the railroads. He began to use Kuhn, Loeb's resources to purchase railroads, playing a key role in consolidating and expanding the burgeoning American railroad network.

On May 6, 1875, Jacob Schiff married Therese Loeb, the daughter of Solomon Loeb, head of the banking firm. Schiff subsequently became a full partner in the firm. The couple moved into a large brownstone at 53rd Street and Park Avenue.

In 1881, when the other members of Kuhn, Loeb realized Schiff's great financial abilities, he was made head of the firm. Schiff's firm developed quickly into one of the most important private investment banking houses in America, playing a pivotal role in America's industrialization during the late nineteenth and early twentieth centuries. Through Kuhn, Loeb, such firms as Westinghouse Electric, U.S. Rubber, Armour, and American Telephone and Telegraph were capitalized.

Jacob Schiff

American Jewish Archives, Cincinnati Campus, Hebrew Union College, Jewish Institute of Religion

In 1897 Schiff joined with E. H. Harriman, who owned the Illinois Central Railroad, to purchase the Union Pacific Railroad. Together, Schiff and Harriman amassed the largest single railroad fortune in the world.

Schiff also served as a director or advisor for many banks, insurance firms, and other companies. He helped float loans to the American government as well as to foreign countries. The most important was the two-hundred-million-dollar bond issue for Japan at the time of the 1904–1905 Russo-Japanese War. Furious with the Russians over their anti-Semitic policies, Schiff called the czarist government "the enemy of government." He was pleased to support the Japanese in their war effort. He also encouraged an armed revolt against the Czar. When the Japanese won the war, Schiff was presented with the Second Order of the Treasure, becoming the first foreigner to receive an official medal at the imperial palace.

In 1910 Schiff was one of several Americans who campaigned to revoke a commercial treaty with the Russians over their mistreatment of Russian Jews. Although the Russians sought him out for loans as well, he was steadfast in his refusals to grant them. Schiff made sure that no one else at Kuhn, Loeb underwrote Russian loans either. He did provide financial support for Russian-Jewish self-defense groups. It was only with the fall of the Czar in 1917 that Schiff dropped his opposition to underwriting the Russian government; he provided some support for the Kerensky government. But, angry at the Russians for refusing to honor the passports of American Jews, he successfully campaigned to abrogate the Russian-American Treaty of 1932.

Schiff remained a conscientious, observant Jew who supported Jewish institutions throughout his life. He said prayers every morning and was a member of New York's Temple Emanu-El. He helped found the Jewish Theological Seminary and regarded the school as one providing a

275

"reasonable Orthodoxy" that would be appealing to the many newly arrived immigrants in New York. He also supported both Yeshiva College and the Hebrew Union College.

Schiff gave the New York Young Men's Hebrew Association (YMHA) a permanent home. He was president of Montefiore Hospital for thirty-five years and paid weekly visits to patients there. He would never allow his name to be used honorifically in any of the institutions that received money from him; the only exception is the Schiff Pavilion at New York's Montefiore Hospital. Schiff also had a strong interest in Jewish literature; he made ample financial contributions to the Jewish Publication Society.

Schiff was a founding member of the American Jewish Committee. In 1914 he helped create the American Jewish Relief Committee, which in time developed into the Joint Distribution Committee.

Schiff's personal wealth was available to help Jews throughout the world. And yet, in some small ways, he was tightfisted. He kept a little notebook on the stand beside the telephone and anyone who made a phone call had to enter the call in the log. At the end of each month, he compared the calls listed in the notebook with those on his telephone bill.

During World War I Schiff and some of his American Jewish peers were assailed by the newer generations of Zionist-leaning leaders for their indifference to Zionism. Schiff had indeed been a strong foe of Zionism, believing it a secular, nationalistic perversion of the Jewish faith and incompatible with American citizenship. He gave some funds to agricultural projects in Palestine, however, and by 1916 he had shifted his beliefs to be in favor of Zionist efforts, openly supporting the notion of a cultural homeland for Jews in Palestine.

A follower of Reform Judaism, Schiff highly respected more traditional Jews and donated money to most standard Jewish causes. One day a young man held a meeting with Schiff to talk about the building of an Orthodox synagogue. Schiff contributed a good deal of money to the project, prompting the man to ask Schiff why a Reform Jew would help the Orthodox. "My dear young man," said Schiff, "if there were no Orthodox Judaism, there would be nothing to reform."

Historians consider Schiff the outstanding figure of American Jewry of his era. His financial acumen and philanthropic efforts made him a leader and a role model for many young men carving out lives and careers in the late nineteenth and early twentieth centuries.

MENACHEM MENDEL SCHNEERSON

Revered Lubavitcher Rebbe

Born April 18, 1902, in Nikolayev, the Ukraine; died June 12, 1994. Renowned rabbi and spiritual leader. Through his charisma and perseverance, Menachem Mendel Schneerson, a Sorbonne-educated rabbi, took the Lubavitcher Hasidic sect, which had been devastated by the Nazis, and rebuilt it into the fastest-growing and most dynamic wing of Orthodox Judaism. After Nazism had spread through Europe, Rabbi Schneerson and his family were given refuge in the United States in 1942. Schneerson became the movement's seventh leader when his father-in-law, the sixth Lubavitcher rebbe, died in 1950. He was regarded by many followers as the Messiah. The *New York Times* called Schneerson "perhaps the best-known Jewish leader in the world."

MENACHEM SCHNEERSON WAS BORN in 1902 in Nikolayev, a port on the Black Sea in the Ukraine, the son of Rabbi Levi Isaac and Channah (Yanovsky) Schneerson. He was a great-grandson of the third Lubavitcher rebbe, who headed a movement founded in the eighteenth century by Rabbi Israel Baal Shem Tov.

When Schneerson was five, his family moved to Yekaterinoslav, where his father had been chosen to be chief rabbi. Schneerson briefly attended a *heder*, a religious primary school, but was mainly educated at home by private tutors. He was considered an *ilul*, or genius, and even his tutors had a hard time keeping up with him. By the time Schneerson was seventeen, he had mastered the entire Talmud, some 5,894 pages, in its Hebrew editions. It is not clear how and when he was ordained a rabbi.

In 1929 Schneerson married Chaya Moussia, the younger daughter of Rabbi Joseph Isaac Schneerson, the sixth Lubavitcher Rebbe. Schneerson took the virtually unprecedented step of studying engineering at the University of Berlin and at the Sorbonne in Paris, making him the first Lubavitcher rebbe to receive a secular education.

In 1940 Schneerson was nearly arrested in Italy for smuggling religious materials to Jews in occupied France. With Nazism spreading its tentacles throughout Europe, in 1942 the family found refuge in the United States. In 1944 Schneerson was appointed director of all Lubavitch publishing and educational activities and established headquarters in New York.

When Rabbi Joseph Schneerson died in 1950, a dispute erupted over who would become

Rabbi Menachem Mendel Schneerson

the new Lubavitcher rebbe. The choice was between Menachem Schneerson and his brother-in-law, Rabbi Samarius Gourary. The elders of the movement decided that Menachem Mendel Schneerson should be the movement's seventh Grand Rabbi.

Schneerson built a loyal group of followers, even though many of them were not Hasidic or even Orthodox. He launched a major program to disseminate information about Orthodox Judaism and popularized the Chabad Hasidic movement, which affected all sectors of American and world Jewry. Chabad is an acronym for three Hebrew words meaning wisdom, understanding, and knowledge. Schneerson set up Hebrew day schools in cities in the United States and Canada.

By the early 1970s, his followers succeeded in setting up Chabad houses throughout the United States. These serve as synagogues, schools, and counseling centers. The target audience is college-age youth. In 1990 there were over 250 such houses throughout the United States.

Schneerson was in the vanguard of the *Baal Teshuva* movement, which saw the return of tens of thousands of American Jews to Orthodoxy. He delivered lengthy weekly talks on such subjects as Hasidism, rabbinic thought, and political issues. Some of his political stands were controversial. He balked at public demonstrations in support of Soviet Jewry, arguing that private government intervention would be more useful. He took a hawkish view with regard to Israel's occupied territories, believing that the Bible commanded Israel to keep all the captured land for itself.

Schneerson was believed by many of his followers to be the Messiah. He always claimed that the arrival of the Messiah was near, but he himself never claimed to be the one. It was left to his proponents to make such an assertion. Because so many of his adherents were convinced of it, the semi official Lubavitch slogan became "We Want Messiah Now."

Schneerson's followers treated him with awe and consulted him on all sorts of personal issues—whom to marry, what career to choose, where to live. At gatherings known as *farbrengens*, Schneerson, simply referred to as the Rebbe, spoke in Yiddish, led a wordless melody, then lifted a glass and offered a toast of *l'chaim* to his listeners.

"He had a way of gesturing minimally that was electrifying," said Chaim Potok, the novelist who has written about the world of Hasidism in his books. "The slightest lift of a finger, the vaguest wave of the wrist. He had the mysterious ability to fill a room simply by being there."

The Lubavitcher sect has over a thousand educational and cultural centers in all parts of the world, particularly in the former Soviet Union. Estimates of its membership vary from tens of thousands to over a million. Schneerson's pictures adorn the "mitzvah tanks" that travel to neighborhoods in large cities as part of an effort to induce Jews to put on *tefilin* (phylacteries) and to observe Jewish law.

Schneerson never visited Israel. The Israeli right-wing politician Geula Cohen once posed the question in the Israeli daily newspaper *Ma'ariv*, "Why won't you [Schneerson] come and give the order [for your followers] to immigrate to Israel?"

Schneerson answered, "My place is where my words are likely to be obeyed. Here I am listened to, but in the Land of Israel I won't be heard. There, our youth will follow only somebody who has sprung up from its own ranks and speaks its own language. The Messiah will be a man of flesh and blood, visible and tangible, a man whom others will follow. And He will come."

Despite his physical absence from Israel, Menachem Schneerson played a major role in Israeli politics, seeking to have the Israeli parliament, the Knesset, change Israel's Law of Return to ensure that conversions performed by non-Orthodox rabbis would not be valid. He was unable, however, to prevail on the issue.

Schneerson left the United States only once—to meet his mother in France when she arrived there from Russia, and to escort her to the United States. He left his headquarters in Brooklyn only for his frequent visits to his father-in-law's grave in Queens. Otherwise he remained at home.

He did not leave home when President Jimmy Carter proclaimed Schneerson's seventy-eighth birthday "Education Day, U.S.A." or when President Ronald Reagan proclaimed Schneerson's eightieth birthday a "National Day of Reflection." The Rebbe was represented at the official ceremonies in Washington, D.C., by delegations of Chabad rabbis. Although his followers built an exact replica of his Brooklyn headquarters (770 Eastern Parkway in Crown Heights) in Israel, the Rebbe never went to visit it.

Schneerson wrote many volumes of Torah commentary and was fluent in ten languages. Sometimes his speeches, broadcast by satellite to Lubavitchers around the world, went on for six hours. Every word was published.

Schneerson died on June 12, 1994, at the age of ninety-two. He was childless and left no designated successor. Many of his followers, convinced he was the Messiah, refused to mourn his death. Still, many of his followers feel lost without his presence.

In October 1994, Schneerson was posthumously awarded the Congressional Gold Medal. The resolution that accompanied it stated that he "inspired people to a renewal of individual values of spirituality, cooperation, and love of learning."

BEN SHAHN

Major Jewish-American Artist

Born September 12, 1898, in Kaunas, Russia; died March 14, 1969. American artist. Ben Shahn's paintings, murals, and posters advocated liberal social or political causes; his artistic compositions were a mixture of poetic surrealism and social realism. Shahn was first recognized and taken seriously by the public for his 1932 series of satirical paintings depicting the trial and execution of Italian-American anarchists Nicola Sacco and Bartolomeo Vanzetti.

BENJAMIN SHAHN WAS BORN in 1898 in Russia, one of five children of Hessel and Gittel (Lieberman) Shahn. Shahn's father was a woodcarver and carpenter. When Ben was eight years old, he immigrated to Brooklyn, New York, with his parents.

From an early age, Shahn wanted to be a painter; he also expressed the desire to become familiar with the America that he wished to depict. At age fifteen, he was apprenticed to a lithographer, which gave him experience in merging image and text. He took night courses at City College, New York University, and the National Academy of Design.

In 1922, when he was twenty-four years old, Shahn married Tillie Goldstein. They traveled to Europe, where they visited the great art galleries. Seven years later, they went to Europe again and spent a good deal of time in Paris. Reading accounts of the Dreyfus Affair while in France, Shahn did a series of paintings in the late 1920s based on original photos of the people involved in the case. The Dreyfus paintings were Shahn's first artistic protest against criminal injustice.

From his family, Shahn developed an intense consciousness about social issues and his art reflected these liberal leanings. Shahn first demonstrated an interest in these issues when he did a series of twenty-three satirical paintings (in gouche or opaque watercolors) that dealt with the trial of Italian-American anarchists Nicola Sacco and Bartolomeo Vanzetti, who were accused of killing a Massachusetts paymaster in 1921. These paintings formed part of a general worldwide outrage at the convictions that many people considered unjustified. Nonetheless, the two men were electrocuted on August 23, 1927.

Shahn's interest in focusing on the poor and downtrodden was sharpened during a 1929 visit to Paris, where his European friends encouraged him to tell the story of America through his art with an emphasis on social commentary. His stay in Europe encouraged him even more to paint American scenes, with an emphasis on providing social commentary through his art and using realistic architectural designs to depict where actual events took place.

In 1933 Shahn was hired by artist Diego Rivera as his assistant on a controversial project.

Rivera was commissioned to produce a fresco to be called *Man at the Crossroads* for the wall of the RCA building in New York City's Rockefeller Center. When people noticed that the labor leader in the fresco bore an unmistakable likeness to the Soviet leader Vladimir Lenin, Rivera was asked to substitute a portrait of an unknown man for the head. When he refused, although he was paid for the job, the mural was chipped from the wall.

Like other American artists, Shahn was subsidized by the government during the Depression. As a participant in the New York City Public Works Art project, Shahn painted eight tempera pictures depicting the Prohibition era in the United States.

Shahn was an accomplished photographer as well. During the 1930s, as a photographer for the Farm Security Administration, he took over six thousand photographs of the unemployed and the poor, as well as of government homestead projects and of small-town American life in general.

Ben Shahn

Shahn's last assignment for that agency was to do a wall fresco for the community center of a garment workers' housing project in Roosevelt, New Jersey. Depicting immigrants arriving from Eastern Europe, the mural illustrated their march toward economic freedom. In the mural, Shahn managed to include artistic references to many of his interests—labor unions, sweatshops, the Triangle Shirtwaist Company fire—as well as to labor and civic leaders.

In 1930 Shahn began a lifetime association with the Downtown Gallery in New York. The gallery displayed his well-known Sacco and Vanzetti paintings as well as his series about the persecuted West Coast labor leader, Tom Mooney, who was found guilty of a bombing and then later pardoned. *Lucky Dragon*, a painting of a Japanese fishing boat that had wandered into a nuclear test zone, was also exhibited.

In 1934 Shahn was commissioned by the Federal Relief Administration to prepare murals for the Riker's Island Penitentiary. The Municipal Art Commission, however, rejected his completed works for reasons that are still not clear.

Shahn's pictures tell stories and emphasize the contrasts between man and his surroundings. They show fundamental aspects of life for workers in factories and on farms, depicting them both poetically and realistically. "I hate injustice," he once said. "I guess that's about the only thing that I really do hate . . . and I hope I will go on hating it all my life."

Other Shahn paintings that have strong social messages are *The World's Greatest Comics* (1946), *Death of a Miner* (1947), *The Victim Player* (1947), and *East Twelfth Street* (1947).

In 1938 Shahn was commissioned to do a mural for the Bronx Central Annex Post Office. Working with his second wife, Bernarda Brysen, he produced thirteen panels that provided a comprehensive picture of life in American cities and farms.

In 1940 Shahn was awarded $19,980 from the Treasury Department's Section of Fine Arts to depict the Social Security program story on the walls of its building in Washington, D.C. On one wall he vividly portrayed a boy on crutches, two girls surveying an accident, a dispossessed family, and a boy with a baseball bat. It is one of his best-known murals.

During World War II, Shahn worked for the Office of War Information, where he designed war posters. In 1944 he painted *Concentration Camp*. The painting sought to suggest the despair felt by Holocaust victims and to confirm the outrage against Nazi persecution felt by many Jewish-American artists. The following year Shahn was selected to be director of the graphic arts division of the Congress of Industrial Organizations (CIO). He worked for a nominal salary because he believed so strongly in the CIO's cause.

In 1943 eleven of Shahn's paintings were included in the "American Realists and Magic Realists" exhibition at the Museum of Modern Art in New York City. In 1947 a retrospective one-man show of Shahn's photographs, mural studies, drawings, and paintings was mounted at the Museum of Modern Art, an indication that he had achieved full public recognition for his work.

Shahn said that he preferred painting in tempera because it was a medium that imposed control and clarity. His colors are bright; some might even say brash. "Often," wrote an art critic for the *New York Times*, "Shahn seems bent upon telling us that this is a terrible and a cruel and a heartbreaking world. Yet there are the stimulatingly swift and keen imaginative flights. And his color can be such as an angel might use."

Until 1950 Shahn focused on social realism in his paintings; he used an intentionally direct style to reach and depict the common man. In his later period, however, he created allegorical and symbolic works, turning more inward, responding to his Jewish and personal beliefs in a greater depth. His early training in Hebrew lithography served as a valuable resource for the Jewish themes that he eventually developed in his art. In fact, Shahn's works adorn a number of American synagogues, including Temple Oheb Shalom in Nashville, Tennessee, and Temple Beth Zion in Buffalo, New York.

In 1954 Shahn was one of two painters (the other was abstract-expressionist Willem de Kooning) whose work was shown at the United States pavilion in Venice, Italy, in an exhibition sponsored by the Museum of Modern Art. Some thirty-four Shahn paintings were included in this exhibit. Among them were *The Red Stairway* (1944), *Spring* (1947), and *Composition with Clarinets and Tin Horn* (1951).

Shahn enjoyed using Hebrew letters in his paintings. As part of a series of interpretive illustrations, Shahn designed a Hebrew alphabet which he named *The Alphabet of Creation* (1954). In 1966 he produced a haggadah which included eleven of his illustrations as well as an original lithograph frontispiece.

From 1945 to 1948, Shahn served as a city council member in his hometown of Roosevelt, New Jersey, where he lived with his second wife and their three children.

Shahn died at the age of seventy in 1969. His colorful and meaningful paintings, murals, and posters largely advocated liberal political causes while still reflecting the heart of American everyday life, which he so vividly depicted. Displayed permanently in a variety of locations, his works provide a unique legacy of life in the nation's mid-century.

SHALOM ALEICHEM

Yiddish Author

Born February 19, 1859, in Pereyalsav, the Ukraine; died May 13, 1916.
Yiddish novelist, dramatist, and story writer. Shalom Aleichem is considered the most talented writer of Yiddish fiction and the greatest Yiddish
humorist. He is most famous for the stories of Tevye and his daughters
that were dramatized on Broadway and in Hollywood as *Fiddler on the
Roof*. Shalom Aleichem tried to finance his writing career through speculation in the stock market, but never became wealthy. His reputation as a
writer, however, soared early in the twentieth century.

SHALOM ALEICHEM WAS BORN Shalom Rabinovitch in 1859 in the Ukraine; his pseudonym
is the traditional Hebrew greeting that means "peace be with you."

The young Aleichem was raised in Voronkov, which became the model for his literary town of Kaserilevke, a symbolic Jewish *shtetl*—small, poor, in an obscure corner of the
world. The fictitious town became a symbol of the self-contained, intimate Jewish enclaves of
Eastern Europe and Russia.

Shalom Aleichem's father was a well-to-do grain and lumber merchant who had a strong
interest in modern Hebrew culture. When his business partner turned dishonest, Shalom
Aleichem's father had to shut down the business. He then opened an inn, which gave his son
an opportunity to get to know the musicians and cantors who frequented the establishment.
Two of Shalom Aleichem's books, *Yosele Solovye* and *Stempenu*, grew out of his boyhood experiences in that small hotel.

At age twelve, Aleichem started to read Hebrew literature. He also tried writing his own
stories. A year later, his mother died of cholera and he was taken care of by his grandmother
until his father remarried. His stepmother was a difficult woman who frequently complained
and swore. She later was to be the inspiration for Aleichem's first work, an alphabetic dictionary of his stepmother's favorite curses. Aleichem colorfully depicted his early life in his 1916
autobiographical book, *Fun Yarid* (*From the Fair*).

When he was sixteen, Aleichem fell in love with the daughter of a cantor who often stayed
at the family inn. Although Aleichem courted her, she eloped with a Russian boy. After that
episode, Aleichem worked as a schoolteacher and became the tutor of the daughter of a rich
landowner named Elimelech Loyev. He lived with the family for three years, but had to leave
when Loyev found out that Aleichem and his daughter were in love. In 1881, however, he
married Loyev's daughter and they had six children.

That same year, when he was twenty-two years old, Aleichem's first articles were published

Shalom Aleichem holding one of his six children.

in the Hebrew periodical *Hamelitz*. When he had tried to write sketches in Russian, editors rejected them. He submitted some works in Yiddish to the Yiddish weekly *Dos Yidishe Folksblat*. To conceal his identity from both his father and father-in-law, he adopted his pen name Shalom Aleichem.

In 1887 Aleichem began writing plays— one-act comedies. One was called *A Khosn, a Doctor* (*A Bridegroom, a Doctor*). The next year he wrote *Der Get* (*The Divorce*).

Aleichem tried to support his literary career by entering the business world and splitting his day between business activity and writing. He described these two identities: " . . . for four hours a day a wheeler-dealer on the bourse . . . but from about five in the afternoon, I am Shalom Aleichem." It was a difficult existence.

In 1885, upon the death of his father-in-law, Aleichem's wife inherited an ample sum of money; he used it to found a Yiddish literary annual called *Di Yidische Folksbibliothek*. In 1888 and 1889, he issued its first two volumes which included, in addition to his own writings, those of that other great Yiddish writer, Mendele Mokher Seforim. Because of his improved financial situation, Aleichem was able in 1884 to publish his first novel, *Natasha*. Between 1884 and 1890, there were five more novels, including *Sender Blank*.

Before the third volume of the literary annual could be published, in 1890, Aleichem lost his money speculating in the stock market. He realized that he was not cut out for the business world and that only through his writing could he make a dependable living.

In 1892 Shalom Aleichem published "London," the first of his Menachem Mendel stories. The following year he wrote his first play and subsequently became a key figure on the Kiev Jewish literary scene as well as a champion of Zionism. By 1899 he was contributing frequently to Yiddish newspapers in Saint Petersburg and Warsaw, and was gaining much popularity through those articles.

Throughout the 1890s, Aleichem wrote sketches centering on his most famous characters, Tevye and Menachem Mendel. Tevye was a poor, hard-working Jewish milkman, deeply honest and very religious. He had seven daughters for whom he had to arrange marriages, a tremendous burden placed upon him. Tevye's life, popularized on the Broadway stage and in Hollywood as *Fiddler on the Roof*, came to exemplify Eastern European and Russian Jewish life at a time when Jews could be persecuted without reason at any moment. Menachem Mendel was a *Luftmench*, a Jewish Don Quixote, a man-about-town who dreamed of becoming rich but had no luck in turning his dreams into reality.

By the early 1900s, Aleichem had become a writer full time. Along with another popular writer of his day, Maxim Gorky, he helped edit a Russian anthology of Yiddish writings. The Russian censors, however, as part of their general anti-Semitic tendencies, barred its publication.

Aleichem's stories and plays turned him into a Jewish folk hero, the authentic voice of his people. More than any other literary figure of his age, he brought the Jews of the Ukraine to life through his writings. He attempted to inject into his works as much humor as possible because, as he wrote in 1911, "I tell you it is an ugly and mean world and only to spite it one mustn't weep! . . . Only to laugh out of spite, only to laugh!"

Following the Kiev massacres and the Russian Revolution, both in 1905, Aleichem fled first to Switzerland, then to London and finally New York, hoping to support himself through his writing and lectures. Two of his plays failed, and in 1907 he returned to Europe, continuing to write plays and giving readings and recitations that turned out to be extremely popular.

In 1908, while on a lecture tour in Russia, Aleichem collapsed. For the next six years, suffering from tuberculosis, he lived in different health resorts on the Italian Riviera, in southern Germany, and in the Swiss Alps. Returning to the United States in 1914, Aleichem suffered new health problems brought on by stress after learning of his son Misha's death in 1915.

One year later, Shalom Aleichem died at age fifty-seven. Nearly every shop and factory on the Lower East Side of New York City closed on the day he was buried, in tribute to a beloved writer whose literary work mirrored and lovingly depicted the colorful daily lives of the Jewish people in Eastern Europe.

YITZHAK SHAMIR

Underground Leader and Israeli Prime Minister

> Born October 22, 1915, in Ruzanoy, Poland. Israeli political leader. In charge of the pre-state underground organization Lehi, Yitzhak Shamir spent nearly a decade as a secret-service operative for Israel's Mossad. He then entered politics, joining the right-wing Herut party, and was elected to the Knesset in December 1973. He served as Knesset speaker from 1977 to 1980 and foreign minister from 1980 to 1983. He was prime minister of Israel from 1983 to 1984 and from 1986 to 1992. For much of the 1980s, Shamir was the main voice of Israel's right-wing political movement.

YITZHAK SHAMIR, whose original last name was Yezernitsky, was born in 1915 in Ruzanoy, Poland. His parents, Shlomo and Penina, were first cousins, Zionists, and not deeply religious; his father attended synagogue regularly and their home was kosher. Shamir, the youngest of three children (the other two were girls), attended only Jewish schools.

Shamir attended Warsaw University, studying law, but dropped out after a year in order to journey to Palestine in 1935. "I didn't think about a career in law," Shamir has said. "I only thought about going to *Eretz Yisrael*. Poland was an episode . . . it didn't interest me at all." Shamir never saw his parents and two sisters again; they were killed in the Holocaust.

To reach British-ruled Palestine, Shamir obtained a student visa and actually registered at Jerusalem's Hebrew University, although even had he wanted to study—which he did not—he lacked the necessary tuition. Shamir quickly linked up with the Irgun, the smaller of the two armed Zionist military units. When the Irgun splintered into two groups in 1938, Shamir sided with the smaller and more violent faction, quickly rising to second in command of its Tel Aviv-based group.

When World War II began in 1939, the Irgun again split. Its larger faction chose to suspend attacks against the British; the smaller one was called Lehi (a Hebrew acronym for Fighters for Israel's Freedom) or the Stern Gang, after its leader, poet-scholar Avraham Stern. Shamir was drawn to Stern because only he and his followers among the Jews were prepared to fight the British.

In 1941 the British arrested Shamir for involvement in terrorist acts, but he escaped from a British detention camp. When in 1942 Stern was murdered, Shamir took over the Lehi, happy in this shadowy existence, adopting a series of aliases; he took one of them, Shamir, as his own. He married one of his agents, Bulgarian immigrant Sarah Levy, code-named Shulamit. They named their first child Yair, Avraham Stern's code name.

Lehi leader Shamir, twenty-eight years old, replaced the group's disorderly bent toward violence with disciplined, cautious operations. In his 1994 memoirs, *Summing Up*, Shamir accepted responsibility for one controversial deed carried out by Lehi: the 1944 assassination in Cairo of Britain's resident minister in the Middle East, Lord Moyne, who had been blocking Jews escaping the Holocaust from reaching Palestine. Shamir monitored the operation carefully, choosing the target and the two young men who were assigned the task.

Shamir was again arrested in the summer of 1946 and exiled to an internment camp in British Eritrea from which he escaped five months later. He fled to Addis Ababa, capital of Ethiopia, inside an empty water tanker, and was granted asylum in France. By the time Shamir returned to Tel Aviv in 1948, he saw that the Lehi's war against the British was over. Shamir and his Lehi comrades, however, continued to fight the Arabs and anyone they considered enemies of the new Jewish state.

Yitzhak Shamir

One of them was United Nations mediator Folke Bernadotte, who wanted to sever Jerusalem from the Jewish state. Shamir wrote in his memoirs that the idea of killing Bernadotte in 1948 was "conceived in Jerusalem by Lehi members operating there more or less independently." Shamir said, "We were asked and we said that we are not against" the deed. However, Israel's Prime Minister David Ben-Gurion decried Bernadotte's assassination and Shamir was branded an outcast by the nation's political leadership. In practical terms, it would be a long time before he would be permitted to hold a government position.

From 1948 to 1955, Shamir operated a chain of six movie houses in Ramat Gan, managed a building firm, and then worked in another construction company. Still a pariah, he sought a job in the Interior Ministry at one stage, but Ben-Gurion sent a note to the interior minister: "I have learned that you are about to hire that terrorist, Yezernitsky. I am against it." Shamir did not get the job.

In 1955 Mossad leaders decided to exploit the intelligence talents of Shamir and other former Irgun and Lehi members; Shamir became a senior operative in the intelligence agency, serving largely in Europe for nearly a decade. He and his family lived a simple, secretive life in Paris under a false name.

In the late 1960s Shamir entered private business again, working at a rubber factory; he also helped run Menachem Begin's Herut party, a forerunner of today's Likud, and in December 1973 was elected to the Knesset.

State of Israel Government Press Office

Yitzhak Shamir (left) with U.S. President George Bush.

Shamir, along with his other former underground colleagues, were no longer considered pariahs once Menachem Begin's party took power in May 1977. Shamir served as Knesset Speaker from 1977 to 1980. When in September 1978 the Knesset voted to approve the Camp David accord, which called for an Israeli-Egypt peace treaty and autonomy for the Palestinian Arabs, Shamir abstained.

Shamir was foreign minister from 1980 to 1983, and when Begin retired as prime minister in August 1983, Shamir was chosen by the Likud to replace him. In the September 1984 elections, neither Shamir's Likud party nor Shimon Peres's Labor party could form a government on its own. So Shamir and Peres agreed to enter into a national unity government and rotate the two top jobs of prime minister and foreign minister. Shamir served as foreign minister from September 1984 to October 1986, after which he replaced Peres as prime minister. In 1988 the Likud narrowly won the election. The national unity government continued with Shamir as prime minister.

In 1990 Shamir's resistance to an American plan for an Israeli-Palestinian peace conference led him to fire Peres, then finance minister, for supporting the idea. This abrupt dismissal ended the unity coalition. Shamir was able to form a new government on his own and, upon taking office, reiterated his vow never to concede Israeli-held land to the Palestinians.

One of Shamir's most important decisions as prime minister came during the 1991 Gulf War when, as a right-wing hardliner, he chose not to retaliate against Saddam Hussein despite Iraq's repeated Scud missile attacks against Israel. By restraining the Israel Defense Forces at the request of American President George Bush, Shamir reduced the prospects that the Arab coalition, joined with the United States and Israel against Saddam Hussein, would turn against Israel.

After lengthy discussions with American secretary of state James Baker, Shamir agreed that Israel would take part in the Madrid peace conference of October 1991, which was aimed at fashioning Israeli peace accords with the Palestinians, Jordanians, and Syrians. Peace talks continued after the Madrid gathering in Washington, D.C., but led nowhere.

Then, in June 1992, the Labor party, under the leadership of Yitzhak Rabin, easily defeated Shamir and the Likud party. Fifteen months later, after secret talks in Oslo, Norway, Israel and the Palestine Liberation Organization (PLO) agreed on a Declaration of Principles that required Israel to evacuate the Gaza Strip and the West Bank town of Jericho.

Shamir was incensed. "Some say that Madrid brought Oslo, " he said. "That's absolutely not true. I never thought about an agreement like Oslo. We wanted, as a result of Madrid, that *Eretz Yisrael* would be in our hands and the Arabs would have a certain autonomy. That's all. And [Jewish] settlement would continue all the time . . . We thought that by the time we got to negotiating a final solution, there would be a half million Jews in Judea and Samaria. We were sure of it."

In early 1996, at the age of eighty-one, Shamir was dividing his time between the Knesset in Jerusalem and his Tel Aviv office. Having been replaced as Likud party leader in March 1993 by Benyamin Netanyahu, Shamir no longer makes headline news. He says he has few regrets about the past. His main hope is that the majority of Jews will come to live in Israel "like all normal people. A people generally resides on its land."

Shamir shared the 2001 Israel Prize for Lifetime Achievement with former Israeli foreign minister Abba Eban and immigration activist Mordechai Ben-Porat. He received his country's highest award for serving, according to an education ministry statement, "as a symbol for generations of youths of the qualities of modesty, love of homeland, and tenacity." The tribute also cited Shamir's leadership as prime minister during the 1991 Gulf War, when Israel exercised restraint and avoided retaliating for repeated Iraqi Scud missile attacks. He "navigated Israeli policy in a way that won worldwide admiration," the statement said.

NATAN SHARANSKY

Soviet-Jewish Dissident

Born January 20, 1948, in Donetsk, the Ukraine. Illustrious Soviet dissident. Natan Sharansky campaigned vigorously for the rights of Soviet Jews to leave for Israel and was then arrested in 1974 and charged with being an American spy. Convicted and sentenced to jail for thirteen years, Sharansky was the object of an international campaign, led by his wife, Avital, to win his release, a campaign that brought immense sympathy to the Soviet Jewish cause. In 1986, after serving nine years, Sharansky was released and flown to Israel. Since 1996, with the exception of eight months in 2000–2001, he has served in a ministerial position in the Israeli government.

H E WAS BORN NATAN BORISOVICH SHARANSKY in 1948 in Soviet Ukraine, but was called Anatoly because his parents, Boris, a filmwriter and journalist, and Ida Milgrom, an economist, trying to keep their Judaism in low profile, were afraid to use his original (Hebrew) name. His father, a Communist, worked as a journalist for a party newspaper. When Sharansky was a youngster, his father died of a heart attack. The family moved to Istra, northwest of Moscow. Sharansky has one older brother, Leonid.

As a child, Sharansky displayed a talent for mathematics. He was the chess champion of his school and later of his home city. Sharansky's dream as a child was to be world chess champion.

After secondary school, Sharansky was admitted to the Moscow Physical-Technical Institute; he studied mathematics and computers there, graduating in 1972. He then worked on computers at the Oil and Gas Research Institute where, Soviet authorities argued, he was exposed to state secrets, the official reason for denying him an exit visa.

His parents, while teaching Sharansky to be proud of his Jewishness, downplayed religion to protect the children from anti-Semitism. Sharansky began to believe that Judaism was a secret sect. The 1967 Six-Day War turned him into an avid Zionist.

In the spring of 1973, Natan Sharansky decided to seek an exit visa to immigrate to Israel. Not only was it denied, but Soviet officials began building a criminal case against him, suggesting that he wanted to go to Israel so that he could kill Soviet soldiers fighting for Egypt.

Meanwhile, Sharansky fell in love with Natalya (Avital) Stieglitz and planned to marry her. Avital received an exit visa. On July 4, 1974, Natan and Avital were married, and the next day Avital left for Israel, confident that Natan would soon follow.

In early March 1977, the twenty-nine-year-old Sharansky was accused in the government newspaper *Izvestia* of passing Soviet secrets to the American Central Intelligence Agency (CIA). Eleven days later he was arrested in an effort to discredit the Jewish emigration movement.

Israel Government Press Office

Natan Sharansky (right) with his wife, Avital.

The Soviet intelligence and security agency, the KGB, threatened Sharansky with the death penalty but told him that if he confessed, he could go to Israel. Sharansky said, "You have to find reasons why you shouldn't cooperate with them." He did. "You feel you were created in the image of God and you must be worthy of it. This feeling was very supportive."

On July 14, 1978, Sharansky was convicted of treason, espionage, and anti-Soviet agitation, and sentenced to thirteen years in prison and labor camp. "I hope that the absurd accusation against me and the entire Jewish emigration movement will not hinder the liberation of my people," Sharansky said during the trial. He vowed that he would one day join his wife in Jerusalem. Avital campaigned vigorously for her husband's freedom, meeting with world leaders and speaking at rallies.

During this time, Sharansky spent 403 days in isolation cells, including one 130-day stretch. Though never physically tortured, he was deprived of food, and suffered from exposure to cold; he was forced to endure long periods of isolation. Avital had given him a Hebrew prayer book, which he read constantly, understanding little but slowly gaining the feeling "as if King David was talking directly to me. That was a pure religious experience, as if King David is explaining to you to be strong against the KGB. That was when I was closest to religion."

Sharansky insisted that he was innocent, and he rejected a Soviet suggestion that he seek a pardon based on ill health, although he did suffer from severe headaches, poor vision, and chest pains.

As part of a major East-West prisoner exchange, Sharansky was freed on February 11, 1986. Arriving in Israel hours later, Sharansky hugged acquaintances, quipping, "I am very glad to have an opportunity to speak to an audience in which my criminal contacts are represented so widely."

Prime Minister Shimon Peres and half the Israeli cabinet were on hand for Sharansky's arrival. "We receive here a great and heroic man, made of unbreakable material, unbreakable spirit," Peres said. Sharansky then spoke to President Reagan by phone. "As you know very well," Sharansky said. "I was never an American spy." He then left for the Western Wall in Jerusalem to pray.

Going straight from prison to Israel and a completely new existence, Sharansky found an intense, complicated experience. He was absorbed both by the opportunities available to him and his new country's shortcomings. "I suspect even when a Jew comes to the next world it's not exactly what he or she expected," he said, half seriously. Prison life was slow compared to the fast-paced Israel. "Here, every half hour, something is happening," Sharansky said. He found the "smallness" of Israel both a virtue and a handicap. "At the same time, we're one big family *and* we can't stand one another."

Most of Sharansky's time is now spent on volunteer activities on behalf of Russian Jewry. He is chairman of the Zionism Forum, a Jerusalem-based group devoted to furthering the cause of Russian Jewry. He wears a green army cap, warding off the pressure of Orthodox Jews to don a yarmulke. He carries a mobile phone, a sign of his being in constant demand. The Jerusalem office from which he runs the Zionist Forum is four times larger than his prison cell was. Sharansky is still observant in his religion—keeping the sabbath, keeping kosher. "The only bad part of Judaism," he joked, "is that we don't have two *Shabbatot* [Sabbaths]."

Early in 1996, Sharansky organized the Israel B'Aliya immigrant-rights party. It won seven seats in the May 29th election, and Sharansky became Minister of Commerce and Industry in Prime Minister Binyamin Netanyahu's new government. The highlight of his service came on January 27, 1997, when Sharansky returned to the former Soviet Union. Accompanied by Avital and his eighty-nine-year-old mother, he was now on the official business of trying to increase Israeli trade. Upon landing in Moscow, Sharansky remarked: "When I was in prison, I often dreamed of landing in Israel in an El Al plane . . . but I never dreamed of landing in Moscow in an El Al plane." During his stay, Sharansky visited the grave of his father and signed an economic cooperation agreement with Moscow Mayor Yuri Luzhov. He winced at the thought that the ceremony took place in a grand hall next door to the building where he had been arrested twenty years earlier.

Following the 1999 elections, Sharansky was appointed Minister of the Interior by Prime Minister Ehud Barak, but in July 2000 he resigned from the post in protest over Barak's willingness to offer unprecedented concessions to the Palestinian Authority. In political opposition, Sharansky fought against the division of Jerusalem and against Israel's capitulation to Palestinian demands under the threat of violence. He was named Minister of Housing in March 2001 in the government formed by Prime Minister Ariel Sharon.

Sharansky fared poorly in the January 28, 2003 elections, as his Yisrael B'Aliya party garnered only two seats instead of the expected four to six. In February 2003, Sharansky was appointed Minister without Portfolio in the newly-formed government of Prime Minister Ariel Sharon.

ISAAC BASHEVIS SINGER

Winner of the Nobel Prize for Literature

Born July 14, 1904, in Radzymin, Poland; died July 24, 1991. Yiddish author. Isaac Bashevis Singer was awarded the Nobel Prize for Literature in 1978. He vividly portrayed Eastern European Jews as they confronted pogroms, false Messiahs, assimilation, and the Holocaust. Singer wrote in Yiddish, a dying language. His novels, short-story collections, memoirs, and children's tales created a cast of Nazi concentration camp survivors who, in settling in the United States, remained a lost generation, stranded between the old and new worlds. Among his better-known works are the novels *The Magician of Lublin* (1966), *Enemies: A Love Story* (1972), and his memoirs, *In My Father's Court* (1966).

ISAAC BASHEVIS SINGER WAS BORN in 1904 to Rabbi Pinchas Menachem Singer, a Hasidic scholar, and Bathsheba (Zylberman) Singer in the town of Radzymin, near Warsaw, then part of the Russian Empire. Both of his grandfathers were rabbis.

At the age of four, the Singer family moved to Warsaw. Singer's father established a rabbinical court at home and the fascinated youngster listened raptly as his father dispensed advice on religious and family matters.

Singer was equally thrilled when his parents related mystical Jewish folk stories to him. "I was born with the feeling that I am part of an unlikely adventure, something that couldn't have happened, but happened just the same," Singer wrote in 1965. "The atmosphere of adventure permeated my home. The astonishment that came over me when I began to read Jewish history has not forsaken me to this day."

His older brother, Israel Joseph, was a well-known Yiddish writer who wrote under the

I.B. Singer

State of Israel Government Press Office

293

I.B. Singer

name I. J. Singer and died in 1944. Singer's sister, Hinde Esther, published two novels and short stories using the name Esther Kreitman. Influenced by his brother, Singer hoped to become a secular writer despite the strong objections of his parents, who wanted him to become a rabbi and a religious scholar.

In the early 1920s, Singer joined his brother in Warsaw, taking a job as a proofreader with a Yiddish literary journal named *Literarishe Bleter*. By 1926 he had begun to write stories and book reviews that were published.

Singer wrote in Hebrew at first, but decided to abandon the holy language in favor of Yiddish, which he knew from his childhood. In 1932 he became coeditor of the Yiddish literary magazine *Globus*, in which some of his stories were published, including his first novel, *Satan in Goray*, which the magazine serialized.

Singer had a mistress named Runya who was a devoted Communist. They lived together on and off for several years in the late 1920s, but were never married. Runya bore Singer's only child, a son named Israel. In 1935 Isaac Bashevis Singer journeyed to the United States to join his older brother, who had moved there a year earlier. Runya and Israel, then five years old, left for the Soviet Union, and eventually immigrated to Israel. In New York City, Singer wrote articles, reviews, and fiction for the *Jewish Daily Forward*, the Yiddish newspaper, and other journals.

"My first impression," he told an interviewer in 1966, "was that here Yiddish literature . . . was dead . . . . It took me about five years . . . to convince myself . . . that Yiddish is still very much alive here."

With the English-language publication of his novel *The Family Moskat* in 1950, Singer gained attention in the United States. Five years earlier, the book had been published in Yiddish. Set in Poland during the fifty years preceding the Nazi invasion, the novel was about the breakup of a leading Jewish family in Warsaw at a time when traditional Eastern European Jewish life was crumbling. The book was awarded several prestigious prizes, including the 1950 Louis Lamed Prize. Critics praised Singer's ability to tell a story about individuals in terms that were immediately universal.

Satan in Goray appeared in English in 1955. It was set in a Jewish hamlet in Poland after the Cossack massacres of 1648 to 1649 and recounted the mysticism and the frantic search for salvation among Eastern European Jews during the time of the self-proclaimed Messiah, Shabbatai Zevi.

Singer's 1960 novel, *The Magician of Lublin*, relates the tale of Yasha Mazur, a philandering circus magician and acrobat who is torn between two worlds, those of the Jewish ghetto and modern society.

One critic noted that Singer's books were filled with "people broken by the Holocaust, the devil in various guises, agonizing rabbis, brutish peasants, fumbling lovers, and failed writers." These colorful and interesting people populated Singer's fictional world and were a reflection of what he had experienced himself. Singer once wrote that, as a child, "I suffered deep crises, was subject to hallucinations. My dreams were filled with demons, ghosts, devils, corpses. Sometimes before falling asleep, I saw shapes. They danced around my bed, hovered in the air." Those childhood dreams were reflected in his writings.

Singer was awarded the Nobel Prize for Literature in 1978. In his Nobel Prize acceptance speech, he noted, "I am not ashamed to admit that I belong to those who fantasize that literature is capable of bringing new horizons and new perspectives—philosophical, religious, aesthetic, and even social. In the history of old Jewish literature there was never any basic difference between the poet and the prophet. Our ancient poetry often became law and a way of life."

Singer's short story "Yentl the Yeshiva Bocher" was turned into a play called *Yentl* and ran on Broadway during the 1975–76 season. A movie version, directed by and starring Barbra Streisand, was released in 1983.

Marion Simon, writing in the *National Observer* in 1968, described Isaac Bashevis Singer as "a small, bird-like man with a barely visible ridge of thin white hair" whose "striking blue eyes betray an innate warmth and lively intelligence." In 1940 Singer married Alma Haimann, a refugee from Munich, Germany.

Singer considered himself religious, although he was not observant of Jewish ritual. "Whenever I am in trouble, I pray. And since I'm always in trouble, I pray a lot." His Jewishness, he said, "is of great importance to me, but I really feel that I am a longtime American and this is my country." Singer became an American citizen in 1943.

As for Israel, Singer's attitude was that "things may look bad [for Israel], but in our history things look bad all the time, and we have outlived scores of nations. We Jews have been living in an eternal, permanent crisis."

Singer's main nonliterary interest was animal welfare. "For animals every day is Treblinka," he wrote in 1972, alluding to the suffering of Jews and others in a Nazi concentration camp. "I one day decided [in 1962] no meat, no fish. I just think it's the wrong thing to kill animals."

In 1987 Singer moved from Manhattan to Surfside, Florida. In 1988 twenty-two new Singer stories were published under the title *The Death of Methuselah and Other Stories*. Singer died in July 1991 at the age of eighty-seven. His most important literary contribution was to provide in his works a sense of the vanished *shtetl* life of Eastern Europe and the experiences of the Yiddish-speaking Jewish immigrants who settled in New York City. His vivid and insightful way of communicating this was unique and thoroughly engrossing for the reader. He was prolific and his writings are widely available in English.

GEORGE SOROS

Financier and Philanthropist

Born in 1930 in Budapest, Hungary. Hungarian-American speculator and philanthropist. A Holocaust survivor, George Soros received his formal education in London, then moved to New York in 1956. There, in 1969, he became the manager of the Quantum Fund, a high-risk hedge fund, and with it has produced the best investment record on Wall Street. In 1981 *Institutional Investor* magazine called Soros "the world's greatest money manager." In September 1992, Soros gained additional fame in the business world by earning nearly one billion dollars for his firm when he predicted correctly that the British would devalue the pound. In 1993 Soros earned a record-breaking $1.1 billion, making his the number one American income, according to *Financial World* magazine. In 1994 he made only seventy million, a significant drop-off from his loftier sums of past years.

GEORGE SOROS WAS BORN in 1930 into an upper-middle-class Jewish family in Budapest, Hungary. His parents were Tivadar and Elizabeth. From his father, who was a prisoner of war during World War I, George acquired a crucial instinct for survival. It served the teenaged George well when the Nazis overran Hungary in 1944.

To avoid having his son's Jewishness discovered, Tivadar Soros arranged for George to pose as the non-Jewish godson of an official of the Hungarian Agriculture Ministry. In that disguise, young Soros traveled around Hungary while an official confiscated the property of landowners who had been transported to Auschwitz. Soros personally delivered notices to prospective deportees who were destined for the gas chambers. During 1944, the year that the Nazis occupied Budapest, Soros, no longer under the protection of the official, moved with his parents from one hiding place to another to avoid detection.

Soros, his parents, and his brother Paul survived the Holocaust. After the war, Soros left his parents behind in Hungary and journeyed to London, where he studied economics at the London School of Economics, graduating in 1952. Soros hoped to become a philosopher, but he abandoned the idea when he realized that he would not be able to fulfill his dream of becoming a philosophy professor at the London School of Economics. He decided to enter the investment world. After a few years of apprenticeship with British firms and learning how financial markets function, Soros moved to New York in 1956 to pursue his chosen career.

At first Soros sold European securities at various brokerage firms, including F.M. Mayer, Wertheim & Co. and Arnhold & S. Bleichroder. At the latter, Soros teamed up with a young

George Soros (left) visits a high school in Bucharest, Romania to which his Soros Foundation donated computers.

Yale graduate from Alabama, James B. Rogers, Jr., to start the Quantum Fund, a fund for an international clientele with money invested in non-American investment funds. Soros was the conceptualizer and the salesman; Rogers had a fundamental flair for spotting the actual monetary value of companies. They began with $250,000 in capital.

The Quantum Fund was, in effect, a series of funds speculating on commodities, currencies, stocks, bonds, and other more sophisticated financial instruments. It became the most successful investment vehicle ever created. Since 1969, the fund's equity has increased about 400 percent; it has realized an unparalleled 35 percent annual return over the years. One thousand dollars invested with Soros then was worth about two million in 1994. No other investment opportunity has produced better results for such a long time. "I have a fascination with risk," Soros once said. "It makes me feel alive. I can get bored just living."

The original Quantum Fund spawned several others associated with it, and Soros, by 1994, was overseeing some twelve billion dollars in investments. Since 1988, however, he has turned over most of the day-to-day running of his funds to others.

Soros has married twice, the first time to German-born Annalise, whom he met in New York; they were married in 1961, had three children, and were divorced in 1981. George married Susan Weber, twenty-five years his junior, in 1983. They have two sons.

Soros claims that his success is due to a financial theory he discovered that he calls "reflexivity." Others assumed that there had to be logic in the way the financial markets worked, that if someone could just get hold of the right set of facts, it would be possible to make predictions about the movements of prices in the financial markets. Soros felt he knew better. He became convinced that what explains financial market behavior is not a rational way of thinking but a reflexive relationship that exists between the biases of investors and what he calls the "actual course of events," another phrase for the economic fundamentals of firms. According to Soros, the bias of investors toward a stock causes its price to rise or fall. At times that bias operates as a self-reinforcing factor that triggers a frenzy of buying on the part of investors. The trick is to discover when the frenzy is about to begin. The key to Soros's success has been in his determining that defining moment accurately time and time again.

By the early 1980s, having made far more money than he needed, Soros sought ways of using his earnings for noble purposes. He decided to try to pry open the "closed societies" of Eastern Europe by giving the citizens of these countries a taste of Western ideas and culture. During the 1980s and early 1990s, he set up philanthropic foundations in the region, underwriting a philanthropic empire so substantial that *Business Week* called him "the single most influential private citizen between the Rhine and the Urals." His financial activities amount to one of the most important private relief efforts of the twentieth century. In time, Soros Foundations blossomed in most of the countries of Eastern Europe and in the former Soviet Union. By the mid-1990s, Soros was giving hundreds of millions of dollars away.

The event that made Soros instantly famous and turned him into a legend on Wall Street and in London was his "bet" in September 1992 against the British pound. At that time Britain had been facing heavy pressure to abandon its membership in the Exchange Rate Mechanism (ERM) system that had kept the exchange rates of European currencies relatively fixed in recent years. The trouble was that with Britain in the economic doldrums in the fall of 1992, the ERM arrangement forced it to keep the pound at far too high an exchange rate. Soros guessed that Britain would have to leave the ERM system and devalue the pound. He bet ten billion dollars, much of that from his Fund, the rest from loans, that Britain would devalue. When it did, on September 15, 1992, he realized nearly one billion dollars in profit.

This September coup against the pound resulted in Soros making the top of the annual list of *Financial World*'s best-paid financiers on Wall Street in 1992. He personally earned $650 million that year, beating out Michael Milken's record of $550 million, set in 1987. This made George Soros a global investment superstar. Fleet Street dubbed him the man who "broke the Bank of England."

In the wake of this event, Soros seemed so powerful that Washington politicians began to worry that new controls might be needed to curb him. Accordingly, in April of 1994, Congressional hearings were held to determine whether George Soros and the other hedge-fund managers should be restrained. The worth of Soros's testimony appeared to weigh heavily in the decision to spare him and the other hedge-fund managers these proposed new controls.

In January 1994, Soros visited Israel and was greeted warmly by Israeli officials. He had been indifferent about being Jewish since surviving the Holocaust. In the early 1990s, however, he had shown signs that he wished to get closer to his religion, perhaps in response to the verbal attacks launched against him by right-wing nationalist groups in Eastern Europe who, angry at his philanthropy in that region, had accused him of being a Zionist agent.

The year 1994 was not a very good financial one for Soros overall. One cause was a disaster that befell him on February 14 of that year. Having bet for some time that the Japanese yen would keep falling against the dollar, Soros discovered that he had speculated incorrectly. The yen suddenly shot up and he lost $600 million dollars in one day. This disastrous loss kept Soros from having another one of the spectacular years he had enjoyed in the past. Soros's Quantum Fund still fared better by the end of 1994 than did the other large hedge funds, although it returned only 3 percent. In 1995, however, the Quantum Fund climbed 39 percent.

Soros spends most of his time engaged in his philanthropy, enjoying field trips to visit his foundations in Eastern Europe and the former Soviet Union. He remains attuned to the business but is active only intermittently, leaving the day-to-day operations to his associates.

Because of his spectacular achievements in the financial markets, George Soros's reputation grew to legendary proportions in the mid-1990s. Many investors, large and small, wanted to learn his investment secrets so that they too might play the markets successfully.

In 1996 the Quantum Fund had a much less remarkable performance than the previous year, ending the year up only 1.5 percent. Early in 1997, *Forbes* magazine put Soros's worth at $2.5 billion. In a major switch of his philanthropy strategy, he decided to expand his charitable efforts to include the United States, having become frustrated at what he called America's failure to help Eastern Europe move toward open societies.

Soros's annoyance led him to reflect on the social and economic problems of the United States. He provided $1 million to a number of programs that aimed at aiding prisoners rehabilitate themselves. One program helped former women prisoners in locating housing; another aided first-time nonviolent offenders find work once out of jail. One of his more controversial activities concerned American drug policy. Soros advocated what he called a "saner" policy, suggesting that heroin and other illicit drugs be made available on prescription to registered drug addicts.

Early in 1997 Soros unleashed an attack against Western capitalist societies, charging them with not sharing their riches with poorer nations. Interviewed on CNN television network, he contended that the West, ruled as it is by the stock market, always left poor people, such as those in Eastern Europe, behind. "The belief that the markets are perfect," he told CNN, "is dangerous, because in fact they are very unstable. And they don't lead to the best allocation of resources because they tend to make the rich richer."

In March 2002, in a book entitled *Soros on Globalization*, the philanthropist asserted that Western governments had placed far too much emphasis on the rapid liberalization of trade and capital markets. Those governments, he affirmed, ought to create institutions that help the world's poor.

According to *Forbes* magazine, in 2002 Soros had a net worth of $6.9 billion, making him the thirty-seventh wealthiest person in the world. Donating $500 million a year to charitable causes, he has made clear his intention to give away most of his fortune by the year 2010.

In 2004, with assets of $7.2 billion, Soros was said to be the twenty-fourth richest American and the fifty-fourth richest person worldwide. During the heated 2004 U.S. presidential election campaign that pitted incumbent George W. Bush against Senator John Kerry of Massachusetts, Soros campaigned actively against Bush, visiting swing states and donating millions of dollars to anti-Bush organizations. Republicans sought to portray Democrat Kerry as beholden to such left-wing luminaries as Soros.

STEVEN SPIELBERG

American Filmmaker

Born December 18, 1947, in Cincinnati, Ohio. American film director and producer. Steven Spielberg turned a childhood fascination with film equipment and picture-taking into one of the most notable filmmaking careers of the late twentieth century. His movies *E.T.* (1982) and *Jurassic Park* (1993) are the two most profitable films ever made. His movies *Jaws* (1975), *Close Encounters of the Third Kind* (1977), and the Indiana Jones trilogy were also all-time box-office hits. Spielberg's 1993 film about the Holocaust, *Schindler's List* (1993), a commercial triumph, won two Oscars, one for Spielberg for Best Director and one for Best Picture of the Year.

STEVEN SPIELBERG WAS BORN in 1947 in Cincinnati, Ohio, the eldest of the four children of Arnold Spielberg, an electrical engineer and computer expert, and Leah (Posner) Spielberg, a former concert pianist. Spielberg's earliest memory is of a brightly lit room filled with old men wearing black hats and with white beards, with a red light at one end—the Cincinnati synagogue into which his parents first carried him when he was six months old.

The family moved to Haddonfield, New Jersey, then to a Phoenix, Arizona, suburb. In Phoenix Steven first exhibited his interest in filmmaking as the "official family photographer." He was a self-described "Jewish nerd" who sought escape from what he perceived to be a humdrum daily routine in science-fiction films and Disney cartoons.

"I wasn't a religious kid," he told *Time* magazine in a 1985 interview, "although I was bar mitzvahed in a real Orthodox synagogue." His family was "storefront kosher." Once his mother bought three live lobsters for dinner, but at that moment, the rabbi drove up to their home. Leah quickly gave the lobsters to her eldest child, who hid them under his bed. When the rabbi reached Spielberg's room, "[y]ou could hear the lobsters clicking and clacking each other with their tails," he recalled. "The rabbi just sort of stared and sniffed the air; he must have wondered what that *trayf* scent was."

Spielberg borrowed his father's eight-millimeter motion-picture camera and took pictures of family outings. He experimented with camera angles and invented story lines for brief horror films starring his three younger sisters. "I killed them all several times," he boasted.

Barred from watching television, Steven was permitted to view Walt Disney movies, but never violent films. At five years old, he was allowed to watch Cecil B. DeMille's circus epic, *The Greatest Show on Earth*, and he remembers hearing his father's reassuring words about the

Steven Spielberg (right) greets Israel President Ezer Weizman at premiere of Schindler's List.

State of Israel Government Press Office

people on the screen: "They can't get out at you." Indeed, Spielberg said later, "They *were* getting out at me. I guess ever since then I've wanted to try to involve the audience as much as I can, so they no longer think they're sitting in an audience."

At age thirteen, Spielberg won a film award for a forty-minute movie he made called *Escape to Nowhere.* In high school he made many film shorts. After taking up stargazing as a hobby, using a homemade reflecting telescope, Spielberg made a feature-length film called *Firelight* which was meant to frighten its viewers. "Things with jaws came out of the ships to gobble up everything in sight," Steven recalled.

By this time, the family had moved to Southern California. Unable to gain admission to the prestigious West Coast film schools, Spielberg settled for attending California State College at Long Beach. In 1969 he received his bachelor's degree in English.

To learn the film business, Spielberg wore a suit, carried a briefcase, and walked self-confidently onto studio lots, which were generally barred to the public. Somehow he got away with it. He watched producers and directors in action. Surprisingly enough, no one gave him any trouble.

His big break came in 1970 when he made a twenty-two minute film, *Amblin'*, about a pair of hitchhikers, a boy and a girl, traveling from the Mojave Desert to the Pacific Ocean. On the basis of this film, Universal Studios awarded Spielberg a seven-year directing contract. *Amblin'* was distributed as a short accompanying the hit movie *Love Story*. When Spielberg later formed a film company, he called it Amblin.

Spielberg's first jobs at Universal were to direct several television shows, including Joan Crawford in the television pilot of *Night Gallery*. He then directed episodes of the TV serials *The Psychiatrists*, *Marcus Welby, M.D.*, *The Name of the Game*, *Owen Marshall*, and *Colombo*. His first opportunity to make a feature film came in 1971 when he produced *Duel*, a made-for-television thriller starring Dennis Weaver; it grossed over five million dollars in Europe and Japan and won several awards, but was never distributed in the United States. Numerous critics called the movie the finest television movie ever made. Other Spielberg television movie efforts, *Savage* and *Something Evil*, were also well received.

Feature film offers flooded Spielberg's office, but he took a year off to develop his own screenplays. The first was the 1974 film *The Sugarland Express*, starring Goldie Hawn, which was based on a true story about a young couple who tried to retrieve their child from a foster home in Sugarland, Texas.

Although the movie fared poorly at the box office, Spielberg's directing talents were applauded sufficiently for him to earn the opportunity to film *Jaws*, Peter Benchley's bestselling novel about a killer shark that terrorizes a shore community. Spielberg's attitude about sharks, he told a reporter, "is that they've had eighty million years to get their act together." The movie was the surprise hit of 1975, earning over four hundred million dollars. It won several Academy Awards and spawned a sequel, which Spielberg did not direct.

Two years later, Spielberg filmed *Close Encounters of the Third Kind*, a tale about UFOs and ordinary people caught up in the mystery and lure of them. Spielberg was appalled at the 1950s films and television series that gave the impression that any arrival of aliens would be unfriendly. He portrayed aliens as benign and unthreatening. Reviews of the film were mixed, but it grossed $154 million in its first six months. Some chastised Spielberg for what they thought was an over-reliance on mechanical devices and optical tricks.

Spielberg appeared to understand the criticism directed at him. "I've been involved in erector sets for five years and I'd like to do people stories very much," he told the *New York Times* in 1978, indicating that future projects would be less dependent on special effects.

His next film, *1941* (1979), was a comedy about war panic in Los Angeles after the Japanese attack on Pearl Harbor. It did poorly at the box office, earning only $26.5 million. However, the 1981 film *Raiders of the Lost Ark* was a smash hit. In the movie, an American archeologist vies with the Nazis to find a sacred relic with cosmic power.

E.T., released in 1982, was one of the highest-grossing movies in history. Audiences, adults and children alike, loved it and saw it more than once. *Jurassic Park* (1993), Spielberg's dinosaur thriller, earned $350 million in the United States and $540 million in international markets, making it the greatest commercial success ever made in Hollywood.

Since 1982, five of the six Universal films that have grossed over one hundred million dollars at the domestic box office have come from Spielberg's Amblin Entertainment Company: *E.T.*, *Back to the Future*, *Back to the Future Part II*, *Jurassic Park*, and *The Flintstones*.

Spielberg's masterpiece, particularly for Jewish audiences, was *Schindler's List* (1993). Filmed almost entirely in black and white, the movie was Spielberg's greatest creative gamble. It is based on the true story of a German businessman who rescued over a thousand Jews from Auschwitz during the Holocaust.

Spielberg said that making *Schindler's List* was an outgrowth of his increasing Jewish self-aware-ness. A commercial hit, grossing $96 million at American box offices, the movie also won seven Oscars, including one for Best Picture and one for Spielberg for Best Director, his first Academy Award. Spielberg had previously been nominated as best director three times, for *Close Encounters*, *Raiders of the Lost Ark*, and *E.T.*; and twice as best producer, for *E.T.* and *The Color Purple*.

Spielberg's interest in the Holocaust did not end with the release of *Schindler's List*. In November 1994 he helped to underwrite a twelve-million-dollar project to videotape thousands of two-hour interviews with Holocaust survivors in order to preserve their stories.

Forbes magazine listed Spielberg as the highest-paid entertainer in 1993–1994. He earned $335 million that year.

Spielberg has been married twice, first in 1985 to actress Amy Irving. They had one son, Max, and were divorced in 1989. He then married Kate Capshaw, also an actress. They have five children, two from previous marriages, three of their own.

In the fall of 1994, Spielberg joined forces with two other Hollywood titans to form a new entertainment firm that some describe as the most powerful in Hollywood. Spielberg's new partners are former Walt Disney studio chief Jeffrey Katzenberg and media mogul David Geffen. Spielberg's Amblin Entertainment Company and Geffen's film unit merged to create a new company called DreamWorks SKG. Geffen's net worth was put at nearly one billion dollars, Spielberg's at more than six hundred million. In late May 1997 *The Lost World*, Spielberg's sequel to *Jurassic Park*, opened and achieved swift success, grossing $229 million. Then came the Spielberg-produced *Men in Black*, another major hit, earning over $300 million worldwide. It was unprecedented to have two such summer hits at the same time.

In October 1997 *Entertainment Weekly* ranked Spielberg as the most powerful figure in Hol-lywood. This distinction notwithstanding, in December of that year *Amistad*, the director's slaveship revolt story, received a poor critical reception and was a financial disappointment.

In the summer of 1998, Spielberg's *Saving Private Ryan*, a Normandy-landing epic starring Tom Hanks, was greeted by unanimous critical approval.

Spielberg has emerged as first among equals among the three DreamWorks chiefs. He signs off on all important decisions and was responsible for a major coup: convincing Robert Zemeckis (of *Forrest Gump* and *Contact* fame) to agree to a five-year nonexclusive directing deal. In its October 1997 issue, *Entertainment Weekly* said: "Ultimately, Spielberg isn't the most powerful person in entertainment because he can alternate high-concept blockbusters with Oscar-friendly dramas. He's the most powerful person because right now anyone on this list [of Hollywood power figures] would sell their spouses, parents, or kids to be in business with him."

In the year 2000, Steven Spielberg produced *The Flintstones in Viva Rock Vegas* and *Gladia-tor*. The film *A. I. Artificial Intelligence*, which he wrote as well as directed, was a disappointing 2001 release. That same year, Spielberg also was executive producer for *Band of Brothers* and *Jurassic Park III*. In 2002 he served as executive producer for the popular *Men in Black II* and directed both *Minority Report* and the well-received *Catch Me If You Can*.

In 2004 Spielberg began production on a movie about the 1972 Munich Olympics, at which Palestinian terrorists tragically killed eleven Israeli coaches and athletes. That same year he also directed *The Terminal*, with Tom Hanks and Catherine Zeta-Jones.

Spielberg's imagination and special ability to create tension and excitement in his films, even before audiences get to see the actual source of that tension (as in *Jaws* and *Jurassic Park*), have made him one of Hollywood's most successful filmmakers.

BARUCH SPINOZA

Philosopher and Excommunicant

> Born November 24, 1632, in Amsterdam, Holland; died February 21, 1677. Dutch philosopher. Baruch Spinoza was the leading thinker of the seventeenth century and his writings provided the basis for modern biblical criticism. Spinoza was forced to endure the most famous excommunication in Jewish history for his heretical views on Judaism. He anticipated secularization, the rise of natural science, the Enlightenment, and the liberal democratic state. For his fellow Jews, Spinoza anticipated the disintegration of ghetto life.

BARUCH SPINOZA WAS BORN in Amsterdam in 1632. His parents had fled Portugal before he was born to escape the Spanish Inquisition and had settled in Holland, where Spinoza's father, Michael, became a successful merchant. His mother, Hana (Devorah) Spinoza, died when Baruch was just a boy of six. His father died when Spinoza was twenty-two years old.

Young Spinoza received a traditional Jewish education, studying the Bible, Talmud, Jewish philosophy, and the Hebrew language. Feeling restricted at the thought of receiving only a religious education, Spinoza also delved into such secular subjects as mathematics, physics, and astronomy. He was a brilliant student.

After his father died, Baruch, together with his brother Gabriel, formed a moderately successful commercial firm to import and export fruit. Although Spinoza had increasing doubts, even heretical thoughts, about his religion, he continued to attend the yeshiva.

His misgivings about Judaism persisted, and Spinoza enrolled in a private school run by Francis Van den Enden, a former Jesuit with a reputation as a free thinker. Latin was associated in Jewish minds with the Inquisition, but Spinoza decided to study it anyway. He also familiarized himself with the Greek and Roman classics, the physical sciences, and the rationalist philosophy of the French philosopher René Descartes. Studying Descartes pulled Spinoza even farther away intellectually from traditional Jewish teachings.

By early 1656, when Spinoza was twenty-four years old, he began to express his heretical views in public, questioning whether Moses wrote the Pentateuch, whether Adam was the first man, and whether the Mosaic law took precedence over natural law. Spinoza had doubts about the existence of angels, the immortality of the soul, and, most importantly, the Divine origins of every word of the Bible.

Synagogue authorities learned with great anguish that Spinoza was studying Latin with Van den Enden; they learned, too, that Spinoza was distancing himself from his religion by failing to perform Jewish rituals and ceremonies. He was given a choice: he would be paid one thousand florins a year in exchange for conforming to synagogue rule, or he would be excommunicated from the Jewish religion. Spinoza was given thirty days to decide. What happened next is not entirely clear, but the fact is that Spinoza never submitted a formal reply to the synagogue authorities. According to one report from this time, an attempt was made on Spinoza's life, but information is virtually nonexistent about who might have been behind the deed.

Baruch Spinoza

A relative by marriage, Samuel de Cacarest, launched a campaign against the accused Spinoza. Summoned to a religious court in 1656, Spinoza was formally accused of heresy. One month later, on July 27, Spinoza was excommunicated from the Nation of Israel for his "evil opinions and acts" and the "abominable heresies practiced and taught by him."

The writ of excommunication read in part: "Cursed shall he be in the daytime, and cursed when he riseth up! Cursed shall he be when he goeth out and cursed when he cometh in! May the Lord forgive his sins. May the Lord's anger and wrath rage against this man, and cast upon him all the imprecations that are written in the Book of the Law! May the Lord wipe his name from under the Heavens; and may the Lord destroy him and cast him out from all the Tribes of Israel with all the maledictions that are written in the Book of Law!" The Jewish community was forbidden to have contact with Baruch Spinoza.

When Spinoza was notified of the ban, he replied by defending his dissident beliefs. Although undoubtedly a stigma for Spinoza, the excommunication had the positive effect of freeing him from guilt he might have felt about his position in the Jewish community. He could now develop his own philosophy without having to consider what other Jews thought of him.

The Amsterdam Municipal Council banished Baruch Spinoza from the city, forcing him to move to a small town in the Dutch countryside called Ouwerkirk. Spinoza, because he had learned the trade as a young man, made a modest living there as an optician and a philosophy tutor. He began working on his *Tractatus Theologico-Politicus*, in which he provided the basis for later biblical criticism. After working on the book for a while, however, he put it aside.

Spinoza believed that everything known by human beings was a manifestation of the all-embracing "substance" that was God. Acquiring knowledge of God's union with nature was the way for people to attain happiness, he thought. Spinoza argued that all men and women were modifications of a single infinite "substance" that was identical with God. And God's will was the same as the laws of nature. To know nature, in his mind, therefore, was to know God.

He viewed this world as all there is, as the only actual being, and the one source of ethical value. The totality of nature was, to him, exactly like God, and God's decrees were written not in the Bible but in the natural laws of reason and nature.

In 1660, when he was twenty-eight years old, Spinoza left the Amsterdam region and settled in Rhijnsburg near Leyden in the West Netherlands. He changed his name to Benedictus (the Latin equivalent of Baric), joined a Mennonite sect called the Collegians, and studied Cartesian philosophy intensively. Spinoza wrote a book called *Principles of the Philosophy of René Descartes*, published in Latin in 1663 and one year later in Dutch. Spinoza remained a bachelor all his life.

A new benefactor, Johan de Witt of The Hague, gave Spinoza a small stipend which permitted him, in 1664, to move to Voorburg, a suburb of The Hague. Spinoza spent his first two years there working on a book he called *Ethics*, which was meant to explain his whole philosophic system. The following year, he suddenly stopped writing the book and returned to the writing of *Tractatus Theologico-Politicus*. He explained that he had returned to that project in order to refute charges of atheism that had been leveled against him and to defend the right to freedom of speech and thought.

Tractatus Theologico-Politicus appeared anonymously in 1670 when Spinoza was thirty-eight years old. The book was perceived as an attack on theologians and religion, and was banned immediately. Somehow it still went through several printings. To prevent further attacks against him, Spinoza called off the publication of a Dutch edition of the *Tractatus*.

Recognized as a philosopher of importance by now, Spinoza was offered a chair of philosophy at the University of Heidelberg. He turned it down, fearful that his freedom of thought would be impaired were he to become part of a large academic institution.

Spinoza settled in The Hague in 1670 to be near his patron, the political leader de Witt, and remained there for the rest of his life. When de Witt was assassinated in 1672, Spinoza was outraged and designed placards with the word "barbarians" on them. He began working on a book of Hebrew grammar, but gave up the project in order to complete *Ethics*, which was published in 1674.

Spinoza developed a pulmonary disease that eventually led to his death in 1677 at the age of forty-five. He was buried in a church in The Hague. In the early 1950s, Israeli Prime Minister David Ben-Gurion tried without success to have the excommunication against Spinoza lifted. But the ideas and philosophy he communicated in his books have lived on, achieving worldwide recognition throughout the centuries since his death.

MARK SPITZ

Record-Breaking Swimmer

Born February 10, 1950, in Modesto, California. American swimmer. Mark Spitz has been described as the greatest Jewish athlete of all time and the most successful swimmer in history. His reputation was made by his incredible feat at the 1972 Munich Olympics, where he won seven gold medals and set a new world record in each event. He tried in vain to make a comeback at the age of forty, when he sought, but failed to earn, a place on the 1992 United States Olympic swimming team.

MARK SPITZ IS THE ELDEST OF THREE CHILDREN. He learned to swim at the age of six. By the time he was eight, his father, Arnold, a construction consultant, and mother, Lenore, entered Mark in a swimming program at the YMCA near their home in Sacramento, California. "I had no idea where I was going when I starting swimming," he said. "It was more or less like a social activity with my friends, and I had goals to be somebody like [pro football star quarterback] Johnny Unitas."

Mark Spitz

To enable Spitz to attend the Santa Clara (California) Swim Club and be coached by the highly successful George Haines, the Spitz family moved to Santa Clara from Sacramento. "Swimming isn't everything," Mark's father said. "Winning is."

In his first year at Santa Clara (1964), Spitz qualified for the national long-course championships in the 400- and 1500-meter freestyle events. The next year, at age fifteen, he finished only fifth in the 1500 meters at the American nationals, but he did win four gold medals and set four new records at the Maccabiah Games in Israel. Spitz acknowledged that winning those races in Israel gave him both more motivation as well as experience.

In 1966, as a high-school sophomore, Spitz became the third man in history to better seventeen minutes in the 1500-meter freestyle; he also won his first national title, the 100-meter butterfly.

Mark Spitz

Mark's first truly outstanding year came in 1967. His achievements included two short-course and two long-course national titles and five American and seven world records in the 100- and 200-meter butterfly races and in the 400-meter freestyle. He also won five gold medals at the Pan-American Games in Winnipeg, Canada. *Swimming World* magazine named him "World Swimmer of the Year."

At the Colorado Springs trials for the 1968 Mexico City Olympics, Spitz experienced a good deal of anti-Semitism from his teammates. His coach, Sherm Chavoor, said, "They tried to run him right off the team. It was 'Jew boy' this and 'Jew boy' that. It wasn't a kidding type of thing either. He didn't know how to handle it."

While he won two gold medals in the relays, a silver in the 100-meter butterfly, and a bronze in the 100-meter freestyle, Spitz finished last in the final of the 200-meter butterfly. He felt disappointed and embarrassed by his defeat.

In 1969 Spitz entered Indiana University, studying to become a dentist. Spitz returned to Israel to participate in the 1969 summer Maccabiah Games. He won six gold medals and was named the outstanding athlete of the games. In 1971, after another solid year of collecting Amateur Athletic Union (AAU) and NCAA titles and world records, Spitz became the first Jewish recipient of the AAU's James E. Sullivan Award, given to the best amateur athlete of the year.

In 1977 he told a reporter for an Israeli magazine, "I feel that being a Jewish athlete has helped our cause. We have shown that we are as good as the next guy. In mentality we have always been at the top of every field. I think the Jewish people have a more realistic way of looking at life. They make the most of what's happening at the present while preparing for the future."

During his championship swimming career, Spitz carried his 170 pounds on a tightly compact, six-foot, one-inch frame. He had the ability to flex his lower legs slightly forward at the knees, which permitted him to kick six to twelve inches deeper in the water than his opponents. His mustache, he said, kept water out of his mouth.

At Munich, where the 1972 Olympics were held, Spitz gave the greatest swimming exhibition ever witnessed. In eight days at the Swimhall, he won four individual (the 100- and 200-meter freestyle and the 100- and 200-meter butterfly) and three relay gold medals, all in world-record time. In trying to explain his Munich performance, Spitz said, "Day in and day out, swimming is ninety percent physical. You've got to do the physical work in training, and don't need much mental. But in a big meet like this, it's ninety percent mental and ten percent physical. Your body is ready, and now it becomes mind versus matter."

When eleven Israeli athletes were killed at the Munich Olympics by Palestinian terrorists, Spitz was put under special guard and then whisked away from the Olympic site. It was felt that he might be next on the terrorists' list.

After his victories at the 1972 Olympics, Spitz retired, and there was talk of his becoming a film star, another Johnny Weismuller perhaps, but nothing developed. For the next four years he became "a major endorsement figure" for several large companies.

He did become the first athlete to capitalize on his athletic career, with endorsement contracts estimated at $5 million. The poster of him posing in a red-white-and blue swimsuit along with his seven gold medals became the most popular-selling poster of a sports figure.

Partially out of boredom, partially entranced with the challenge, he decided in the summer of 1989 to try to make a comeback as a swimmer. He was thirty-nine years old and his goal was to win another gold medal, this time at the 1992 Olympics in Barcelona. He chose to concentrate on his best event, the 100-meter butterfly, which was the one men's event in which times had not dropped measurably. Pablo Morales held the record of 52.84 seconds. Spitz's 1972 time of 54.27 seconds would have given him seventh place at the 1988 Olympics. To make the 1992 United States Olympic team, Spitz thought he needed to swim in the low 53s.

Because so few athletes continued in their chosen sports into their forties and because Spitz granted frequent interviews, his comeback garnered a great deal of publicity. Many were skeptical. Spitz himself seemed to vacillate between robust self-confidence and curiosity.

Though he tried hard, Spitz ultimately found the competition too tough for him. Shorn of his mustache, four pounds heavier than he had been twenty years earlier, Spitz was beaten badly in two exhibition 50-meter butterfly races in the spring of 1991.

When Spitz failed to qualify for the Olympic swimming trials in early March of 1992, he announced that he was giving up his comeback attempt. "I'm fighting something unavoidable and not exclusive to me. It's called 'old age,'" he explained. Mark is living in Los Angeles with his wife and thier two sons, Matthew and Justin. After he failed to qualify for the 1992 olympics, Spitz stopped swimming for three months; but he later resumed working out with the UCLA masters swim team.

In 1997, forty-seven-year-old Spitz was without his famous mustache and twenty pounds heavier than when in his prime. His back had become arthritic and a skiing accident left him with two screws in his left leg. By the fall of 2002, Spitz had become a motivational speaker and a real estate investor. He continued to work out four times a week at the UCLA swimming pool.

Spitz has tried not to dwell on the Munich Olympics, even on the occasion of its thirtieth anniversary in September 2002. "I never think about it, he said, because what I did was so conclusive. If I had lost a race, I could tell myself if I had done this or that, I would have won, but since I didn't lose, I have no misgivings."

During his competitive career, from 1965 to 1972, Mark Spitz won nine Olympic gold medals, one silver, and one bronze; five Pan-American gold medals; ten Maccabiah gold medals; thirty-one national AAU titles, and eight NCAA championships. During those years, he set thirty-three world records and was named "World Swimmer of the Year" in 1967, 1971, and 1972. His name will forever be synonymous with excellence.

ALFRED STIEGLITZ

Father of Photography as Art

Born January 1, 1864, in Hoboken, New Jersey; died July 13, 1946. American photographer. Alfred Stieglitz sought to turn photography into an art. Before his efforts, photography was not considered an art form, and because of this bias, photographs were not exhibited in museums. Stieglitz changed that perception. His photographs were the first to be accepted for showing in American museums. Stieglitz became well known for his innovative work and experimentation in photography. He wanted to show in his art the truth and simplicity of such elemental forces as clouds, snow, and rain.

ALFRED STIEGLITZ WAS BORN in 1864 in Hoboken, New Jersey, the eldest of six children of prosperous German-Jewish parents. His father was a wool merchant who, in 1881, when Alfred was seventeen years old, took his six children to Berlin to be educated. Every summer they returned to the family estate on Lake George in New York State. The picturesque area became the setting for many of Stieglitz's photographs. Although the Stieglitz ancestors had been observant Jews in Europe, Alfred's parents led an assimilated life.

Stieglitz studied engineering at Berlin Polytechnic. At some point he purchased a camera and began studying photochemistry. He took serious interest in the emerging field of photography. His teachers instructed him in its traditional methods, but Stieglitz sought to break away from those traditions by using new techniques and materials. In his photography, Stieglitz focused on natural elements rather than stilted poses and portraiture. The first acclaim he won for his photography was for snow scenes in New York City, and for scenes of Europe.

In 1887, when he was twenty-three years old, Stieglitz sent twelve of his prints to the London amateur photographer competition and captured the first prize. He won more than 150 medals throughout his career in other international competitions.

Stieglitz became famous for his discovery of the painter Georgia O'Keeffe (1887–1986), whom he married in 1924 after divorcing his first wife, Emmy Obermeyer. O'Keeffe inspired some of Stieglitz's best-known photographs. Lewis Mumford called those photographs "the exact visual equivalent of the report of the hand as it travels over the body of the beloved."

For twenty years Stieglitz studied the sensuality of O'Keeffe with his camera. "I've given the world a woman," he said of his photos of her. Stieglitz photographed her thousands of times and these portfolios were exhibited at major art museums.

So, too, were his photographs of clouds, trees, weather patterns, and skies. He used no tricky lighting effects in his photography; he used only natural light. Stieglitz was convinced that a photograph did not have to rely upon the personality of the subject or the drama in the photo itself for its merit and that it was possible to give to photographs of grass and snow and rain the same high emotion and excitement that one could find in portrait work. No serious photographer had ever tried to record the "real world" of pure nature—snow, rain, clouds, and trees—before Stieglitz. He called these photographs of the outside world "Equivalents."

In 1890 Stieglitz returned to New York from Europe, continuing to experiment with scenes of everyday urban life, machines, and buildings. He especially liked to work with the play of light and shadow in nature.

Stieglitz founded the influential photography magazine *Camera Work* in 1903. Fifty editions of the periodical were published over the next fourteen years. The quality of Stieglitz's photo-engraving for the magazine was very impressive. Once, when photographs from his first gallery, the Photo-Secession in New York, were lost on their way to an exhibition in Brussels, the exhibition committee used reproductions from *Camera Work* to replace them.

In 1905 Stieglitz opened the Little Gallery on New York's Fifth Avenue, where he exhibited photography along with the work of American and European artists. A champion of modern art, Stieglitz staged the first American shows of works by Pablo Picasso and Henri Matisse at another gallery called 291, which took its name from its Fifth Avenue address. These shows caused a sensation in the New York art world. By 1908 Stieglitz had introduced to the American public the drawings of Auguste Rodin and, in addition to Matisse and Picasso, the work of Henri de Toulouse-Lautrec and Constantin Brancusi.

In 1911 Stieglitz published controversial Rodin drawings in *Camera Work*, and half of his subscribers cancelled their subscriptions. He was undeterred, however, in his effort to be a pioneer. He published Gertrude Stein's earliest work. But in 1917 he suspended publication of the magazine because of financial difficulties.

Stieglitz felt committed to showing the work of artists whom he considered sensitive and enlightened. He introduced many of these in The Intimate Gallery and An American Place, two of his other galleries. Among the artists he introduced were John Marin, Arthur Dove, Georgia O'Keeffe, Marsden Hartley, and Max Weber.

In 1916 Stieglitz mounted a show at the Albright Museum in Buffalo, New York, that explained the notion of photography as art. Stieglitz was active in lobbying museums to collect and exhibit photographs.

In 1924 the Royal Photographic Society of Great Britain presented him with its highest award, the Progress Medal.

Stieglitz achieved fame and a measure of respect for his talent and trailblazing. In 1934 a book called *America and Alfred Stieglitz—a Collective Portrait* was published. It contained interpretations of Stieglitz's work by leading poets, writers, artists, and photographers.

In everything Stieglitz did, he tried to achieve purity and simplicity, and to avoid all ornamentation and sentiment. "All art," he once said, "all living work . . . life itself, is abstract in the deepest sense." Stieglitz associated himself with highly regarded writers and critics of his day, including Gertrude Stein, Sherwood Anderson, William Carlos Williams, Van Wyck Brooks, and Paul Rosenfeld, all of whom worked to develop a distinctive and original American voice in the arts.

Stieglitz summed up his principles this way: "I was born in Hoboken. I am an American. Photography is my passion. The search for truth my obsession . . . . Art or not art—that is immaterial. There is photography. I continue on my way seeking my own truth, ever affirming today." As if to mirror his photographs, he dressed only in black and white. He believed that the artist had to open himself, to express what was within and "see all." This was about as close as Stieglitz came to a set of religious beliefs.

For many years Stieglitz suffered ill health. In 1946, at the age of eighty-two, he suffered a stroke at his gallery and died a few days later. He willed twenty-seven of his photographs to the Boston Museum of Fine Arts and his collection of the work of photographic pioneers to New York's Metropolitan Museum of Art.

Following Stieglitz's death, Georgia O'Keeffe donated much of his collection of paintings and photographs to New York's Metropolitan Museum of Art and to Chicago's Art Institute. Stieglitz had already donated his collections of African art and many of his paintings to Fisk University in Nashville, Tennessee. His fifty thousand letters went to the Yale University archives.

Alfred Stieglitz was largely responsible for photography being accepted as a valid form of artistic expression. He also played a key role in discovering and exhibiting the works of previously unknown artists who were pioneers in abstract expressionism, cubism, and futurism. Stieglitz worked especially hard to win recognition for American arts. *Life* magazine, in its special Fall 1970 issue, ranked Stieglitz as one of the hundred most important Americans of the twentieth century.

JOHN VON NEUMANN

Mathematician and Computer Pioneer

Born December 28, 1903, in Budapest, Hungary; died February 8, 1957. Hungarian-American mathematician and computer pioneer. One of the world's foremost mathematicians, John von Neumann discovered how to detonate the atomic bomb. He also devoted his energies to machines that would bear his name: von Neumann computers. In the 1940s he designed what became the basic scheme of the computer five decades later. While debate existed over the inventor of the stored-program computer, von Neumann is generally credited with bringing the idea to the public's attention. More than anyone else, von Neumann stimulated people's interest in the mysterious, often intimidating subject of computers.

JANOS NEUMANN CAME FROM AN UPPER-CLASS Hungarian background that produced other giants in the fields of mathematics and physics. His father, a Jewish banker named Max Neumann, earned sufficient Hapsburg respect to add the honorific "Margattai" to his family name (later changed, by John, to "von"). Janos was the eldest of three sons. He called himself John after he moved to the United States in 1930.

Even as a small child, von Neumann loved mathematics; he constantly tried to adapt its logic to the world at large. Once, when he saw his mother look up from her crocheting to stare into space contemplating, he asked her, "What are you calculating?" He was a very bright child who also learned language early. From the age of six, he joked with his father in classical Greek.

A private tutor was hired for von Neumann when he was ten, but he also attended the Lutheran gymnasium—from 1914 to 1916—in Budapest, becoming its best mathematician.

When the Communist regime of Bela Kun took power in Hungary in 1919, banks were expropriated, forcing Max von Neumann to flee with his family to their home in Venice out of fear that in the chaos that prevailed, they might be in physical danger. The von Neumanns returned to Budapest in August 1919, two months after the fall of Kun. The episode turned young von Neumann into a lifelong anti-communist.

Although he enrolled in the University of Budapest in 1921, von Neumann acquired much of his education at other institutions as well. Most of his time, especially from 1921 to 1923, was spent at the University of Berlin. There he listened to lectures by Albert Einstein. Von Neumann also went to the Swiss Federal Institute of Technology in Zurich, where he received a diploma in chemical engineering in 1925. A year later, on March 12, 1926, at age twenty-two, he was awarded his doctorate *summa cum laude* in mathematics from the University of Budapest.

Institute for Advanced Study, Princeton, New Jersey

John von Neumann

Between 1927 and 1930, von Neumann was a lecturer in mathematics at the University of Berlin. During his first year, he published five papers. Three of them, by setting forth a mathematical framework for quantum theory, were of great importance for that field. A fourth paper was a pioneering effort in game theory. The fifth dealt with the link between formal logic systems and the limits of mathematics.

Although von Neumann was uninterested in religion, he never hid his Jewish origins. His first wife, Mariette Koevesi, was a Hungarian-born Catholic whom he married in 1929; she left him in 1937. Von Neumann married again the following year. His second wife was Klara Dan, the daughter of a wealthy Hungarian-Jewish family. They had one daughter, Marina.

In 1929 von Neumann was invited to become a visiting lecturer at Princeton University, which was a turning point in his career. By the 1930s, von Neumann was recognized as one of the world's leading mathematicians. He became a tenured professor at Princeton in 1931. In 1933, when the Institute for Advanced Study was founded at Princeton, von Neumann became one of the six original professors in its school of mathematics, a post he held for the rest of his life.

Anecdotes about von Neumann focus on his uncanny ability of instant recall. He could read a book, then years later quote it verbatim. Equally amazing was the speed with which he did calculations in his head.

Von Neumann worked on the building of the first atom bomb at Los Alamos in the early 1940s and, while there, he came to appreciate the value of computers. Fellow scientist J. Robert Oppenheimer persuaded him to become a mathematical consultant for the secret Manhattan Project late in 1943. Von Neumann's key contribution was helping discover how to detonate the atomic bomb. He built an implosive lens which generated a strong spherical shock wave that imploded or compressed a ball of plutonium or uranium isotope. When a critical point was reached, the chain reaction was set off. Proven effective during the Alamogordo testing of the bomb, von Neumann's technique was employed in World War II in the detonation of the Nagasaki bomb which spurred the Japanese surrender.

During the summer of 1944, von Neumann was eager to find speedier ways to compute numbers. He learned of a confidential project at the University of Pennsylvania where a computer was being built that could perform 333 multiplications per second. Von Neumann was intrigued by the idea and visited the project in September. He became the scientific patron of the computer, named ENIAC, or the Electronic Numerical Integrator and Computer. His interest and presence gave respectability to a project that others thought was a waste of time.

Sensing the vast potential for ENIAC, von Neumann envisioned better-designed, better-made computers that would extend far beyond ENIAC's capabilities.

ENIAC lacked memory capacity and von Neumann understood that only with a stored-memory computer could there be more sophisticated, more powerful machines with a greater capacity to perform tasks. A dispute has raged for decades over who specifically devised the notion of a stored-memory computer—von Neumann or others before him. Whatever the actuality, von Neumann is generally credited with bringing the idea to the public's attention.

Von Neumann's talents were many. In 1944 he and Oskar Morgenstern published a classic work, *Theory of Games and Economic Behavior*. In it they analyzed simple games like poker and coin-matching in order to demonstrate that a "best-possible" method of play existed and was mathematically determinable. Their game theory could be applied to many areas of interest, including both economic and sociological dilemmas. In this book, von Neumann and Morgenstern made the first step toward a broad theory of mathematical economics.

After World War II, von Neumann was interested in building his own computer at the Institute for Advanced Study. Others there balked, hoping to keep their establishment an idyllic ivory tower rather than a place cluttered with unattractive pieces of machinery. Von Neumann, however, got his way. His plan was to build a fully automatic, digital, all-purpose electronic calculating machine, the fastest of its time, intended for scientific research, rather than the commercial market. The IAS computer, named for the Institute for Advanced Study, begun in 1946, was completed five years later.

Von Neumann, more than anyone else, has been credited with stimulating public interest in the field of computers. He sensed the potential they had for use in the sciences, and in speaking out enthusiastically about that potential, acquired a reputation as the leading force behind the computer age.

In 1948 von Neumann produced more pathbreaking work. He and Norbert Wiener published their famous *Cybernetics, or Control and Communications in the Animal and the Machine*. The book discussed the possibility that electronic brains could take over human tasks. In October 1954, von Neumann was appointed a member of the Atomic Energy Commission, which had as its main concern the stockpiling and development of nuclear weapons.

Von Neumann held decidedly right-wing views. In a posthumously published article for the February 25, 1957, edition of *Life* magazine, which came out soon after his death, von Neumann proved himself an avowed advocate of preventive warfare against the Soviets: "If you say why not bomb them tomorrow, I say, why not today? If you say today at five o'clock, I say why not one o'clock?"

When von Neumann was dying, the secretary of defense, his deputies, the secretaries of the Army, Navy, and Air Force, and all the military chiefs of staff gathered around his beside at Walter Reed Hospital in Washington, D.C., for a meeting. He was still that important to their deliberations.

John von Neumann died of bone cancer on February 8, 1957, at the age of fifty-three.

Not as well known as Einstein or Freud, John von Neumann possessed one of the greatest minds of the twentieth century and his contributions to scientific knowledge have been immense. His instincts about how important computers would become were incredibly accurate.

SELMAN WAKSMAN

Nobel Prize Recipient and Antibiotics Researcher

Born in Priluka, the Ukraine, July 2, 1888; died August 16, 1973. American biochemist. Selman Waksman won the 1952 Nobel Prize for Physiology and Medicine for his research into antibiotics and his discovery of the antibiotic streptomycin. Although his research interests were originally in soil microbiology, Waksman was best known for his revolutionary research on antibiotics. Streptomycin became one of the most important antibiotics ever discovered because it proved to be effective against many kinds of bacteria, including the tubercle bacillus. It was Waksman who coined the term "antibiotic" to describe disease-fighting "wonder drugs." Antibiotics are credited with saving millions of lives.

SELMAN WAKSMAN WAS BORN in 1888 into a religious family in a small town near Kiev in the Ukraine. His father taught him the Bible and Talmud, and he received a modest secular education. Living in a farming community, intrigued by the earth, Waksman took a strong interest in the soil. He took note of the rich black dirt of the Ukrainian steppe, which produced impressive grain harvests. This interest in the soil influenced him later to study agriculture and microbiology in depth.

If a love of the soil would lead him to his eventual field of study, so, too, would the calamity that struck his family. When he was nine years old he watched helplessly as his sister suffocated to death from diphtheria. Tragically, although a new antitoxin had already been discovered and was in use in Europe, it was not yet available to residents of the Ukraine. His sister's death had an immense impact on Waksman. He resolved to try to save other children struck down with the dreaded disease.

As a teenager, Waksman was always eager to help others. Together with his friends, he organized a school for poor children, he cared for ill people, and he helped organize a youth group for the purpose of trying to protect his town from persecution by the Russian authorities.

In 1910, when he was twenty-two years old, Selman Waksman immigrated to the United States. He chose to study microbiology. As an undergraduate and graduate student at Rutgers University in New Brunswick, New Jersey, Waksman also elected to study agriculture and bacteriology. Waksman did his advanced studies at the University of California, receiving his doctorate in 1918.

Waksman spent most of his forty-year career at Rutgers. In 1927 he wrote *Principles of Soil Microbiology*, which was one of the most comprehensive works on the subject at that time and became a standard in the field. He was first a lecturer in soil microbiology at Rutgers and later was named professor, serving in that post from 1930 to 1940.

Waksman undertook research into micro-organisms in the soil. He wrote his first paper, at the age of twenty-seven while still a newcomer in the field, on soil. He consulted with industry experts and helped develop strategies for finding the best methods of producing nutritional substances and enzymes derived from fungi and bacteria.

During the summers, Waksman traveled to Woods Hole on Cape Cod in Massachusetts, where he worked at a laboratory that conducted research into marine microbiology. He headed the Institute of Microbiology at Rutgers from its founding in 1949 until he retired in 1958.

It was Selman Waksman's work with soil organisms that led him to his pathfinding research in antibiotics. His specialty was the role of fungi and bacteria in the decomposition of organic matter. Although his original research interests were in these aspects of soil microbiology, Waksman became known for his work on antibiotics, especially streptomycin, which grew out of these other projects.

Dr. Selman Waksman

American Jewish Archives, Cincinnati Campus, Hebrew Union College, Jewish Institute of Religion

The discovery of penicillin had prompted targeted investigations by scientists for other drugs that would conquer dangerous bacteria. Then, with all of the casualties caused by World War II, the search for new antibacterial substances to treat infections was intensified. Waksman entered the search, encouraged by the discovery of penicillin's therapeutic potential. He began his search for antibiotic substances in the 1930s after many years of studying a group of soil microorganisms or fungi known as actinomycetes. He was quite familiar with their prevalence, distribution, taxonomy, and growth pattern.

Waksman hoped to find what he called new "antibiotics," or "substance[s] produced by one organism that kills other microorganisms." Through his research, Waksman was able to develop numerous specialized techniques that were of value in cultivating microbes and in isolating and purifying active antibiotics.

Streptothricin, the first antibiotic substance that he isolated from an actinomycete, was considered too toxic for therapeutic use. Waksman then returned to a species of fungus—Streptomyces griseus—that he had first described in 1916. In 1943 he isolated from this soil mold the antibiotic known as streptomycin through a method called adsorption, a chemical process of gathering dissolved substances on a surface—such as, as in this case, charcoal. Streptomycin affected gram-negative bacteria (those that easily lose the gram stain). Its greatest victory was over the penicillin-resistant tubercle bacillus, the cause of tuberculosis, but the new drug proved to be effective against numerous other bacteria as well. Waksman's discovery was thus categorized as a broad-spectrum antibiotic.

Waksman and his colleagues started to elucidate the chemical structure of streptomycin; other investigators completed the task. Streptomycin became one of the most important antibiotics ever discovered and was considered a major breakthrough in the area of chemotherapy. What was especially pleasing to Waksman was the fact that some of his discoveries were used to help in the fight against childhood diseases—a victory of sorts for him after the loss of his sister to diphtheria.

Waksman and his research team worked on discovering other antibiotics and isolated several; one was called neomycin and was employed to treat bowel infections and local skin or eye infections.

In 1952 Selman Waksman won the Nobel Prize for Medicine and Physiology. He was supported in his research by Merck and Company, one of the larger pharmaceutical firms, as well as by the Mayo Clinic.

Waksman published his memoirs, *My Life with the Microbes*, in 1954. He summarized the book as "the story of the life of an immigrant boy who went from the steppes of the Ukraine to the New World in search of a better education and better opportunities to do what he wanted with his life . . . I tried my best." His discoveries have translated into lifesaving medicines—the "wonder drugs of the twentieth century"—for his fellow human beings.

CHAIM WEIZMANN

First President of the State of Israel

Born November 27, 1874, in Motol, Russia; died November 9, 1952. Zionist statesman and first president of the state of Israel. Through his timely discovery of a way of manufacturing acetone, which was vital to the British war effort, Chaim Weizmann endeared himself to the British authorities. To reward him for his great contribution, the British agreed to support, through the Balfour Declaration of 1917, the establishment of a Jewish homeland in Palestine, which Weizmann advocated early on and campaigned for throughout the 1930s and 1940s. After the Jewish state was founded in 1948, Weizmann served as its first president for four years.

CHAIM WEIZMANN WAS BORN in 1874 in Motol, Russia, one of fifteen children. Weizmann's father, Ozer, was a timber merchant who made a living by floating the wood along the Vistula River for processing and export to Danzig. Weizmann's mother was named Rachel Leah.

Although few of the children of Motol had the opportunity to advance in their studies beyond the village's classrooms, Weizmann was determined to break out of that trap. Raised in nearby Pinsk, he showed special talent for science.

In 1885, at age eleven, Weizmann exhibited leadership qualities by writing a letter in which he asked why Jews should look to England to take compassion on them and "give us a resting place." He ended it with: "In conclusion, to Zion: Jews—to Zion let us go."

When he was eighteen, Weizmann enrolled at the universities of Damstadt in Berlin and Freiburg in Switzerland to study chemistry. During this time he also grew close to the new Zionist movement being estab-

Chaim Weizmann

lished by Zionist leader Theodor Herzl. Weizmann became one of the new young leaders of the movement, receiving recognition for his organizational and fund-raising abilities.

Weizmann attended his first Zionist Congress in 1898 and became the leader of the Democratic Faction, which sought to introduce Jewish traditions, culture, and heritage into the Zionist movement. In contrast, Theodor Herzl wanted to place the emphasis on diplomacy and organizational efforts.

Herzl's Zionism also focused on securing wealthy patrons to donate money to develop agriculture in Palestine. Weizmann, on the other hand, stressed the importance of encouraging the common people to lend their support to Palestine. Influenced by his training as a chemist, Weizmann advocated what he called "synthetic Zionism," combining diplomacy to achieve a Jewish homeland and Jewish efforts to build the land for themselves.

A strong believer in educating the Jewish community in Palestine, Weizmann wanted to build a university there and to promote Jewish culture. He was especially attracted to the Zionist thinker Ahad Ha'am's strong convictions that Jewish culture was only realizable in a national homeland. To Weizmann, Palestine was too poor in natural resources to rely only upon an agricultural base; it had to become scientifically and technologically advanced.

In 1898 Weizmann completed a doctorate in chemistry at Freiburg University. He then worked in a German chemistry laboratory before being appointed lecturer in chemistry at England's Manchester University in 1906. Weizmann began publishing scientific papers and working on inventions in the field of chemistry.

In 1901 he married Vera Chatzman and they moved to Geneva. The Weizmanns had two sons, Benjamin and Michael.

Weizmann was deeply involved in the effort to scuttle the plan for Jews to establish a homeland in Uganda. The British Foreign Secretary, Lord Lansdowne, had offered Jews some territory in the African country of Uganda. Inclined to accept the offer, Theodor Herzl ran into heavy opposition at the Sixth Zionist Congress in August 1903. Weizmann was against this location plan and hoped to defeat it. As a result, Herzl agreed to renew his efforts to promote a Jewish homeland in Palestine.

In 1916, while World War I still raged on, England was having problems producing munitions. As a research chemist, Weizmann sought a way of helping the British. To that end he developed a new process for producing acetone from ordinary chestnuts, which were plentiful in England. The process was essential to the making of cordite, an explosive used by the Navy.

Weizmann had befriended several British politicians, including David Lloyd George, who became prime minister of England, and James Balfour, who served as foreign minister. These influential British friends were so grateful for his discovery that they wanted to make Weizmann a knight. He politely declined and instead asked that the British government proclaim its readiness to support the idea of a Jewish homeland in Palestine.

When in 1917 the British issued the Balfour Declaration endorsing the plan, it was in great measure due to Weizmann's timely scientific discovery. The Declaration marked the first time that a world power had thrown its weight behind the idea of a Jewish return to Palestine.

In July 1918, Weizmann laid the cornerstone for Jerusalem's Hebrew University. He also played a leading role in establishing the *Keren Hayesod* (the Foundation Fund), which became the fund-raising arm of the World Zionist Organization.

Weizmann's achievement in attaining the Balfour Declaration from the British established

Dr. Chaim Weizmann (right) with U.S. President Harry S Truman.

him as a leader of the Zionist movement. He was elected president of the World Zionist Organization (WZO) at a conference in London in July 1920, and served in that position until 1931. He was president again from 1935 to 1946.

Over the next two decades, Weizmann spent all of his time traveling around the world to promote a Jewish state in Palestine—seeking out world leaders, addressing mass meetings of Zionists—all in pursuit of this dream. He especially urged others to help in raising the intellectual level of the Jewish community in Palestine by building schools and universities there.

His pro-British views, which had served him so well previously, turned against him in the 1930s. Following the 1929 Arab riots in Palestine, the British government issued a White Paper that, for the first time, made Jewish immigration to Palestine contingent upon how well Palestine could absorb Jews. In protest, Weizmann resigned as WZO head, and the British policy was rescinded. A year later, however, he was not reelected as WZO president because he was considered too pro-British.

In 1942 Weizmann's son Michael volunteered for the British Royal Air Force and was lost in combat. Weizmann, however, did not let this heartache keep him from continuing to work in different parts of the world on behalf of a Jewish state.

After the war was over, Weizmann traveled to the United States to seek the help of the new president, Harry S Truman in fighting the newly announced British ban on further Jewish immigration to Palestine. After meeting with Weizmann, Truman developed a warm, close relationship with him; the American president pleaded with the British to rescind their ban, but to no avail. Weizmann was successful in his pleas for help from the United Nations which, in 1947, voted to support a plan to partition Palestine into two states: one Jewish, one Arab.

Within hours after the new Jewish state was proclaimed in May 1948, Weizmann was elected the first president of Israel.

A few days later, Weizmann visited President Truman in Washington. "You will never know what this means to my people," he told the president. "We have waited and dreamed and worked for this moment for two thousand years." Weizmann assured Truman that the president's support for the Jewish people would not be forgotten.

Weizmann was in poor health for the four years he served as president, a largely ceremonial position with no real political power. Described as bitter that he had not been given a greater decision-making role in the new state's government, Weizmann devoted most of his time to the new scientific research center in Rehovot, which became a hub for the study of cancer, nuclear physics, immunology, electronics, and mathematics. It developed into one of the major centers of its kind in the world and is named the Weizmann Institute of Science.

Weizmann had not been an observant Jew and, as president, he sought to assure Jews in Israel that religious Jews would not become politically powerful in the new state. "I think we must make it clear from the outset that, while we respect religious feelings, the state will not be able to set the clock back and let religion become the principal vehicle in running the country. Religion will be restricted to synagogues, family, and schools. It will not be allowed to supervise the workings of the government offices."

Weizmann completed his memoirs, *Trial and Error*, in 1949.

One of Weizmann's great disappointments was his inability to reach a friendly understanding with Arab leaders on cooperation between the two groups. He died in 1952 at the age of seventy-eight and is buried at the Weizmann Institute for Science.

ELIE WIESEL

Nobel Peace Prize Recipient and Witness to the Holocaust

Born September 30, 1928, in Sighet, Romania. American Jewish intellectual. During the 1950s and 1960s, when the Holocaust and its victims appeared to be forgotten, Holocaust survivor and intellectual Elie Wiesel became the eloquent voice of the Six Million. Through his writings, especially his autobiographical work *Night* (1956), Wiesel created enormous interest in and provoked fresh sympathy for Holocaust victims. Winner of the 1986 Nobel Peace Prize for his human-rights work, Wiesel cast light on the sufferings of Soviet Jewry as well.

ELIE WIESEL WAS BORN in 1928 in Sighet, Romania, a Hungarian-speaking town in Transylvania. His father, Shlomo Wiesel, was a storekeeper. Young Wiesel studied the Talmud and spent hours studying the Kabbala with Hasidic rabbis.

Courtesy of Boston University

Elie Wiesel

In 1944, when Wiesel was sixteen, the Nazis deported the fifteen thousand Jews of Sighet, half of the town's population, to the concentration camp at Auschwitz. Wiesel, his father, his mother Sarah, and his three sisters, were among them. Wiesel's mother and youngest sister died in the gas chambers there. His two older sisters survived the war.

Wiesel and his father were sent from Auschwitz to the concentration camp at Buchenwald. Wiesel was forced to endure the horror of watching his father die a slow death from disease and starvation. That memory was seared into the young man's mind.

In 1946, liberated with other Jewish orphans and shipped to France, Elie became the ward of a French Jewish children's agency.

From 1948 to 1951, Wiesel attended the Sorbonne, studied philosophy, and worked as a journalist. In addition, he taught Hebrew and the Bible and served as a choir director. In the early 1950s, Wiesel was a stringer for the French newspaper *L'Arche*, official publication of organized French Jewry. He was also a correspondent for the Israeli newspaper *Yediot Aharonot*. He was known in those days by his full name of Eliezer Wiesel.

During this time, he traveled to Morocco and India, and began a doctoral dissertation comparing Jewish, Christian, and Buddhist concepts of asceticism. He never completed it, however.

In 1954 he interviewed the Catholic philosopher François Mauriac for an article. Mauriac played an important role in Wiesel's life by acknowledging Christian responsibility for the Holocaust and encouraging Wiesel to write about his wartime experiences.

In 1956 Wiesel went to New York as the United States correspondent for *Yediot Aharonot*. There he also wrote for the Jewish *Daily Forward*. He also continued to write for *L'Arche*.

Speaking about who influenced him the most, Wiesel has said: "Harav Shushani in Paris, Rabbi Saul Liberman in New York City, and—as a child in Sighet—the Wizhnitzer rebbe."

The 1956 publication of Wiesel's first book, *Night*, launched his career as a novelist, but it was not until the book appeared in the United States four years later that he began his career as a spokesperson for Holocaust victims. First published in Buenos Aires in Yiddish, *Night* was called *Un di velt Hot Geshvign* (*And the World Has Remained Silent*). François Mauriac wrote a moving introduction to the book when it appeared in French.

A slender volume, *Night* told Elie Wiesel's personal story. He introduces himself as "witness," and recounts the horrific experience of watching his father slowly die before his eyes. The author's questioning of faith is powerful. The book was Wiesel's chance to bear witness before the world as to what he and other Jews had undergone.

Condensed and translated into French as *La Nuit* in 1958, the 1960 American version, called *Night*, sent shock waves through the American Jewish community. For nearly two decades, little had been written or spoken publicly about the Holocaust. After the appearance of Wiesel's book, the Holocaust became a legitimate subject for public discussion among Christians as well as Jews. Elie Wiesel became a hero, praised for being a spokesman for world Jewry, termed by some a "modern Job."

"I wanted to show the end, the finality of the event," Wiesel said. "Everything came to an end—history, literature, religion, God. There was nothing left. And yet we begin again with *Night*. Only where do we go from there? Since then, I have explored all kinds of options. To tell you that I have now found a religion, that I believe—no. I am still searching. I am still exploring. I am still protesting."

An important segment of Wiesel's career was devoted, through his writing and lectures, to bringing the Holocaust to the attention of the public. He achieved notable success and became one of the leading figures in American Jewry.

Night was the beginning of a whole new genre of literature in which readers learn about horrible events drawn from everyday life, not from the author's imagination. To Wiesel, the role of the artist was to remember and to re-create, not to imagine, since reality was far more shocking than anything that could be imagined.

Night, as it turned out, was Wiesel's only book to deal directly with the Holocaust, yet that event is at the center of all of his writing. In four future novels, he explored a different option open to the Holocaust survivor: murder in *Dawn* (1961), suicide in *The Accident* (1962), madness in *The Town Beyond the Wall* (1964), and faith and friendship in *Twilight* (1988).

In *The Accident*, Wiesel tells the story of a Jewish immigrant journalist who is struck by a cab and lies in critical condition in a hospital, an incident Wiesel experienced himself. As the sole survivor of his family, the victim develops great guilt, and struggles against God, but tries to accept life and love as part of his existence.

Dawn recounts the tale of a concentration-camp survivor who joins the pre-state underground in Palestine and is ordered to kill a British officer in retaliation for the sentencing to death of a Jewish partisan. Wiesel examines the moral problems incurred by murder, concluding that all murder is ultimately suicide.

Wiesel also wrote *A Beggar in Jerusalem* (1970), *The Oath* (1973), and *The Fifth Son* (1985). *Beggar* is a fictionalized version of the 1967 Six-Day War. To Wiesel, that war marked a turning point in Jewish history, ending the cycle of despair Jews had faced until then, and providing a new hope for the Jewish people. *The Oath* begins before the era of the concentration camps and examines the death of a Carpathian town, its Jewish inhabitants, and the spiritual anguish of its only survivor, and is seemingly autobiographical. *The Fifth Son* is about a child of survivors who tries to learn about the past despite efforts to keep it hidden from him.

Wiesel developed a number of themes in his writing, including being a witness and the necessity to establish dialogue between peoples. Linked with biblical and Hasidic lore in his books, these themes form the basis of his effort to suggest how to have a meaningful existence despite the Holocaust.

Making use of his popularity as a writer and philosopher, Wiesel turned his attention to the plight of Soviet Jews who were prevented from immigrating to the West by the Soviet government. He began his campaign to help them in 1965 with a series of articles in *Yediot Aharonot*, the *Forward*, and the *Saturday Evening Post*. In a book, *The Jews of Silence* (1966), and a play, *Zalmen, or The Madness of God* (1974), Wiesel shed light on the Soviet-Jewish community and praised it for not becoming assimilated despite Stalinist terror tactics. "How can it be explained?" he asked. "I don't know. The temptation to assimilate was tremendous."

In 1963 Wiesel became an American citizen. In 1969 he married Marion Erster; they had a son, Shlomo-Elisha, three years later.

Wiesel taught at the City University of New York from 1972 to 1976; Yale University in 1982 and 1983, and since 1976 he has been the Andrew W. Mellon Professor in the Humanities at Boston University. He served as chairman of the President's Commission on the Holocaust in 1979 and 1980, and on the United States Holocaust Memorial Council from 1980 to 1986.

Wiesel visited Cambodia and Thailand in 1979 to help suffering Cambodian refugees. It was his form of protest against permitting people to die and be forgotten, stemming once again from his Holocaust experience. Wiesel was awarded the Congressional Medal of Achievement in 1984, and two years later, in 1986, the Nobel Peace Prize, in recognition of his fight for human rights.

During a visit to Israel in 1991, Wiesel noted that "Whenever I write, I always have in front of me a picture of the house where I was born. We must always ask, 'Where do I come from?' and 'Where are we going?' There must be a sense of history. If I had to sum up my mission in one sentence, it would be: not to make my past your future."

Wiesel has continued to write novels based on the World War II era and his view of the Holocaust. His 1992 novel *The Forgotten* tells the story of World War II survivor Elhanan Rosenberg, a retired professor living in New York City.

Wiesel's *Wise Men and Their Tales: Portraits of Biblical, Talmudic, and Hasidic Masters* was published in 2003.

STEPHEN S. WISE

American Rabbi, Social Activist, and Zionist Leader

> Born March 17, 1874, in Budapest, Hungary; died April 19, 1949. American Zionist leader. Stephen Samuel Wise was a revolutionary force in twentieth-century American Judaism, arguing that rabbis should be permitted to speak their minds and should be active in helping to ease society's ills. An ardent Zionist, Wise worked tirelessly on behalf of Jewish statehood and immigration to Palestine. He helped establish the National Association for the Advancement of Colored People and the American Civil Liberties Union. He was a founder of the American Jewish Congress and was a leader of the Zionist Organization of America for twenty years.

STEPHEN SAMUEL WISE WAS BORN in Budapest in 1874, a descendant of a long line of rabbis. His father was Rabbi Aaron Weisz. His mother, Sibine, was the daughter of Moritz Fisher, founder of the world-famous porcelain industry in Hungary.

The Weisz family reached the United States in 1875, when Stephen was an infant, settling on East Fifth Street in New York. They Americanized the spelling of their last name to Wise.

At age fifteen, Wise entered the City College of New York. Meanwhile his father tutored him in rabbinic studies. Two years later, in 1891, Stephen transferred to Columbia University and won honors as a Greek and Latin scholar. His first love intellectually, however, was English; he devoted much time to reading the works of the great English poets and prose writers. Wise graduated from Columbia in 1892; he was only eighteen years old.

In 1893 Wise traveled to Vienna, where he was ordained a rabbi by the city's chief rabbi, Adolph Jellinek. That same year, Wise was installed as assistant rabbi and then rabbi of the prestigious Conservative Congregation B'nai Jeshurun on New York's Madison Avenue.

During this time, Wise heard reports of the Dreyfus Affair in France and of pogroms in czarist Russia, events that encouraged him to join the embryonic Zionist movement. He wanted to put an end to the assault on world Jewry. He founded the Zionist Federation in New York on July 4, 1897.

In 1898 Wise met Theodor Herzl, the founder of modern Zionism, at the Second Zionist Congress in Basel; Wise was selected as American secretary of the Zionist movement. The following year, he went on a speaking tour on behalf of Zionism and was asked to become rabbi at the Reform Temple Beth Israel of Portland, Oregon. The offer suited Wise because he was looking for a small city where he could settle and have the opportunity to read, study, and write. He also believed that he would be more comfortable in a Reform congregation. In 1900 he married the artist Louise Waterman and soon thereafter was installed as rabbi of Temple

Beth Israel in Portland. They had two children: James Waterman Wise (1901–1983) and Justine Wise Polier (1903–1987).

Wise's marvelous talents as a forceful, liberal rabbi took hold during the six years he spent in Portland. His goal was to make Judaism come alive in contemporary society. He urged improved civic and social service efforts and championed interfaith activities, at the same time revolutionizing the traditional role of the rabbi.

To show that he was not just preaching, he agreed to take on gratis the job of Oregon Commissioner of Child Labor. In that role, he helped to improve the horrendous conditions faced by young boys and girls who were forced to work long hours for small pay. Oregon's state and city governments were filled with corruption. Rabbi Wise joined the movement to institute honorable government at the local level.

During his Portland years, Wise also found time to translate the Book of Judges, providing the first contemporary translation of that biblical text. Wise's translation was included in the authorized Jewish translation of the Holy Scriptures.

In 1902 Wise received his doctorate from Columbia University for his translation and editing of Solomon ibn Gabirol's *Improvement of the Moral Qualities*.

Wise returned to New York in 1907 and founded the Free Synagogue (now the Stephen Wise Free Synagogue), which was his attempt to change the nature of synagogue Judaism. His synagogue honored freedom of speech from the pulpit; it supported the idea of free seating without having to pay dues. Such liberal, egalitarian principles, not surprisingly, collided with the more conservative Jewish establishment of New York who preferred their synagogues to be hierarchial rather than democratic.

Forever seeking to deal with social injustices, Stephen Wise created the Free Synagogue's Social Service Division in 1908, and the following year he helped found the National Association for the Advancement of Colored People.

Wise was an ardent supporter of the labor movement. In 1911, after the Triangle Shirtwaist Factory fire in New York City, Wise argued in a speech that all human life should be valued and the meaning that should be taken from the fire was that "the life of the lowest worker in the nation is sacred and inviolable." The fire encouraged Wise to take a more activist attitude toward helping the downtrodden.

In 1915 Wise was active in the American Union against Militarism and the League to Enforce Peace. That same year, along with attorney Louis Brandeis, Wise founded the American Jewish Congress. He acted as a key intermediary with President Woodrow Wilson and his advisor, Colonel Edward House, in formulating the text of the Balfour Declaration by which the British pledged support for a Jewish homeland in Palestine.

From 1918 to 1920, Wise was vice-president of the Zionist Organization of America. In 1920 he helped establish the American Civil Liberties Union. Two years later he planned and founded the Jewish Institute of Religion, the Reform rabbinical seminary that provides training for rabbis from all branches of Judaism.

Wise was cochairman, from 1919 until 1945, of the American Zionist Emergency Committee (ZEC), perhaps the most important Zionist lobbying group of its time. He joined with moderates within the ZEC who were prepared to compromise on the idea of a Jewish state in return for obtaining the support of non-Zionists for unrestricted immigration to Palestine.

In 1936 Wise became president of the Zionist Organization of America (ZOA) and chairman of the United Palestine Appeal. He remained president of the ZOA until 1943, when he was ousted by Abba Hillel Silver and his followers.

Despite their occasional differences, Wise worked closely with other notable Zionist leaders—Chaim Weizmann, David Ben-Gurion, and Abba Hillel Silver. In contrast with other more moderate voices, Wise was among the first of the American Jewish leaders to warn of the dangers of Nazism. Utilizing his close links to President Roosevelt, Wise encouraged him to put pressure on the German government to end its persecution of Jews.

In 1930 Wise coauthored, with Jacob De Haas, *The Great Betrayal*, an indictment of the British government for failing to implement the promises it had made in the Balfour Declaration. From 1933 to 1935, Wise led the American Jewish Congress in organizing boycotts against Nazi Germany and in opposition to the 1936 Olympic games being held in Berlin. In 1936, he organized the World Jewish Congress and served as its president until 1949.

After World War II, Wise was deeply disturbed that he had not done enough to persuade the American government to help in the rescue of the Jews in Europe during the Holocaust. In 1945 he visited the displaced-persons camps in Europe where war refugees were housed. This experience convinced him that a Jewish state had to be established at once.

In 1948 Wise was instrumental in the merger of the Jewish Institute of Religion with Hebrew Union College in Cincinnati, Ohio. He finished his memoirs, *Challenging Years* (1949), shortly before his death at the age of seventy-five.

Wise was a major influence on many fronts—as a responsible, concerned citizen, as a rabbi, and as a Jew—fighting for justice for the labor force and the common people, encouraging freedom of speech among rabbis, and, most of all, serving as a leader of American Jewry during the critical years leading up to the Holocaust and the birth of the state of Israel.

HERMAN WOUK

Bestselling American Novelist

Born May 27, 1915, in New York City; American novelist. Herman Wouk catapulted into fame with his bestselling novel *The Caine Mutiny*, winner of the Pulitzer Prize in 1951. Since then he has written widely about American Jewish life and World War II, significantly affecting the way readers viewed those two phenomena. Wouk's fiction combines detailed and substantial background information and a strong story line. Two of his most popular books are *The Winds of War* (1971) and its sequel, *War and Remembrance* (1978). Many of his novels have been turned into Hollywood films or television miniseries. His books *The Hope* (1993) and *The Glory* (1994) depict the history of the state of Israel.

HERMAN WOUK WAS BORN to Russian immigrant parents Abraham and Esther (Levine) Wouk in New York City in 1915. Abraham Wouk was a laundry laborer earning three dollars an hour. The Wouks emerged from poverty in 1932 when Abraham became successful as a well-known leader in the laundry industry. The family moved to the more well-to-do West Side, the background for Wouk's famous novel *Marjorie Morningstar* (1955).

David Hume Kennerly

Herman Wouk

David Hume Kennerly

Herman Wouk

As a child growing up in the Bronx, Wouk was religious. He wrote that his Jewish education was "up to the level of proficiency in Talmud study. My grandfather, arriving in the USA when I was thirteen, was my main Talmud teacher, and with my father and mother, the main influence for Jewish identification."

In 1932, Wouk graduated from Townsend Harris High School. At Columbia University he majored in philosophy and comparative literature, edited the college humor magazine, and wrote two varsity shows.

While in college, Wouk was exposed to all sorts of secular temptations, and for a while was lax in his observance of Jewish traditions, but soon returned to them. After his 1934 graduation, he worked as an advertising and radio scriptwriter. He wrote gags for radio comedians, including Fred Allen.

He married Betty Sarah Brown in 1945; she was a convert to Judaism. The Wouks had three sons, but their eldest child died at an early age. The family created a philanthropic fund in his memory, calling it the Abe Wouk Foundation.

During World War II, Wouk enlisted in the United States Navy. To while away long hours in port between campaigns in the South Pacific, he began a novel called *Aurora Dawn* (1947). The setting was the fast-paced, frenetic atmosphere of radio advertising which Wouk knew so well. It became a Book-of-the-Month-Club selection. *City Boy: The Adventures of Herbie Bookbinder* (1948) was Wouk's next book. It told of a heavyset Bronx boy's experience in school and in summer camp, and is still widely used in schools and anthologies.

Wouk gained national recognition with his third book, the Pulitzer-Prize-winning novel *The Caine Mutiny* (1951). Wouk drew upon his Navy experiences on the destroyer *Zane*. The novel describes the conflict of values between personal rights and professional duty when a ship's captain is removed from duty by his executive officer, who has concluded that the captain is psychotic.

Wouk's novels have usually made the bestseller lists. These include *Marjorie Morningstar*, which some reviewers found to be an overly long book (565 pages) and tedious. One critic called it "a soap opera with sociological and psychological props." But it was hailed by thousands of readers as a great read. One critic lovingly called the novel a "Jewish *Vanity Fair*."

In *Marjorie Morningstar*, Wouk wrote about a middle-class young Jewish woman who falls in love with a man and enters show business; she eventually settles down and lives an ordinary life as a suburban housewife. The book became famous for its delineation of the new Jewish stereotype—the so-called Jewish-American princess—who likes clothes, goes in for ostentatious wealth, and makes sure to attach herself to a professional husband of high status.

Wouk, an observant Jew, explained his faith in Orthodoxy in a nonfiction book *This Is My God* (1959), written soon after the death of his son. The book has been credited with encouraging many Jewish men and women to take a new look at their Judaism. He attends synagogue frequently and devotes part of each day to study of the Talmud.

In that book Wouk wrote, "Judaism is part of my life and of my family's life . . . . Religious people tend to encounter, and among those who are not, a cemented certainty that belief in God is a crutch for the weak and the fearful. It would be just as silly to assert that disbelief in God is a crutch for the immoral and the ill-read . . . ." To him, the survival of the Jewish people "looks like the hand of Providence in history." He credited Jewish survival to the law of Moses. "I believe it is our lot to live and serve in our old identity, until the promised day when the Lord will be one and his name one in all the earth. I think the extinction of Jewish learning and Jewish faith would be a measureless tragedy."

Wouk wrote the novel *Youngblood Hawke* in 1962. His next novel, *Don't Stop the Carnival* (1965), told the story of a middle-aged Broadway press agent who sells his business and purchases a problem-ridden hotel in the Caribbean. His Jewishness makes him feel alienated and out of place there.

Wouk's *The Winds of War* (1971) was number one on the *New York Times* bestseller list for twenty-four weeks. The sequel, *War and Remembrance* (1978), also a *New York Times* bestseller, dealt, like the first book, with the Holocaust and the major battles of World War II. When these two books were published in the People's Republic of China, Wouk immediately became the most popular living foreign novelist in that country.

Wouk wrote his World War II novels in order to increase readers' knowledge of events that seemed far away in time and removed from contemporary life. "World War II," he said in an interview with *Publishers Weekly*, "was an Everest of human experience, and as always, you cannot see the mountains until you get some distance away. It started with a horse-drawn army moving into Poland and ended with the atom bomb. Its outcome was crucial to the human race and it is important to realize how close an outcome it really was."

331

Hollywood films and several television miniseries based on many of Wouk's books were produced following their publication.

Derided by some critics for not being a great writer, Wouk has been assailed for lacking a writing style and for caring too little about symbolism. Many others, however, have praised him for being a Jewish phenomenon. The critic Pearl K. Bell lauded Wouk for being "an unembarrassed believer in such discredited forms of commitment as valor, gallantry, leadership, patriotism." He has also been heralded for being a Jewish-American writer who is not embarrassed at being Jewish.

Although Wouk is a very private man, his novel *Inside Out* (1985), which recounts the story of a one-time Jewish gag writer, is clearly somewhat autobiographical. He has shied away from public speaking, and recently stated that "I have not met with a journalist for twenty-five years." A stipulation he makes when giving a public speech to a Jewish fund-raising meeting is that the food served be strictly kosher.

Wouk's novels *The Hope* (1993) and *The Glory* (1994) depict the history of the state of Israel chronologically. "Perhaps some people will think it's 'chutzpah' for me—an American living in the Diaspora—to write on Israel's history," he said. "But I believe this is not just an Israeli story; it is a world story, with the framework being one of great global events."

In April 1997 the musical *Don't Stop the Carnival* opened in the Coconut Grove Playhouse, in Miami, Florida. Wouk and singer-songwriter Jimmy Buffett wrote the musical. Based on Wouk's book, which he wrote for the show, the play tells the tale of a middle-aged theatrical press agent who retires to run a tropical hotel on the fictitious Caribbean island of Kinja. "An engaging story, melodies that will rumble in your head for days, lyrics both wry and wrenching, a great cast . . . and loads of visual flash," wrote Christine Dolen in the *The Miami Herald*.

Herman Wouk's *The Will to Live On*, a further exploration of the subject matter covered in his religious-themed *This Is My God*, was published in 2000. This was followed, in 2004, by a novel entitled *A Hotel in Texas*, about which *Publishers Weekly* wrote: "Still working more than fifty years after he won the Pulitzer for *The Caine Mutiny* and more than thirty years after *The Winds of War*, Wouk, now nearly ninety, has license to write what he pleases: in this case, a light, sprightly story about lost love, high-energy physics and the machinations of Washington."

YIGAEL YADIN

Israeli Leader and Archeologist

Born March 21, 1917, in Jerusalem; died June 28, 1984. Israeli military leader and archeologist. As premier archeologist and military leader, Yigael Yadin embodied the Zionist model of the soldier-scholar. As acting chief of staff, Yadin led the state of Israel to victory in its 1948 War of Independence. Then, after being appointed chief of staff, he built up the modern Israel Defense Forces. He earned fame for his archeological digs in Israel—in 1958 at Hazor, then in 1964 near the Dead Sea—uncovering the letters of Simeon Bar Kochba, the famous ancient Jewish rebel, and the remnants of the Jewish martyrs at Masada. In his later years, Yadin entered politics, becoming deputy prime minister of Israel and the leader of a new political party.

YIGAEL YADIN WAS BORN in Jerusalem in 1917. His father was a well-known professor of archeology, Eliezer Sukenik.

His mother, Chassia (Feinsod) Sukenik, was the founder of the first kindergarten in Palestine early in the twentieth century. At age fifteen, Yadin joined the underground defense organization known as the Haganah, serving in a number of command and training posts, among them head of the Jerusalem district and director of the officers' school. In 1944, at twenty-seven years old, he was an operations officer for the group.

When Yadin was eighteen years old, he began studying archeology and Semitic languages at Jerusalem's Hebrew University. He continued his studies for another decade. Meanwhile he climbed the military ranks to become, in 1947, at age thirty, chief of operations. He was given the personal code name Yadin, which became his surname. On December 22, 1941, Yadin married Carmella Ruppin. They had two daughters.

While Israel's War of Independence was being fought in the late 1940s, Yadin was the acting chief of staff (the actual chief of staff, Ya'acov Dori, was ill). Yadin advised David Ben-Gurion, the political leader of the *Yishuv*, to proclaim Israel's independence, even though he put the odds of victory at no more than fifty-fifty.

Yadin the military leader benefited from his familiarity with archeology. When the Israeli army was able to outflank the Egyptian army in the Negev, it was because the Israelis used an ancient Roman road that Yadin knew about from his studies.

In 1949 Yadin served as leader of the Israeli delegation to the postwar peace talks held on the Greek island of Rhodes. Appointed chief of staff that year, he shaped the modern Israeli army, designing its unique system of supplying reserve forces, which requires Israeli men to devote one month a year to military service until age fifty-five. It was that method that enabled Israel to prevent the much larger Arab armies from overwhelming them on the battlefield.

When Ben-Gurion, the country's first prime minister, wanted to make drastic cuts in the defense budget, Yadin resigned. Ben-Gurion had always thought of Yadin as a possible political heir. Even with his resignation, Yadin remained Ben-Gurion's protégé.

In 1953 Yadin began studies at the Hebrew University in Jerusalem. He was awarded a doctorate in archeology in 1955. That same year, his book *The Scroll of the War of the Sons of Light against the Sons of Darkness* was published. The book described one of the Dead Sea Scrolls, the manuscripts that were preserved intact for centuries in inaccessible caves near the Dead Sea. The next year, Yadin was presented with the Israel Prize in Jewish Studies for the book; this is the highest honor Israel can bestow upon one of its citizens.

Yadin hoped, through his archeology research, to connect the Jewish people in Israel with their ancient past. In 1955 he took thousands of volunteers on a dig at the former great city of Hazor, north of the Sea of Galilee. Hazor, recognized as one of the most important fortress cities of ancient times, had been inhabited by the Israelites under Joshua and by Canaanites, Persians, and Greeks. Spending five years at the site, and with a Bible as his main guide, Yigael Yadin peeled back the layers of ancient civilization and eventually found artifacts and evidence of Joshua's major battle against Hazor in the thirteenth century B.C.E. Also found were courtyards, chariots, palaces, temples, reservoirs, and messages.

In 1961 Yadin led another dig at Ein Gedi, along the Dead Sea. His search was for solid evidence of the existence of Simeon Bar Kochba, the leader of a rebellion against the Romans following the destruction of the Temple in 70 C.E. The only way to reach the caves in question was to fly Army helicopters directly above the narrow entrances and then lower a volunteer from a rope. Swinging back and forth, the volunteer threw himself into the slit entrance of the ancient and smelly caves. Through this method of investigation, Yadin and his team discovered fifteen letters from Bar Kochba issuing orders to his lieutenants to continue the campaign against the Romans.

In 1963 Yadin was appointed professor of archeology at the Hebrew University in Jerusalem. A year later, he focused his attention as an archeologist on the flat-topped mountain fortress of Masada near the Dead Sea. Masada, known as the place where approximately a thousand Jewish men, women, and children, determined to continue their resistance, camped after the Romans destroyed the Temple in 70 C.E. When it became clear that the Romans would soon overtake them, Jews took their own lives rather than surrender.

Yadin found ancient coins, letters, arrows, and skeletons of the martyrs as well as an ancient palace built by King Herod with a throne room, reception halls, servants' quarters, and workshops. Yadin also found uncovered jars containing food. In the living quarters, he found such household items as stoves, basins, and dishes. Sandals were strewn about. Also found were a *mikveh* (ritual bath) and the remains of a synagogue.

Ben-Gurion was indifferent at first to the tale of the site where Jews chose suicide over fighting and sure defeat, but Yadin arranged exclusive coverage of the discoveries with a British newspaper and gained international attention for his dig and its view into ancient Jewry. In 1965 Masada became a national shrine in Israel. "Masada will not fall again" was the new slogan for Israelis. Future officers of the Israel Defense Forces took their oath of loyalty to the state of Israel standing on top of Masada.

At Yadin's initiative, the Shrine of the Book was built on the grounds of Jerusalem's Israel Museum. Inside the Shrine are fragments of the Dead Sea Scrolls along with some of the Bar Kochba letters and other ancient artifacts.

Yadin's digs contributed to the advancement of archeology in Israel, especially to the way digs should be conducted and artifacts preserved. Yadin also wrote about his archeological adventures. His best-known books are *The Message of the Scrolls* (1957), *Masada* (1965), and *Bar Kochba* (1971).

During the 1967 Six-Day War, Yadin served as a military adviser to Prime Minister Levi Eshkol. Following the 1973 Yom Kippur War, he was appointed one of five members of the blue-ribbon commission set up to investigate the causes for Israel's lack of military preparedness on the eve of that war.

In 1977 Yadin founded a new political party called the Democratic Movement for Change (DMC), which sought to attract Israelis who had grown tired of the corruption

Yigael Yadin

State of Israel Government Press Office

scandals of the early 1970s and who wanted a change in the nation's electoral system. Yadin's party surprised everyone when, in the May 1977 election, it won fifteen seats, an extraordinarily high number for a "third" party (other than Labor and Likud).

The following October, the Likud Prime Minister Menachem Begin took Yadin's DMC into his coalition government and Yadin became deputy prime minister. Disappointed that he was not able to realize the electoral and social reforms that were his goals, Yadin stepped down from politics as his party disintegrated in 1980. He died in 1984 at the age of sixty-seven, having influenced Israeli Jews for posterity, both through his active political career and his archeological research into the nation's past.

THUMBNAIL
SKETCHES

AGAM, YA'AKOV

Born in 1928 in Rishon Letzion, Palestine.
ISRAELI PAINTER AND SCULPTOR.

Ya'acov Agam studied at Jerusalem's Bezalel School of Arts and Crafts; then at the Johannes Itten School in Zurich, and finally at the Academy of Abstract Art in Paris. He introduced geometrical abstraction to Israeli art. His *Transformable Painting* and *Transformes Musicales*, painted in 1951 and 1952, marked the start of an artistic effort into the third dimension. In 1955 he took part in the first international exhibit where kinetic art was shown to the public in Paris. Agam's originality, as anyone viewing his art learns almost immediately, lies in his ability to make the composition appear to change as the viewer moves. His sculpture is relief-like in style. Agam's works hang in such prestigious places as the president's residence in Jerusalem, Lincoln Center in New York, and the Élysée Palace in Paris. In 1963 Agam won the first international prize in the São Paolo Biennale. He ranks as one of Israel's most talented and most creative artists.

AHAD HA'AM

Born in 1858 in Skivira, Ukraine; died in 1927.
ZIONIST INTELLECTUAL.

Through his many short, succinct essays, Ahad Ha'am acquired the reputation of being one of the major intellectual figures of the Zionist movement despite the fact that he never held any related public positions. Ahad Ha'am—in Hebrew, "one of the people"—was his pen name (his birth name was Asher Ginsburg), and, as an adult writer, he became known by it. His most famous essay was written in 1891, shortly after his first visit to Palestine, and was called "Emet me'Eretz Yisra'el" ("Truth from the Land of Israel"). Ahad Ha'am urged that the large Arab population in Palestine be recognized and that Jews avoid thoughtless acts and supremacist policies against the Arabs. A debate arose between Ha'am and Zionist leader and theorist Theodor Herzl over how best to develop a Jewish homeland in Palestine. Herzl favored a "political" approach, utilizing diplomacy in order to win over world leaders to the idea of that homeland. Ha'am, in contrast, thought that Jews themselves had to be more active and, in particular, take a greater interest in Jewish culture—that interest in Jewish culture would, in turn, spur Jews to immigrate to Palestine. In that way, Jews themselves would create a Jewish homeland rather than obtain it by gaining the blessings of world leaders. The debate was never in fact resolved. Future Zionist leaders used a mixture of the two approaches in forging the Jewish state that was created in 1948. Ahad Ha'am called for a cultural renaissance in the Diaspora in his first essay, "Lo zeh haDerech" ("This Is Not the Way"), published in 1899. He also insisted on the need for an ethical content within Zionism. In 1907, when he was forty-nine years old, he moved to London. In 1922, at the age of sixty-four, he moved to Palestine. He died at the age of sixty-nine in 1927.

AMICHAI, YEHUDA

Born in 1924 in Wurzberg, Germany; died September 22, 2000.
ISRAELI POET.

Yehuda Amichai was regarded as the unofficial poet laureate of the state of Israel. Amichai's family, whose original name was Pfeuffer, was from southern Germany. His grandparents were farmers; his father, an Orthodox Jew, was a businessman. Arriving in Palestine in the 1930s, Amichai lived in Petach Tikvah, then Jerusalem, where he went to Ma'aleh, the elite religious high school. A year or so after his bar mitzvah, Yehuda abandoned his religion. He served in both the British Army and the Palmach, the pre-state commando unit of the Jewish defenses forces in Palestine. Amichai published eleven volumes of original poetry in Hebrew; many of them became bestsellers. He also wrote two novels, including *Not of This Time, Not of This Place* (1963), and a number of short stories. Considered his country's greatest poet, Amichai's poems often question the militarism that has permeated certain segments of Israeli life. While the early Jewish pioneer Joseph Trumpeldor said, "It is good to die for our country," Amichai, in contrast, wrote "I want to die in my own bed." In 1982 Amichai won the Israel Prize for literature. In November 1994 he was one of eighteen writers to receive the New York Public Library's annual "Literary Lion" prize. He married twice and had three children. Amichai's literary work has helped to shape Israel's national identity. Rochelle Furstenberg, writing in the *Jerusalem Report*, noted that "[i]n his ability to draw from traditional Jewish sources while speaking in an accessible way to universal humanist concerns, Amichai represents the best of Israeli culture." In 1995 *Yehuda Amichai: A Life of Poetry 1948-1995*, one of several collections that cover the poet's entire career, was published. The following year marked the English-language publication of two projects on which he collaborated with photographers: *Open-Eyed Land*, with Franz Wieler, and *Poems of Jerusalem*, with Aliza Auerbach. He lived in the Yemin Moshe quarter, overlooking Jerusalem's Old City, until his death in 2000.

APPELFELD, AHARON

Born in 1932 near Czernowitz, then Romania.
ISRAELI FICTION WRITER.

Aharon Appelfeld is Israel's leading literary voice for the Jewish victims of the Holocaust. His stories are drawn from his own experience during and after World War II. He was born to a middle-class German-speaking family. When the Nazis invaded Romania in the summer of 1941, Appelfeld's life was quickly disrupted. His mother was murdered, his father taken prisoner. He, then a child of only nine, had to manage by himself. He escaped from a labor camp at Transnistria and lived among Ukrainian peasants until 1944, when Soviet forces liberated the region. Joining other orphan refugees, he reached Italy, then Palestine, in 1946. Appelfeld studied at Jerusalem's Hebrew University and decided to be a writer as part of his attempt to rehabilitate himself. He chose to write about Holocaust victims, a rare thing for a Hebrew-language writer in Israel to do in the late 1950s and early 1960s. His group of stories *Ashan* (*Ashes*), published in 1962, was the first literary attempt in the Hebrew language to portray

Holocaust victims. Appelfeld's writing helped to legitimize this new genre in Hebrew letters. Avoiding descriptions of life in the ghettos or death camps, he concentrated on what happened to Jewish victims immediately before and after the war, not during the fighting. Appelfeld's view was that describing what happened in the camps would be grotesque and obscene. Most of his stories, which were published in twelve volumes during the 1960s, focus on survivors trying to resettle in Israel or in the transit camps in Europe. In *Badenheim 1939*, he noted the false quiet of European Jewry before World War II. His short novel, *Abyss*, was published in 1993. His tenth novel, *Unto the Soul*, was published in 1994. His novel *Iron Tracks* was a National Jewish Book Award winner in 1996. Appelfeld's *The Story of a Life: a Memoir*, a retrospective on the last seven decades of his life, was released in 2004.

ASCH, SHOLEM

Born in 1880 in Kutno, Poland; died in 1957.
POLISH WRITER.

Sholem Asch started out writing in Hebrew but, falling under the influence of I.L. Peretz, the Polish writer considered the founder of modern Yiddish literature, Asch turned to Yiddish by the time he was twenty years old. His version of Yiddish was quite removed from the everyday language of his fellow Jews and considerably more clumsy than that of the noted writer Shalom Aleichem. Nevertheless a prolific and a popular writer, Asch was able to attract non-Jewish readers, taking Yiddish literature to a wider readership. This was considered his greatest achievement. Asch's best-known works include *Moyshele* (an affectionate nickname of Moses, 1900); *Dos shtetl* (*The Village*, 1904); *Motke ganev* (*Motke the Thief*, 1971); and *Kidesh hashem* (*Martyrdom*, 1920). His plays, especially *Got fun nekome* (*God of Vengeance*, 1907), attracted large audiences. Many of his Jewish readers were distressed to find that his later works were attempts to reconcile Jesus with the Jewish faith. These included *The Nazarene* (1939), *The Apostle* (1943), and *Mary* (1949). Asch settled in Israel in 1954, where he wrote *Der novi* (*The Prophet*, 1955). He was seventy-seven years old when he died in 1957.

BAECK, LEO

Born in 1873 in Lissa, Poland; died in 1956.
GERMAN THEOLOGIAN.

Leo Baeck studied at the Breslau rabbinical seminary and the Hochschule für die Wissenschaft des Judentums in Berlin, as well as simultaneously at the universities of Breslau and Berlin. The author of a number of influential books, Baeck wrote *Das Wesen des Judentums* (1905) translated into English as *The Essence of Judaism* in 1936, in which he saw the basis of Judaism as morality and asserted that his religion was superior to Christianity. Baeck's reputation, however, was gained not so much from his

Leo Baeck

writings and teachings as by his efforts to guide and support the German-Jewish community during the Holocaust. He served as rabbi in Oppeln (Upper Silesia), Düsseldorf, and, beginning in 1912, in Berlin. He taught at Berlin's Hochschule, where he had himself studied. After the Nazis rose to power in 1933, Baeck chose to remain in Germany and, as president of the *Reichsvertretung* (the representative body of German Jewry), defended Jewish rights. His goal was to preserve Jewish dignity and integrity as a means of overcoming Nazi persecution. Twice arrested by the Gestapo, he resumed his activist work upon his release on both occasions. In 1943 Leo Baeck was deported to the Theresienstadt concentration camp. He survived and settled in London after the war. In his final years Baeck was chairman of the World Union of Progressive Judaism and taught at the Hebrew Union College in Cincinnati. He died at the age of eighty-three.

BEN-ZVI, YITZHAK

Born in 1884 in Poltava, Ukraine; died in 1963.
SECOND PRESIDENT OF THE STATE OF ISRAEL.

Yitzhak Ben-Zvi was a labor leader, historian, and ethnographer of Jewish tribes and communities. He cofounded, with Ber Borochov, the Zionist Socialist Poalei Zion party in 1905 in his native Ukraine. In 1907 Ben-Zvi immigrated to Palestine and was one of the founders of the Jewish Watchmen's Association called *Hashomer*; he was also a founder of its predecessor, Bar Giora. Ben-Zvi served on the editorial board of the first Hebrew socialist magazine in Palestine, called *Ha'ahdut*. A close colleague of David Ben-Gurion, Ben-Zvi and the future Israeli prime minister studied law together in the years before World War I in Istanbul, where they tried to establish contact with the Young Turk leaders. When the war began, the two returned to Palestine, championing a pro-Ottoman policy; soon thereafter, however, both were expelled from the country. They eventually reached the United States, where they sought to turn young people into Zionists; they also organized the American Battalion of the British Army's Jewish Legion. Ben-Zvi was one of the founders of a number of the major pre-state institutions of the Jewish community in Palestine. In 1919 he helped found the political party Ahdut ha'Avodah and a year later the Histadrut, the major labor federation. In 1930 he was a founder of the political party Mapai. He was a member of the Va'ad Le'umi, the Jewish National Council, becoming its chairman in 1931 and president in 1944. Ben-Zvi also held key posts in the Histadrut and the Jerusalem municipality. From 1949 to 1952, he was a Knesset (parliament) member. In 1952 he was elected the second president of the state of Israel upon the death of Chaim Weizmann. Ben-Zvi served as president until his own death in 1963 at the age of seventy-nine.

BERLE, MILTON

Born July 12, 1908, in New York City; died March 27, 2002.
AMERICAN ENTERTAINER.

Milton Berle was born Milton Berlinger; his career began at age five, when his mother entered him in a Charlie Chaplin look-alike contest—and he won. During the 1920s, Berle appeared in numerous silent movies; he then performed on stage and on radio. In 1948, he became the first variety-show host on the new medium of television. Known affectionately as "Uncle Miltie" to his many viewers, Berle kept the entertainment moving as host of *Texaco Star Theater*. The program became a regular Tuesday night fixture on TV for seven seasons. Because television was so new and expensive, viewers crowded outside appliance-store windows to watch the comedian. Berle was television's first superstar and was an important early influence on the medium. His fans called him "Mr. Television." Berle built upon his vaudeville background to develop his special brand of slapstick comedy, which in-

Milton Berle

cluded dressing in outlandish costumes. In April 1997 he launched a new venture: a luxury gambling magazine entitled *Milton*. Targeted at men in the twenty-five to thirty-nine age group, its motto is: "We Drink! We Smoke! We Gamble!" In 1998 Berle attended "Milton Berle's 90th Birthday Roast" at the Westbury Music Fair, cracking jokes, quipping to reporters that the secret of his long life was never drinking and never smoking—though he has been smoking cigars since he was twelve years old."

BLOCH, ERNEST

Born in 1880 in Geneva, Switzerland; died in 1959.
SWISS-AMERICAN COMPOSER.

Ernest Bloch began his full-time music studies in violin and composition when he was fourteen years old. In his later teenage years he studied in Brussels and Frankfurt. Although he returned to his native Geneva to work, still a teenager, in his father's clock business, Bloch took on conducting assignments from time to time in Neuchâtel and Lausanne. He is known largely as a Jewish composer. The sounds of the *shofar* can be heard in his compositions, as can the music of Jewish chants in the synagogue. He wrote Jewish music "not for the sake of self-advertisement," he once said, "but because it is the only way in which I can produce music of vitality.... It is the Jewish soul that interests me, the complex, glowing, agitated soul that I feel vibrating through the Bible." One of his most famous works is the largely orchestral

Jewish Cycle (1911–1918). In 1916 Bloch immigrated to New York, where his music won great praise. In 1920 he became the first director of the Cleveland Institute of Music, a post he held for five years. In 1923 he returned to writing Jewish-inspired compositions, including *Baal Shem* and *Abodah* for violin and piano, and *From Jewish Life* for cello and piano. None of the first thirty of Bloch's one hundred works was published; only one of those thirty (*Fantasie*) was ever recorded. From 1930 to 1938, Bloch lived in Europe, where he composed *Avodath haKodesh* (*Sacred Service*) and *Voices in the Wilderness*. From 1939 until he died in 1959 at the age of seventy-nine, Bloch lived on the West Coast of the United States.

BLOOMBERG, MICHAEL R.

Born February 14, 1942, in Medford, Massachusetts.
AMERICAN EXECUTIVE, LATER MAYOR OF NEW YORK CITY.

The son of the male bookkeeper at a local dairy, Michael graduated from Johns Hopkins University in 1964 and earned an MBA from Harvard in the summer of 1966. He was hired by Salomon Brothers to work on Wall Street, becoming a partner by 1972. Soon after, he was supervising all of Salomon's stock trading, sales, and, later, its information systems. Bloomberg was fired in 1981 after another company acquired Salomon, and he used his stake from the Salomon sale to start his own company, which revolutionized the way businesses acquired financial information. He created and sought subscriptions to a financial information computer (known as a "Bloomberg") that collected and analyzed various combinations of past and present securities data, delivering the information immediately to the user. In 1990 Bloomberg L.P. launched a news service, followed by radio, television, Internet, and publishing operations. Bloomberg, who had become a billionaire, wrote a best-selling memoir entitled *Bloomberg by Bloomberg* and, in November 2001, successfully ran for the mayoralty of the City of New York. In 2004 Mayor Bloomberg was winning mixed reviews for his policies of raising taxes, cutting costs, and banning cigarettes in bars and clubs.

BRONFMAN, EDGAR M., SR.

Born June 20, 1929, in Montreal, Canada.
LIQUOR MAGNATE AND JEWISH RIGHTS ADVOCATE.

Edgar M. Bronfman, Sr., was born in 1929 in Montreal. His father, Sam Bronfman, was a refugee from czarist Russia who arrived in Canada in 1889 and in 1924, formed Distillers Corporation, an alcoholic beverage company based in Montreal. Four years later, he acquired Joseph E. Seagram & Sons of Waterloo, Ontario, and built it into a successful business. His son Edgar, one of four children, earned a bachelor's degree in history from McGill University in Montreal in 1951. Two years later he joined the merged corporation, now called the Seagram Company. Bronfman soon moved to New York, where he worked in the firm's United States operation. In 1959 he became a naturalized American citizen. When his father died in 1971, Edgar Bronfman assumed overall control of the company. Bronfman diversified the firm, acquiring office buildings, shopping malls, and other businesses. In time Seagram's became the leading worldwide producer and marketer of distilled spirits, wines, coolers, juices, and soft drinks, with $6.1 billion in sales in 1993. Still chairman of Seagram's, but no longer taking an active role in daily business operations (his son, Edgar, Jr., is now president of the company), Bronfman has remained one of the richest men in America. According to the *Forbes* magazine 1995 list of the richest four hundred people in the country, Edgar Bronfman, Sr. is thirteenth and worth $2.7 billion. Bronfman has been president of the World Jewish Congress since 1981 and devotes much of his time to negotiating with world leaders on the status, welfare, and rights of Jews in many countries, especially those of the Soviet Union. He has been credited with helping bring to light the startling disclosure that former United Nations Secretary-General Kurt Waldheim had a Nazi past. Bronfman lives in New York City. He has been married four times (twice to the same woman) and has seven children. Bronfman received an honorary doctorate from Jerusalem's Hebrew University in June 1997. He was honored for "his important work on behalf of the Jewish people, and in appreciation of his friendship for and support of the Hebrew University."

Edgar M. Bronfman, Sr.

CANETTI, ELIAS

Born July 25, 1905; died August 13, 1994.
BULGARIAN WRITER AND NOBEL PEACE PRIZE RECIPIENT.

Of Spanish-Jewish descent, Elias Canetti was educated in Zurich, Frankfurt, and Vienna, and in 1929, prior to becoming a writer, earned a doctorate in chemistry. He was preoccupied with the question of how political and social forces affected the individual, particularly with what he called the "dissolution of the individual in a crowd," and with the "human acceptance of death," which he resisted. In the early 1930s, Canetti began writing plays and novels. His only novel, *Die Blendung* (1935, published in 1946 in English as *Auto-da-Fé*), dealt with a professor's descent into madness. With the rise of Nazism, Canetti was forced to leave Austria, settling in Britain in 1939. He did not develop a wide following among German readers until the publication of the first volume of his major work, *Crowds and Power* (1960), a psychosociological study of crowd behavior. Both books earned him critical praise. He won the Nobel Prize in Literature in 1982 because, the Nobel committee said, his writings "were marked by a broad outlook, a wealth of ideas, and artistic power." With fame came a chosen life of reclusiveness. It was only through his three vol-

345

umes of memoirs, published in the 1970s and 1980s, that the public learned more about him. Beginning in 1988, Canetti made his permanent home in Switzerland. He died at the age of eighty-nine in 1994. At his request, he was buried in Zurich next to the grave of James Joyce.

CANTOR, EDDIE

Born in 1892 in New York City; died in 1964.
AMERICAN COMEDIAN AND VAUDEVILLE PERFORMER.

Eddie Cantor

One of the best-known Jewish entertainers of his era, Eddie Cantor was a successful comedian in vaudeville, on Broadway, in the movies, on radio, and on television. He was born Isidor Iskowitch on the Lower East Side of New York; he never finished elementary school. In 1907, when he was fifteen years old, he won an amateur contest at a music hall, then he began touring with a comedy blackface act. In time, he appeared regularly on the vaudeville circuit, breaking records for long runs at the major American variety houses. Between 1917 and 1919, Cantor toured Europe's music halls and later gained top billing in the *Ziegfeld Follies*. During the 1920s, Cantor worked in films. In 1923 he starred on Broadway in *Kid Boots*, a musical that ran for three years. Among his most popular movies were *The Kid From Spain* (1933), *Roman Scandals* (1934), and *Ali Baba Goes to Town* (1937). He died in 1964 at the age of seventy-two.

CAPA, ROBERT

Born in 1913 in Budapest, Hungary; died May 25, 1954.
AMERICAN WAR PHOTOGRAPHER.

Robert Capa's birth name was Andrei Friedmann, but he changed it in the belief that people would be more likely to purchase photographs from someone named Capa. His first published photograph was taken of Leon Trotsky, the Russian revolutionary, at a meeting in Copenhagen in 1931. Robert Capa was considered the greatest war photographer, always taking risks, and able to capture the essence of the sad, tragic stories on the battlefield. He was the first to photograph the horror of war at close quarters. His photo of a Loyalist soldier, taken during the Spanish Civil War, just as the soldier was shot, has become one of the most memorable combat photos of the twentieth century. Capa's photographs appeared in *Life* magazine from 1936 until his death in 1954. "War is like an actress who is getting old," he once said.

"Less and less photogenic and more and more dangerous." Following World War II, Capa and two fellow photographers, David Seymour and Henri Cartier-Bresson, founded Magnum Photos, the international photographic agency. In the same period he had a love affair with movie actress Ingrid Bergman. In 1948 Capa photographed the military action during Israel's War of Independence. He was taking photos of French troops on a mission near Hanoi on May 24, 1954, when he stepped on a land mine and was killed. He was forty-one years old.

CHAYEFKSY, PADDY

Born January 29, 1923, in New York City; died August 1, 1981.
AMERICAN PLAYWRIGHT AND SCREENWRITER.

The son of Russian immigrant parents, Chayefsky graduated from DeWitt Clinton High School in the Bronx and was awarded a bachelor's degree in 1943 from the City College of New York. He was wounded during World War II while serving in Germany with the United States armed forces. Chayefsky began his career by writing scripts for a radio show called *Theater Guild of the Air*, which adapted plays for radio. In 1953 he became an integral part of the "Golden Age of Television" when he began writing teleplays for the *Philco Television Playhouse*, focusing on character studies of "little people" drawn from lower-middle-class New York society. Many of these hour-long plays had Jewish themes. *Holiday Song*, his first play for television, recounted the story of a cantor whose crisis of faith ended after he miraculously reunited two Holocaust survivors. Paddy Chayefsky's most famous teleplay was *Marty* (1953), which he adapted into a feature film the following year. His first Broadway play, *Middle of the Night*, dealt with a middle-aged, widowed Jewish garment manufacturer who falls in love with a much younger non-Jewish employee. Like *Marty*, the play focused on loneliness and the redemptive power of love. Chayefsky's most important theatrical effort was *The Tenth Man* (1959), loosely based on the Yiddish classic, *The Dybbuk*. His greatest popular successes came in Hollywood, where he wrote the original screenplays for *The Hospital* (1971) and *Network* (1976), both touching on the question of how modern institutions let the individual down. He is the only person ever to win three Oscars for screenwriting—for *Marty*, *The Hospital*, and *Network*. Chayefsky died at the age of fifty-eight in 1981.

COSELL, HOWARD

Born March 25, 1918, in Winston-Salem, North Carolina; died April 23, 1995.
AMERICAN SPORTS BROADCASTER.

Born Howard William Cohen, Cosell grew up in Brooklyn, hoping to become a newspaper reporter. His parents, however, urged him to enter law school. Changing his name to Cosell, Howard graduated from New York University's law school in 1940, began to practice law, and then enlisted in the United States Army in

December 1941. In 1953 an ABC Television program manager, a friend of Cosell's, asked him to host a Saturday public-service radio program in which Little League baseball players questioned professional players. Three years later, ABC offered Cosell $250 to do ten five-minute sports broadcasts each weekend. Bored by his postwar law career, Cosell eventually took up broadcasting fulltime. In response to the vocal support he gave controversial heavyweight boxer Cassius Clay (later, by the 1960s, renamed Muhammed Ali), Cosell gained much public notice—plus condemnation. In 1970 Cosell, whose voice and delivery were very distinctive, became the outspoken commentator on ABC-TV's "Monday Night Football," a job he kept for the next four-

Howard Cosell

teen years. Cosell revolutionized the sports broadcasting profession by going beyond simple play-by-play descriptions to give strong opinions on players and issues. He retired from active broadcasting in 1992. Described as "the most dominant sportscasting personality of his time," Howard Cosell was also dubbed the most famous talker in America.

DELL, MICHAEL S.

Born in February 1965, in Houston, Texas.
AMERICAN COMPUTER EXECUTIVE.

Michael Dell's mother was a financial advisor and his father an orthodontist. He studied engineering and computer science for two years at the University of Texas, but upon discovering that he was successful at selling computers from his dorm room, Dell dropped out and, with a $1,000 investment, went into business. He founded Dell Computers in 1984. His strategy of not selling computers in stores, but rather of marketing customized computers directly to consumers, proved an overwhelming success. By 2004 Michael Dell was worth $13 billion, making him the eighteenth wealthiest person in the world. Dell Computers continued to dominate the personal computer market and was capturing a significant segment of the market for servers and printers.

DOCTOROW, E.L.

Born January 6, 1931, in the Bronx, New York.
AMERICAN NOVELIST.

Edgar Laurence Doctorow is the grandson of Russian immigrants. In 1948 he graduated from the prestigious Bronx High School of Science, and in 1952 from Kenyon

College. He began to study for his master's degree at Columbia University and spent a year there, but left before completing it. In 1953 Doctorow was drafted into the United States Army, where he served in the Signal Corps for two years. After being discharged, he began working as a reader for Columbia Pictures. He started to write novels at the same time. His first, *Welcome to Hard Times* (1960), focused on an evil individual who destroys the town of Hard Times in one day. *Big as Life* (1966) was a science-fiction tale of two gigantic nude figures who travel around New York City, frightening residents. Some critics thought Doctorow used the figures to symbolize nuclear weapons, but the author was silent about his intent. Beginning in 1959, Doctorow worked as a fulltime book editor, first for New American Library, then, beginning in 1964, as editor-in-chief of Dial Press, a position he held for five years. In 1971 his next novel, *The Book of Daniel,* appeared; it dealt with the execution of the accused Jewish atomic spies, Julius and Ethel Rosenberg, and the great impact their espionage had on their two small sons. In 1975 Doctorow achieved greater recognition as a first-rate novelist with the publication of *Ragtime,* a book populated with such historical figures as Harry Houdini, Sigmund Freud, Carl Jung, Emma Goldman, Teddy Roosevelt, Woodrow Wilson, and Albert Einstein. In 1976 *Ragtime* won the National Book Circle Critics Award; it sold more than two hundred thousand copies in hardcover and was made into a successful film. By the 1970s, Doctorow had resigned from book publishing in order to write fulltime. His other books include *World's Fair* (1985), a re-creation of a Jewish boy's New York childhood in the 1930s, and *Billy Bathgate* (1989), in which the title character, a brazen youngster, insinuates himself into the inner circle of the infamous Dutch Schultz gang. Doctorow's 1994 novel *The Water Wheel,* like many of his other books, was a bestseller. His novel *City of God* appeared in 2000. In describing the book, one reviewer noted: "There's a mystery here, along with a romance, a chilling Holocaust narrative, and a deep-focus portrait of fin-de-siècle Manhattan."

DOUGLAS, KIRK

Born December 9, 1916, in Amsterdam, New York.
AMERICAN ACTOR.

Kirk Douglas was born Issur Danielovitch in the carpet-mill town of Amsterdam, New York. He began working when he was seven years old to help his family make ends meet. Anti-Semitism accompanied Douglas as a youngster; he was often beaten up on the way home from Hebrew school. Douglas began saving for a college education when he was eight years old, but gave the three hundred dollars he accumulated to his father for some other unidentified reason. In 1939 he enrolled in the American Academy of Dramatic Arts in New York City.

Kirk Douglas

He served in the United States Navy during World War II. At war's end, he returned to New York to pursue an acting career. Cast on Broadway in the role of the Unknown Soldier in *Wind Is Ninety* (1945), he gained the notice of Hollywood. He was then cast opposite the great actress Barbara Stanwyck in *The Strange Love of Martha Ivers*. The film that made Kirk Douglas a big star, however, was *Champion* (1949). Other movies followed: *The Big Sky* (1952); *Lust for Life* (1956), *Gunfight at the O.K. Corral* (1957); *Spartacus* (1958), and *Cast a Giant Shadow* (1966). In 1955 Douglas formed his own film company, Bryna Productions, named for his mother, which produced *Spartacus*. Douglas was not afraid to credit Dalton Trumbo, who was blacklisted, with the screenplay during a time when other studios were still frightened of the McCarthy witch hunts. So sensitive was the topic of mental institutions in Hollywood that Douglas fought for ten years to make *One Flew Over the Cuckoo's Nest*. When the film, produced by Kirk's eldest son, actor Michael Douglas, appeared in 1975, it won five Oscars, including Best Picture. Kirk Douglas's memoir, *The Ragman's Son* (1988), was on the bestseller list for thirty-four weeks. Since then the actor has published three well-received novels. Douglas and his wife, Anne, have four sons. No stranger to close calls, Douglas survived a helicopter crash in 1992 and suffered a stroke early in 1996. The autobiographical *Climbing the Mountain: My Search for Meaning* and *The Broken Mirror*, a story for children with a Holocaust theme, were both published in September 1997. In *Climbing the Mountain*, Douglas confessed that the most important thing he learned from his Torah studies was that all of the major biblical figures came from dysfunctional families. "That made me happy. It was reassuring to find out that they, like us, all had problems that they had to overcome." In 1997 a deeply depressed Douglas acknowledged putting a gun in his mouth and considering suicide. In 2003 he and son Michael costarred in *It Runs in the Family*, a film about a dysfunctional New York family and their attempts to reconcile.

DREYFUS, ALFRED

Born in 1859 in Mulhouse, Alsace, France; died in 1935.
FRENCH ARMY OFFICER.

The name Alfred Dreyfus is one of the best-known in modern Jewish history, symbolizing the victims of the true evils of anti-Semitism. Dreyfus was accused of treason and became the central figure in the famous Dreyfus Affair, a legal case that divided France, and created fresh worldwide revulsion against anti-Semitism. Dreyfus studied at the École Polytechnique and joined the army as an engineer, achieving a lieutenant's rank. Despite anti-Semitic pressures, he was appointed captain on the general staff, the only Jew. In 1894 a French intelligence agent discovered what he thought was a suspicious document in the wastebasket of the German military attaché; the paper contained a promise to deliver a secret French artillery manual to the Germans. An intelligence chief, Major Hubert Joseph Henry, argued persuasively that Dreyfus had been behind the espionage, although experts could not identify the handwriting on the document in question. Indicted for treason, Dreyfus was forced to face a military court martial. The court had difficulty reaching a verdict but, perhaps influenced by public opinion, which favored a conviction, Dreyfus was found guilty, expelled from the army, and sentenced to life imprisonment in exile. Having been publicly humiliated, he was transferred, in chains, in disgrace, to a prison on Devil's Island, off the coast of Guyana, South America. He continued to protest his innocence. Strong evidence that another person was responsible for the deed that Dreyfus was convicted of led to that individual's trial, but he was found innocent. After the famous novelist Émile Zola published an open letter entitled *"J'Accuse"* ("I Accuse") in the newspaper *L'Aurore*, in which he accused those who denounced Dreyfus of malicious libel, Zola himself was found guilty of libel and had to flee to England. The article, however, convinced French authorities that Dreyfus had been unfairly convicted. In the summer of 1898, the continued uproar over the case led a new war minister to reopen the case. When Henry, Dreyfus's original accuser, was shown evidence that the charges against Dreyfus had been based on forgery, he committed suicide. Dreyfus was then brought back to France to stand trial for a second time. He was again found guilty, but this time his jail sentence was reduced to ten years. With solid evidence that he had been framed, Dreyfus was soon pardoned and, seven years after the second trial, exonerated by a court of appeal. Distressed by the Catholic Church's encouragement of anti-Semitism, a new French government legislated the separation of church and state, one of the most significant developments in the continuing Dreyfus Affair. Dreyfus was reinstated as a major in the army; he retired a year later, but rejoined the army during World War I and was promoted to lieutenant colonel in 1916. He was awarded the Legion of Honor, also in 1916. After the war, Dreyfus retired and lived in Paris. He died at the age of seventy-six in 1935. In September 1995 the French military acknowledged that Dreyfus had been framed and was, after all, innocent.

DUBINSKY, DAVID

Born February 22, 1892, in Brest-Litovsk, Russia; died September 17, 1982.
AMERICAN LABOR LEADER.

Although Russian by birth, the famed labor leader grew up in Lodz, a largely industrial, slum-infested city in Poland. Dubinsky attended school only until age eleven; he then began to work as a baker, following in the footsteps of his eight older brothers. Having observed the exploitation of workers firsthand, Dubinsky supported the idea of a bakers' union, and when one was founded, he became its secretary, mainly because he was one of the few members literate in both Polish and Yiddish. The bakers called a strike, and Dubinsky, along with other union organizers, was arrested; his activism would land him in jail more than once.

Fleeing to New York in 1911, Dubinsky became a member of the Cutters' Union of the International Ladies Garment Workers Union (ILGWU), quickly rising to leadership status and eventually being elected to its general executive board. In 1932 he became the union's president, holding that position until 1966. By then, the ILGWU had overcome its financial troubles and become a major force in the U.S. Under Dubinsky's helm, the union was a pioneer in gaining pensions, welfare, and paid vacations for its workers.

DUBNOW, SIMON

Born in 1860 in Mstislavl, Russia; died in 1941.
RUSSIAN HISTORIAN.

Simon Dubnow's life work was the study of Jewish history and its sociological interpretation. He succeeded Heinrich Graetz as the Jewish "national" historian, but as a secularist, he rebelled against all religious attachments. Dubnow received a traditional Jewish education, but at age eleven he tired of religion and traveled to Dvinsk, Vilna, and to St. Petersburg in search of a secular education. In 1880, when he was twenty years old, Dubnow moved to Odessa, then a great center of Jewish literature. In 1903 he moved to Vilna and later to Matislaw. By 1906 he finally settled in St. Petersburg, where he held a chair in Jewish history at a progressive university there. Dubnow regarded Jews not as a religious community but as a sociological concept. To him, Jewish history was the recounting of the history of autonomous centers of Jewish national creation and hegemony; at any given time one of those centers could become more dominant and creative than the others. He was not clear which part of the Jewish world he thought should become such a center in the near future, but he seemed to suggest that he did not favor Palestine as the leading choice. In Dubnow's view, Judaism was the highest form of culture. Rejecting the Zionist movement, he believed that the entire world was the homeland of the Jews. His book *History of Hasidism* (1930) urged Jews to cooperate with other nations through the adoption of a secular culture. In 1922 he left Russia for Berlin. Publication of his ten-volume history of the Jews, *World History of the Jewish People*, occurred between 1925 and 1929. After Hitler's rise to power, Dubnow returned to Russia and settled in Riga. In 1941, when the Nazis rounded up the Jews of Riga, Dubnow was shot by a drunken Latvian guard. His final words were: "Brothers, don't forget! Recount what you hear and see—record it all."

EBAN, ABBA

Born February 2, 1915, in Cape Town, South Africa; died November 17, 2002.
ISRAELI DIPLOMAT.

Abba Eban was born Aubrey Solomon and educated at Queens College, Cambridge. He was brilliant in the study of language and an outstanding orator and debater. In

1942 Eban served the Jewish community in Jerusalem as Allied Headquarters' Liaison Officer for the training of volunteers. In 1944 he became Chief Instructor at the Middle East Arab Center in Jerusalem. Taking on political tasks after World War II, he joined the Jewish Agency in 1946 and was Liaison Officer with the United Nations Special Committee on Palestine the year after. For the next thirteen years, Eban served abroad in different capacities for the state of Israel. He in effect became the chief spokesman for the fledgling state and, with his gift for language and oratory, was able to articulate the Jewish state's case with great effectiveness—at the United Nations, on American television, and before other American audiences. Eban was appointed representative of the Provisional Government of Israel to the U.N. in 1948; from 1949 to 1959, he was Israel's Permanent Representative to the U.N.; from 1950 to 1959, he also served as Israel's ambassador to the United States. Eban yearned to return to Israel and become a political leader there, but the years spent abroad and his lofty manner of speech gave him little electoral appeal. He spent the years from 1958 to 1966 as president of the Weizmann Institute in Rehovot. In 1959 he was elected to the Knesset (parliament) for the first time, as a member of the ruling Mapai party. He joined the cabinet in 1959 as minister without portfolio, served as minister for education and culture from 1960 to 1963, and as deputy prime minister from 1963 to 1966. He was minister for foreign affairs from 1966 to 1974, serving during both the 1967 Six-Day War and the 1973 Yom Kippur War. Together with Prime Minister Golda Meir and Defense Minister Moshe Dayan, Eban was forced to resign from the government in March 1974 because of overwhelming public criticism of the government for permitting Israel to be caught so unprepared on the eve of the Yom Kippur War. Eban returned briefly to the limelight when he was chairman of the Knesset Foreign Affairs and Security Committee in 1984. He wrote a number of well-received books and memoirs, especially *Voice of Israel* (1957), *My People* (1968), *My Country* (1972), *The New Diplomacy* (1983), *Personal Witness* (1990), and *Diplomacy for a Next Century*, (1998).

ESHKOL, LEVI

Born October 25, 1895, in Oratowo, Ukraine; died February 21, 1969.
ISRAELI POLITICAL LEADER.

Levi Eshkol's original family name was Shkolnik; his father was a poverty-stricken schoolteacher. When Levi was nineteen years old, in 1914, he left home to join other Jewish idealists going to Palestine and was one of the early settlers of Kibbutz Degania Bet on Lake Kinneret (the Sea of Galilee). He quickly showed talent as a manager, taking charge of the kibbutz's successful farming and industrial enterprises. He was appointed head of the agriculture section of the Jewish Agency, in effect the "minister of agriculture" of the Jewish community in Palestine. After the state of Israel was established, Eshkol was appointed minister of agriculture; then, from 1952 to 1963, minister of finance; and in 1963, prime minister. He led the country prior to, and during, the 1967 Six-Day War. Eshkol's apparent lack of confidence on the eve of the war was sadly reflected in his infamous radio address to the nation on May 28, 1967, during which he frequently stammered and lost his place, and seemed generally unsure of himself. Yet Eshkol did lead his country to one of its most important military victories against overwhelming odds. He was not a great orator, but was down-to-earth and got along well with all kinds of people. His philosophy was that there was no time to waste, the state had to be built; homes and factories had to be constructed immediately so that immigrants could be absorbed properly. One of Eshkol's proudest achievements was the completion of the National Water Carrier Project, which enabled large supplies of water to be brought from the northern part of the country to the arid south. He died in February 1969 at the age of seventy-four.

FOX, WILLIAM

Born January 1, 1879, in Hungary; died in 1952.
AMERICAN FILM EXECUTIVE.

William Fox's original last name was Fried; before his first birthday, he was brought from his native Hungary to the United States. As a young adult, he sensed that motion pictures were going to become a huge industry, and he began acquiring movie houses when he was in his twenties. Realizing that the suppliers of films were making a good deal of money, Fox started the Greater New York Film Rental Company. He became one of the most successful of the independent film distributors. In 1914 he entered film production, calling his new firm the Box Office Attractions Film Rental Company, which became more widely recognized under its later name—Fox Film Corporation. In 1916 Fox moved to Hollywood and headed his own movie studio, where his films featured such stars as Theda Bara and Tom Mix. During the 1920s, Fox brought the German director F. W. Murnau to the United States to work on his films. He also helped to nourish the talents of American directors John Ford and Howard Hawks. Fox's was the first Hollywood studio to adopt a sound-on-film system. Nearly four months before the first talkie appeared on screen (Warner Brothers' *The Jazz Singer*, 1927), the Fox Movietone newsreel enabled American audiences to hear as well as to see such newsmakers as Charles Lindbergh, the great American aviator, on the big screen with accompanying voiceovers. By 1929 Fox had acquired numerous movie theaters, including one of the largest in the world, the Roxy in New York City, as well as the rights to both American and foreign sound-on-film systems. He also purchased controlling interest in Loew's, the parent company of MGM. By the 1930s, Fox's rivals had ousted him from his own company. In 1936 just one year after Darryl F. Zanuck's Twentieth Century Productions had merged with the Fox Film Corporation, William Fox declared bankruptcy. In 1941 he was convicted of an attempt to bribe a judge presiding over his bankruptcy hearing and he spent six months in prison. Fox died at the age of seventy-three in 1952.

GAON, SAADIAH BEN JOSEPH

Born in 882 C.E. Upper Egypt; died in 942 C.E.
BABYLONIAN COMMUNITY LEADER.

Born to a poor family, Saadiah Gaon moved to Tiberias in Palestine as a young man. By the time he was twenty, he had completed a Hebrew dictionary and rhyming lexicon, and had written a polemic against the schismatic Karaites, who had rejected rabbinical Judaism. Living for a while in Syria, Saadiah later settled in Sura, Babylonia, where he taught at the academy. He and the leading scholar in Palestine, Aaron ben Meir, differed over who should regulate the Jewish calendar—the Babylonian Jewish community or the one in Palestine. The Babylonians won out, implying the supremacy of the Babylonians over the Palestinian sages. By 928, Saadiah Gaon had became head of the academy, making important contributions to most branches of Jewish knowledge. He translated the Bible into Arabic for the first time and added his own commentary, helping Jews of the Arabic-speaking world gain a greater understanding of Judaism. He devised a fresh way of studying the Bible by trying to ascertain the literal meaning of the text. His goal was to make the Bible accessible not only to Arabic-speaking Jews but to the world of Islam as well. So appealing was the Arabic translation that it was read along with the Hebrew text of the Torah in the synagogue. Gaon was also a Talmudic authority whose decisions were legally binding. He produced the first authoritative *siddur*, or prayer book, for worshipers. His most famous theological work is called *Sefer Emunot v'Deot* (*Book of Beliefs and Opinions*). He attempted to show that Judaism's most basic beliefs can be explained by reason and that the Torah should be regarded as revealed reason.

GOLDBERG, ARTHUR

Born August 8, 1908, in Chicago, Illinois; died January 19, 1990.
UNITED STATES SUPREME COURT JUSTICE AND CABINET MEMBER.

Arthur Goldberg

Library of Congress

The youngest of eleven children, Goldberg was the first in his family to graduate from high school. He attended a community college and then DePaul University. He graduated, however, from Northwestern University in 1929. The following year he was awarded a doctorate in law, graduating first in his class. Goldberg entered private practice and soon became deeply involved in the labor issues growing out of the aftermath of the Depression and New Deal programs. He became the legal adviser to most of Chicago's union leaders. During World War II, Goldberg was director of the labor division of the Office of Strategic Services. In 1949 he was general counsel for two major unions, the

Congress of Industrial Organizations (CIO) and the United Steelworkers (USW). In 1955 he was a primary negotiator in the merger between the CIO and the American Federation of Labor (AFL). Newly-elected president John F. Kennedy selected Goldberg as his secretary of labor in 1961. The following year, Kennedy nominated Goldberg to serve on the Supreme Court, giving him the so-called Jewish seat previously held by the retiring Felix Frankfurter. Goldberg frequently took the liberal side of issues. For instance, he voted to reverse the convictions of civil rights sit-in demonstrators and in a major Florida case he reversed the contempt conviction of a leader of the National Association for the Advancement of Colored People from Miami who had refused to provide membership rosters to state officials. In 1965 Goldberg resigned from the Supreme Court after President Lyndon B. Johnson urged him to become the new United States Ambassador to the United Nations, a position he accepted. Goldberg incurred the wrath of Arab representatives when he called for a cease-fire at the time of the 1967 Six-Day War without stipulating that Israel withdraw from occupied territories. In 1968 Goldberg resigned from the U.N. post over a disagreement with President Johnson's policies in Vietnam and returned to his private law practice in New York. From 1963 to 1969, Goldberg was chairman of the Jewish Theological Seminary board of overseers, and in 1968–69 he was president of the American Jewish Committee. In 1970 Goldberg ran unsuccessfully for governor of New York State. He died at the age of eighty-two in 1990.

GOLDMANN, NAHUM

Born July 10, 1895, in Visznevo, Lithuania; died August 29, 1982.
ZIONIST LEADER.

Nahum Goldmann

State of Israel Government Press Office

Nahum Goldmann was born in Lithuania, but was educated in Germany, where he received a law degree from the University of Heidelberg in 1920 and a doctorate in 1921. A skilled linguist and diplomat, Goldmann devoted his life to lobbying for Jewish causes. He was a cofounder (along with Jacob Klatzkin) of the Eshkol Press, which between 1928 and 1934 published ten volumes of the *Encyclopedia Judaica* in German and two volumes in Hebrew. After World War I, while the Versailles Peace Treaty was being drafted, Goldmann worked for the Committee of Jewish Delegations, trying to protect Jewish rights in Palestine. In 1935 he traveled to New York to represent the Jewish Agency at the League of Nations. In 1936 the Committee of Jewish Delegations became the World Jewish Congress (WJC); Goldmann served as its president from 1936 to 1977. He served as president of the World Zionist Organization from 1956 to 1968. Laboring aggressively on behalf of the state of Israel, Goldmann was controversial and iconoclastic; he rarely hesitated to speak his mind. For instance, he assailed the Jewish state for failing to recognize the legitimacy of Diaspora Judaism and for not taking into account Arab rights. Goldmann was best known for the crucial role he played in negotiating German reparations after World War II. He first organized the centralized Conference on Jewish Material Claims. He then met, in December 1951, with West Germany's Chancellor Konrad Adenauer and created the framework for a settlement that called for payments in cash and goods to the state of Israel as well as to individual Jewish claimants. It was one of his most important achievements. Goldmann died at the age of eighty-seven in 1982.

GOMPERS, SAMUEL

Born in 1850 in London, England; died in 1924.
AMERICAN LABOR LEADER.

Samuel Gompers was born into a working-class family in London and as a forceful, energetic labor leader had an overwhelming impact upon the development of the American labor movement. He entered the Jewish Free School at the age of six, where he studied Hebrew, Talmud, reading, writing, and arithmetic. When he was ten, his family was unable to afford to continue with his schooling so Samuel became an apprentice shoemaker, earning sixpence a day. He then served as an apprentice cigar maker, working in his father's trade. In 1863, at the age of thirteen, Gompers immigrated with his family to the Lower East Side of New York City. There he joined the local branch of the Cigar Makers' National Union and, while in his twenties, became one of its leaders. In 1886 Gompers played a crucial role in creating the American Federation of Labor (AFL) and served as its president, virtually uninterrupted, from its founding until 1924. He also edited the AFL journal from 1894 for thirty years, until his death at the age of seventy-four. Gompers became the spokesman for organized labor in the United States. He adhered to the popular slogan "Reward your friends and punish your enemies." Though an immigrant, he favored restrictions on immigration in order to protect the American working force. Gompers had a strong personality and was known for dominating any meeting he attended. He opposed socialism and was convinced that the American worker would be best served by using the capitalist techniques of collective bargaining and direct negotiation with employers. In 1896 William Jennings Bryan sought the support of organized labor in his presidential bid. Promising Gompers a cabinet post in exchange for his support, Bryan failed to win it because the labor leader opposed the politicization of the labor movement. During World War I, Gompers mobilized support for the American war effort within the labor movement and was appointed by President Woodrow Wilson to the Commission for International Labor Legislation, whose goal was to achieve better labor laws.

GREENBERG, HENRY "HANK"

Born January 1, 1911, in New York City; died September 4, 1986.
AMERICAN BASEBALL PLAYER.

Hank Greenberg was the son of Orthodox Jewish parents from Romania who immigrated to the United States. He attended James Monroe High School in the Bronx and was an athletic star who lettered in four sports. He began playing baseball for the Bay Parkways in New York and eventually became one of baseball's greatest right-handed hitters. In baseball's first century (1839–1939), Greenberg is generally considered the best Jewish player. He played for the Detroit Tigers from 1933 to 1947, and the Pittsburgh Pirates in 1947. His career batting average was .313 in 1,394 games. He had 1,628 hits in 5,191 at-bats, with 331 home runs (including 11 grand-slam homers) and 1,276 runs batted in (RBIs). Greenberg was the first National Leaguer to earn one hundred thousand dollars a year. He was Most Valuable Player in both 1935 and 1940, and was selected to the All-Star teams every year from 1937 to 1940. He led the American League in home runs and in RBIs four times. In 1934, as the season neared its autumn finale, Detroit was in a tight pennant race, and fans were concerned that if Greenberg did not play on Yom Kippur, the Jewish Day of Atonement, the team's chances of winning the pennant would fade. When Yom Kippur arrived, Greenberg refused to play and although the Tigers lost the game, he won the city's respect. The Tigers went on to win the pennant, but lost the World Series. Hank Greenberg died at the age of seventy-six in 1986.

GREENSPAN, ALAN

Born March 6, 1926, in New York City.
CHAIRMAN OF THE FEDERAL RESERVE BOARD.

A child of the Depression who rose to become one of the most influential Americans of the late twentieth and early twenty-first centuries, Alan Greenspan was President Gerald Ford's chief economic adviser during the mid 1970s and became chairman of the Federal Reserve Board shortly before the stock market crash of 1987. Often dubbed the second most powerful man in America, he is the son of a stockbroker and retail worker. After high school, Greenspan studied music at the Juilliard School, and his first job was as a clarinet and saxophone player in a swing band. At age nineteen, he became an economics student at New York University, obtaining a B.A. *summa cum laude* in 1948; he received a doctorate from the same school in 1977. Greenspan and bond trader William Townsend founded a financial consulting firm, New York's Townsend-Greenspan & Co. Inc., which flourished until 1987, when Greenspan dissolved the firm to become the Federal Reserve chairman. He remained at that post through four presidencies; he was expected to serve until 2009. As Fed chief, Greenspan controls U.S. monetary policy by influencing short-term interest rates and, in turn, the cost of credit to American companies and consumers. Every word he utters publicly about the economy affects the stock market. He married his second wife, NBC journalist Andrea Mitchell, in April 1997.

HALEVI, JUDAH

Born circa 1075 in Toledo (Or Tudela), Spain; died in 1141.
SPANISH RELIGIOUS THINKER AND POET.

Judah Halevi was one of the great Jewish poets of the Middle Ages. (The other major one was Solomon Ibn Gibirol.) Halevi was born to a family of means either in Toledo or Tudela, Spain. He received both a rabbinical and a secular education and became a doctor in Toledo. The Christian persecution of Jews in Toledo forced him to move to Cordova, where he continued to work as a physician. Halevi was also a poet; his early works were mainly secular in subject matter, dealing with friendship and love, marriage, and riddles. He developed an increasing awareness of the plight of Jews and, later, his poetry became filled with religious references. His series of *Songs of Zion* spoke of the tragedy of the Jews as a homeless people and of his love for Zion. Halevi wrote many religious poems as he grew older; among them were poems that became part of the liturgy. He is also famous for a prose work called *Sefer ha Kuzari* (*The Book of the Khazars*), which was written in Arabic and based on the story of the conversion to Judaism of the Khazars, a tribe in the lower Volga region. *Kuzari* became one of the most popular Jewish books of theology. To Judah Halevi, Judaism was superior to other religions because it was the basis upon which other religions had been founded. Because of this, Jews, as the fount of spirituality in the world, had a special obligation to the world to behave in a particular way, he believed. When Jews suffered, it was meant, in his view, to be an act of purification, one which would precede their eventual return to their land. Halevi had a deep yearning to move to the Land of Israel, believing that only there could he lead a full Jewish life. Setting out to accomplish this, he reached Egypt, but was delayed there for some time, never reaching Israel and thus unable to fulfill his dream. He died in Egypt while in his sixties.

HECHT, BEN

Born February 28, 1894, in New York City; died April 18, 1964.
AMERICAN SCREENWRITER, PLAYWRIGHT, NOVELIST.

Ben Hecht was born on New York City's Lower East Side to Russian immigrant parents; he grew up speaking Yiddish. The family moved to Racine, Wisconsin, when Hecht was still a youngster. Years later, after three days at the University of Wisconsin Ben dropped out, convinced he could learn more in the outside world. He was only sixteen at the time. He went to Chicago, on his own, and began working as a journalist, first for the *Chicago Journal*, then for the *Chicago Daily News*, which sent him to Berlin as a correspondent from 1918 to 1920. Hecht's first novel, *Eric Dorn*, was published in 1921 and was based on his experiences in Berlin. Back in New York, Hecht teamed with Charles MacArthur to write the highly successful play *The Front Page* (1928), which was the duo's most famous joint literary work. A popular play to this day, it took a cynical, romanticized view of journalism. Hecht was most famous for his screenwriting. He was the first Hollywood writer to earn a thousand dollars a day and he became the highest-paid script writer of his era. He said screenwriting was no harder than "a game of pinochle." Thanks to his scripts for *Underworld* (1927) and *Scarface* (1932), Hecht has been credited with inventing the gangster film. *Underworld* won the first Oscar for best original story. Hecht, unimpressed by the honor, used the Oscar statuette for a doorstop. He also wrote the scripts for two of Alfred Hitchcock's most famous movies, *Spellbound* (1946) and *Notorious* (1948). Credited on screen in only a small number of the 150 films on which he actually worked, Hecht was known for his speed in writing, and was said to have written the first nine reels of *Gone with the Wind* (for which he was given no screen credit) in a week, although he had not read the novel. The infamous book *A Jew in Love* (1931), one of his eleven novels, dealt with Jewish self-hatred. He expressed regret at writing it; he was never able to live it down. He had all but discarded his Jewishness until the 1930s, when Hitler's rise to power encouraged him to become a zealous defender of the Jewish faith, even though he was opposed to Zionism. Disillusioned with David Ben-Gurion's pre-state policies, Hecht accused him of being cowardly toward the British. Hecht wrote a vicious attack on Zionism, a book called *Perfidy* (1961), which was boycotted in both Israel and Great Britain. He died in 1964 at the age of seventy.

HEIFETZ, JASCHA

Born February 2, 1901, in Vilna, Russia; died December 23, 1987.
AMERICAN VIOLINIST.

A child prodigy, Jascha Heifetz began studying the violin at the age of three. During his lifetime, he was considered one of the greatest masters of the violin. Heifetz's father, Ruvin, was thrilled to learn that his young son stopped crying whenever music was played. Buying his three-year-old son a violin, Ruvin Heifetz was astonished at the child's progress in just a year. When Heifetz's father asked Elias Malkin, a professor at the Royal School of Music in Vilna, whether his son was ready for formal training, Malkin at first suggested that they wait three years—until he heard the child play; Malkin accepted him as a student at once. Heifetz first performed publicly at age seven. When he was nine years old, he played in a variety of Russian cities and needed police protection to escape from the enthusiastic crowds. He studied with Leopold Auer at the age of ten and performed with the Berlin Philharmonic at age eleven. He embarked on his first European concert tour in 1914. His New York debut came at the age of sixteen and established him at once as one of the world's musical greats. On October 27, 1917, musicians came from great distances to hear him play at Carnegie Hall. Before he finished his first selection, thunderous applause swept the hall. Heifetz performed in Russia during the Russian Revolution, in Ireland during the Sinn Fein uprising, and in Japan during an earthquake. In 1925 he performed in Tel Aviv, donating his concert fees to the promotion of music in that city. Heifetz returned to Russia in 1934 for the first time in seventeen years and devoted admirers came from remote Siberian outposts to hear him play. "That," said Heifetz, "was the greatest emotional experience of my life." George Bernard Shaw once visited Heifetz backstage after a London recital and scolded him for playing too perfectly. "Nothing may be perfect in the world or the gods become jealous and destroy it. So would you mind playing one wrong note every night before you go to bed?" Shaw said. It was impossible for Heifetz to comply with the request. In Israel, in 1953, Heifetz played a work by Richard Strauss, whose works were not performed in the Jewish state because of the composer's connections to Nazism. An angry Israeli assaulted Heifetz with an iron bar outside Jerusalem's King David Hotel, slightly injuring his arm, but the injury caused no permanent harm, nor did it interfere with his playing. By 1947, at forty-six years old, Heifetz had played one hundred thousand hours of concert time and traveled two million miles touring. He summed up his life by saying that "I played the violin at three and gave my first concert at seven. I have been playing ever since." When he stopped playing publicly, Heifetz became reclusive and granted no interviews. He died in 1987 at the age of eighty-six.

HERSHKO, AVRAHAM AND CIECHANOVER, AHARON

Hershko: *Born December 31, 1937, in Karcag, Hungary.*
Ciechanover: *Born October 1, 1947, in Haifa, Israel.*
ISRAELI BIOCHEMISTS.

Avraham Hershko and Aharon Ciechanover became the first two Israelis to win a Nobel Prize in the sciences when they captured the chemistry award in December 2004, sharing the $1.25 million prize with Professor Irwin Rose of the University of California. Hershko and Ciechanover's research, conducted in the 1980s, aimed at determining how the human body marks faulty proteins for destruction in order to defend against illnesses such as cancer. The Israeli-born Ciechanover directs the Rappaport Family Institute for Research in Medical Sciences at Haifa's Technion, where the Hungarian-born Hershko is a professor. The duo discovered that potentially threatening proteins are "marked" for destruction by a molecule called *ubiquitin*, which sends the proteins to the body's "waste disposal" units known as *proteasomes*; there, the marked proteins are chopped to pieces. When such degradation does not work properly, degenerative brain diseases, cervical cancer, and cystic fibrosis can develop. "We are not a building that stays still; we are all the time exchanging our proteins, synthesizing and destroying them," said Ciechanover. "Some proteins get spoiled. We discovered the process by which the body exercises quality control." Although the work of Hershko and Ciechanover has already led to the development of numerous drugs for degenerative diseases and malignancies, Ciechanover said his work has never been motivated by economic considerations, pointing instead to his pride in contributing to Israel's strong reputation in medical research. "I have never thought of money. We earn very small salaries in Israel," he said. "It is more the honor for Israel, for myself, that a small country can make it. . . . I am as proud for myself as I am for my country."

HERZOG, CHAIM

Born September 17, 1918, in Belfast, Northern Ireland.
PRESIDENT OF THE STATE OF ISRAEL AND MILITARY COMMENTATOR.

Chaim Herzog was the son of Rabbi Isaac Herzog, the Chief Rabbi of Israel (1921 to 1936) and later of Palestine and Israel (2936 to 1948). After studying at the Merkaz HaRav and Hebron yeshivas, and at the Government of Palestine High School of Law, Herzog completed his education at the University of London and Cambridge University. Herzog served in the Haganah during 1936-1939 Arab Revolt, and during World War II, in the British Army in Europe. In 1948, he became operations officer in the 7th Brigade of the Israel Defense Forces (IDF) during Israel's War of Independence. From 1948 to 1950, and from 1959 to 1963, Herzog was head of military intelligence of the IDF. From 1950 to 1954, he served as military attaché in Washington, D.C. He was commanding officer of the Jerusalem district from 1957 to 1959 and commander of the Southern Command from 1957 to 1959. He retired from the IDF in 1962, and spent the next ten years as managing director of an investment firm. In 1965 Herzog joined David Ben-Gurion's breakaway Rafi party. By 1967 he had begun work as the military commentator for Israel Radio. Among his best-known achievements were the detailed, calmly delivered, and authoritative military commentaries he provided during the 1967 and 1973 Israeli-Arab wars. Following the Six-Day War, Herzog became military governor of the West Bank and Jerusalem. He was a senior partner in a Tel Aviv law firm from 1972 to 1983. Between 1975 and 1978, he served as Israel's ambassador to the United Nations. In November 1975, when the U.N. General Assembly adopted the "Zionism Equals Racism" resolution, Herzog angrily tore up the text of the resolution in public. In 1981 he was elected to the Knesset (parliament) as a Labor party member, and in 1983 he was chosen Israel's sixth president, serving in that position for the next decade. Herzog was most proud of having developed close contacts with the Israeli Arab community, In *Living History: A Memoir*, published in 1996, Herzog wrote: "During all my years in the military, in Security, in politics, in the law, in journalism, in economics, in diplomacy, and in government, I was inspired by my belief in the eternity of Israel and the compulsion to work toward it. Beyond every setback I see the saga of remarkable achievements in every field of life. The tragedies that befell the Jewish people in my lifetime have no equal. But our victories and achievements have surpassed the dreams of generation." Herzog died of heart failure as a result of pneumonia on April 17, 1997. He was seventy-eight years old.

HESCHEL, ABRAHAM JOSHUA

Born in 1907 in Warsaw, Poland; died December 23, 1972.
AMERICAN PHILOSOPHER AND JEWISH SCHOLAR.

Abraham Heschel was the heir to a Hasidic dynasty. As a young adult, he moved from his native Warsaw to Germany, where he studied philosophy at the University of Berlin. In 1938 he was expelled from Germany with all other Polish Jews who did not hold German citizenship, and was brought to Cincinnati, Ohio, in 1940, when he was thirty-three years old, by the Reform movement's Hebrew Union College. He devoted most of his scholarship to his heritage. After teaching at Hebrew Union College in Cincinnati for five years, Heschel became a faculty member of New York's Jewish Theological Seminary of America, the seminary of Conservative Judaism. He remained there until his death in 1972 at the age of sixty-five. Heschel proved a maverick, fitting in with neither Reform nor Conservative Judaism's mainstreams. His book *God in Search of Man: A Philosophy of Judaism* (1955) articulated his belief that the Jewish religion is grounded in God's search for human righteousness and spiritual yearning, not in man's need for cosmic order. He attacked those who reduced Judaism to a series of inert rules and perfunctory rituals. He exposed an entire generation of Jews to "aggadic" Judaism, with its focus on interpersonal concern and spiritual quest in contrast with halachic (legal) obligations. "Man is not for the sake of good deeds," Heschel wrote. "The good deeds are for the sake of man. Judaism asks for more than works, for more than the *opus operatum*. The goal is not that a ceremony be performed; the goal is that man be transformed—to worship the Holy in order to be holy. The purpose of the *mitzvot* (God's commandments) is to sanctify man . . . ." From the mid-1950s until his death, Heschel supported a number of political causes, advocating fair housing, care for the aged, educational reform, and progress for African-Americans.

HIRSCH, SAMUEL

Born in 1815 in Thalfang, Prussia; died in 1889.
AMERICAN REFORM RABBI.

Samuel Hirsch was a leader of both the German and American Reform Jewish movements. He was born in Prussia and studied at universities in Berlin, Bonn, and Leipzig. Chief rabbi of Luxembourg from 1843 to 1866, he became a leader of American Reform Judaism. When he was twenty-seven years old, Hirsch published *The Jewish Philosophy of Religion* (1842), which attempted to put Judaism side by side with Christianity as "absolute religions" in order to give both religions equal validity. He saw Christianity's function as proclaiming God to a pagan world and called it an "extensive" religiosity; Judaism, on the other hand, in his view, was an "intensive" religiosity since it already had God in its midst. Hirsch stressed social justice and this emphasis became a central part of the American Jewish Reform movement.

HUROK, SOL

Born April 9, 1888, in Pogar, Russia; died March 5, 1974.
AMERICAN IMPRESARIO.

Sol Hurok came to the United States from Russia in 1906, when he was eighteen years old, with only three rubles in his pocket. At first he held a series of jobs, including peddling needles and running a streetcar, but, after deciding that what he really liked was listening to music, Hurok hoped for a career in that field. He started to arrange concerts for clubs and labor organizations. Soon, whenever a charity group in Brooklyn wanted to organize a concert, Hurok was asked to make the arrangements. By age twenty-one he was renting Madison Square Garden in New York and offering concerts there. In 1914, when he was twenty-five, Hurok became a naturalized American citizen. By 1916 he was routinely presenting important artists at New York's Hippodrome Theater, the early signs of his growing talent as an impresario. He organized concerts for labor organizations and arranged an appearance by the well-known violinist Efrem Zimbalist as a benefit performance for the Socialist party. He coined the frequently quoted expression, "When people don't want to come, nothing will stop them." He became best known for his importing of foreign talent. It was Hurok who organized the American visits of the *Habimah* Theater (1926) and the Moscow Art Players (1935). He also arranged tours for Britain's Sadlers' Wells Ballet, France's D'Oyly Carte Opera Company, and the Russian Bolshoi and Kirov ballet companies. "S. Hurok Presents" was a phrase that grew more and more familiar as he increased his bookings. Performers he presented included Isadora Duncan, Anna Pavlova, Feodor Chaliapin, Isaac Stern, Maria Callas, and Rudolf Nureyev. Hurok treated each star grandly and with consideration. He also discovered performers who went on to great fame, such as the contralto Marian Anderson. In 1953 a Hollywood movie, *Tonight We Sing*, told Sol Hurok's life story. He had become legendary by this time. He retired in 1969 and died at the age of eighty-six in 1974.

IBN EZRA, MOSES

Born circa 1055 in Granada, Spain; died 1135.
SPANISH HEBREW-LANGUAGE POET.

Moses Ibn Ezra's family was well established in Granada, Spain; his three brothers were well-known scholars. Ibn Ezra obtained a solid Jewish and Arabic education. When the Jewish community in Granada was destroyed in 1090 by fanatic Moslems, Ibn Ezra escaped, wandering throughout Spain for much of his life. He spent a good deal of time searching for patrons to back his literary efforts. At one stage he fell in love with his niece, but his father insisted that she marry Ibn Ezra's younger brother. The sadness Ibn Ezra felt as a result of the outcome of this love affair influenced his poetry. He has been described as one of the great masters of Hebrew-language poetry; he produced more than 300 secular poems and 220 religious ones. His poetry was filled with a morose feeling, but some of it was also cheerful. For example: "A beautiful woman, a cup of wine, a lovely garden, the song of a bird, the murmur of a brook, are the cure of the lover, the joy of the lonely, the wealth of the poor, and the medicine for the sick." *Sefer hanak (Necklace)* is his most famous secular work, with its 1,210 verse couplets. Each line ends in a homonym. One work that he wrote in Arabic on rhetoric and poetics became a key source concerning the Hebrew-language poetry of medieval Spain. His religious verses were his most important contribution, particularly his penitential poems (*Selichot*). Ibn Ezra's poetry expresses Jewish sadness at being in exile and urges people to examine their behavior. Many of his poems can be found in Sephardic prayer books. He died in 1135 at roughly the age of eighty.

ISSERLES, MOSES

Born in 1525 in Cracow, Poland; died in 1572.
SCHOLAR OF RELIGIOUS LAW.

Moses Isserles's father, Israel, was a well-to-do leader of the Cracow community in Poland. Isserles was born there, then went to Lublin to study. He returned to Cracow to become its chief rabbi, a position he held until his death at the age of forty-seven in 1572. Moses Isserles, known by the acronym Rema, was considered an authority on Judaism because of his prodigious learning as well as his wealth and social position. Many people throughout Europe had great respect for the rabbinic academy that he founded in Cracow. His replies to queries on subjects of rabbinic law, known as *responsa*, helped build his scholarly reputation. Accepted as authoritative, his decisions were known for the leniency they reflected, particularly when it came to the underprivileged classes. Isserles wrote commentaries on the Bible and rabbinic literature. It was, however, his supplements to the work of Joseph Caro, his contemporary, for which he is best remembered. Caro published a comprehensive work on Jewish law called *Beit Yoseph* (*The House of Joseph*). Isserles then wrote *Darchei Moshe*, (*The Ways of Moses*), which was meant to serve both as commentary and critique of Joseph Caro's work. Isserles emphasized the significance of local custom in Jewish law; he also made it clear that he felt that the views and practices of the Central European, or Ashkenazi, rabbis and communities should not be ignored; Caro had neglected them because he had been writing out of the Sephardi (Spanish) tradition. When Caro published his *Shulchan Aruch* (*Prepared Table*), a shortened version of *Beit Yoseph*, Isserles was concerned that Ashkenazi Jews would accept it as authoritative and forget their traditions. Accordingly, to "cover" the *Shulchan Aruch*, Isserles wrote *Mappah* (*Tablecloth*), which supplemented the thoughts and practices of the Ashkenazim. The combined work of the *Shulchan Aruch* and the *Mappah* became the standard by which Jews learned how to practice Judaism.

JABOTINSKY, VLADIMIR

Born October 18, 1880, in Odessa, Russia; died August 3, 1940.
ZIONIST LEADER.

Vladimir Jabotinsky is most famous for being the mentor of Israel's Prime Minister Menachem Begin. He was also the leading intellectual force behind the militant brand of Zionism, which serves as the ideological underpinning for the Israeli right wing. Jabotinsky was born into a middle-class Russian family. He studied law in Berne and Rome. Excelling as a journalist and linguist, he traveled extensively as a columnist for a number of Russian newspapers. In 1903 Jabotinsky became active in Zionist affairs. In 1918 he served as an officer in Palestine and later, during the April 1920 Arab riots, became active in the Jewish defense of Jerusalem. Imprisoned by British authorities and sentenced to fifteen years for confronting Arab crowds with his troops, Jabotinsky was released from Acre Prison in 1921 after great protest. "I want a state with an army," he once said. "I don't want a 'national home' for the Jewish people in Palestine. The Jewish people are not ready to retire to a home for the aged and the obsolete." He formed the Revisionist Zionist Organization and the Betar Youth Movement in 1925, and the New Zionist Organization in 1935.

JOSEPHUS, FLAVIUS

Born circa 38 C.E. *in Jerusalem; died after 100* C.E.
JEWISH HISTORIAN.

Flavius Josephus lived at the time of the revolt of the Jews against Rome; his writings are considered the most important source for Jewish history during this highly significant first century C.E. He was born Joseph ben Mattathias. All that is known about him comes from his own pen. He describes himself as a child prodigy who was consulted by high priests and others on religious and legal matters. When he was sixteen years old, he began studying the three Jewish schools of thoughts—Pharisees, Sadducees, and Essenes—but chose to spend the next three years living with a desert hermit. He eventually joined the Pharisees and became commander of Galilee when the Jewish War began in 66 C.E. Flavius Josephus began to prepare for a defense against an inevitable Roman counterattack; despite his copious writings on the subject, what happened in his defense is not clear. It appears that he was not a successful military commander and that the cities under his command eventually gave way to the Romans. In order to survive, he fled with forty men from Jotapata when that city fell. He eventually surrendered to the Romans and was scheduled to be executed. To stave off death, Josephus made it known, upon the death of Nero, that he had prophetic powers and predicted that Vespasian would become Roman emperor. Rewarded for his accurate prophesy, Josephus was given his freedom and accompanied Titus, the commander of the Roman army, to Jerusalem; there Josephus tried to convince the Jewish rebels to surrender. The Jews considered him a traitor; the Romans thought him a spy. Following the fighting, Josephus settled in Rome, living in Vespasian's former villa. He wrote three important works: *The Jewish War*, *Jewish Antiquities*, and *Against Apion*, which included his autobiographical work *The Life*. Josephus's account of the Jewish War, meant to be objective, actually had a bias toward the Roman side and played down the Jewish role in the revolt. *Jewish Antiquities* was a history of the Jewish people, a book that Josephus hoped would educate non-Jews about Jews.

KAHNEMAN, DANIEL

Born in 1934 in Tel Aviv.
ISRAELI-AMERICAN PSYCHOLOGIST.

Daniel Kahneman was awarded a Nobel Prize in economics in December 2002 for his research using insights from psychology to analyze human decision-making. He shared the prize with Vernon Smith of George Mason University. A dual American-Israeli citizen, Kahneman received a B.A. in psychology and mathematics in 1954 and a doctorate in psychology from the University of California at Berkeley in 1961. He served in the Israeli army and set up a system for interviewing recruits that remained in place for several decades. Kahneman has been professor of psychology and public affairs at Princeton University since 1993. The work for which he received the Nobel Prize was the result of an unusually close collaboration with the late Amos Tversky, in which they conducted experiments to reveal how human judgment under uncertainty adheres to systematic rules of thumb or shortcuts.

KERTÉSZ, IMRE

Born November 9, 1929, in Budapest, Hungary.
HUNGARIAN WRITER.

Imre Kertész received the 2002 Nobel Prize for literature "for writing that upholds the fragile experience of the individual against the barbaric arbitrariness of history." He spent a year at Auschwitz as a teenager, about which he later mused: "I always have the feeling that I was obliged to be Jewish. I am Jewish, I accept it, but to a large extent it is also true that it was imposed on me." Kertész's first novel, *Fateless* (1975), deals with the young Köves, who is arrested and taken to a concentration camp but conforms and survives. In his 1990 novel, *Kaddish for a Child Not Born*, Kertész presents a consistently negative picture of childhood and from this pre-history derives the paradoxical feeling of being at home in the concentration camp. In granting him the Nobel Prize, the Swedish Academy noted that "for him, Auschwitz is not an exceptional occurrence that, like an alien body, subsists outside the normal history of Western Europe. It is the ultimate truth about human degradation in modern existence."

KOCH, EDWARD I.

Born December 12, 1924, in the Bronx, New York.
AMERICAN POLITICIAN.

Ed Koch, a congressman who became the mayor of New York, is one of America's most popular and controversial politicians. One of his better-known expressions is "How'm I doing?", which he asked of his constituents all the time—and to which he usually responded, "I'm doing fine." Koch was born in the Bronx in 1924. His father,

Louis, a furrier, and his mother, Joyce (Silpe) Koch, came from Poland. The Koches moved to Newark, New Jersey, during the 1930s. Koch earned a law degree from New York University in 1948. Elected mayor of New York City in 1977, he was only the second Jew to hold that post—his predecessor, Abe Beame, was the first. He was nationally famous, one writer noted, "for his brash style, a bald pate and a voice that sometimes seemed to emanate from his nose." Koch failed in his 1982 bid to become governor of New York. He served as mayor, however, for twelve years before losing to David Dinkins in 1989. In 1995 he wrote a mystery novel called *Murder in City Hall*; this was followed a year later by *Murder on Broadway*. A third mystery novel, *Murder on 34th Street*, was published in early 1998. The sleuth in all three novels is the mayor himself. In the late 1990s, Koch was also the presiding judge in a television show called *The People's Court*. In 2004, in addition to his duties as a partner in the law firm of Bryan Cave LLP, Koch was hosting a Saturday program on Bloomberg radio and was writing a column for *New York* magazine.

KOOK, ABRAHAM ISAAC

Born in 1865 in Grieve, Russia; died in 1935.
RELIGIOUS THINKER.

Abraham Kook was the key figure of the religious Zionist movement in Palestine. His supporters called him simply the Rav, or Rav Kook. He was the first Chief Rabbi of Palestine. Kook was a child prodigy who studied in the well-known yeshiva of Volozhin, Lithuania. He then served as rabbi to Jewish communities in Lithuania and Latvia. In 1904, when Kook was thirty-nine years old, he moved to Palestine and became the rabbi of Jaffa and the burgeoning Zionist settlements there. In 1909, he had to deal with the problem arising from the sabbatical year when biblical law enjoins that the land remain fallow. He ruled leniently and permitted the land to be sold nominally to a non-Jew. This liberal ruling permitted Jews to continue to cultivate the land. Although some of his colleagues disagreed with him at the time, the ruling has been regarded as authoritative in Israel ever since. Kook spent World War I outside Palestine. He had gone to Europe in 1914 to participate in a rabbinical conference that never took place, and because of the fighting he was not able to return to Palestine until war's end. At first he lived in Switzerland; then he became rabbi of the Mahzikei Hadas congregation in London. Kook helped negotiate the Balfour Declaration in 1917. Returning to Palestine in 1919, he became chief Ashkenazi rabbi for Jerusalem. There he founded a rabbinic academy called Merkaz haRav (The Center of the Rabbi), where he imbued his students with Jewish religious nationalism. The ultra-Orthodox Jews opposed him and set up their own central rabbinical institution. Rav Kook was an outstanding Torah scholar. Most Orthodox Jews opposed Zionism because of its basic refusal to wait for divine redemption to return the Jews to their land. Kook, however, thought Zionism was holy, making him an attractive figure to nonreligious Jews in Palestine. He thought anyone who immigrated to Israel was inspired by holiness, since they were creating the basis for messianic redemption. Kook became the first Ashkenazi chief rabbi of the Jewish community in Palestine in 1921, helping to shape this new institution, believing that it would help the Jews attain self-government. He held the post until his death at the age of seventy in 1935.

LEONARD, BENNY

Born April 7, 1896, in New York City; died April 18, 1946.
AMERICAN BOXER.

Benny Leonard

Some consider Benny Leonard the greatest Jewish sports figure of all time and the best Jewish boxer in history. Boxing expert Nat Fleischer ranked him the second-greatest lightweight fighter ever. From 1917 to 1924, Leonard held the world lightweight title. His career record was 209 bouts with eighty-eight wins (sixty-eight by knockout), five losses, one draw, and 115 no-decisions. Leonard's birth name was Benjamin Leiner. He was the son of Orthodox Jews and grew up fighting Italian and Irish kids on the street, not only with his fists but also with sticks, stones, and bottles. In part because of some of the beatings he took, Leonard disliked this kind of fighting intensely. At age eleven, he fought with gloves for the first time. He used the name Benny Leonard in his early fights so his parents would not learn that he was boxing. When he was in his thirties, Leonard bought a hockey team and taught boxing at City College of New York. The 1929 stock market crash, however, wiped out all his savings and so, in 1931, at age thirty-five, he tried to make a comeback as a welterweight. This decision has been described as the greatest mistake in his boxing career, for in 1932 he was soundly defeated by Irish fighter Jimmy McLarnin. He began working as a referee in 1943. Three years later, he was refereeing a match at New York's St. Nicholas Arena when, during the seventh bout, he collapsed in the ring and died of a brain hemorrhage at the age of fifty. Leonard died a legend, due in part to the claim that no one had ever messed his slicked-down hair in over two hundred fights. Perhaps the greatest tribute to Benny Leonard came from Hearst Publishing editor Arthur Brisbane, who said, "He has done more to conquer anti-Semitism than a thousand textbooks." Leonard was posthumously named a member of the Jewish Sports Hall of Fame in Israel.

LEVITT, WILLIAM

Born February 11, 1907, in Brooklyn, New York; died January 28, 1994.
AMERICAN HOME BUILDER.

William Levitt's mass-production building techniques gave hundreds of thousands of middle-class Americans the ability to buy their own homes after World War II. Realizing that returning soldiers would be eager to settle down, Levitt built modest homes at affordable prices, lining American suburbs with what came to be known as "Levittowns." This new type of housing development symbolized the postwar American boom. Levitt's father was Abraham Levitt, whose parents were Russian-Jewish immigrants. Abraham Levitt was in real estate on Long Island. In 1941 Bill Levitt, then thirty-four years old, and his brother Alfred were awarded a government contract to build 2,350 war workers' homes in Norfolk, Virginia. They analyzed the construction process, figuring out how to speed it up by dividing the work into twenty-seven different teams. Before World War II, Levitt had taken an option on a thousand acres of farmland near Hempstead, Long Island; this became the site where he first implemented his vision of building inexpensive large-volume housing. He called his development Levittown. Its homes were simple, with four and a half rooms designed for young families; each house stood on a 60-by 100-foot lot, of which the home took up only 12 percent. A basic Levittown home sold for $7,990. Between 1947 and 1951, Levitt mass-produced rows of concrete and wood houses, creating instant suburbs and revolutionizing the single-family housing market.

LIEBERMAN, JOSEPH I.

Born February 24, 1942, in Stamford, Connecticut.
UNITED STATES SENATOR AND VICE PRESIDENTIAL NOMINEE.

In November 2000, when U.S. Democratic presidential nominee Al Gore selected him as running mate, Joe Lieberman became the first American Jew to be nominated for the vice presidency. On Election Day, the Gore-Lieberman ticket won more popular votes than did the Republican ticket of George W. Bush and Dick Cheney, but the Bush-Cheney team ultimately triumphed by garnering more electoral votes in a hotly contested and highly controversial race. Lieberman had the distinction of receiving more votes for vice president than any Democrat in history. Having earned a bachelor's degree from Yale College in 1964 and a law degree from Yale Law School in 1967, Lieberman was elected to the Connecticut State Senate in 1970, serving there for the next ten years, the last six as majority leader. From 1982 to 1988, he served as Connecticut's attorney general. He was first elected to the U.S. Senate in 1988 and won reelection in 1994 and 2000. In 2004 Lieberman sought the Democratic Party's presidential nomination, but bowed out early after a dismal showing in the primaries. He and his wife, Hadassah, have four children.

LIPCHITZ, JACQUES

Born August 22, 1891, in Druskienikl, Lithuania; died May 26, 1973.
FRENCH SCULPTOR.

Jacques Lipchitz was one of the most extraordinary sculptors of the twentieth century. His father, a building contractor, wanted his son to be an engineer. Lipchitz, however, at eighteen years old, studied sculpture in Paris and found his calling. He concentrated on ancient, medieval, and primitive art. In 1912, at the age of twenty-one, Jacques had to return to Russia to do military service; he was eventually discharged for poor health. In 1915 he produced some of the first sculptures to employ the principles of cubism in three dimensions. In 1916, anticipating a technique used by other sculptors in later years (especially Henry Moore and Barbara Hepworth), Jacques Lipchitz bored a hole in his sculpture *Man with a Guitar* in order to create space within the sculpture. Lipchitz became a French citizen in 1925 and worked in Paris as a sculptor for many years. Turning away from the popular cubist approach, he used what was described as a more expressive and exuberant style in his sculpture, including his well-known work *Joie de Vivre* (1927), probably the earliest revolving sculpture. He produced abstract, open-work constructions using bands of metal. A famous example of this technique is *The Couples* (1929). Characterizing his work after 1930 were mythological and violent themes as well as solid monumental forms, including his *Prometheus* (1937). In 1941 Lipchitz left Paris for New York. His work after World War II was rich in symbolism as he tried to express the suffering of Europeans in the previous decade. Lipchitz died in 1973 at the age of eighty-two.

LUCKMAN, SID

Born November 21, 1916, in Brooklyn, New York; died July 5, 1998.
AMERICAN FOOTBALL PLAYER.

Sid Luckman

Sid Luckman's father sparked his son's interest in the game when he gave his eight-year-old son a football. Luckman attended New York's Erasmus High School, where he played football. Despite offers of athletic scholarships for his sports activities from forty universities, Luckman planned to attend the United States Naval Academy in Annapolis, Maryland. But after meeting Columbia University Coach Lou Little, Luckman decided he wanted to play for him and he entered Columbia. His college football years (1936–1938) produced a disappointing 10–14–1 record, but Luckman, who displayed superior skill on the playing field even while his team lost more than half its games, was hardly to blame. He became one of the best triple-threat men in college football. In his final year at Columbia, 1938, he was named All-American, even though the team finished only 3–6. He was the first modern T-formation quarterback. Sid Luckman was also regarded as the greatest long-range passer in pro football of his time. A genius at football strategy, he led the Chicago Bears, for whom he played from 1939 to 1947, to five Western Conference titles and four National Football League (NFL) championships. In twelve years with the NFL, Luckman attempted 1744 passes, had 904 completions for 14,686 yards, and passed for 139 touchdowns. The year 1943 was Luckman's greatest. On November 14, 1943, playing at the Polo Grounds in New York, he gave the finest performance of his life, passing for a record seven touchdowns against the New York Giants, surpassing the previous record of six set by Sammy Baugh. That year Luckman guided the Chicago Bears to an 8–1–1 record. The twenty-eight touchdowns he tossed in ten games in 1943 remained a record until the Baltimore Colts' Johnny Unitas broke it in 1959 with thirty-two in twelve games. Luckman also passed for five touchdowns in the NFL title game when the Bears defeated the Washington Redskins 41–21. He was elected to the Pro Football Hall of Fame in 1965.

MARSHALL, LOUIS

Born in 1856 in Syracuse, New York; died in 1929.
AMERICAN JEWISH COMMUNITY LEADER.

Louis Marshall was one of the most dynamic American Jewish community leaders of the twentieth century and was at the forefront of some of the most important American Jewish organizations at their founding. Born to German-Jewish immigrants, Marshall entered Columbia Law School in 1876, completing the two-year law school program in one year. Between 1878 and 1894, Marshall argued more than 150 cases in front of the New York State Court of Appeals. He played a leading role in the Syracuse Jewish community, and in 1891 he was included in a national delegation that visited President Benjamin Harrison on behalf of Russian Jewry. In addition, he served as president of Manhattan's Temple Emanu-El, the leading Reform Congregation in the United States; president of the American Jewish Relief Committee; and chairman of the Board of Directors of the Jewish Theological Seminary. He was president of the American Jewish Committee, which he helped found, from 1912 to 1929. He played a major role in the successful campaign to abrogate the 1832 United States Commercial Treaty with Russia when the czarist government refused to recognize the passports of American Jews; his efforts helped obtain religious liberty for American Jews traveling abroad. Marshall was the official president and spokesman for the Committee of Jewish Delegations to the 1919 Paris Peace Conference and was instrumental in gaining minority rights for the Jews of Eastern Europe. He died in 1929 at the age of seventy-three.

MONTEFIORE, MOSES

Born in 1784 in Leghorn (Livorno) in Italy; died in 1885.
ENGLISH JEWISH LEADER.

Moses Montefiore was born in Italy but lived much of his life in England. He was the first Jew to be knighted when Queen Victoria gave him that honor in 1837. At an early age, Montefiore became an apprentice in a firm of food and tea merchants; later, he and his brother, a partner in the company, set out on their own. Montefiore's wealth accumulated and by the age of forty he retired in order to devote himself to charitable works. He spent the next sixty-one years in these endeavors. Married to a Rothschild, but childless, he spent time visiting orphanages and schools. His motto was "Think and thank," meaning use your mind and show your gratitude by helping the less fortunate. He was six feet three inches tall and cut an impressive, authoritative figure. He showed little regard for Judaism when young, but after visiting Palestine seven times, he became an observant Jew. He traveled with a personal *shochet*, a ritual slaughterer, to make sure his meat and poultry were strictly kosher. He sought to purchase large pieces of land in Palestine for future Jewish settlement and aided in setting up a number of early farming colonies. He built a windmill in Jerusalem—which still stands— in an attempt to introduce a source of energy to the holy city. The Yemin Moshe quarter in Jerusalem was named in his honor. In 1837 Montefiore was the first Jew to be elected sheriff of the City of London. Queen Victoria noted in her diary: "Today I knighted the Sheriffs. One of them was Mr. Montefiore, a Jew, an excellent man, and I was glad to be the first to do what I consider quite right." Montefiore's greatest accomplishments were in preventing pogroms among threatened Jewish communities. In the 1840s, Montefiore visited czarist Russia and persuaded the Russian authorities to reduce their attacks against Jews. He performed much the same task in Morocco and Romania. Montefiore died at the age of 101 in 1885.

MORGENTHAU, HENRY, JR.

Born May 11, 1891, in New York City; died February 5, 1967.
AMERICAN AGRICULTURAL EXPERT AND POLITICIAN.

Henry Morgenthau, Jr., was born and educated in New York City. His father, Henry Morgenthau, Sr., was a financier and diplomat. At age sixteen, Henry, Jr., attended the New York State College of Agriculture, a part of Cornell University, but, having contracted typhoid fever, he had to drop out of school. While recuperating, Morgenthau acquired a great love for the outdoors. His father had purchased a 1,700-acre farm in East Fishkill, New York, where Morgenthau spent his time. Over the years Morgenthau developed ten varieties of apples. In 1922 he purchased the journal *American Agriculturalist*, using it to disseminate his views to the American government, especially on reforms in rural education. One of his neighbors near his Dutchess County farm happened to be Franklin Roosevelt, governor of New York and subsequently president of the United States. In 1934, President Roosevelt appointed Morgenthau secretary of the treasury, the highest political office ever held by an American. Morgenthau became one of the president's closest associates. He is best remembered for the abortive Morgenthau Plan of 1945 that would have partitioned postwar Germany into an essentially agrarian society. He died at the age of seventy-six in 1967.

Henry Morgenthau, Jr. (left) chats with David Ben-Gurion.

MUNI, PAUL

Born September 22, 1895, in Lemberg, Austria (now Lvov, Ukraine); died August 25, 1967.
AMERICAN ACTOR.

Paul Muni

Paul Muni was born Muni Weisenfreund. His parents were traveling players in Austria, but the family moved to the United States when Paul was seven. At age twelve he debuted on the stage in Cleveland's Yiddish theater. Six years later, his father died. Muni began touring on his own as an actor in Yiddish-language plays. He appeared briefly with the theater company of Jacob Kalich and Molly Picon, but ceased working during the 1919 influenza epidemic. Later that year, Maurice Schwartz signed Muni for his Yiddish Art Theater in New York. Muni spent the next eight years with Schwartz's theater and earned praise for his appearances in Gogol's *Inspector General* and Romain Rolland's *Wolves*. In 1926 Muni appeared before an English-speaking audience on Broadway for the first time in *We Americans*; his next Broadway role was as an ex-convict in *Four Walls*. Fox studios signed him to make two films; both were

374

unsuccessful at the box office. Muni then returned to the stage. A third Hollywood attempt led him to play in the gangster classic *Scarface* and his success in this role made him a larger star in Hollywood than on Broadway. However, he continued to appear on stage. He got fine reviews from his performance in Elmer Rice's *Counsellor-at-Law*. Muni signed a new long-term contract with Warner Brothers and made the classic *I Am a Fugitive from a Chain Gang*. Muni was nominated for an Oscar several times; the only time he won was for *The Story of Louis Pasteur*. Muni often used heavy make-up, which helped him excel as a character actor. He also starred in *The Life of Émile Zola* and *Juarez*; he played a Chinese peasant in *The Good Earth* (1937). When his film career slowed down in the mid-1940s, Muni returned to the stage, receiving good notices for his work in such plays as *Key Largo* and *Inherit the Wind*. He appeared in a film for the last time in 1959, playing an elderly Jewish doctor in *The Last Angry Man*. He died at the age of seventy-two in 1967.

NETANYAHU, BINYAMIN

Born October 21, 1949 in Tel Aviv.
ISRAELI POLITICAL LEADER.

Binyamin Netanyahu "Bibi" is one of the most charismatic and articulate Israeli leaders in history. His brother was Jonathan Netanyahu, the commander of the highly successful Entebbe rescue operation of July 1976. Binyamin was a soldier and officer in an elite unit in the Israel Defense Forces (IDF) from 1967 to 1972. After he received his bachelor of science degree from the Massachusetts Institute of Technology (MIT) in 1974, he earned a master of science degree from the university's Sloan School of Management. He joined a Boston company as a management consultant from 1976 to 1978, and later, in Israel, was part of the senior management of Rim Industries in Jerusalem from 1980 to 1982. From 1982 to 1983, Netanyahu served as Israel's ambassador to the United Nations and as deputy chief of mission to the United States. He was elected to the Knesset (parliament) for the first time in 1988. Netanyahu served as deputy foreign minister from 1988 to 1991 and as deputy minister in Prime Minister Shamir's office in 1991 and 1992. He was a member of Israel's delegation to the Madrid Peace Conference in October 1991 and the subsequent peace talks in Washington, D.C. He appeared so frequently on American television news programs during the Gulf War that he was dubbed "Mr. CNN," a reference to the Cable News Network. In March 1993, Netanyahu replaced Yitzhak Shamir as the leader of the Likud party following Shamir's defeat by Yitzhak Rabin in the June 23, 1992, Knesset elections. Netanyahu was the Likud's candidate for prime minister when elections were held in Israel in May 1996. Defeating Labor Prime Minister Shimon Peres by a narrow margin, Netanyahu took office as Israeli's prime minister on June 18, 1996. Netanyahu surprised left-wing critics by working out terms with the Palestinians for an Israeli troop withdrawal from the sensitive West Bank city of Hebron. Seeking reelection in May 1999, Netanyahu was handily defeated by the Labor party candidate, Ehud Barak. Following that setback, he temporarily left politics and lectured widely in the U.S., for which he was handsomely paid. Although in late 2000 polls showed him leading in a race against Prime Minister Ehud Barak, Netanyahu declined to run, claiming that if victorious he would have a hard time governing because his own Likud had too few Knesset seats. Late in 2002, after Labor left the Sharon-led National Unity Government, Sharon appointed Netanyahu foreign minister. Sharon then soundly defeated Netanyahu in the Likud party race for prime minister, and following his victory in the January 2003 elections, Sharon appointed Netanyahu finance minister.

NIZER, LOUIS

Born February 6, 1902, in London, England; died November 10, 1994.
AMERICAN LAWYER.

Louis Nizer was born in London and moved to Brooklyn, New York, as a child. He graduated from the Columbia Law School in 1924. In 1926 he cofounded a law partnership with Louis Phillips that grew into the prestigious New York-based law firm of Phillips, Nizer, Benjamin, Krim & Ballon; Nizer was a senior partner. He became an authority on contract, copyright, libel, divorce, plagiarism, antitrust, and entertainment law. Nizer was an expert at preparing and presenting legal arguments. Much of his legal work involved the film industry and at one stage he had as clients eighty-five percent of the producers and distributors of copyrighted film programs used on television. In his long career as a trial lawyer, Nizer represented a host of famous people, among them Johnny Carson, Charlie Chaplin, Salvador Dali, Eddie Fisher, Alan Jay Lerner, Mae West, the basketball star Julius "Dr. J" Erving, and Spyros P. Skouros, former board chairman of Twentieth Century-Fox films. His autobiography, *My Life in Court* (1962), remained at the top of the bestseller list for seventy-two weeks, making Nizer nationally famous. The book included stories of court cases such as the famous libel suit in which Nizer successfully defended writer Quentin Reynolds in a lawsuit against the columnist Westbrook Pegler. Nizer also wrote *The Implosion Conspiracy* (1972) about the Julius and Ethel Rosenberg espionage case. Nizer died at the age of ninety-two in 1994.

PERES, SHIMON

Born August 21, 1923, in Wolozyn, Poland.
ISRAELI POLITICAL LEADER AND NOBEL PEACE PRIZE RECIPIENT.

Shimon Peres, whose original family name was Persky, emigrated from his native Poland to Palestine in 1934 with his family. In 1948, at the relatively young age of twenty-five, Peres became the first head of Israel's navy. He was director-general of the ministry of defense from 1953 to 1959. In 1959 he was elected for the first time to the Knesset (parliament) as a member of the ruling Mapai party; he resigned in 1965 and helped lead Ben-Gurion's breakaway Rafi party, which won ten Knesset seats in that year's national election. Between 1974 and 1977, Peres served as defense minister in the Labor party government led by Yitzhak Rabin. When Rabin resigned suddenly in April 1977, Peres became acting prime minister, although he lost the general election in May to Menachem Begin's Likud party. Leader of the Labor party opposition from 1977 to 1984, Peres took a more conciliatory attitude toward resolving Israel's problem with the Palestinians than did the right-wing Likud party. Following the September 1984 election, Peres's Labor party and Yitzhak Shamir's Likud party were forced to form a National Unity Government. The two men entered into a power-sharing arrangement, rotating the posts of prime minister and foreign minister over the next four years. Peres served as prime minister from 1984 to 1986 and was regarded as highly competent in the position. After the 1988 election, the national unity government remained in power and the rotation agreement was eliminated. Peres served as finance minister until two years later, when Shamir dismissed Peres because he had given support to American proposals for an Israeli-Palestinian peace conference. In February 1992, Peres was defeated for the Labor party's leadership by Yitzhak Rabin, who went on to become prime minister the following June, whereupon he appointed Peres his foreign minister. For his role in securing the Oslo peace accord between Israel and the Palestine Liberation Organization (PLO), which led to Israel's departure from the Gaza Strip and the West Bank town of Jericho, Peres was awarded the 1994 Nobel Peace Prize. (The prize was shared with Rabin and PLO chief Yassir Arafat.) Peres became acting prime minister on November 4, 1995, after Rabin's assassination. Shortly thereafter, the Labor party and then the Knesset approved his appointment as prime minister. In an election held on May 29, 1996, the Likud's Binyamin Netanyahu defeated Peres in the race for prime minister. Even after Ehud Barak's triumph as Labor party leader, Peres appeared to be working behind the scenes to establish a National Unity Government that would provide him with a senior cabinet position. In July 1999, Peres became Minister for Regional Cooperation in Barak's new government. In February 2001, when Ariel Sharon formed a National Unity Government with Labor, Peres became foreign minister, serving until Labor left the government toward the end of 2002. In 2004 Peres led the Labor party opposition to the Sharon government.

PERLMAN, ITZHAK

Born August 31, 1945, in Tel Aviv.
ISRAELI VIOLINIST.

Itzhak Perlman's parents, Chaim, a barber, and Shoshana, were both natives of Poland. A child prodigy, Perlman wanted to play the violin from a very early age. He practiced on a toy fiddle before getting a secondhand violin, which his parents bought for six dollars. Perlman was stricken with polio when he was four years old and left permanently disabled; he walks with leg braces and crutches and is the only violin soloist who plays sitting down. Perlman played his first public violin recital at the age of nine. He attended the Shulamit Conservatoire and the Tel Aviv Academy of Music. At thirteen, Perlman traveled to the United States to study at the Juilliard School in New York. He also appeared on the television variety program *The Ed Sullivan Show* as well as touring the country for two months. Deciding to remain in New York, Perlman debuted at Carnegie Hall on March 5, 1963. In 1964, when he was only nineteen, he won the coveted thousand-dollar Levintritt Memorial Competition. In much demand as a soloist and still considered one of the finest violinists in the world, Perlman plays on a Stradivarius violin valued at several hundred thousand dollars.

PHILO

Born Circa 25 B.C.E. *in Alexandria, Egypt; died 50* C.E.
JEWISH PHILOSOPHER.

The first well-known Jewish philosopher, Philo was born Philo Judaeus and was known as Philo of Alexandria. He was born into a wealthy, upper-class Jewish family in Alexandria, which was at the time the second most important Jewish center outside Palestine. Raised as a Jew, Philo received a Greek education. His brother Alexander became a senior official in the Roman administration in Egypt. Philo devoted himself to his studies and writing. In 40 C.E., anti-Jewish riots erupted in Alexandria. They were due to the Jews' refusal to put up a statue of the Roman Emperor Caligula in the Jerusalem Temple. Philo led a delegation to Rome to appeal (in vain) to Caligula to cancel the edict. However, the assassination of Caligula the following year was followed by the selection of a more sympathetic emperor, Claudius, who did cancel the edict. Philo wrote vividly of the incident, then retired from public life and spent the rest of his life writing full time. He wanted to synthesize Greek and Jewish thought in order to demonstrate that Judaism was compatible with Hellenism. His commentaries on the Bible were interpreted through Greek allegorical tradition. Philo believed that the Bible contained philosophical truths and that God was a transcendent being who revealed himself to people through the Divine Word known as the Logos, which mediates between God and humanity. Writing in Greek, Philo worked from the Greek translation of the Bible. It is not clear whether or not he knew Hebrew. His works were largely forgotten by Jews until they were rediscovered during the Renaissance. Philo also deeply influenced Christians, who thought highly of his theory of the Logos and his use of allegory.

RAMON, ILAN

Born June 20, 1954 in Tel Aviv, Israel; died February 1, 2003.
FIRST ISRAELI ASTRONAUT.

When, on January 16, 2003, Ilan Ramon and six other astronauts began a journey into space aboard the shuttle *Columbia*, the Israeli public was ecstatic. "He was the face of Israeli exceptionalism," wrote the English-language *Jerusalem Post*. "He showed us there was no limit to what a person can accomplish as a Jew." Sixteen days later, when the *Columbia* blew apart and all seven astronauts perished just minutes from touchdown in Cape Canaveral, Florida, the joy turned to devastation. The first

Israeli astronaut, Ramon had graduated as a fighter pilot from Israeli air force flight school in 1974, and later became one of his country's first pilots trained to fly F-16s. In June 1981, he participated in Israel's successful destruction of the Iraqi nuclear reactor, although his involvement was made public only in the days immediately preceding the *Columbia* launch. Ramon's mother and grandmother had survived Auschwitz, and although Ramon himself was a secular Jew, he ate kosher food aboard the shuttle and carried a small Torah that had survived the Bergen-Belsen concentration camp. Married and the father of four, the forty-eight-year-old Ramon e-mailed Israeli President Moshe Katzav from space: "All that's needed is the right leadership to bring the people of Israel to the heights of heaven."

ROSENWALD, JULIUS

Born in 1862 in Springfield, Illinois; died in 1932.
AMERICAN MERCHANT.

Julius Rosenwald was born to a family of German immigrants. He held odd jobs while in school, including pumping a church organ, selling newspapers, and carrying bags for tourists. When he was sixteen, Rosenwald moved to New York, where he worked in his uncle's clothing store. At age twenty-one he opened his own retail clothing store, then shifted to manufacturing summer clothing. In 1895 he joined with one of his main customers, Sears, Roebuck, and became vice-president the following year. Rosenwald introduced a money-back-if-not-satisfied guarantee that was a big hit with customers. Soon the growing firm opened its own factories to produce its goods. In 1909 Rosenwald was chosen president of Sears; he became chairman of the board in 1925. He helped revolutionize the retail merchant business through the introduction of the famous Sears mail-order catalog, making him one of the first to offer dry goods by mail. At the time of his death at age seventy in 1932, Sears, Roebuck and Company's mail-order catalog was distributed to more than forty million homes and offices. Rosenwald attributed his wealth to luck, and liked to say, "Don't ever confuse wealth with brains." His business success was soon overtaken by his philanthropic work; he gave away more than fifty million dollars, mostly to causes that benefited African-Americans.

ROTHKO, MARK

Born September 25, 1903, in Russia; died February 25, 1970.
AMERICAN PAINTER.

Mark Rothko was brought to the United States from Russia as a boy of ten, and he and his family settled in Portland, Oregon. From 1921 to 1923, he studied at Yale University; he began to paint in 1925. He studied with Max Weber, the American cubist painter. Aside from a short period at the Art Students' League, Rothko was largely self-taught. In 1935 he cofounded the post-fauve expressionist group called

"The Ten." By the mid-1940s, however, he had adopted an abstract surrealist manner in his painting. Around 1947 Rothko began to paint pictures that consisted of several large, soft-edged rectangular areas of delicate, deep color. He created a luminous effect in his paintings through the interaction of colors; his pictures were quite large. Rothko sought to envelop his viewers in the painting's emotion. During World War II, Rothko was deeply influenced by European surrealist painters who reached New York at this time. He began painting misty canvasses with mythical figures who appeared to float in space. As of 1948, Rothko started to focus his painting style on the large fields of translucent color that made him internationally known. He had one-man exhibitions at the Venice Biennial and many other large important galleries and museums. In 1971 the Rothko Chapel was dedicated in Houston, Texas; it was decorated with fourteen of the artist's works. To Rothko, painting was a religious experience which he tried to convey in his work. In the last decade of his life the colors in his paintings took on more somber tones, a reflection, apparently, of personal depression that led to his suicide in 1970 at the age of sixty-seven.

RUBINSTEIN, ARTUR

Born January 28, 1889, in Warsaw, Poland; died December 20, 1982.
AMERICAN PIANIST.

Artur Rubinstein

Courtesy of the Academy of Motion Pictures Arts and Sciences

The youngest of seven children, Artur Rubinstein is considered one of the finest pianists of his era, as well as the most successful interpreter of Chopin. A child prodigy, Rubinstein studied under Joseph Joachim, Heinrich Barth, and Max Bruch. In 1900, when he was only twelve years old, Rubinstein made his Berlin debut, playing Mozart's A Major concerto; the debut was received enthusiastically. Studying briefly with Paderewski, Rubinstein then toured in Europe, the United States, and South America. In 1932 he married Aniela Mylnarski, the daughter of a Polish musical conductor; they had four children. In 1934 Rubinstein retired from the concert stage for three years in order to refresh his technique and repertoire. In 1946 he became an American citizen. For the next thirty years, he gave numerous concert tours and made many recordings, including ones of the complete works of Chopin and three cycles of the Beethoven concertos. Once, in 1953, in New York, Rubinstein gave five concerts in less than two weeks. His last concert was in London in 1976, when he was eighty-eight years old. He wrote a two-volume autobiography, *My Young Years* (1973) and *My Many Years* (1980). Artur Rubinstein died at the age of ninety-three in 1982.

SHARON, ARIEL

Born in 1928 in Moshav Kfar Malal, Israel.
Israeli Military Commander and Prime Minister.

Ariel Sharon is considered one of Israel's greatest military commanders, and one of its most controversial. His family's former name was Sheinerman. "Arik," as he is known to all, attended high school in Tel Aviv and joined the Haganah in 1945. A platoon commander in Israel's 1948 War of Independence, Sharon was wounded in the unsuccessful Battle of Latrun, but recovered. He studied history and Asian studies at Jerusalem's Hebrew University in 1952 and 1953. He was then selected to lead the newly formed 101 Commando Unit, which carried out retaliatory raids against Arab terrorist groups. In January 1954, Sharon became commander of a group that united Unit 101 and a paratroop regiment; his retaliatory raids across enemy lines continued. In 1956 Sharon became commander of a paratroop corps that carried out an attack on the Mitla Pass in the Sinai during the Sinai Campaign. He was accused by superiors of insubordination for seeking permission from them to send in a patrol to rescue a trapped group of Israeli soldiers but going well beyond his orders by sending in a far larger force than agreed upon; in the ensuing battle, thirty-eight Israelis lost their lives, though the mission was a success. Sharon was not punished. He held various military posts over the next seven years and in 1964 was appointed Northern Front Commander. He was promoted to major general in 1966. During the 1967 Six-Day War, Sharon commanded an armored division and was cited for his tactical brilliance. In 1969 he was appointed Southern Front Commander and, in this capacity, led Israeli forces in the War of Attrition over the next year. In 1970 and 1971, Sharon sought to eliminate terrorist cells from the Gaza Strip. He resigned from the Israel Defense Forces (IDF) in June 1972, when his chances to become chief of staff seemed small. He then ran for the Knesset (parliament) as a member of the Liberal party within Menachem Begin's newly-formed Likud, which Sharon himself had helped establish. When the 1973 Yom Kippur War began, Sharon was called back to active military service and commanded an armored division. For nine months in 1975 and 1976, Sharon served as a special advisor on military affairs to Prime Minister Rabin. Sharon's newly formed party, Shlomzion, won two seats in the 1977 Knesset elections, but then ceased to exist when Sharon joined the Herut party soon thereafter. Begin appointed Sharon minister of agriculture and chairman of the Ministerial Committee for Settlement; in those capacities, he became a kind of czar of the Jewish settlement drive. Begin then appointed Sharon minister of defense in August 1981. Controversy pursued Sharon; he was accused of misleading Begin by allowing IDF troops to reach Beirut rather than restrict their occupation to southern Lebanon. The Kahan Commission, appointed to investigate the circumstances surrounding the massacre of

Palestinians by Christian Phalange soldiers at the Sabra and Shatilla refugee camps in September 1982, urged in its February 1983 report that Sharon be removed as defense minister. Although he left the defense ministry, Sharon remained in the government as minister without portfolio. In the 1984 National Unity Government, he became minister for industry and trade. Sharon sued *Time* magazine for publishing an article that, he said, made false claims—that a secret appendix of the Kahan Commission report contained evidence that Sharon had encouraged the Jamayel family to take revenge against the Palestinians by carrying out the massacre at Sabra and Shatilla. Although the jury found the accusation untrue and the article defamatory, the jury decided that the article had been published without malicious intent. Sharon was unable to collect the fifty million dollars he had demanded in compensation from *Time*. Sharon became head of the opposition Likud party in the summer of 1996. The Palestinian leadership blamed Sharon's visit to the Temple Mount in late September 2000 for sparking a new round of violence between Palestinians and Israelis. When Ehud Barak handily defeated Binyamin Netanyahu for prime minister in 1999, Sharon assumed leadership of the Likud party, which he led to an easy victory over Prime Minister Ehud Barak in the February 2001 elections. The Palestinians escalated the violence, especially in March 2002, as a wave of suicide bombings took numerous Israeli lives. Sharon responded with increased military force against the Palestinians on the West Bank and in the Gaza Strip. In elections held on January 28, 2003, Sharon's Likud party decisively defeated Labor, under the leadership of Amram Mitzna. In 2004 Sharon was struggling in his bid to implement unilateral Israeli disengagement from the Gaza Strip.

SILVER, ABBA HILLEL

Born January 28, 1893, in Sirvintos, Lithuania; died November 28, 1963.
AMERICAN REFORM RABBI AND ZIONIST LEADER.

Abba Hillel Silver was brought to the United States in 1902. His father was a rabbi and a Hebrew teacher. Though Silver was raised in an Orthodox environment, he chose to become a Reform rabbi and was ordained by the Hebrew Union College in Cincinnati in 1915. He also graduated from the University of Cincinnati that year. Later Silver was awarded doctoral degrees from Western Reserve University and Hebrew Union College. For two years, he served as rabbi in Wheeling, West Virginia. He was then chosen rabbi of the influential Congregation Tifereth Israel in Cleveland, where he served from the age of twenty-four until his death. A great orator, Silver identified himself with numerous social causes in Cleveland. He and Stephen S. Wise headed the American Zionist Emergency Council during World War II. In 1941 Silver proposed the establishment of a Jewish commonwealth in Palestine and championed a far more activist policy in favor of a Jewish state than did fellow American Zionist leaders. Because of his conflict with Zionist leaders over these issues, Silver was forced to resign from the Emergency Council in 1944. He wasn't silent for long, however. He returned to positions of Zionist leadership in

1945, becoming president of the Zionist Organization of America as well as chairman of the American section of the Jewish Agency. He was the chief spokesman of the Jewish Agency during the discussions that led to the United Nations resolution of November 29, 1947, supporting the idea of a Jewish state, and ultimately the creation of that state. Silver died at the age of seventy in 1963.

SIMON, NEIL

Born July 4, 1927, in New York City.
AMERICAN PLAYWRIGHT.

Neil Simon grew up in a middle-class environment, graduating from DeWitt Clinton High School in the Bronx. He left New York University early, however, when the Army Air Force Reserve stationed him in Colorado. He later wrote about his childhood and military experiences in several of his memorable Broadway plays. In 1948 Simon began writing material for comedians performing skits at hotels, and for radio and television comedy shows. Among the television personalities for whom he wrote were Sid Caesar, Imogene Coca, Phil Silvers, and Gary Moore. He won an Emmy award in 1957 for his work on *The Sid Caesar Show*, and in 1959 for *Sergeant Bilko*, which starred Phil Silvers. His first full-length play, *Come Blow Your Horn* (1961), ran for 677 performances on Broadway. His second, *Barefoot in the Park* (1963), had 1,530 Broadway performances. Both have been performed on stages throughout the country countless times since then. A long list of plays, books for musicals, and film scripts has made Neil Simon one of the most familiar and successful writers on Broadway and in Hollywood. His plays include *The Odd Couple* (1965), *Plaza Suite* (1968), *Brighton Beach Memoirs* (1983), *Biloxi Blues* (1984) and *Broadway Bound* (1987). Many of his plays have been adapted for the film, usually by Simon himself. In his plays, Simon finds humor in everyday life, focusing on ordinary people in ordinary situations. Many of his plays are set in New York City. One play, *Chapter Two* (1977), examines his feelings both for his first wife, who died, and his second wife, actress Marsha Mason. While his characters are often Jewish, Simon does not examine their Jewishness. Simon's play *London Suite* opened; it marked the first time that a Neil Simon play had been performed off-Broadway. Simon chose the venue because he feared that a Broadway production, with its huge costs, might too easily become a financial failure. In 1996, *Rewrites: A Memoir*, an autobiographical account of Neil Simon's early career and life, was published. Simon's play Proposals, opened on Broadway in the fall of 1997, but did not fare well. His film *Odd Couple II* opened in the theaters in April 1998.

SOLOVEITCHIK, JOSEPH DOV

Born in Pruzhan, Poland, in 1903; died in 1993.
TALMUDIC SCHOLAR.

Joseph Dov Soloveitchik has been a role model for the modern Orthodox Jewish community in the United States as it attempts to acculturate to American life. He has shown others how to live a full Jewish life without closing off from modern society as found in the United States. One of the world's great Talmudic scholars, he is the only well-known Talmudist in the United States who is also a philosopher and theologian. Soloveitchik is a member of a leading Lithuanian rabbinic family; he received his Jewish education from tutors under his father's guidance. He is a master of his grandfather's revolutionary analytic method of Talmudic study known as the Brisker method. In 1922 Soloveitchik left Poland for Germany and studied at the University of Berlin where, in 1931, he received his doctorate, having written his dissertation on German philosopher Herman Cohen's work. Arriving in the United States in 1912, Soloveitchik was a rabbi for a large part of Boston's Orthodox Jewish community. He resigned his post after numerous battles with other Orthodox leaders about how to supervise Jewish dietary laws. During the late 1930s, Soloveitchik established an Orthodox Jewish day school, the Maimonides School, in Boston. Appointed professor of Talmud in 1941 at Yeshiva University in New York, he succeeded his father, Rabbi Moshe Soloveitchik. Joseph Soloveitchik has educated most of America's Orthodox pulpit rabbis. He has served as chairman of the Halakah Commission of the Rabbinical Council of America, setting strict guidelines for cooperating with non-Orthodox Jewish groups. He is strongly pro-Zionist, yet he turned down an invitation in 1959 to become the Ashkenazi Chief Rabbi of Israel. Among his better-known philosophical essays are "The Lonely Man of Faith" (1965), "The Halakhic Man" (1983), and "The Halakhic Mind" (1986). He retired from Yeshiva University in 1984 at the age of eighty-one due to illness.

SONDHEIM, STEPHEN J.

Born March 22, 1930, in New York City.
AMERICAN COMPOSER AND LYRICIST.

Stephen Sondheim is one of America's great musical theater composers. He wrote several full-length musicals when he was still in college. At that time, he studied with composer Milton Babbitt in New York City. In 1956 Sondheim wrote incidental music for the show *Girls of Summer*. He then wrote the lyrics for the 1958 production of *West Side Story*, collaborating with Leonard Bernstein, who wrote the music. *West Side Story* is considered one of the classics of the Broadway stage. Sondheim also wrote the lyrics for *Gypsy* (1959) with Jule Styne, who wrote the music, and *Do I Hear a Waltz?* (1965) with Richard Rodgers. He has written both words and music for his own shows, including *A Funny Thing Happened on the Way to the Forum* (1962), *Anyone Can Whistle* (1964), *Company* (1970), *Follies* (1971), *A Little Night Music* (1973), *Sweeney Todd* (1979), and *Into the Woods* (1987). The last five musicals won both the New York

Drama Critics' Circle and Tony awards for best musical score. Sondheim also wrote music and lyrics for *Assassins* (1991). His play *Sunday in the Park with George* (1983) won him a Pulitzer Prize. He has also written music for films, including *Stavisky* (1974), *The Seven Percent Solution* (1977), and *Reds* (1981). In 1976 a show that used a collection of his songs was staged in London and called *Side by Side by Sondheim*. A pair of other shows, *Marry Me a Little* (1981) and *You're Gonna Love Tomorrow* (1983) were also based on anthologies of Sondheim's songs. Sondheim spent 1990 as Visiting Professor of Drama at Oxford University. The 1994–95 Broadway season saw Sondheim's *Passion* open to mixed notices, and it wasn't until nine years later, in 2004, that a new Sondheim musical, *Bounce*, made a bid for Broadway. However, having received less than stellar notices in out-of-town tryouts, *Bounce* never came into New York. On a more positive note, that same year the Roundabout Theatre Company's Broadway revival of *Assassins* was enthusiastically received, garnering the 2004 Tony Award for Best Musical Revival, and in 2005 Roundabout returned Sondheim's *Pacific Overtures*, originally presented in 1976, to Broadway in an innovative new production.

SOUTINE, CHAIM

Born in 1893 in Similovitchi, Russia; died in 1943.
FRENCH PAINTER.

Chaim Soutine, one of the best representatives of the artistic school of Paris, painted in the expressionist tradition, using bright colors. He was born in western Russia in 1893 into a poor Orthodox Jewish family. His father mended clothes for a living. Soutine was the tenth of eleven children. The absence of money led Soutine to steal a small amount from his home to purchase a colored pencil; he was punished by being locked in the cellar for two days. When he asked the local rabbi to pose for a portrait, the rabbi's son beat Soutine up so badly that the rabbi had to pay Soutine's mother twenty-five rubles in damages. Using this money, Soutine traveled to Minsk in 1909, when he was sixteen, to attend art school, and then a year later to Vilna, where he became a brilliant student at the School of Fine Arts. He remained at the school for three years, painting subjects that were morbid and sad, including Jewish burials, and scenes of desolation and misery. He died in Paris at the age of fifty in 1943.

SPITZER, ELIOT

Born June 10, 1959, in Riverdale, New York.
AMERICAN LAWYER AND STATE ATTORNEY GENERAL.

Since becoming the State of New York's Attorney General on January 1, 1999, Eliot Spitzer has been a champion in the causes of investor protection, personal privacy, and criminal law enforcement. His bold first-time investigations of conflicts of interest on Wall Street have led to major reforms in America's financial services industry. His prosecutions of white-collar crimes have resulted in some of the nation's largest fraud recoveries. Spitzer clerked for United States District Court Judge Robert W.

Sweet and, later, was an associate at Paul, Weiss, Rifkind, Wharton, and Garrison. From 1986 to 1992, he was an assistant district attorney in Manhattan, eventually becoming chief of the Labor Racketeering Unit, where he successfully prosecuted organized crime and political corruption cases. A 1981 graduate of Princeton and a 1984 graduate of Harvard Law School, Spitzer is politically ambitious. In December 2004, he announced his candidacy for the governorship of New York in 2006.

STEINSALTZ, ADIN

Born July 11, 1937, in Jerusalem.
ISRAELI RELIGIOUS SCHOLAR.

Adin Steinsaltz was born in Jerusalem in 1937 into a nonobservant family. His father, Avraham, was a socialist, but proudly Jewish. Steinsaltz's Jewish education was modest and at first he was skeptical about religion. But he eventually embraced Judaism, noting later that "religion was the truth that I was searching for." Steinsaltz studied Judaism, mathematics, and chemistry at Jerusalem's Hebrew University. At age twenty-four, he became the youngest school principal in Israel. Three years later, in 1964, he decided to embark upon the ambitious task of creating a modern Talmud. "It was a kind of hubris," he acknowledged. The Talmud was completed 1,500 years ago in two versions, both named for their places of origin: one is the commonly used Babylonian text of 2.5 million words; the other, the Jerusalem (or Palestinian) Talmud, is far less known and half as long as the Babylonian Talmud. To Steinsaltz, Judaism was in peril if "an essential part of our people are cut off from the Talmud." Until he came along, most Jews *were* "cut off" from the Talmud, as indicated by one 1988 poll that showed that eighty-four percent of Israeli Jews had never read any of it. This was not surprising, given how complex, obscure, and unintelligible parts of the Talmud are, making it accessible to only highly trained scholars. Standard editions of the Talmud were virtually unreadable because the Hebrew was printed without vowel notations or punctuation. Steinsaltz inserted vowel marks and punctuation; he also translated Aramaic sentences into modern Hebrew and explained the many words from other languages that appear in the Talmud. He also provided his own commentary to the Talmud to go with those of Rashi and other rabbinical commentators. In 1965 Steinsaltz founded the Israel Institute for Talmudic Publications and began work on his massive project of translating and reinterpreting the Talmud. By 2004 Steinsaltz had completed thirty-eight of the sixty tractates. The Steinsaltz project has made the Talmud accessible to tens of thousands of Hebrew-language speakers, enabling the masses to read the Talmud as they would any other book. In 1989 Steinsaltz began producing an English edition of this Talmud; however, after twenty-volumes were issued, the project was halted. A number of Jewish authorities in Israel and elsewhere have described Steinsaltz's Talmud project as the most important Judaica publication of the twentieth century. In 1988 Steinsaltz received the Israel Prize, Israel's highest honor, for his work on the Talmud and for furthering Jewish education. Steinsaltz had made the Babylonian Talmud so accessible that some yeshiva high schools urged their students to bypass his edition so they could become proficient in Talmud by using their own logic instead of relying only on the Steinsaltz viewpoint.

STERN, ISAAC ·

Born July 21, 1920, in Kremenetz, Soviet Union; died September 22, 2001.
AMERICAN VIOLINIST.

Isaac Stern was called America's greatest musical ambassador. An internationally famous virtuoso violinist, Stern came to the United States as a child. He began studying violin when he was eight years old, dropping out of grade school in order to study music full time in a small conservatory. When he was twelve years old, he began studying with Naoum Binder, the concertmaster of the San Francisco Symphony. Stern made his debut with the San Francisco Symphony Orchestra when he was sixteen years old. In 1937, just seventeen, Stern gave a recital at New York's Town Hall, which was followed by six years of cross-country touring. His triumphant debut concert at Carnegie Hall occurred in 1943, when he was twenty-three years old. Stern was prominent soloist with orchestras in the United States and abroad. He was also a leading figure in the successful attempt to save Carnegie Hall from being demolished in 1960. He served as president of the American-Israel Cultural Foundation and sponsored numerous Israeli artists as well as other performers. Stern became an honorary fellow of Tel Aviv's Diaspora Museum in late 1996. The following September he gave a concert in Moscow in the Conservatoire, performing the violin concerts by Mozart and Bach. Although he had visited the former Soviet Union in the 1950s and 1960s, he had refused to return until this visit in protest against the government's treatment of human rights activists. "Thanks God, the times have changed in Russia, and I am glad to meet the Muscovites again," Stern said.

STRASBERG, LEE

Born November 17, 1901, in Budzanow, then Austria-Hungary; died February 17, 1982.
AMERICAN ACTING TEACHER.

Lee Strasberg was born Israel Strassberg in what was then Austria-Hungary. At the age of seven, he immigrated with his family to the United States and grew up on the Lower East Side of New York. Strasberg's brother-in-law introduced him to the theater by giving him a small part in a Yiddish-language production that was being performed by the Progressive Dramatic Club. He then became a member of the Chrystie Street Settlement House's drama club. Philip Loeb, casting director of the Theater Guild, sensed that Strasberg could act, although he was still not thinking of a fulltime acting career; he was working as a shipping clerk and bookkeeper for a wig company. When he was twenty-three years old, however, Lee enrolled in the Clare Tree Major School of the Theater. He eventually left the school to study with students of the Russian acting teacher Constantin Stanislavsky—Maria Ouspenskaya and Richard Boleslavsky—at the American Laboratory Theater. In 1925 Strasberg had his first professional appearance in *Processional*, a play produced by the Theater Guild. By

1931 he had decided to abandon acting in favor of a career in directing and teaching. That year, along with Cheryl Crawford and Harold Clurman, he formed the Group Theater company. Influenced strongly by Stanislavsky, Strasberg became famous for teaching performers an acting technique he called "The Method," which had the advantage, he believed, of letting actors and actresses use their psyches and subconscious minds in creating characters for the stage. Method acting required a series of physical, emotional, and vocal exercises that made the actor try to learn more about himself personally in order to become the character he was portraying. Leaving the Group Theater in 1936, Strasberg went out on his own. In 1948 he became the guiding force of the Actors' Studio and was selected as its artistic director three years later. Among the actors influenced by Strasberg and his Method acting technique were Anne Bancroft, Al Pacino, and Maureen Stapleton. Strasberg founded the Lee Strasberg Theater Institutes in New York and Los Angeles, and was nominated for best supporting actor for his role in the 1974 film *The Godfather, Part II*. Strasberg served as the Actors' Studio's artistic director until his death in 1982 at the age of eighty-one.

THALBERG, IRVING

Born May 30, 1899, in Brooklyn, New York; died in 1936.
AMERICAN FILM PRODUCER.

Irving Thalberg was a frail child; he suffered from a rheumatic heart condition and was confined to bed for lengthy periods during his childhood. Because of this, he became a voracious reader. With his appreciation of literary quality, he was also able to form a great respect for quality in motion pictures. As a young adult, Thalberg became an assistant manager of an export company and, soon thereafter, a secretary at Universal Pictures' New York office. A few months later, Thalberg became the general manager of the Universal City studio in Hollywood. In 1923 he produced the successful film *The Hunchback of Notre Dame*. Only one year later, Thalberg became Louis B. Mayer's right-hand man. Soon Thalberg was running the newly formed MGM studio. From 1924 until 1933, Thalberg produced some of the era's greatest movies, including *Ben Hur, The Crowd, Hallelujah, Anna Christie, Private Lives, Grand Hotel, The Barretts of Wimpole Street*, and *Mutiny on the Bounty*. He also produced several Marx Brothers comedies. He never put his name on the screen for a credit in his movies, and once said, "If you're in a position to give yourself credit, you don't need it." Thalberg was the inspiration for F. Scott Fitzgerald's hero in *The Last Tycoon*. Among the performers he made famous were John Gilbert, Greta Garbo, Clark Gable, Joan Crawford, and Norma Shearer, whom he married in 1927 after she converted to Judaism. (She returned to Christianity in 1942.) Thalberg's final movie was the widely acclaimed adaptation of Pearl Buck's bestseller *The Good Earth*. In 1933, at the age of thirty-four, Thalberg suffered a heart attack; he died of pneumonia in 1936 when he was only thirty-seven years old. That year, the Academy of Motion Picture Arts and Sciences instituted a special award in his name that is given every year to the producer who shows "the most consistently high level of production achievement," as the Academy defined the award.

TROTSKY, LEON

Born in 1879 in Yanovka, Southern Ukraine; died August 21, 1940.
RUSSIAN REVOLUTIONARY.

Leon Trotsky was born Lev Davidovich Bronstein in southern Ukraine. Although he studied mathematics at Odessa, he soon turned to revolutionary politics and in 1896, at the age of seventeen, joined the illegal Social Democratic party. Two years later, he was arrested for his activities as a political activist and served two years in jail. He then took the name Trotsky, the name of one of his jailers. Exiled to Siberia, Trotsky escaped to London, where he joined Vladimir Lenin in the editing of *Iskra*, a Social Democratic journal. Trotsky formulated the theory of permanent revolution, with its main tenet that a bourgeois revolution in Russia would, by its inner momentum, lead rapidly to the socialist stage, even before the socialist revolution in the West. Trotsky became one of the key organizers of the October Revolution that established the Soviet regime in 1917. Lenin asked Trotsky to head the new government or become commissar for home affairs; Trotsky, however, turned down these offers, believing that his being Jewish could embarrass the new regime. Trotsky believed that there was no future for Jews as a separate people; he favored their assimilation. He was appointed commissar for foreign affairs and selected as head of the delegation to the Brest-Litovsk peace talks. Trotsky and Lenin quarreled over the issue of peace with Germany. Trotsky believed the German revolution was imminent and therefore opposed signing a peace treaty that would turn over large parts of Russian territory to imperial Germany; he urged stopping the war unilaterally. Yet he was also against making peace under unfavorable conditions, calling for "neither war nor peace." Lenin, however, was skeptical and demanded that the peace treaty be signed in order to prevent another Russo-German war. In 1918 Trotsky was appointed commissar for military affairs. His mandate was to prepare the new republic to fight both the threat of foreign military intervention and the antirevolutionary armies still operating in Russia. Organizing the Red Army with great skill, Trotsky led it to victory. With Lenin's death in 1924, Stalin, as part of his maneuvering to replace Lenin, managed to push Trotsky out of a key role in party leadership. When Trotsky and Stalin had a complete falling out, Trotsky moved from one country to another in the 1920s and 1930s until he was finally assassinated in 1940 at the age of sixty-one, in Mexico, apparently by Stalin's associates.

WARBURG, FELIX

Born in 1871 in Hamburg, Germany; died in 1937.
AMERICAN FINANCIER AND PHILANTHROPIST.

Felix Warburg was a major figure in the German-Jewish elite that dominated the American Jewish community in the early part of the twentieth century. Warburg was one of seven children of Moritz Warburg, who was head of the banking firm of M.M. Warburg and Co. When Warburg was sixteen years old, he left school and was sent to Frankfurt, where he went to work for relatives on his mother's side, the

Oppenheims, in their precious-stones business. Warburg moved to New York in 1894 when he was twenty-three years old. He married Frieda Schiff, the daughter of the American financier Jacob Schiff, who gave Felix a job with his firm, Kuhn, Loeb and Company, in 1895. Eventually becoming a senior partner of the firm, Felix Warburg helped finance the industrial development of North America. His reputation as a financier and philanthropist was widespread. He helped support the Henry Street Settlement, which offered, among other things, open-air playgrounds for children in crowded settlement areas of the city. He was also a supporter of the Educational Alliance, which sought to absorb and help immigrants in the United States. In 1902 Warburg was appointed commissioner of the New York Board of Education, holding that post for many years, introducing reforms in the public school system. He helped pass a probation bill that enabled the courts to improve their handling of juvenile delinquency. In 1907 Warburg was appointed the first state probation commissioner. He helped to establish a babies' hospital and a tuberculosis prevention center for children. From 1914 until 1932, he was the chairman of the American Jewish Joint Distribution Committee. He directed the census of food supplies in New York City during World War I. In 1917 he was the major force in forming the Federation for the Support of Jewish Philanthropic Societies of New York, serving as its president for twenty years. Not an ardent Zionist, Warburg did aid the Jewish community in Palestine by supporting the Palestine Economic Corporation. In 1929 he was the cofounder, with Louis Marshall, of the Jewish Agency, and chairman of its administration committee. He resigned from the committee in 1931, however, in protest against the British restrictions on Jewish immigrants to Palestine. In 1933 Warburg led the campaign to raise money to help the oppressed Jews in Nazi Germany. His New York home on Fifth Avenue eventually became the site of the Jewish Museum. He died at the age of sixty-six in 1937.

WEIZMAN, EZER

Born in 1924 in Tel Aviv.
PRESIDENT OF THE STATE OF ISRAEL.

Ezer Weizman is the nephew of Israel's first president, Chaim Weizmann. During World War II, Weizman served in the Royal Air Force and was stationed in Egypt and India. From 1946 to 1948 he was a member of the military organization Irgun. He also served in the Air Service, a forerunner of the Israel Air Force (IAF), flying ammunition and provisions to the embattled Negev and Gush Etzion regions in 1948. He was sent to Czechoslovakia to learn how to fly Messerschmidts and bring one back to Israel. Weizman served in the Israel Air Force until 1966. From 1958 to 1966, he headed the IAF and shaped it into the force that operated with such startling effectiveness in the opening hours of the 1967 Six-Day War. From 1966 to 1969, Weizman served as head of the Operations Branch of the Israel Defense Forces (IDF) and was deputy chief of staff. He wanted to become chief of staff, but that did not occur. In 1969, having joined the right-wing Gahal political party, Weizman was appointed minister of transport in the National Unity Government. From 1971 to 1972, he was chairman of the Herut party's executive committee. In 1977 he ran the Likud party's election campaign and was credited with engineering its surprise upset victory. Appointed defense minister, Weizman served for the next three years, playing a major role in helping Israel finalize its peace treaty with Egypt. Weizman developed close relations with the late Egyptian President Anwar Sadat, which helped both before and after the peace treaty to keep Israel-Egypt relations from worsening at times of stress. Weizman eventually resigned as minister of defense in May 1980 when he opposed efforts by Menachem Begin and Ariel Sharon to increase Jewish settlement in the occupied territories and to thwart the granting of autonomy to Palestinians there, as called for in the Camp David agreement of September 1978. From 1980 until 1984, Weizman remained in the Knesset (parliament), but spent a certain amount of time in business activities. In March 1984, he established the dovish Yahad party, which won three seats in elections the following September. The following August, the party joined the Labor Alignment; Weizman was appointed minister without portfolio. In January 1985, he was appointed coordinator of Arab affairs. In October 1986, Weizman joined the Israel Labor party along with other members of his party. In early 1993, he was elected president of Israel, and in March 1998 he won reelection to that post. Weizman retired from office in the summer of 2000 in the wake of a financial scandal for which he was not indicted.

WINCHELL, WALTER

Born April 7, 1897, in New York City; died February 20, 1972.
AMERICAN RADIO COMMENTATOR AND NEWSPAPER COLUMNIST.

Walter Winchell was the father of the modern gossip column. Ninety percent of American adults either tuned in to his radio show or read his daily syndicated newspaper column. With a single utterance or printed sentence, Winchell could make or break a celebrity. "Good evening, Mr. and Mrs. America, and all the ships at sea." That was the way Walter Winchell, with his nasal, staccato voice, opened up his radio news program once a week. Winchell was born into a poor Jewish immigrant family. He tried vaudeville for twelve years and contributed theatrical gossip to a theater chain's employee publication. During World War I, Winchell served in the United States Navy. In 1920 he offered gossip material to *Billboard* and the *Vaudeville News*. Two years later, the *Vaudeville News* gave him his own column. In 1924 Winchell's "On Broadway" column moved to the *New York Evening Graphic*, and in 1929 to the *New York Daily Mirror*. The popular, widely syndicated column appeared in the *Mirror* for the next thirty-four years. In 1932, Winchell started his weekly radio program, which was on the air twenty years. He had a way of reporting show business and political gossip with great conviction. Using a rapid-fire delivery and a deeply serious voice, Winchell possessed a unique style that made what he was saying seem to be bordering on the hysterical, yet urgently important. Millions of listeners tuned in to his radio program. He had an estimated reading public of over thirty-five million as a syndicated columnist. Winchell's disclosures, often sensational, were what made him famous. He was considered a great molder of public opinion. Walter Winchell was the first columnist to write of the behind-the-scenes world of Broadway. He constantly boosted Federal Bureau of Investigation director J. Edgar Hoover in his columns. Among his sources for information were presidents and kings, industrial leaders, show-business personalities, and racketeers. Winchell hung out at his own table at Manhattan's celebrity meeting place, the Stork Club, hobnobbing with politicians, entertainers, even gangsters. Winchell's slang idiom, which seemed original, was widely imitated and became part of the English language. He pursued subjects while they were "cupidating" until they "middle-aisled," welcomed a "blessed event" or "storked," and, ultimately "renovated." Even with the Depression at its height, Winchell was earning $431,700 a year. From 1930 until 1950, Winchell was at the zenith of his popularity. In the 1950s, his popularity sagged, as did his power to influence people with his words and "inside" information. In the 1960s, Winchell was the moderator for the television series *The Untouchables*, based on a book by Eliot Ness, the federal agent who became famous for his exploits in chasing down hardened criminals. In his later years, Winchell was remembered less for his newspaper columns and radio programs than for his narration of that TV show, one of the most popular of the decade. Walter Winchell retired in 1969 and lived in California until his death three years later at the age of seventy-four.

YEHOSHUA, AVRAHAM B.

Born in 1936 in Jerusalem.
ISRAELI NOVELIST.

Avraham B. Yehoshua was born a fifth-generation Jerusalemite. His father wrote stories about Jerusalem's Old City. He himself is one of the most widely read contemporary Israeli authors. One critic noted that "Yehoshua wrote suspenseful allegorical tales reminiscent of the existentialist dimension of Franz Kafka and S.Y. Agnon but often with a tense political-cultural level of engagedness." Yehoshua writes about sexual tensions in such stories as "Shelosha Yamin Vayeled" ("Three Days and a Child", 1965). But those tensions appear to be a metaphor for the frustrations of Israeli society. In other stories, he offers strong indictments of the basic principles of the Zionist state, especially in "Massa ha'Erev shel Yatir" ("An Evening in Yatir Village", 1959). His novel of the 1973 Yom Kippur War, *Hame'ahev* (*The Lover*, 1977) was well received. Yehoshua's style is between the real and the grotesque, and is said to reflect Israel's traumatized society. His novel *Gerushim Me'uharin* appeared in Israel in 1982 and was translated into English, entitled *A Late Divorce*, in 1984. In his fiction, according to another writer, Yehoshua "portrays some of the 'neurotic' deviancies attendant upon flirtation with the Diaspora and with *yeridah* (the Hebrew word for emigration that also connotes abandonment of the state of Israel)." Yehoshua has also written several plays, including *A Night in May* (1974) and *Objects* (1986).

INDEX

Descartes, René, 304
De Toulouse-Lautrec, Henri, 311
De Witt, Johan, 306
Dilthey, Wilhelm, 76
Dinkins, David, 367
Director, Rose, 120
Disney, Walt, 196, 300
Disraeli, Benjamin, 14
Doctorow, E. L., 348–49
Dori, Ya'acov, 333
Douglas, Kirk, 349–50
Douglas, Michael, 350
Dove, Arthur, 311
Dreiser, Theodore, 41
Dreyfus, Alfred, 104, 134, 214, 238, 280, 326, 350–51
Drury, Allen, 241
Dubinsky, David, 351
Dubnow, Simon, 352
Dulles, John Foster, 180
Duncan, Isadora, 364
Durkheim, Émile, 103–05
Durros, Daniel, 265

Eban, Abba, 352
Edward, VIII (King of England), 253
Ehgram, Sidney, 207
Ehrlich, Paul, 106–08, 253
Eichmann, Adolf, 169–70
Einstein, Albert, 13–14, 109–11, 198–99, 242, 313, 315, 349
Eisenhower, Dwight D., 59, 244, 273
Eliot, T. S., 50
Elizabeth, II (Queen of England), 210
Ellington, Duke, 129
Enders, (Dr.) John F., 268
Enesco, Georges, 207
Erving, Julius ("Dr. J"), 376
Eshkol, Levi, 170, 353–54

Farrow, Mia, 27–28, 139
Fast, Howard, 349
Fay, Frank, 49
Feldman, Charles K., 26
Feller, Bob, 173–74
Ferber, Edna, 157
Fermi, Enrico, 244
Fisher, Eddie, 376
Fitzgerald, F. Scott, 178, 388
Fleischer, Nat, 369
Ford, Gerald, 164
Ford, Henry, 89, 370
Ford, John, 354

Fortas, Abe, 75
Fox, William, 354
Francis, Dr. Thomas, Jr., 268
Frank, Jacob, 70
Frankfurter, Felix, 112–15, 356
Frederick, II (King of Prussia), 201
Freud, Sigmund, 13, 116–18, 315, 349
Freund, Miriam, 85
Friedman, Milton, 7, 119–21

Gabirol, Solomon ibn, 327
Gable, Clark, 196, 388
Gaon, Saadiah, 355
Garbo, Greta, 126, 195–96, 388
Garland, Judy, 196
Garrison, Jim, 160
Garson, Greer, 196
Gaugin, Paul, 214, 236
Geffen, David, 168, 303
Gelb, Arthur, 259
Genovese, Kitty, 259
Gershwin, George, 17, 122–24
Gershwin, Ira, 122–24
Gilbert, John, 388
Gilmore, Gary, 187
Ginsburg, Ruth Bader, 15, 75
Gleason, Jackie, 28
Godfrey of Bouillon, 251
Goldberg, Arthur, 73, 191, 355–56
Goldman, Emma, 349
Goldman, Ronald, 100
Goldmann, Nahum, 356–57
Goldwater, Barry, 120
Goldwyn, Sam, 14, 125–27, 195
Goldwyn, Sam, Jr., 126
Gompers, Samuel, 357
Goodman, Benny, 128–30
Gore, Al, 370
Gorky, Maxim, 285
Goulden, Joseph C., 260
Graetz, Heinrich, 189, 352, 358
Graham, Martha, 96
Green, Adolph, 64
Greenberg, Hank, 17, 358
Greenspan, Alan, 358
Griffith, D. W., 195
Gropius, Walter, 200

Ha'am, Ahad, 68, 320, 339
Hagar, 20–21
Halevi, Judah, 359
Halkin, Hillel, 155
Halprin, Rose, 85